Modernization and Revolution in China

Modernization and Revolution in China

From the Opium Wars to the Olympics

FOURTH EDITION

JUNE GRASSO • JAY CORRIN • MICHAEL KORT

An East Gate Book

M.E.Sharpe
Armonk, New York
London, England

An East Gate Book
Consulting Editor: Doug Merwin

Photos for chapters 1 through 4 are courtesy of the Library of Congress Prints and
Photographs Division. Photos for chapters 7 through 9 are from *China Reconstructs*.
The photo for chapter 12 is courtesy of Mengna Luo.

Library of Congress Cataloging-in-Publication Data

Grasso, June M., 1951–
  Modernization and revolution in China : from the Opium Wars to the Olympics / by June
Grasso, Jay Corrin, and Michael Kort.—4th ed.
    p. cm.
"An East Gate Book."
Includes bibliographical references and index.
ISBN 978-0-7656-2390-4 (cloth: alk. paper)—ISBN 978-0-7656-2391-1 (pbk.: alk. paper)
1. China—History—19th century. 2. China—History—20th century. I. Corrin, Jay P., 1943–
II. Kort, Michael, 1944– III. Title.

DS755.G7 2009
951.05—dc22   2009009131

Contents

Preface   vii
A Note on the Pronunciation of Chinese Names   xi

1. The Middle Kingdom   3
2. Patterns of Traditional Chinese Life   10
3. Imperial Breakdown and Western Invasion   32
4. The New Chinese Republic   65
5. Nationalists and Communists   88
6. China at War   111
7. Creating the New Order: 1949–1957   130
8. The Great Leap and the Bad Fall   163
9. The Cultural Revolution   189
10. A Second Revolution: The Reforms of Deng Xiaoping   219
11. The Era of Jiang Zemin   239
12. China in the World   259
13. The Fourth Generation   277

Notes   307
Suggested Readings   317
Index   323
About the Authors   337

Preface

Modernization and Revolution in China has been written primarily with the undergraduate college student and lay historian in mind. There are many fine textbooks on China, but the authors of this book always had problems trying to find a survey of Chinese history in one volume that could serve the needs of a course that focused on the modern era. We found that most textbooks on Chinese history were either too lengthy and detailed in their coverage of the imperial period or, if devoted to the Communist era, incomplete in their treatment of the all-important nineteenth-century background. It is this gap in the literature that this history of modern China hopes to fill.

The authors of this book believe that an understanding of contemporary China requires an appreciation of the rich historical traditions that molded its past. China is one of the world's oldest, geographically contiguous civilizations, and for this reason alone, history probably looms larger in the Chinese consciousness than it does in the minds and thoughts of most other peoples. There are very few civilizations that have shown such reverence for the wisdom of the ancestral past. A deep sensitivity and respect for historical traditions also has meant that the Chinese have had to travel down a much longer road to accommodate their culture to the demands of "modernization," that is, the panoply of forces that move a society away from old habits and customs in the direction of urbanization, industrialization, and the rationalization of thought and behavior.

The central themes around which we have woven our narrative are those of modernization and revolution. These processes of change can be seen in the crucial nineteenth century—hence the great amount of space devoted to that period in this text—and partly were the product of outside influences. Yet from the outset there was an ongoing struggle between external forces and internal difficulties and differences that shaped the outcome of China's efforts to modernize. As such, they posed challenges that were far greater than those confronted by other states that came late to modernization, especially Russia and Japan, countries against which China's attempts at modernization are frequently compared. The manner in which the Chinese employed their past to overcome these challenges had a seminal influence on the ways in which the Communists structured their revolution and, we believe, continues to weigh heavily on the course of events in China today.

Modernization is a difficult concept to define. This is partly due to the complexity of changes associated with it as well as the wide variety of ways in which nations have gone through the experience. We define modernization here as the process by which societies move from a rural, agrarian base to urban, industrial structures of living via the application of science, technology, and rational modes of thought. Elements commonly associated with such restructuring of the social order include sustained economic growth, specialization of labor, increased public education, broader distribution of income, expanded life expectancy, an increasing reliance on bureaucracy, and mass political participation. Once set in motion, modernization affects all parts of a country's social structure as well as the consciousness of its citizens. When such changes take place rapidly they naturally have a revolutionary impact on the society undergoing the experience.

The onset of modernization certainly brought revolution to China. Revolutions, we believe, do not constitute mere alterations in the political framework of society. They are instead traumatic upheavals in the core fixtures of a culture. Revolutions bring about radical changes in the economic and political orders of a country; they produce shifts in consciousness and social structures and are always marked by the emergence of a new ruling elite, whose values achieve legitimation through acceptance by the larger society. It has been said that revolutions are "ruptures of conscience." Mao would have agreed, for one of the purposes of his Cultural Revolution was to compel a break with China's past by touching the very souls of every Chinese.[1]

The changes wrought by modernization first began in Western Europe; then spread to North America and, with much turmoil and pain, to the rest of the globe. The model for such change in the West employed by the "first-comers" (mainly Britain, France, and the United States) was democratic capitalism. This paradigm had little success in other parts of the world, most notably in Russia and China, both of which were "latecomers" to modernization.[2] The principles of free market economics and liberal, participatory forms of governance fell on arid soil in much of the non-Western world. Instead, local cultural traditions combined with imperialist pressures made command economics and authoritarian political ideas of the right and left more appealing. In the case of Russia and China, it was the preeminent paradigm of the left, Marxian socialism, which provided the blueprint for modernization.

It should be noted that we use the term *modernization* rather than *Westernization* to describe these processes of social change. The latter term suggests that the first-comer experience is somehow the only possible model and that modernity itself reproduces Western ways. In fact, social change outside the first-comer core has been so dramatically unique and variable as to nullify the term *Westernization* as applied to the global experience. Moreover, the most modernized nation in the twenty-first century may well be Japan, whose experiences in this direction have certainly not been the result of merely replicating Western cultural forms.

Studying China requires the analytical approach that the German sociologist Max Weber called *Wertfrei* ("value free"). By this Weber meant the necessity of evaluating social facts without the distortion of one's own cultural bias. As the historian Paul Cohen has noted, histories of China often have relied too heavily on the vocabulary, concepts, and analytical constructs borrowed from the West. The result has been a distortion of Chinese history by either placing too much importance on the role of the West or by misconstruing its influence on China. The challenge, says Cohen, echoing Weber's dictum, is to reduce the distorting pull of the outsider perspective and to view Chinese history on its own terms.[3]

At the center of current Chinese history is an ongoing struggle between the forces of modernity and the pull of tradition. Some elements of Chinese civilization were prepared for change, others resisted it, and still other indigenous aspects of Chinese culture interacted with outside stimuli to produce new elements not found anywhere else in the world. The dynamic of these tensions has given birth to a social, cultural, and political order that is unique, vital, and yet still in transition. What follows is the story, albeit by necessity abbreviated, of how China as we know it today came to be.

A Note on the Pronunciation
of Chinese Names

English-speaking students often have difficulty pronouncing Chinese names because certain consonants and vowels used in the *pinyin* system of romanization have sounds unlike their English counterparts. Some approximate equivalents are as follows:

pinyin	*English*
zh	j
q	ch
x	sh
c	ts
a	a (as in *father*)
ui	ay

In Chinese names, the surname is written first.

Modernization and Revolution in China

1

The Middle Kingdom

The throne room of the Imperial Palace in the "Forbidden City."

The Chinese have never doubted their place in the world. In ancient times they called their land "Zhongguo"—the "Central Territory" or, as it is more commonly translated, the "Middle Kingdom." They also proudly called their emperor the "Son of Heaven." Chinese tradition and mythology affirmed that their emperors ruled over "all under heaven" in a universe composed of concentric circles of which China was the core and which became progressively less civilized the farther one strayed from the glorious center. Traditional beliefs further affirmed that it was China's earliest emperors who gave humanity fire, hunting, agriculture, writing, silk, musical instruments, and most of the other prerequisites of civilized life.

Whatever the problems of geographic or historical accuracy these names and claims pose, there is still much that has made China extraordinary and even unique among the nations of the world. Although the Chinese were not the first to develop civilized life, their civilization of about 4,000 years, starting with the Xia dynasty, has been the world's most enduring. It also has been one of the most creative and productive. Its basis was a highly efficient agricultural system utilizing sophisticated and extensive water control and irrigation techniques that enabled the Chinese to grow enough food to support what already in ancient times was the largest concentration of human beings in the world. Ancient China also developed an original writing system, one that spread to and influenced much of eastern Asia, and one that is still in use today. China has a rich philosophical tradition. Its core is Confucianism, an ideological and ethical system dating from the sixth century B.C.E. whose primary concern is maintaining a stable and humane social order. The venerable and varied Chinese literary tradition encompasses lyrical poetry, drama, prose, and an encyclopedic wealth of scholarship, particularly history. In fact, fully one-half of all the world's books printed before 1750 were printed in Chinese. China's artistic heritage includes superb technique in calligraphy and stunning achievements in landscape painting. And considerable skill was evident in Chinese sculpture, especially at its peak during the middle of the first century C.E.

The Chinese also were adept at combining art and function, as can be seen in their delicately balanced gardens and an architecture that sought harmony with nature. The bronzes of the ancient Shang dynasty (sixteenth to eleventh century B.C.E.) have never been surpassed. Porcelain, perhaps China's best-known synthesis of art and function, was the standard of the world for so long that it is simply known as "china." Chinese craftsmen also made many other products desired throughout the world. In particular demand was silk, which was woven into clothing, tapestries, and embroideries of rich variety and decoration. Chinese cottons and woolens also reflected extraordinary craftsmanship and artistic sense.

Chinese civilization was technologically adept. The Chinese were outstanding metallurgists. Aside from the great bronzes of the Shang era, they developed techniques for casting iron and making steel centuries before they were known in Europe. Chinese technical innovation gave the world not only the deservedly lionized "four inventions" of printing, paper, the magnetic compass, and gunpowder, but also, among other things, the modern horse collar (vital to transportation and agriculture), the watertight ship compartment, canal locks, suspension and segmented bridges, the crossbow, and the humble but ever so useful wheelbarrow. Chinese engineering accomplishments—from flood control and irrigation systems along the Yellow River in the second millennium B.C.E. to the building of the 2,000-mile-long Great Wall beginning in the second century B.C.E. and the construction of the 1,200 mile Grand Canal in the sixth century C.E.—matched any in the ancient world. Chinese medicine was comparable or superior to medical practice anywhere in the world until the nineteenth century. Anesthetics in surgery and acupuncture have been practiced in China for two millennia. China's first medical college was established 1,000 years ago, and over the centuries the empire's medical practitioners developed many useful drugs for various maladies.

In the pure sciences, China's international standing is less formidable, in part because the scientific method that since the seventeenth century has transformed the world was the product of European thinking. Still, Chinese mathematicians probably invented coordinate geometry, and they certainly computed the ancient world's most accurate value for *pi*, used negative numbers 1,000 years before the Europeans, and discovered the algebraic triangular pattern for coefficients (called "Pascal's Triangle," in honor of its European discoverer) about 500 years before it was known in Europe. The Middle Kingdom's astronomical tradition stretches back to 1300 B.C.E. and includes the world's first study of sun spots, the observation of the Crab Nebula supernova in 1054 C.E., and centuries of cataloging and mapping the stars. China's efforts in botany included extensive studies of flowers and fruits, and its blend of alchemy and primitive chemistry produced the world's first gunpowder. Whatever the later shortcomings of Chinese science, it is likely that China was the world's leading technological society for some 700 years, from the seventh to the fourteenth centuries C.E.

Perhaps the most remarkable achievement of Chinese civilization was in the realm of government. Most great empires have been relatively short-lived, lasting for a few generations or at best several centuries. It was Rome's great accomplishment to maintain political unity in the Mediterranean basin for about 500 years. But China's achievement dwarfed Rome's. The Chinese were the first, more than two millennia ago, to develop a relatively efficient bureaucratic system of government, one that they improved on in succeeding generations. This not only enabled the Chinese emperors to govern more effectively but also helped to maintain central authority as individual emperors came and went. Once political unity was established in 221 B.C.E., despite invasion, conquest, civil war, and disorder that intervened for centuries at a time, it became a phoenix that continued to rise and reassert itself for more than 2,000 years.

Even before they achieved political unity, the Chinese became and remained the world's most numerous people. Although much of China south of the

Yangzi River was once populated by ethnic groups such as Thais, Tibeto-Burmans, Miao, and Khmers, these people either have been assimilated or reduced to the status of small minorities in their ancient homelands, while the Chinese have spread and multiplied. Thus, when Rome was at its height, more people lived under the Chinese "Son of Heaven" than under the Roman Caesar. When 4 million souls in wild and primitive North America established their ambitiously titled "United States of America," and Russia, the most populous country in Europe, contained about 35 million people, there were 200 million Chinese. Today, more than 1 billion people—one human being in four—live in China, twice the population of the United States and the former Soviet Union combined.

The physical immensity of China likewise places it in an exclusive category among the nations of the world. Today only Russia and Canada have territories that exceed China's 3.7 million square miles. (The United States, including Alaska, is about 3.6 million square miles.) Within that huge territory there are several major divisions and great diversity. The most basic division is ethnic rather than geographic: the division between "China proper," where ethnic—or "Han"—Chinese have predominated for several millennia, and the outlying territories populated by a variety of ethnic and religious minorities. China proper, an area of approximately 1.5 million square miles, is itself divided into four regions: the North China Plain drained by the Yellow River; the upper course of the Yangzi River, in particular rich and fertile Sichuan Province; the lower course of the Yangzi; and the southern coastal region drained by the West River and its tributaries.

China proper's most fundamental geographic division, however, is between north and south. North China, the ancestral home of the Han Chinese and the area where Chinese civilization first took shape about 4,000 years ago, is a large plain through which flows one of the great streams of the world, the Yellow River. It is a region both blessed and cursed by nature. The soil of the North China Plain, called loess, extends in places to a depth of 150 feet, and it is fertile and easily worked. Therefore, even though the rainfall of north China is marginal for successful agriculture—averaging about 20–25 inches per year—the Yellow River valley was a natural spot, much like the river valleys of Egypt and Mesopotamia, for neolithic man to make the transition from a hunting and pastoral existence to a sedentary agricultural life.

While it was the Yellow River with its life-giving waters that made this transition possible in the face of inadequate and unreliable rainfall, the river also has presented a major problem for the people who have farmed and lived near or on its banks. The loess soil is easily eroded, and that soil, floating in the Yellow River as sediment, gave the river its color and its name. It also gave the river a second name: "China's Sorrow." Meandering along its gentle and sometimes barely sloping course to the sea, the Yellow River deposits the sediment in its bed, inexorably rising as the endless process continues and therefore constantly threatening to overflow its banks. When this has occurred, despite the best efforts of generations of Chinese to maintain the dikes built along those banks, the river, at points flowing 20 feet above the valley floor on its ever-rising bed of sediment, has brought famine and death instead of sustenance and life to China. On several dreadful occasions, the sedimentation process actually caused the Yellow River to change its course. As the river irresistibly cut its new route home to the sea, it destroyed countless human lives in the process.

South China has its own great river, the Yangzi, but a different set of problems. The Yangzi, like the Yellow River, rises in western China, flows through its majestic and daunting gorges in Sichuan Province midway between its source and mouth, draws water from many tributaries and lakes, and after a course of 3,200 miles empties into the East China Sea. Although the Chinese did not settle the Yangzi basin until well after their civilization was established in the north, the region eventually became, and has remained, the agricultural heart of China. South China, warmed by Pacific sea breezes and bathed by annual monsoon rains, has a climate suitable for the cultivation of rice, a crop that permits more intensive husbandry than does the wheat or millet grown in the north. The relatively infertile soil—leached of its nutrients for millennia by heavy rains and eroded by floods that occurred when forests were cut down to make room for rice paddies—has not prevented double cropping of rice, which has sustained not only the population of south China but much of the population of the north as well. This has never been easy. Generations of mountain-moving human labor have drained swamps, irrigated dry land, and terraced hills to make them suitable for planting. Still, 450,000 square miles, less than a third of China proper, is arable.

Most of China proper lies in regions drained by three major rivers and their tributaries: the above-described Yellow and Yangzi, and the West, which drains the southernmost parts of the country before reaching the South China Sea. But China also includes vast areas inhabited by ethnic minorities. To the west is Xizang (Tibet), the 500,000-square-mile "roof of the world." Much of that huge plateau, the world's highest, is more than 12,000 feet above sea level; it contains the Himalayas, the world's tallest mountain range, crowned by Mt. Everest, the world's loftiest peak. Today the Tibetan people, once warlike and formidable in their ability to resist Chinese authority, are being submerged by a sea of Chinese immigration into their homeland. To the northwest is Xinjiang, a stark region of desert and mountains speckled with numerous, but shrinking, oases. It is home to about 12 million Turkic-speaking Muslim people and a growing Han minority. Directly to the north is Mongolia, the windswept cradle of Genghis Khan's great empire, where grasslands give way to semi-aridity and then to the great Gobi Desert. And to the northeast is Manchuria, homeland of the Tungus people. In 1644, the Manchus, a Tungus group, conquered China and ruled it as the Qing dynasty until 1911, when the dynastic system that had existed for more than 2,000 years collapsed. Despite a severe continental climate of hot summers and cold winters, Manchuria is a rich region, unlike Xizang or Xinjiang. Manchuria's flatlands are fertile and well-watered, its mountains cloaked by forests, and its subsoil laced with valuable minerals, including coal. It has long tempted China's neighbors, notably Russia and Japan. Today Manchuria is an area of considerable economic importance, particularly for China's future industrial development.

The number of people living in the outlying areas—the Tibetans, Mongols, Uighurs, Tungus, among other groups—has always been small relative to the number of Han Chinese. But their impact on China has been enormous. Because large parts of these regions are poorly suited to agriculture, many of their inhabitants, in contrast with the settled agriculturists of China proper, developed a nomadic lifestyle. These wanderers of the inner Asian heartland moved with their flocks of sheep, cattle, or yaks from pasture to pasture, their movements dependent on the vagaries of nature. They relied on the horse, and so became superb horsemen and therefore capable, in a world before firearms, of militarily threatening the more numerous Han Chinese, particularly when the latter suffered from internal disorder. The impact of the marauding nomadic horsemen often could be serious, such as when they made the ancient silk road leading westward through the Tarim Basin in Central Asia impassable, or when nomad hordes ravaged large parts of China itself. At other times the impact was calamitous, when certain nomad groups were able to unify their disparate bands and actually conquer part or all of China and establish ruling dynasties. This occurred in the fourth and fifth centuries when various Tibetan, Mongol, Tungus, and Turkic dynasties divided up north China, in the tenth century when the Khitans conquered most of north China, and in the thirteenth century when the Mongols established their Yuan dynasty to rule over all of China. Finally, in the seventeenth century, the Manchus conquered China and founded one of its greatest dynasties, the Qing, which endured for almost 300 years.

A measure of the seriousness with which the Chinese regarded the nomad threat and the resources they devoted to containing it is the 2,000-mile-long Great Wall, which spans northern China from inner Asia to the sea. Built and rebuilt over many generations, wide enough to hold a two-lane highway, the Great Wall is the most massive structure ever built.

As it turned out, what ultimately posed the greatest threat to the Chinese and their civilization did not come from horsemen beyond the Great Wall, but from sailors across the sea. For it was the inhabitants of a remote corner of the Eurasian continent known as Western Europe, riding the crest of their scientific and industrial revolutions, that gave them technological and military capabilities far beyond those of the Chinese, who, after 1750, became a challenge that threatened not only the political integrity of China but the very Confucian roots of Chinese life.

Several key questions immediately arise from any examination of China's legacy and accomplishments. Why were the Chinese able to bring cultural and political unity to such vast and varied domains? Why did China ultimately sink into such a deep malaise during the nineteenth century? Finally, why did China, a nation so dedicated to order and stability, have to endure one of history's most violent and thoroughgoing revolutions before it could begin to restore its former greatness? In order to answer these questions, we must turn to a brief overview of how the Chinese ordered their lives before the crises of the nineteenth and twentieth centuries that so shook and almost shattered the land they called the Middle Kingdom.

2

Patterns of Traditional Chinese Life

Canton, China. Row of cubicles for the triennial Ku-yan examinations.

Nature and geography provided some conditions that helped promote unity over the broad expanse destined to become China. The cradle area of Chinese civilization in the Yellow River Basin was laced with rivers linking the various civilized centers in the region. This permitted a variety of interchanges that promoted cultural and ethnic homogeneity over a much larger area than was the case in other ancient civilized areas such as Egypt and Mesopotamia.

natural boundaries

At the same time, China was relatively more protected—although not cut off—from other powerful and potentially threatening civilized centers by its surrounding mountains, deserts, and seas. But these natural and geographic advantages only created a certain potential; in the end Chinese unity was a human effort, the product of cultural, technological, social, economic, and political institutions built over the course of the country's long history.

Maintaining unity and continuity was a constant challenge. There has been an ebb and flow to Chinese civilization, periods of progress and periods of regression, of unity and power, and of fragmentation and weakness, of confidence and assertiveness, and of hopelessness and despair. In a way, Chinese civilization, as it endured its ebbs and flows and bridged the crises and triumphs, became a testament to the validity of the ancient concept of *yin* and *yang*, which postulates that while the world is made up of opposing forces, those forces are nonetheless complementary and vital to each other.

The Four Orders

Whatever the variables of the Chinese experience, there were a number of fundamental constants that underlay its 4,000-year history. The most basic of these is that Chinese civilization has always rested on an agrarian, peasant base. Since earliest times, between 80 and 90 percent of China's population has consisted of peasant farmers. Foreigners observing China have reserved their admiration for the work of the nonpeasant classes, particularly the philosophical and literary works of China's educated elites or the paintings, silk, and ceramics of its artisans. But ultimately it was the backbreaking labor of China's peasant masses that created the highly productive agricultural foundation on which China's other classes built the marvelous edifice that was Chinese civilization.

Chinese thinkers themselves accorded the peasantry's contributions partial recognition. In their view of society—described as the "four orders"—the peasantry was assigned second place in terms of status, inferior only to the scholar-officials who governed the state. Social reality, as opposed to official status, was another matter. Chinese peasants generally lived and died in their own encapsulated world; in fact, one of the most important divisions in traditional Chinese society was that between the masses who lived in their villages and spent their days working the soil and the various groups who lived in the towns.

Urban China housed the other three orders: the highest, the governing officials and the class of large landowners from whom most governing officials sprang; the two remaining lower orders, the artisans and the merchants; and a mixed bag of people whose occupations excluded them from membership in the four orders at any level. The last group included soldiers, actors, prostitutes, and others whose work was considered menial or disreputable.

The difficult conditions in which the Chinese peasants lived and worked shaped their institutions and values. Since ancient times the population of China's river valleys has been high; that is, there always has been a large number of people relative to the resources, especially land, needed to sustain them. Along with this unrelenting overcrowding, China's agriculture has long depended on controlling water, both in the north, where inadequate and unreliable rainfall had to be supplemented by irrigation, and in the south, where rice cultivation required alternate flooding and draining of the fields. This meant that survival, to say nothing of prosperity, depended on close cooperation at the ordinary, everyday level of life and the mobilization of the labor power of masses of people for large water control projects. The end result was a value system radically different from that of the West, where, since the Renaissance, the individual has been exalted and personal freedom has been a key standard for judging the merits of a society. In China the group always was paramount and the individual consistently and often mercilessly subordinated to it. Each individual had to contribute to the general welfare and do nothing to disrupt the order and stability deemed so vital to the functioning of the system on which community life depended.

The individual first was subordinated to the family, the basic economic, political, and moral institution of Chinese society. It was the family, not the individual, that owned property, paid taxes, and frequently took responsibility for the legal or moral transgressions of one of its members. The family therefore was crucial to maintaining social discipline and keeping people in their place.

This was done through an autocratic and hierarchical structure headed by the grandfather or father. The family patriarch had almost absolute authority over the other family members, from his wife, whom he could divorce almost at will, to his children, over whom he frequently held the power of life and death. Children owed their father what was known as filial piety. This concept actually went beyond absolute deference to one's father to include subservience to any superior and, by extension, submission to the state. Chinese children were told the heroic saga of Wu Meng, whose filial piety led him to endure being eaten by mosquitoes to divert them from attacking his parents. More compelling was the tragic tale of a youth named Deng. Having stabbed his father by accident while trying to ward off several men who were attacking his esteemed parent, poor Deng was executed nonetheless because filial piety forbids striking one's father under any circumstances.

Aside from their duty to the father, the young in a family were subordinated to the old. So carefully ordered was the family, for example, that there is no single word in Chinese for "brother"; rather there are terms only for "elder brother" and "younger brother" and one's relationship to them. Even the way one addressed a brother, or anybody else, depended on one's position in the family hierarchy.

While every member of a Chinese family endured tyranny, the women suffered special deprivations. Chinese philosophy, which assigned to women the darkness and cold (or "*yin*") qualities of the *yin/yang* duality ("*yang*," the male symbol, signified brightness and warmth), and language itself, in which the written character used to designate "wife" was derived from pictographs signifying a female and a broom, left little doubt about a woman's value and her place. Chinese women had few property rights. They could be cast out by their husbands or compelled to share him with concubines. Bound to an arranged marriage, and compelled to move into her husband's household, a Chinese woman had to endure not only her husband's tyranny but that of her mother-in-law as well. Generally speaking, the only way out of an unbearable marriage was suicide. Adding physical injury to the social insult of Chinese women was the practice of footbinding. Dating from the Northern Song dynasty (960–1126), this was the painful and crippling custom of binding the feet of little girls so that their toes were forced back under their arches rather than allowed to grow out normally. It created the tiny and presumably beautiful "lily feet" associated with the popular image of Chinese women. For several centuries footbinding was limited to women of the upper class, but it then began to spread so that by the nineteenth century more than half of all Han Chinese women bound their feet. As they limped through life on their twisted toes and broken arches, they were expected to smile and look graceful and beautiful.

While the peasants fed China, a class called the gentry did the governing. Although in China the gentry for the most part were the large landowners, formal membership in the gentry was based on something else. Gentry members had to be highly educated and able to pass an extremely difficult qualifying examination based on the classic Confucian texts (although sometimes good connections or money could do the job as well). Upon passing this exam and earning what was known as a scholarly degree, these "scholar-gentry" were eligible for the next, even more difficult, level of exams. These three-day examinations qualified the approximately 1 percent who passed them to be government officials. These select few then were eligible for the highest-level exams, during which they were confined to tiny cubicles for seven exhausting days. Very few candidates passed (only 24,874 during the entire 267-year Ming dynasty, for example). From this *crème de la crème* came the top officials of the realm.

Two characteristics made the Chinese scholar-gentry unique among traditional societies. First, those who passed the first level of examinations shouldered much of the responsibility for local government. Their responsibilities included maintaining law and order, overseeing public works (especially the critical irrigation and flood control infrastructure), collecting taxes, and organizing public ceremonies. This service traditionally was done voluntarily and therefore drastically reduced the expense of governing the vast expanse of China. This in turn made a major contribution to China's long-term unity, for one of the things that helped break down vast empires in the era before modern communications was the great expense and hence the great tax burden of controlling a large geographic area. Also, China's local government was in the hands of educated men whose years of study gave them a set of values and capabilities that made them at once more loyal to their sovereign and more capable of carrying out the state's dictates than the paid officials of other states and empires. Of course, gentry service was hardly altruistic. Holding official gentry status and serving in local government brought many honors and opportunities to enrich oneself and one's family.

A second special characteristic of the Chinese scholar-gentry was that formal gentry status was not inherited. True, both considerable wealth and leisure time were required to prepare for even the lowest-level exams (which most candidates failed in any case) and therefore most gentry members did in fact come from the wealthy landowning class. One can therefore speak in a general sense of the Chinese gentry as the large landowning class that provided most of the successful candidates for the state examinations and consequently the scholar-gentry who governed China. In a given generation any particular landowning family might not have a son who was capable of passing the exams and achieving formal gentry status. By virtue of its wealth, however, the family remained part of the gentry in the broader, informal sense, likely to produce a successful examination candidate farther down the generational line. Still, formal gentry status and the honor and privileges that went with it required passing the first level of exams and qualifying as a scholar, something that each individual had to do by himself, regardless of his family background or wealth.

The right to take those examinations was open to most male Chinese. This small opening permitted a tiny but steady and unending stream of highly talented peasant men to rise from their class of origin and enter the gentry. A typical formula for success was for a village to finance the education of a particularly talented son, whose success would bring great honor and benefits to the village itself. This meant that over the centuries the Chinese ruling class consistently received infusions of new talent from below. China's unique method of keeping government service open to talent helped make the Chinese gentry far more vibrant and durable than the strictly hereditary upper classes of other societies. This in turn contributed to the overall durability of Chinese civilization itself.

The examination system developed over time, with a formal system of exams initially being instituted in the first century C.E., during the Han dynasty. After a period of decline, the examinations and service system dependent on them were revived and greatly improved during the Tang dynasty (618–906). Thereafter the gentry dominated Chinese society and government for more than 1,000 years.

Living alongside the gentry families in the towns were the merchants. Confucianism did not consider commerce a productive endeavor since merchants themselves merely bought and sold what others made, rather than creating new wealth. Yet commerce was widespread and enduring in traditional China, stimulated by the Middle Kingdom's wide variety of products and its excellent transportation network. But China's merchants never were able to establish the independence of action merchants in Europe enjoyed. This was largely because early on Chinese merchants faced a unified state that had developed the strength to control many human activities, including commercial life. In Western Europe, on the other hand, the merchant class was able to maneuver and grow in the urban cracks and crevices of Western Europe's decentralized medieval society. A typical problem for the Chinese merchants was that whenever a great demand for a product developed, the government would move in and set up a monopoly to generate revenues for itself. Moreover, China's merchants tended to invest in land and in the education of their sons, and so aspire to gentry status. Ultimately this meant that China's merchants, whatever their wealth, did not develop into a self-conscious entrepreneurial class like the bourgeoisie of Western Europe, a class that one day was to be the driving force behind the development of commercial capitalism and, subsequently, the Industrial Revolution.

Whatever disadvantages this ultimately posed for China, for several millennia the Chinese social structure, with most people welded firmly in their place, proved remarkably stable and enduring. Governed by strict rules of conduct, it was to a large degree self-regulating. To the extent that it was not, as we shall see later, the Chinese devised governing institutions that did a superb job of filling in the gaps.

The Dynastic Cycle

China's long history prior to the twentieth century is generally divided according to the various dynasties that ruled the country and the periods of disunity interspersed between them. The dynasties themselves rose and fell according to a pattern that has come to be called the "dynastic cycle." Each dynasty was established by force. Those that survived for a lengthy period (some lasted only a generation or two) in turn followed a common pattern of growth and decay. They typically began with several generations of effective emperors and efficient government. The state bureaucracy functioned relatively well and maintained public works, social services, and public order. Social stability existed because the peasantry had enough land to support itself and pay the taxes necessary to maintain the government. Eventually, however, the quality of the emperors would decline. They, their ministers, and the entire bureaucracy became increasingly corrupted. Landlords tended to accumulate larger holdings, driving the peasantry to tenancy or landlessness and to poverty. Peasants were unable to pay their taxes; landlords, who could pay, managed to evade them. All this inevitably undermined the state's ability to govern. Social discontent grew, often exacerbated by natural disasters whose impact was magnified by the government's inability to respond to the crisis. Rebellion (and/or invasion) followed. The old, decrepit dynasty fell, followed after an interregnum of varying length by a new, vigorous dynasty, and the start of a new cycle.

Chinese tradition provided an explanation for the dynastic cycle. The failure of the old dynasty was proof that it had lost the support of the gods, what was called the "Mandate of Heaven." The loss of this mandate gave the people what was called the "right to rebel." The new dynasty's ability to establish itself was proof that it had inherited the prized and vital Mandate.

The earliest periods of Chinese history, the years before the sixteenth century B.C.E., have left a wealth of archaeological artifacts but an historical record shrouded in myth and legend. A documentable history begins with the Shang dynasty of the sixteenth to twelfth centuries B.C.E. Controlling several provinces of northern China, the Shang were skilled workers of bronze, carvers of jade, and weavers of silk, as well as adept warriors. Most significantly, their inscriptions carved on oracle bones are the first examples of a script identifiable as the origins of Chinese writing. The Shang were overthrown by their neighbors, the Zhou. This dynasty officially lasted from the twelfth century B.C.E. until the end of the third century B.C.E., but its actual existence as a functioning state lasted at most until the eighth century B.C.E.

The period that followed, between about 770 B.C.E. and 221 B.C.E., was rent by disunity, nomad invasions, and chronic internecine war. Yet, it also was one of the most creative and important periods in China's history. There were major technological innovations in agriculture that promoted more efficient farming and the expansion of arable land; this supported the first major spurt in China's population. Other advances included the development of iron tools and improved methods of harnessing animals. Together these and other developments promoted economic development and growth that encompassed both domestic and foreign trade. Political developments were equally significant. Although China lacked a unified centralized state, centralized power was developing *within* the various Chinese states. Monarchs began to use paid employees—in effect creating a primordial civil service bureaucracy—to administer their territories directly and limit the power of the landed nobility. Another factor promoting centralized state power was technological changes in warfare. The invention of the crossbow was one of several developments favoring mass armies of infantry and cavalry at the expense of chariots manned by the nobility.

Most important were the seminal intellectual developments of this era. Here the Chinese were not alone. During the 500 years in the middle of the first millennium B.C.E. the Eurasian land mass became a huge intellectual tidal pool, where the lightning of new insights seemed to strike again and again to create powerful new systems of thought whose moral and ethical standards would not only dominate large parts of the ancient world but also remain pervasive influences to this day. Along the western fringe of what was then the civilized world, the Greek city-state of Athens reached its glorious height as the genius of teachers, philosophers, and scientists like Socrates, Plato, and Aristotle were laying the intellectual foundation of Western civilization. On the Mediterranean's eastern shore, in the tiny principalities of Judea and Israel, the Hebrew prophets were developing a religious code that provided Western civilization with much of its ethical foundation. Just to the east, Zoroaster founded the religion that was to predominate in the Persian empire for more than 1,000 years until the Muslim conquests of the seventh century C.E. On the eastern side of the Hindu Kush the Gautama was laying the basis for Buddhism, another of Asia's great religions.

Meanwhile, where Eurasia meets the Pacific, the Chinese were developing and expanding their intellectual tradition. Between 551 and 479 B.C.E., Confucius, China's most important thinker, outlined his ideas about how to secure social harmony and good government. Confucius's thinking reflected deeply rooted Chinese concepts, and many of the classic Confucian texts and writings attributed to the great master really antedate him by centuries. Additional insights came from later Confucian scholars, the most important of whom was probably Mencius (373–288 B.C.E.).

Confucianism faced rival systems of thought. Daoism, a doctrine with deep, ancient roots stressing harmony with nature, emerged as a major religion in China about the same time as Confucius was expounding his ideas. Legalism, a body of thought dedicated to maintaining social order, evolved during the fourth century B.C.E. and gained many important adherents. While these three doctrines had many points of disagreement and competed with each other for followers, they eventually came to coexist, although Confucianism, rendered more flexible by Daoist influences and tempered by Legalist doctrines, ultimately emerged as the prevailing thought system in China. Another important influence was Buddhism, which beginning in the fourth century C.E. became the only foreign doctrine to gain a wide following in traditional China. What finally emerged from all of this has come to be known as the Confucian outlook, a way of thinking and acting that retained a central core of continuity and dominated China for 2,000 years.

The Confucian Outlook

The prime directive of Confucianism was to maintain social order and good government. Confucianism assumed that the harmony and order required by society could not be imposed solely from above. This meant that all individuals had to understand and accept their place in society. Government in turn must be based on rules and codes of behavior that commanded respect and were enforceable. A key assumption was that people could be educated to internalize values and thus accept their place and perform the duties associated with it. Confucianism therefore was a strictly hierarchical outlook assigning places to most people from birth. And while it assumed that government was based on a moral code, Confucianism always stacked the deck against the individual and in favor of authority, from the peasants at the base of the power structure to the emperor at its pinnacle.

A concept that perhaps best illustrates the essence of the Confucian outlook is the concept of *li*—proper conduct according to status. In the contemporary West, people are accustomed to rules of conduct and codes of law that are applied equally to all individuals. According to *li*, however, nothing could be more dangerous. Instead (at least when dealing with the upper classes; the lower classes were to be controlled more by strict laws and punishments), each position in the social hierarchy was governed by specific rules. Therefore, the classic texts relate that Confucius himself "when conversing with higher great officials . . . spoke respectfully." However, when dealing with someone of lesser status than himself, Confucius "spoke out boldly." The law clearly reflected *li*. Since a husband was superior to a wife, it was quite proper for him to strike her, while a wife could strike a husband only on pain of receiving 100 blows from the state. Whatever the wife's complaints on this score, they were worse for a son, who could be beaten by his father and subject to execution if he struck back. So strong were the sanctions of *li* that if a gentleman of the upper classes committed certain transgressions, it was presumed that no criminal proceedings would be necessary; rather, he was expected to recognize the gravity of his offense and take the opportunity to commit suicide, thereby at least honoring *li* with his final act.

Lest anyone from any level of society have any doubt of how to behave, Confucian scholars provided four other virtues to complement *li*: benevolence, righteousness, wisdom, and good faith. The scholars also gave the people the "three bonds." These bonds required the loyalty of the subject to the ruler, subordination of the son to the father, and faithfulness of the wife to her husband (who himself could enjoy the pleasure of other wives and concubines without hindrance from *li* or anything else). Two additional relationships— between younger and older brother and between friends—rounded out the picture. Only one of all these relationships, that between friends, was one of equals; the others were between people who were superior or inferior to each other on the social ladder.

Harmonious society also required good government. The key to this according to Confucius, as it was to Plato living a century later and half a world away, was that governing be done by carefully selected and properly trained people. Confucius was convinced that his knowledge and teaching held the secret to good government, and he seems to have spent a good deal of his time wandering from state to state in what was then a divided China looking for a ruler willing to sample his intellectual and political wares. Confucius's claims hardly fit the modest image he usually projected. "If someone would employ me," he is said to have promised, "in a month I would have my system working. In 3 years, everything would be running smoothly."

Confucius postulated that good government began with a ruler knowing how to behave. Naturally, the foremost experts in proper behavior were none other than those with a mastery of Confucius's teaching and a broad education and knowledge of Chinese culture. Therefore, Confucian scholars were the perfect and only choice to serve as the ruler's advisers, administrators, and officials. Over time, once Confucianism was accepted and became the official ideology of the Chinese state, a complex and sophisticated system based on a rigorous system of examinations was developed for training and selecting these men.

Another important dimension of Confucianism that helps to explain its success over such a long period of time is its tolerance and flexibility. Although Confucianism venerated the past and the old—whether customs, traditions, learned texts, ancestors, or society's elders—and therefore resisted change, it was sufficiently flexible to tolerate or even absorb elements from other systems, both secular and religious. It therefore was perfectly acceptable for a Confucian official to observe Daoist rituals in his home, even if they were at variance with the strict Confucian etiquette he observed in public life. Nor would that official have any problems with the ancient religions and pantheon of gods of the Chinese masses.

Confucianism meanwhile absorbed important elements from several competing intellectual systems. Legalism fortified the Chinese administration of justice. Buddhism, a religion from India that for a time challenged Confucianism and was consequently subject to a period of severe persecution, added some of its insights to the Confucian tradition. Confucian scholars of the sixteenth and seventeenth centuries were able to tolerate Catholic visitors from Europe. Confucianism, then, was flexible enough to accommodate, swallow, and adapt so long as its core principles remained uncompromised, a quality that helped it ride out many storms. It is, after all, a Chinese insight that it is the tree that bends a little, not the one that stands absolutely rigid, that survives in a strong wind.

Imperial China

In the end it was force, not philosophy, that produced unity in China. The Middle Kingdom's political fragmentation finally came to an end in 221 B.C.E. when much of China proper was unified under the Qin dynasty (221 B.C.E–206 B.C.E.). Qin Shihuangdi, the dynasty's first emperor, became known as much for his ruthlessness and cruelty as for his achievements as a unifier. His merciless pursuit of power claimed countless Chinese lives. In order to break local traditions and loyalties, he ordered the infamous "burning of the books," the destruction of all local records and philosophical works that predated his reign. He also broke the power of the local landlords, codified China's laws, standardized the writing system and weights and measures, and largely completed the Great Wall. While his policies amounted to a human tragedy, and a crime in cultural terms, Qin Shihuangdi's relentless attacks on local traditions and autonomy are credited with contributing significantly to forging the unity of China's vast length and breadth.

Stigmatized by its founder's harshness, the Qin dynasty outlived Qin Shihuangdi himself by only 4 years. But his work was continued, albeit with greater moderation, during the Han dynasty (206 B.C.E.–220 C.E.), founded after several years of civil war. Under the Han, Confucianism became official state doctrine, and the system of examinations for selecting officials was introduced for the first time. Though considered by some historians to be two dynasties (the Western, or Former, Han [206 B.C.E.–9 C.E.] and the Eastern, or Later, Han [25–220 C.E.]), the long-lived Han dynasty was marked by another development of fundamental importance: ethnic Chinese expansion beyond the Yellow River cradle area into the rich Yangzi valley to the south. The final collapse of the Han empire in C.E. 220 led to 400 years of disunity. Despite the many problems of the immediate post-Han period, this era also witnessed developments that strengthened China in the long run, particularly the agricultural growth of the Yangzi valley and its transformation into China's breadbasket.

As it turned out, the Qin and Han had done their work well, for even without external political bonds, internal cultural and ethnic sinews helped prevent the kind of permanent fragmentation that occurred in Europe after the fall of the Roman Empire. In 590 c.e., China was politically reunited under the Sui dynasty. Destined, like the Qin, to collapse under the weight of its harsh exactions in barely a generation, the Sui dynasty still managed to contribute to China's long-term unity by completing one of the engineering and construction marvels of the ancient world: the 1,200-mile-long Grand Canal linking north China with its new breadbasket in the Yangzi valley to the south. Over the next 500 years—under the Tang (618–906) and Northern Song (960–1126) dynasties—Chinese civilization achieved new heights in what has been called its medieval flowering. A dazzling array of technological breakthroughs transformed agriculture. Advanced water management techniques (including improved dams and the invention of the sluicegate), improved and faster ripening seeds (which permitted double-cropping), and new and better fertilizers produced vastly expanded crop yields. This once again allowed the population to grow. Woodblock printing spread the knowledge of these developments and techniques, while the growth of commerce, itself the product of better land and water transportation, allowed different regions to specialize in crops best suited to local conditions. Progress was across the board: from medicine and public health (drainage systems in the cities, improved knowledge of anatomy, even the invention of the toothbrush), to textile manufacturing (including a machine for reeling silk), to metallurgy (using coal to produce iron), to the technology of warfare (to which the Chinese added gunpowder, firearms, and even bombs). China became the world's most technologically advanced and urbanized society; quite likely it also was the best governed under the reorganized civil service bureaucracy developed by the Tang.

The Chinese Bureaucracy and Governmental System

The roots of the Chinese bureaucracy reach back prior to the Qin unification. During Confucius's time, China's competing states worked to improve their administrative systems by using hired employees rather than hereditary nobles to oversee their domains. In the second century c.e., the Han dynasty set up the first formalized bureaucracy selected by an examination system. However, the system set up under the Tang was a substantial improvement on what had gone before, so much so that despite subsequent improvements, the Chinese bureaucracy probably was at its best under the Tang (618–906) and its immediate successor, the Northern Song (960–1126). The Tang established six major administrative divisions, or boards, each with a specific area of responsibility: public administration, revenue, military, rites, public works, and justice. These six boards, centralized in the capital of Xi'an, were the fulcrum of the Chinese bureaucracy until the twentieth century. The Tang also divided the empire into smaller, more manageable administrative units, from provinces (which often were bigger than entire European countries) down to local counties. The most significant post-Tang addition to this basic structure was the Censorate, an agency for supervising and checking the work of the rest of the bureaucracy. What made the Censorate so effective and important was that it bypassed normal bureaucratic channels and reported directly to the emperor.

The key to the Chinese bureaucratic system was the preparation, selection, and self-discipline of the men who staffed it: a governing group that came to be known as the Mandarinate, after the language—Mandarin—used in all official government communications and business. The preparation consisted of years of study. Selection for office was based on the examination system.

During his years of study, a prospective candidate was immersed in the deep, broad sea of China's culture and values. He studied history, literature, fine arts, calligraphy, and more, receiving traditional China's version of what Westerners consider a liberal education, the assumption being that those who best understood China's traditions would know best how to conduct themselves and therefore how to run the country. He memorized and learned to accept the ancient Confucian system of values and behavioral rules; he did not learn, as is the tradition in the West, to think critically and question what he was told. Rather than being trained in specific governing techniques, he was drilled in proper Confucian behavior and the management of people in general.

The examination system during China's later dynasties was a grueling rite of passage. The Chinese claimed that to pass the provincial examinations that qualified one to be a government official—a three-day ordeal spent entirely in a tiny cubicle—required the "spiritual strength of a dragon horse, the physique of a donkey, the insensitivity of a woodlouse, and the endurance of a camel."[1] Candidates for the very top jobs then had to pass a seven-day writing marathon in the capital, after which they received a final grading in an oral examination from the emperor himself. What all this did, aside from putting many of the empire's best minds through hell and breaking many of them, was to create a class of men committed to governance, deeply schooled in a common set of values and traditions, and indoctrinated to be loyal to the system they served. Armed with this value system and body of knowledge, it was assumed that the Mandarinate, composed of what were called "gentlemen" or "superior men," would govern in large part by virtue of the example they set.

Confucian ideology and the Chinese themselves were too realistic and practical to assume that example alone would be enough to control the population or, for that matter, that every official would exhibit model behavior.

The Chinese over time therefore developed administrative institutions and techniques to limit the impact of human imperfections or inadequacies. One of these was the Censorate. Another, the "law of avoidance," precluded officials from serving in their home regions. This reduced the possibility of someone using his power for personal gain or to build up his own fiefdom. The principle of "circulation" reinforced this by requiring officials to shift from place to place every 3 to 6 years. To further keep them honest, officials had to observe the rule of "mourning." This required a period of sabbatical and study on the death of one's father, during which an official was re-immersed in the Confucian classics and the values, rules, and ethics contained therein. The use of Mandarin—one of many Chinese dialects—as the official language of government helped build cohesiveness by giving the Mandarinate a common tongue in an empire where many dialects were spoken and, in effect, setting it off from much of the general population. A later technique introduced by the alien Manchus during the Qing dynasty (1644–1911) was to appoint two officials—one Chinese and one Manchu—to certain governmental posts. Each would then act as a check on the other. In this case, efficiency was sacrificed for control, a technique that served the Manchus well for at least the first half of their dynasty.

The position of the Mandarinate was reinforced by Chinese law. The legal system in China did not function as it does in the modern West, where a well-developed civil code regulates relations between individuals and law is viewed as protecting the individual against not only criminal acts committed by other citizens but against abuses by the state. In China, law was subordinated strictly to the interests of maintaining order. The punishment for a particular act depended on one's social status, hence the fate of the unfortunate Deng, executed for striking his father while trying to protect him from harm. The law served the state, not its subjects. There were more than 600 capital offenses in traditional China, and execution was often a long and cruel process. Torture was used to extract confessions. Furthermore, guilt was collective; entire families could be punished and even executed for the transgressions of one of their members. No wonder that the people were expected and sincerely tried to settle most disputes among themselves.

Finally, the Chinese bureaucracy rested on the gentry. Local government, from public works to religious celebrations to legal matters, which easily could have swamped a state governing an area as large as China in the era before modern communications, was the gentry's responsibility. And it did the job so well that at any given time the vast Chinese empire, from Han times well into the nineteenth century, could be governed by at most 30,000 to 40,000 officials.

All of this is not meant to give the impression that the Chinese had the perfect governmental system. The emperor who stood at its head had absolute power, and the quality of the government often rose and fell with the quality of the emperor. Emperors could destroy the careers and lives of even the highest and most competent officials on a mere whim. A top adviser or administrator could find himself one day suddenly being publicly whipped or otherwise tortured, and executed the next. Officials were poorly paid and, in fact, expected to supplement their income by accepting favors (called the "squeeze") or through other forms of corruption. Sometimes this was kept within tolerable limits, but when the central government was weak, corruption could rage out of control.

Several factors tended to mitigate the harshness of the system. While the emperor was considered all-powerful, he was nonetheless bound by Confucian precepts, which limited his behavior in the temporal realm. The Confucian principles according to which the state justified its existence were rooted in a dualistic vision of the world, one which recognized that the secular sphere of politics had to be subordinated to a higher set of moral standards. One of the Censorate's functions was to make sure that "harmony" prevailed between "heaven" and the emperor's earthly domains. In principle, the scholar-gentry was obliged to serve the court only so long as the ruler's behavior conformed to loftier laws that existed beyond the claims of the state. In effect, the emperor was expected to provide good government. If he did not and things went wrong, it was assumed that the requisite bonds of harmony had been broken, the emperor had lost the "Mandate of Heaven," and the people as a whole had the right to rebel. In this way the administration of justice, however severe, was held in check by Confucian morality and ethics. Administrative techniques such as the circulation of officials and supervision by the Censorate helped limit abuses of power by both the executive and his bureaucracy.

For centuries the Chinese bureaucracy managed to exercise extraordinary control over the lives of the people. The Mandarinate dominated Chinese life and enjoyed the privileges that life provided. In its official capacity it controlled public works, supervised commerce, and controlled education and public ceremonies. It could interfere in many areas of what Westerners consider to be "private" life. Overall, this elite's power and pervasiveness in Chinese life make it reasonable to call traditional China a bureaucratic society, ordered and restrained by the administrative system to which in ancient times it had given birth.

China's Last Dynasties

The golden age of the Chinese bureaucracy and the medieval flowering of Chinese civilization ended with the final collapse of what is known as the

Southern Song dynasty in 1279. This glorious era was followed by a national catastrophe, the first foreign (or "barbarian," as the Chinese saw it) conquest of all China by the Mongols, the nation of nomads whose terrifying and merciless cavalry overran and decimated Russia in three years and drove into Europe to the shores of the Adriatic. In China, however, the conquest was a bitter decades-long struggle that absorbed the energies of both great Mongol conquerors: Genghis Khan (1167–1227) and his grandson Kublai Khan (1260–1294). Yet the Mongols, so invincible as conquerors, were less formidable as rulers; their dynasty (the Yuan) lasted fewer than 100 years (1279–1367) before being overthrown by Chinese rebels who went on to establish the Ming.

The Ming dynasty (1368–1644), victorious over the alien and hated Mongols, represented a national vindication for the Chinese. The new dynasty also had to its credit other major accomplishments, among them the rebuilding of the Great Wall and the reconstruction and extension of the Grand Canal, the latter reflecting major advances in engineering technology. Before long, however, the first signs of problems, which proved to have serious long-term implications, appeared. Although Ming sailors, under Zheng He, carried out remarkable explorations to Arabia and Africa between 1404 and 1433, China subsequently turned inward. The Ming was less interested in what it found across the sea than in securing its frontiers with inner Asia, whence had come the hated Mongols. Also, centuries of cultural contact between Ming China and various foreigners shrank, thus decreasing the stimulation provided by alien ideas and techniques. Intellectual life began to stagnate; it was during the Ming dynasty that the notorious "eight-legged essay," a complex form of writing stressing form at the expense of content, became the required method of answering the civil service examinations. Technological progress in many areas, including agriculture, ebbed to what was probably its slowest pace in China's history. The Chinese began to fall behind in military techniques; they made much less progress in the use of firearms, for example, than did their Japanese neighbors to the east. Far more important, however, was the technological lag relative to the distant inhabitants of Western Europe, who were learning to overcome many technological problems, including how to travel global distances by sea, and who, in the person of Portuguese merchants, made their first landing in China at the southern city of Guangzhou (Canton) in 1514.

For a time, these small groups of Portuguese and other Europeans were hardly a problem for the Ming. During the seventeenth century, with the dynasty in decline, the Ming fell victim to new invaders from the north. In 1644 the Manchus became the second foreign group to conquer all of China. The Manchus, whose dynasty is known as the Qing, began their rule in a vigorous enough fashion. Their conquests extended the Chinese empire to its greatest extent ever, and although some of that territory was eventually lost, the Manchu policies of replacing tribal rule with imperial administration and systematic sinification deserve credit for welding several outlying areas from Xinjiang to Inner Mongolia into what China is today.

From the latter part of the seventeenth century until the middle of the eighteenth, China was the most populous and possibly the most prosperous country in the world. The Manchus strengthened interregional ties, promoting both prosperity and unity. Meanwhile, their ability to impose order for more than a century contributed to a spectacular and unprecedented growth in China's population. This proved to be a dangerous development, as China's population began to outrun its available natural resources, paving the way for overpopulation to become what it remains today: China's most daunting domestic problem. Overall, while maintaining their distance from the Chinese masses who surrounded them (and forbidding Chinese settlement in their Manchurian homeland), the Manchus accommodated themselves to China and Chinese ways far better than the Mongols had. This gained their dynasty, initially considered alien, a degree of acceptance that helped make it one of the most long-lived of all of China's dynasties.

The Tributary System

Initially, the Manchus, by restoring the empire's military strength, were successful in controlling the encroachments of the European powers who hoped to open China for trade. Dealing with the Europeans was a complicated problem. For the Chinese, relations between nations were based on the idea of Confucian hierarchy, in which each member state held a prescribed position. Just as in the Confucian social order the father or the emperor was supreme in his realm, so China in the world of nations stood at the top. China was the center of the world; all the peripheral states held inferior positions. China therefore could never recognize others as equal trading partners because anyone not a part of Chinese culture *ipso facto* was a "barbarian." Any state wishing to establish relations with the Middle Kingdom first had to fit itself into what was known as the tribute system. According to this scheme, barbarians were given the right to honor the emperor by bringing gifts to China. In presenting their gifts, barbarians were obliged to perform the kowtow, a ritual of prostrating oneself three times in front of the emperor while gently knocking one's head on the floor. Having thereby established beyond any doubt who was superior, the Chinese magnanimously would present gifts to the barbarians in return. That done, the Chinese were willing to engage in trade and maintain peaceful relations, provided it remained on their terms.

This logic, if not every detail of the traditional system, was applied to the new visitors from Europe. As with China's Asian neighbors and traditional tributaries who presented their tribute and traded only at designated locations, the Europeans were confined to several port cities. The Portuguese, the first European traders to arrive, were restricted by the Ming dynasty to Macao, a fortified port the Portuguese built near the Chinese city of Guangzhou. The Portuguese were soon joined by the British and the Dutch, with the British eventually becoming the dominant European country trading with China.

The British arrived in China in 1637 and were permitted to establish a trading post at the city of Guangzhou. From the first, however, they found the situation unsatisfactory. One problem, for which nobody was to blame, was that while there was a large British demand for Chinese goods—especially tea—there was little Chinese interest in British goods. The British therefore had to pay for much of what they wanted with silver and gold bullion, all the while searching desperately for something the Chinese might want or need. The other British problem was the treatment they received from the Chinese. Like other barbarians—Asian, European, or whatever—the British traders were confined to a designated place, in this case Guangzhou. This angered the British, who were, after all, a rapidly expanding colonial power and not in the habit of being told what to do. Making matters worse, the conditions at Guangzhou were hardly conducive to promoting the type and level of trade the British desired. Foreign merchants at Guangzhou could not do business directly with most Chinese merchants. They had to deal with a special group of Chinese traders organized into a guild called the "cohong." The cohong was composed of six to twelve firms and was responsible for all Western trade and held a monopoly over it. All foreigners had to adhere to strict regulations imposed by the cohong. They also had to live in designated areas called "factories" outside Guangzhou itself, lest these foul-smelling barbarians—whom the Chinese called "big noses," "hairy ones," and similar epithets—contaminate the civilized Chinese. All women were banned from the factories. Thus to the insult of isolation and the injury of limited trade was added the frustration of celibacy, at least according to official regulations.

Despite all these problems, the Guangzhou System was quite profitable for the individual Europeans engaged in it, even as it drained the West of gold and silver. Trade peaked under this system between 1760 and 1840, with the greatest beneficiary being the famous British East India Company, holder of the monopoly on all tea imported into Great Britain and its possessions until 1833. But the British remained unable to sell their manufactured products in China, which might have reduced their trade imbalance with the Middle Kingdom and stemmed the flow of gold running from London to Beijing. This frustration only grew worse as the British thirst for tea grew to where the tea trade provided London with one-tenth of its tax revenues as well as the entire profits of the East India Company.

The British and other Europeans ultimately solved their trade deficit problems by selling the Chinese opium, whose increased use was a good barometer of growing social problems in the Middle Kingdom. The profit that could be made from opium was staggering: ten dollars of opium grown in Britain's possessions in India sold for about 600 dollars in China. Addicts in the early nineteenth century were mostly young men from wealthy families, but the habit soon spread to people from all walks of life. In 1800, when an emperor's edict prohibited opium use, China consumed about 200 chests of the drug (each weighing about 133 pounds); by 1839, the figure was more than 40,000 chests. Meanwhile the opium trade spread from Guangzhou up and down the China coast as the enormous wealth that it provided corrupted Chinese officials and brought all sorts of Western adventurers, called free traders, to China to make their ill-gotten fortunes, a situation that became far worse after the East India Company lost its monopoly on the tea trade in 1833. By then opium accounted for well over half of China's foreign imports, every bit of it needed to feed the habits of an estimated 4 to 12 million opium smokers. The opium trade probably had become the largest single-commodity commerce of its kind in the world.

As its ties grew with Great Britain and other Western nations, China developed a similar but somewhat special relationship with an expanding Eurasian power—the Russian Empire. The Russians came to China not by sea from the south, but by land from the north. In 1689, with the treaty of Nerchinsk, the Chinese put a limit on Russian territorial ambitions in eastern Asia. What made Nerchinsk special was that it was a treaty on the European diplomatic model rather than a tribute relationship. A generation later, in 1728, a trade agreement reached at the Mongolian town of Kiakhta regulated Russian trade with the Middle Kingdom. Again the agreement was special, reflecting the threat of territorial expansion the Russians alone posed. The Treaty of Kiakhta permitted the Russians a small permanent mission in Beijing, something no other European nation was allowed. Still, China's relations with the Russians on the one hand and with the British, other Western Europeans, and the Americans on the other were hardly satisfactory to any of these uninvited intruders. These relationships depended on China's power to make them stick, and that power, as it turned out, began to ebb just as the Guangzhou trade was reaching its peak.

Part of the difficulty was that by the late eighteenth century the Qing was entering the period of dynastic decline so familiar in Chinese history. But something new was happening as well. While the Manchus were beginning their century-long fall from their throne in Beijing, all of China was starting a far greater slide from its traditional historical perch. This was an event of far greater moment than simply the decline of a dynasty. The decline and fall of the Manchus alone would have been like an iceberg, albeit a huge one, breaking off from its mother glacier and melting into the sea of history. Little in the global historical landscape would have been affected. By contrast, in an historical sense, the decline of China as a civilization represented far more than the disappearance of a mere iceberg, or even a glacier; it was more like the demise of a continental icecap, a structure of such mass and magnitude that even its partial submersion by historical forces dramatically changed a significant part of the world's historical and political landscape, much as the melting of a massive icecap changes global geographic features.

The process of Chinese decline was both relative and absolute and had two parts, as during an earthquake, when two geological plates, one rising and one falling, grind against each other. One plate of this historical earthquake consisted of the various Western nations, propelled upward first by their commercial revolution of the seventeenth and eighteenth centuries and then by their industrial revolution of the nineteenth century. The other plate was China, finally, after centuries as the top crust of world civilization, being pushed inexorably downward by a series of forces, some internal, emanating from deep within its own history, and some external, generated by the rising and immensely powerful European mass that was crashing with increasing force against the vulnerable Middle Kingdom.

The internal factors undermining China were deeply rooted and extraordinarily difficult to counteract. There was little China could muster against European technology, especially after the Industrial Revolution was under way. Chinese technology lagged in part because China had not developed the scientific method of thinking and research whose products were making the Europeans so strong. It is not that the Chinese lacked a history of scientific achievements; indeed the opposite is in fact the case. But the systematic application of theory, experimentation, and practical application that developed in Europe after 1600 and produced a veritable explosion in scientific and technological advances there did not take place in China.

Several factors help account for this. The Confucian tradition stressed memorization and rote, not critical thinking and the creative development of new ideas. It also tended to separate intellectual and practical work, with hands-on labor consigned to an inferior position. Yet many of the early machines of the Industrial Revolution were the result of the marriage of intellectual work and mechanical skills. Even the Chinese language itself was an obstacle to scientific achievement. Because it has a picto-ideographic script rather than an alphabet, it was extremely difficult for one to become literate in it. In addition, stifling formality and tradition surrounded not only Confucian ideas but the written ideographs that expressed them, and this formality—as made manifest in the eight-legged essay—had grown since Ming times. All of this, in a sense, encased Chinese thought inside an intellectual great wall that was far more effective against new ideas than the Great Wall of stone was against new invaders.

A related factor in China's weakness was the failure of the Chinese economy to grow and expand like the economies of the West. Western economic growth, after all, was both a cause and effect of the scientific and technological progress that made these new barbarians so irresistible. The question, then, is why—with her ancient economic might that included technical achievements in all sorts of productive enterprises, as well as impressive commercial activity that characterized various periods of its history—did China not undergo a commercial capitalist revolution and then an industrial revolution?

Part of the explanation of the failure to develop capitalism may lie in the anticommercial traditions of Confucianism and the suffocating impact of the Chinese imperial state and its bureaucracy on merchant activities. But it is not enough just to blame obscurant scholars and meddlesome bureaucrats for China's economic underdevelopment. There is, in fact, an element of ethnocentrism in the Western assumption that China somehow should have been expected to follow a particular course simply because that is the way things happened in the small corner of the world that is Western Europe. It makes more sense to look at the conditions in China and to try to understand what happened there in light of the problems, prospects, and choices the Chinese faced.

Ironically, the problems China faced at the time of the European incursion may well have been a function of what once had been China's strength: its size, its deeply rooted traditions, and its sophistication. China's large population, once a source of power, seems to have reached a point, no later than the eighteenth century and possibly several centuries earlier, when it began to weigh China down. At least two developments are important here. As China's population passed a certain point, the amount of land available per family began to decrease. As this continued, in a country lacking modern industrial technology, per capita production began to fall, a process that may have begun as early as the twelfth century. Over time, this fall in productivity gradually transformed China from a rich country into a poor one. In addition, China's huge population made human labor so cheap that it became unnecessary to introduce new, labor-saving technology. Well before European missionaries and traders began to arrive in China in significant numbers, Chinese technological progress had ground to a halt, leaving the Middle Kingdom at a great disadvantage vis-à-vis the new, aggressive adventurers from across the sea.[2]

The problem of strength transformed into weakness may be looked at from another perspective. One of the reasons Great Britain and several other European nations were able to "take off" economically was that the mass to be launched was relatively small and light. In other words, there was a tremendous amount of resources readily available (much of it from the rich, easily exploitable Americas) to transform the economy of a relatively small country like Britain. China, however, was far larger than Britain, so much so that even the resources of North America (to which China did not have access) would not have been enough to overhaul its gigantic economy.[3] In short, given the size and traditions of their country, and whatever their attitude toward change, there is little the Confucian scholars could have done to overcome a legacy transformed by the alchemy of time from a golden pedestal into a leaden anchor.

Whatever the precise causes of its difficulties, by the nineteenth century China was impaled on an unprecedented two-pronged challenge, one prong being its own decline and the other the technologically superior nations of Europe. As a result, in effect the Middle Kingdom was forced to perform a long and painful kowtow at the feet of foreign barbarians, so that it would be a century and a half before a Chinese leader—a peasant-born revolutionary named Mao Zedong—could truthfully say that once again, "The Chinese people have stood up!"

3

Imperial Breakdown
and Western Invasion

During the Boxer Rebellion, Allied forces entered Beijing [Peking]
through a breach in the wall.

The Qing Dynasty Declines

Along with Western incursions, by the end of the eighteenth century the
Qing dynasty also was being seriously threatened by a multitude of internal problems. First, there was the state's inability to sustain an enormous
increase in population. Because of a century of peace and relative prosperity, China's population apparently doubled under the Manchus, reaching
the level of about 300 million by the end of the eighteenth century. The
expansion of agricultural production was unable to keep up with such rapid

demographic growth. By 1800, arable land had increased by less than 5 percent, woefully inadequate to support a population that had expanded by more than 100 percent. Rather than accept unemployment or starvation, many Chinese peasants turned to banditry or joined rebel movements to ease their misery.

Population growth and food shortages were compounded by poor government leadership, which, even before the arrival of Westerners, was becoming increasingly corrupt. Local tax collectors consistently increased their demands on peasants in order to line their own pockets. This placed additional burdens on the local populace, while less and less revenue for the maintenance of public works was sent to the imperial court. By the mid-nineteenth century there were serious food shortages and floods resulting in mass death. During one 25-year period (1796–1820), for example, the Yellow River flooded seventeen times. This was a sure sign that responsible officials were pilfering money designated for dike control. The central government was unable to check such local corruption. Because the Manchus feared the growth of regional power sources, they devised a complex series of bureaucratic checks and balances that prevented the gentry from building up bases of local power. This system was good at maintaining the status quo, but not sufficiently responsive when quick, forceful action became necessary. The official gentry also were spread too thin and hence overwhelmed by their administrative tasks and the sheer numbers of people for whom they were responsible.

At the same time, the Manchu elite military apparatus, the soldiers who had conquered China with their daring cavalry skills, also was riddled with corruption and in decline. The combined pressures of population growth, corruption, famine, and floods, made worse by ineffective government, spawned the dark omens of dynastic decline: banditry, riots, and rebellion.

The Qing lost control of a significant portion of rural society during the course of what was called the White Lotus Rebellion, the first of a chronic series of upheavals that, along with Western incursions, would ultimately destroy the regime. Social and economic unrest, brought on by heavy-handed tax collectors and poor government administration, was aggravated by the malicious behavior of imperial troops on their way to quell an uprising in the remote southwest of China. "The officials force the people to rebel" soon became the battle cry of angry peasants. By 1796 these sentiments had swelled into a major uprising, led by the anti-Qing White Lotus secret society. Its aim was to overturn the Manchus and restore the former Ming dynasty. The ensuing struggle was a long and costly one, not ending until 1804. It was suppressed primarily through the efforts of the gentry who organized their own local militias. The White Lotus Rebellion was just one of a series of internal upheavals that threatened the Qing. The glaring ineffectiveness of the Manchu military, plagued with indiscipline and corruption, caused the Manchu soldiery to lose its reputation as an invincible fighting force.

The British and the Opium Trade

It was in the midst of such internal disturbances that the Qing dynasty was obliged to consider British demands for the regularization of trading relations and, at the same time, deal effectively with an illegal opium trade. Both issues were serious challenges to China's traditional social and political order.

Britain's insistence on trade with China along lines acceptable to European diplomatic practice ran contrary to the traditions of the tributary system, the basic principle of which recognized the inequality of states rather than the equality inherent in Western international law. Opening up additional ports for trade with the Middle Kingdom, something emperors never did for any other "inferior" state, would break down this traditional structure of Chinese superiority.

A crucial factor in this arrangement was the deportment of the outsider. The Chinese saw a direct link between external affairs and inner order, one being directly dependent on the other. Just as the Confucian social structure was based on correct ceremonial form (*li*), the assumption being that proper behavior according to status influenced the deportment of the beholder and established in his mind the authority of the ruler, official, or parent, so a nation's status within the tribute system contained certain role expectations that confirmed its place in the wider world order. When barbarians abroad did not submit to their prescribed status, people within China might be encouraged to do the same. Most dynasties had collapsed under the twin blows of "inside disorder and outside calamity": the breakdown of the external regulating mechanism led to foreign invasion, and this encouraged domestic rebellion. Consequently each dynasty was obliged to make its foreign relations comply with the theory according to which it claimed to rule China from within.

The opium issue can be seen in this wider context of Chinese international relations and moral traditions. By the late 1830s the opium problem was becoming too serious for the Manchus to ignore. Opium not only was wreaking physical and economic havoc as China's store of precious metals was depleted to pay for it but opium use was also becoming a serious ethical problem. According to Confucian custom, the body was not something that the individual possessed for his own use but was rather entrusted to him by his ancestors as a link between the past and the future. Hence the habitual use of opium, which defiled the body and compromised one's social responsibilities, was a gross affront to filial piety, the core of the Chinese moral system. At the same time, the illegal increases in opium sales, and the emperor's inability to control or check them, exposed to governmental critics the political weakness of the Manchu regime. The illicit opium traffic, added to which was the British insistence on regulating trading relations on the basis of Western law, became an internal political issue that centered on the Manchus' growing inability to control centrifugal regional forces within the empire.

The First Opium War and the Unequal Treaties

On March 10, 1839, Lin Zexiu, viceroy of Hubei and Hunan, an accomplished poet nicknamed "Lin the Clear Sky" for his moral rectitude, arrived at Guangzhou as special imperial commissioner charged with putting an end to the opium trade. Commissioner Lin was a model Han scholar, representing both the best virtues of the Confucian tradition as well as the limitations of its world-view.

As a scholar, Lin had emancipated his thinking from the purely classical literary tradition and developed an interest in and knowledge of political affairs, history, geography, economics, and science. Although he was keenly interested in the West and hoped to use its technical knowledge to benefit China, Lin, like other scholar officials of his day, still had a singular Chinese concept of foreign relations and, in accordance with the principles of the tributary system, arrived at Guangzhou to dictate, not to negotiate. From the outset, he made the mistake of failing to recognize Britain as a great power and not a vassal state like Korea or Japan, thus grossly underestimating British military power. Nor did Lin adequately appreciate Britain's position in the opium trade, in particular the triangular economic role that the trade played among China, India, and Great Britain (the government of British India was largely funded through the export of Indian opium to China). This was a fatal oversight in his approach to resolving the issue.

At first Lin and his advisers appealed to the British with moral suasion. Lin wrote a letter to Queen Victoria highlighting the depravity of the opium traffic and suggesting that the English monarch must be secretly ashamed of such conduct. Certainly, Lin argued, public morality and upholding international law, which had declared opium traffic illegal, was more important than private gain. Unfortunately, this ethical approach had faint effect on a nation driven by a capitalist quest for wealth and power.

When Lin arrived in Guangzhou that March, he ordered coastal defenses strengthened, Chinese opium dealers arrested, and foreign traders to deliver inventory lists of their opium stocks. Lin announced that he would not leave Guangzhou until the flow of opium was stemmed. He solemnly pledged to see that matter dealt with, and nothing would be allowed to obstruct his mission. If the traffic in opium were not stopped, "a few decades from now we shall not only be without soldiers to resist the enemy, but also in want of silver to provide an army."[1]

In response, the superintendent of British trade at Guangzhou, Charles Elliot, protested and ordered the opium ships to flee and prepare for battle. Lin then quarantined the foreign dealers in their warehouses and kept them from communicating with their ships in port. At this juncture Elliot changed his tactics and ordered British traders to surrender their opium stocks, promising both the British and the American dealers that they would be compensated. Elliot, in his capacity as representative of the British government, announced that the private opium stocks were "held" by the British government. This in effect made the opium the property of the British crown and meant that its subsequent destruction would require Chinese compensation.

During April and May 1839, British and American dealers surrendered 20,283 chests and 200 sacks of opium, which were publicly destroyed on a beach outside of Guangzhou. During the following months, Lin maintained his prohibitionist policy. He forced ship captains to sign an agreement never to carry opium to China and to accept an agreement that allowed for the confiscation of any opium found.

Meanwhile, in England, members of Parliament and several municipal Chambers of Commerce openly pushed for a declaration of war. British Foreign Secretary Lord Palmerston announced in September 1839 that the only way to deal with China was to give it a good beating and explain afterward; on October 1 the British declared war. In April 1840 they sent to Guangzhou a force of 16 men-of-war bristling with 540 cannon, 20 transports, 4 armed steamers, and 4,000 sailors.

The Chinese military was no match for the steam-powered ships and superior firepower of the British. The Manchus also were severely handicapped by their ignorance of Western military power and their anachronistic fighting tactics. One provincial governor-general, for instance, submitted to the throne a military strategy written by a Tang official in the eighth century. Other mandarins, a bit more up to date, had some respect for Western sea power, but were convinced that the Europeans could easily be defeated on land. Numerous Chinese military officials argued that the English had such close-fitting garments that they could not maneuver easily on shore and that if simply pushed over, they would be incapable of getting up again. The British occupation of Ningbo, in the spring of 1842, gave the Chinese an opportunity to test their strategies. The emperor's best troops were dispatched to the scene, but the commander, having consulted the oracles as to the most propitious time to attack, made his move at the height of a rampaging rainstorm. His troops became hopelessly bogged down in the mud. Even if they had managed to engage the British, the emperor's soldiers would have had little impact because the Chinese used obsolete flintlock guns that could not fire in the rain. Meanwhile, a force of Chinese marines became seasick and was sent elsewhere, and reinforcements for soldiers attacking Ningbo failed to materialize because their frightened commander escaped his travails by smoking himself into an opium torpor. The ensuing slaughter of Chinese troops was so bloody that even the most seasoned British soldiers were sickened by it.

The Qing emperor was now forced to negotiate with Britain, for further losses would have signaled dynastic weakness and encouraged rebellion. The Treaty of Nanjing, the Supplementary Treaty of the Bogue (Humen), and two French and American agreements (all of which were signed between 1842 and 1844), the first of the so-called "unequal treaties" that opened China to imperialist exploitation, brought an end to the Opium War. The terms of these treaties undermined China's traditional mechanism of foreign relations, the method of controlled trade via the tribute system. Five ports were opened for trade, gunboats, and foreign residence: Guangzhou, Xiamen, Fuzhou, Ningbo, and Shanghai. Hong Kong was ceded to the British and was made a free and open port. The cohong system was abolished, and a system of "fair and regular" tariffs was to be established, which the Treaty of the Bogue set at an average of 5 percent. But the most significant terms of the treaties were those establishing extraterritoriality (exempting Westerners from Chinese law) and most-favored-nation treatment. According to the latter, any concession granted by China to one power was automatically extended to other treaty signatories as well.

The fixed tariff, extraterritoriality, and the most-favored-nation clause were particularly injurious to China and were accepted only because the mandarins were at the wrong end of the gun. The most-favored-nation concept meant, in effect, that it would be impossible for China to negotiate with other states on an individual basis and that one nation's gain was automatically extended to all others. A major difficulty for China, from the beginning of negotiations, was that the mandarins failed to appreciate the revolutionary implications of what was occurring and tried to accommodate Western international law within traditional Confucian diplomatic and political parameters. For example, they viewed the most-favored-nation clause as simply another dimension of their old policy of playing off the barbarians against one another; it also seemed to complement the traditional notion that the emperor treated all barbarians alike. In addition, they saw no reason to oppose the clause because the other powers probably would seek to trade surreptitiously under British auspices, and, of course, the officials would have difficulty identifying them because all Westerners looked alike and spoke in unintelligible tongues.

The principle of extraterritoriality guaranteed that Westerners would be exempt from Chinese authority in the treaty ports and would instead be subject to their own civil and criminal codes. The combination of the right to reside in the newly opened ports and extraterritoriality gave the foreign communities a special position in China, eventually allowing them to become autonomous units with little control by any higher authorities. Once again, however, the Manchus viewed this in terms of their traditional practice of easing the task of governance by allowing the barbarians to regulate their own affairs and keeping them separate from the Chinese communities so as not to pollute cultural life, a policy that had been used so successfully with the tribes of inner Asia that had penetrated the empire throughout history. And the 5 percent tariff was readily accepted because it was higher than tariffs on native goods, though this prevented the Chinese from raising future duties to protect domestic industries.

Finally, the treaties failed to address the opium problem. Transactions continued, because too many influential Western traders and Chinese officials made profits from it. In fact, opium addiction increased after the treaty settlement, its importation ultimately doubling the 1830s figures. Transactions in opium finally were regulated in later treaties drawn up in 1858 and 1860, which both legalized opium and placed duties on its importation. As a final humiliation, China was obliged to pay 21 million silver dollars as a war indemnity, part of which was used to compensate Western traders for damaged pocketbooks after Commissioner Lin destroyed their opium stocks.

Even more serious in the long run was the Qing's acceptance of Westerners into the office for the collection of imperial customs. This occurred a few years after the promulgation of the treaties, when internal rebellion threatened to shut down the orderly collection of customs on foreign goods coming into the country. Because the Qing government's inability to control the collection of taxes on imported goods threatened the entire trading network established by the treaty system, the British convinced the Manchu court to accept Western help in running the office responsible for collecting China's maritime customs. By the late 1850s one of the most important bureaucracies in the Manchu government, the so-called Maritime Customs Service, was partially staffed and managed by Westerners.

The treaty arrangements brought a multitude of new problems to the ailing Qing dynasty. For one thing, extraterritoriality could be used to protect the hustlers and racketeers who emerged to take advantage of international trade. By acquiring British nationality, Chinese were able to claim legal protection in the treaty ports, and the unscrupulous could use this status to shield their criminal activities from Chinese law. During times of economic depression and social disorder this criminal community linked up with local secret societies, constituting a serious challenge to political order. Another problem for the court was carrying out the terms of its treaty obligations. Complying with the agreements had the effect of making the Manchus look weak in the eyes of their subjects. In fact, the court could gain popular support only by defying the treaties, but this brought additional punishment, humiliation, and increasing demands from the foreigners. This dilemma became more acute after 1860, when Christian missionaries were given the right to enter the interior of China. No longer restricted to the treaty ports, the Westerners' presence now became even more pervasive. Local gentry and the peasant masses, most of whom had only heard stories of the new barbarians, now came face to face with the real thing, flesh and blood intruders against whom they could direct their economic frustrations.

The Second Opium War

As problematic as the treaties proved to be for the Qing, they seemed even less satisfactory to the Western powers. After the cohong system was eliminated and ports opened to Western commerce, a flourishing trade with China still had failed to materialize. The major reason for this was the self-sufficient nature of the Chinese economy, although Western businessmen were convinced that it was owing to high internal taxes and an insufficient number of ports open for commerce. More significant for China, however, was that the Western diplomats became frustrated with Beijing's refusals to treat their official representatives in an acceptable manner.

By the 1850s all foreign governments, unhappy that the emperor was shielding the court through obstreperous intermediaries at the provincial level, demanded a revision of the treaties. The Chinese refused to yield, but in the autumn of 1856 the Westerners used the pretext of the murder of a French missionary and the seizure of a British-registered ship by Chinese authorities to force the revision of the treaty system. When the Chinese failed to apologize for these actions, a combined Anglo-French military expedition under Lord Elgin and Baron Gros was dispatched to the city of Tianjin to resolve the disagreements to the satisfaction of the West. After the city was overwhelmed by the Anglo-French forces, the Chinese were obliged to sign what were called the Treaties of Tianjin (1858).

The signatories included China, Britain, France, the United States, and Russia, the latter having begun to move rapidly on the western frontier region of China after recognizing the increasing weakness of the Qing dynasty. The settlement allowed for the opening of eleven new treaty ports; the legalization of opium trade, which could now be taxed; permission for foreigners to travel in the interior, with France securing agreement for toleration of missionaries and converts in all areas of China; foreign navigation and commerce on the Yangzi River; and Western diplomatic representation and residence in Beijing.

The Chinese, however, refused to ratify these treaties in Beijing. In response, the Europeans prepared to move their forces to the capital itself. The Chinese chose to repel them, and a clash occurred outside of Tianjin. After meeting considerable resistance, the Anglo-French forces pushed on toward Beijing with a terrible vengeance, looting and pillaging along the way. As cannonfire and wrathful destruction worked its way toward the capital, the emperor and his court fled Beijing for the safety of the royal hunting lodge beyond the Great Wall.

Beijing, the administrative core of the Qing dynasty, was now at the disposal of foreigners. The plundering reached its senseless crescendo when the Europeans arrived at the Summer Palace outside Beijing. Here lay one of the artistic marvels of mankind, a vision of beauty so vast that a British chaplain on the scene wrote that a man must be a poet, a painter, an historian, a virtuoso, and a Chinese scholar to describe it. The Summer Palace was an 80-square-mile sculptured park sprinkled with some 200 exquisitely designed buildings (two of which were tiled with roofs of gold) containing priceless works of art, and libraries of rare, irreplaceable books and manuscripts. The palace was the repository of tribute gifts and other treasures collected over the centuries of Chinese civilization. These, along with magnificent pagodas, temples, and lakes, presented "a concentration of visual beauty, artifice and wealth as neither existed nor could once again have been brought into being anywhere else in the world."[2] It was at this idyllic spot that what little Western discipline remained completely collapsed, and for twenty-four hours the Palace was subjected to an orgiastic rampage of looting. Within hours the French army alone had packed off 300 wagons loaded with treasures. What could not be carried away was smashed. One French officer wrote home that for two days he had walked on jewels, silks, porcelain, and bronzes worth more than 30 million francs, and that the ensuing destruction was certainly worse than anything since the sack of Rome. As a final insult to civilization and as a perverted form of punishment for the departed emperor, Lord Elgin ordered the Summer Palace to be burned to the ground. Years later, when asked what might be learned about art from the opening of China, Elgin, in an epic display of what his country had yet to learn, opined:

> The most cynical representations of the grotesque have been the principal products of Chinese conception of the sublime and beautiful. Nevertheless I am disposed to believe that under this mass of abortions and rubbish there lie some hidden spark of a divine fire, which the genius of my countrymen may gather and nurture into a flame.[3]

The destruction of the Summer Palace and the subsequent occupation of the Qing capital brought forth the Convention of Beijing. This agreement guaranteed British diplomatic representation in the capital; China's war indemnity was increased; and Tianjin was opened to trade and foreign residence. The British gained the Kowloon Peninsula, opposite Hong Kong, and French missionaries were given the right to own properties in the interior of China. The biggest winner of all was Russia, which had not even fought in the war. The Russians wrested significant territorial concessions east of the Ussuri River and legalized the acquisition of territories taken under a previous treaty signed in 1858, thereby completing a successful advance into the Amur region of China begun nearly 20 years earlier. Without firing a shot, the Russians won 400,000 square miles of territory along with considerable commercial concessions. The second set of treaties signed between 1858 and 1860 completed the structure through which the Middle Kingdom would be opened to the West. China would not be liberated from this system of imperial exploitation until 1943.

The Impact of the Unequal Treaties

How damaging were the so-called unequal treaties to China's sovereignty? Certainly the treaty arrangements made it more difficult for the Qing to control its own economy. The low, fixed tariff limited the competitiveness of Chinese industry vis-à-vis Western manufactured items. The right to travel freely and the added protection of extraterritoriality provided foreigners with special positions beyond the reach of Chinese laws. Within the treaty ports, where foreigners even gained the right to control the collection of customs, a concentration of industry (with access to cheap Chinese labor) and Western education centers developed. Under the protection of Western law and customs there grew up within the treaty ports a new Westernized socio-economic class of Chinese. Known as the "compradores," this group would play an important role in the subsequent efforts to modernize China. Clearly, the long-term result of the unequal treaties was an intensification of the Western challenge to the Chinese way of doing things. Moreover, the Western barbarians were now within the Great Wall of China; indeed, they resided in the capital city itself.

Unfortunately for the Qing, what was happening to China in the fading years of the nineteenth century was not considered revolutionary or even unusual. It was not deemed extraordinary because the treaty system and the foreign-administered Maritime Customs Service, the two devices by which the Western powers maneuvered China into the international capitalist system, were seen to be in line with Chinese tradition. The Qing essentially met the Western challenge through institutions and preconceptions that had developed over centuries of contact with pastoral nomads (witness the court's position on extraterritoriality and the most-favored-nation clause). The treaties, for example, were seen simply as a means of "bridling and reining in" the powerful sea barbarians, essentially a traditional device for accommodating outsiders and giving them a place within the Chinese world. Thus, unlike the Japanese who worked diligently to have their treaties revised, the Chinese saw them primarily as a mechanism to keep foreigners in bounds. In practice, this meant that the Manchus would try to improve conditions within the framework of the agreements, rather than abrogate them, but that they would generally prefer the status quo because antagonizing the West would lead to confrontation and further unacceptable demands.[4]

China's response to the West was severely handicapped by her lack of information about the outside world. The dynasty's approach to the opium issue, for instance, was marked by an ignorance of Western affairs and the role of commerce in its economic life. For the most part, Qing officials viewed the Westerners as just another group of barbarians, essentially akin to earlier intruders in search of higher civilization. Thus they failed to recognize that the Westerners indeed were a different species who could not be accommodated within the traditional Confucian system. During times of dynastic decline, or when outsiders put pressures on the court, Chinese rulers frequently allowed foreigners to participate in the political order. Whenever foreign invaders from inner Asia became too powerful, the Chinese would acquiesce and, in extreme circumstances, the foreigner could become the dominant power in the Chinese state, though in virtually every instance he became "sinicized," and there was no real alteration in the traditional socio-political structure.[5] The Manchus themselves were invading foreigners, who, once taken into the system, became loyal upholders of Chinese culture. As opposed to prevailing Western norms, it was not the idea of the nation that was important to the Chinese. What mattered was the Confucian order, and every intruder who arrived at China's gate was absorbed into this cultural entity.

A fatal defect in the Qing's traditional approach to handling barbarian affairs was that it failed to appreciate that the Westerners had not come to partake in the promise of a superior civilization. The Westerners were far more powerful than previous interlopers and were in search of wealth and national glory, objectives ultimately destructive of the Confucian world order.

The Taipings

As Westerners proceeded to encroach on Chinese territory and gain control over parts of the Chinese economy, the Qing dynasty was confronted with an even more serious problem: the immediate threat to the Manchu social and political order by the Taiping Rebellion (1850–1864), an uprising that triggered one of the most destructive wars the world has ever seen, possibly killing more people than World War I.

The word "rebellion" may be somewhat of a misnomer, for as the historian Franz Michael has observed, a major consequence of the turmoil of the Taipings was a rearranging of China's political, social, and intellectual traditions. Although unsuccessful, the Taipings propagated ideas and organizational schema that set the stage for transforming state and culture into previously unrecognizable configurations. "One may well say," wrote Michael, "that modern Chinese history begins with the Taiping Rebellion."[6]

The seedbed of the Taipings was the southern provinces of Hunan and Guangxi, two areas that were geographically removed from the strong arm of the central government in Beijing. The region had experienced serious economic dislocation brought on by the Opium War and the subsequent shift in trading activity as ports were opened farther north. After the first war against the British, many soldiers found themselves without jobs when the special armies were disbanded. With increasing unemployment many turned to banditry. Their ranks were swelled by destitute laborers and transport workers thrown out of work as trade moved away from Guangzhou to other ports. Intense ethnic rivalries that developed between the local Chinese population and groups who, over the years, had migrated into the area from outlying provinces exacerbated the situation. These disaffected social elements were increasingly exposed to a whole complex of alien ideas that worked their way into the interior from Guangzhou, giving considerable political overtones to their struggle for survival.

The Taiping movement began among an ethnic minority known as the Hakkas ("guest settlers"), migrants from central China who had never been assimilated into the mainstream Han Chinese culture of Guangxi. Centuries of economic, social, and political squabbling had made the Hakkas particularly resentful of the local Han. Maintaining their own distinctive dialect and cultural traditions, the Hakkas were a permanent but embittered "out-group" who at times had taken up arms against their Han oppressors. To make matters more volatile, by the middle of the nineteenth century many Hakkas had come to embrace Christianity, adding yet another source of friction to their relations with local groups.

The founder of the Taipings was a frustrated Hakka scholar, Hong Xiuquan, who suffered the indignity of failing the civil service examinations for entrance into the scholar class no less than four times. During the course of his checkered academic career Hong had encountered Christianity. The experience must have been a profound one, for after failing his third exam Hong suffered a nervous breakdown during which he had visions revealing to him not only his true identity, that of the younger brother of Jesus of Nazareth, but also a mission: to assist his "Elder Brother" in cleansing the world of idolatrous demons and to establish a "heavenly kingdom of great peace" (Taiping Tianguo). After enduring a delirium lasting forty days, which neither doctors nor sorcerers could abate, Hong emerged, according to all who knew him, an entirely different person in both physical appearance and personality. He supposedly became taller, stronger, and enormously self-confident. For the next few years Hong studied Biblical tracts, mostly from the Old Testament, and became passionately convinced of his mission to destroy the idols of false religions.

Hong's emerging world-view was a hodgepodge of Confucian teachings and misunderstood Christianity. Having made converts among friends and relatives, he decided to embark on a more ambitious mission and established what was called the "Society of God Worshipers." In 1844 some of Hong's followers went into Guangxi Province and organized a branch of the society, winning thousands of converts. Attacking opium, gambling, and drinking, and with an emphasis on the equality of all men and women, the society appealed mostly to those who were down and out and distressed minorities, such as the Hakkas. Convinced of their infallibility, and buttressed by religious visions, Hong and his lieutenants took advantage of deteriorating conditions in south China by organizing local communities into military units for protection against banditry and the onerous exactions of government officials. By 1850 the Taipings had devised a surprisingly effective military organization which, fueled by a revolutionary ideology and fanatical adherents, swept aside all government troops in the provinces of Guangxi and Hunan. As the Taipings surged into the Yangzi River valley, tens of thousands of discontented peasants well beyond the traditional Hakka enclaves joined their ranks. When in 1853 they overran the important city of Nanjing, where Hong set up a government and declared a new dynasty, their converts had reached the millions.

The Taiping Rebellion was a unique event in Chinese history. Its objective was not only to eliminate the Qing, which was considered a "foreign" dynasty, but to replace the entire Confucian system with a pseudo-Christian society. The movement's basic document, "The Land System of the Heavenly Kingdom," served as a sort of constitution for the new Taiping social structure. The "System" insisted on the communal sharing of wealth and property under the direction of a theocratic state. The family was to remain the basic unit of organization, but it would be stripped of its paramount economic and social functions, which were to be transferred to the government. The leadership also promulgated strict laws promoting social equality. The accumulation of private wealth and privilege were outlawed, and the sexes were declared equal (among other things, this meant the end of footbinding and polygamy).

Hong's version of Christianity, which focused on the Ten Commandments, interwove through all Taiping institutions. The leader's interpretation of the Bible was mandatory reading for every citizen, and to facilitate the task, the

Taipings utilized the vernacular in writing instead of the difficult classical style, the language used by the Mandarinate. Plain language and writing also were used in civil service examinations, these being based on certain Christian teachings and open to men and women alike.

Another radical aspect of the new regime was its unification of military duties with civil administration and civilian life. Much of this was derived from the ancient classic *The Rites of Zhou* and earlier practices developed by the generals of the Ming dynasty but never systematically put into practice. Essentially, peasants served simultaneously as soldiers, and all army officers were given both military and civilian duties. Each basic social unit, which consisted of twenty-five families, was incorporated into an overreaching bureaucratic structure in which every aspect of human affairs was controlled by military-civilian authorities. Each person in Taiping society, for example, was assigned to twenty-five-person squads where he lived, fought, and worked with his "brothers and sisters." Hence membership in the Taiping commonwealth was total, demanding the sacrifice of both self and property to the group. Yet this formalized egalitarian edifice was under the sway of an elitist leadership, dominated by a father figure who served as a latter-day Jehovah, his heavenly authority flowing from top to bottom via the chosen apostles of his kingdom on earth.

Unfortunately, the ethic of self-sacrifice expected of the Taiping rank-and-file was not reciprocated by their standard-bearers. The Taiping leadership embraced a double standard that betrayed the egalitarian ideals of its theocratic social code. For example, although wealth was to be shared by the commonwealth, the movement's apostles were given a far greater share of community property and managed to accumulate huge personal fortunes. Taiping chieftains lived in luxury, while followers were relegated to a harsh existence in military and labor camps, frequently starving to death when provisions ran short. Sexual and even personal contact between men and women was forbidden on penalty of death, but Taiping leaders enjoyed personal harems. The size of a leader's harem seems to have been determined by his rank. Hong Xiuquan, for instance, kept eighty-eight concubines; the East King, thirty-six; the North King, fourteen; and, a sure sign of diminished status, an Assistant King had a mere seven.

Perhaps the most threatening dimension of the Taiping uprising, which set it apart from all previous dynastic rebellions, was its intention to destroy the Confucian value system, thereby eliminating the dual role of the educated gentry elite as governing officials and moral and social leaders. It was this special dual function that made imperial China's political and social order unique. Dynasties rose and fell throughout China's history, yet in the midst of these social and political upheavals the Confucian order remained unchanged and, consequently, the gentry provided an elastic recuperative agent for the new conquerors, who needed them to construct and administer the new dynasty. The Taipings, however, sought to replace both the dynasty and the traditional autonomy of the Confucian order with a new set of monotheistic religious teachings in which the state would have pervasive power.

The special character of the Taiping Rebellion lay in its unique combination of religious elements, nationalism—the movement was vehemently anti-Manchu—and social forces rooted in an uprising of land-starved, destitute peasants. It is for such reasons that this important episode in Chinese history has been such a great inspiration to and the subject of careful study by the Chinese Communists. In fact, all subsequent revolutionary movements in China have articulated their indebtedness to the Taipings.

The religious zeal and military discipline of the Taipings under the leadership of capable generals enabled Hong Xiuquan's armies to score numerous victories over Qing forces with relative ease. Early in 1855 a Taiping general defeated a formidable Qing counteroffensive and extended Taiping control over the whole of the fertile lower Yangzi valley. Securely entrenched in Nanjing, the Taiping treasury was reputed to have six times the wealth of the imperial government; it seemed only a matter of time before its superior armies would subdue Beijing itself. At this juncture, however, the seemingly invincible Taiping military machine began to sputter, as a series of internal squabbles greatly weakened the rebels' fighting and administrative effectiveness.

The initial success of the Taipings was eventually undermined by bloody infighting among the leaders and the mental breakdown of Hong Xiuquan, who escaped these problems by retreating into a world of sensual pleasure. After this the Taipings never recovered their dynamism, and after a few more years of unrelenting carnage, they succumbed to new, revitalized armies loyal to the imperial government.

Ironically, it was the dynasty's reaction to the Taipings, rather than the rebellion itself, that proved to be the most damaging to its own future. In order to defend the threatened basic Confucian traditions, the Qing was obliged to turn to those who had the most to lose in the Taiping order, namely the scholar-gentry class. It was the gentry's creation of a new type of army based on regional loyalties that ultimately crushed the rebellion. But in doing this, the Manchus called into play a host of power bases that would ultimately weaken the central government. The whole elaborate system of checks and balances based on carefully contrived divided authority and overlapping responsibilities ceased to function effectively after the emergence of regional strongmen. The erosion of the power of the central government naturally meant the weakening of Manchu authority, for the new regional leaders were Han and represented an emerging nationalism. Hence, politically, the rebellion hastened the transfer of governmental power from the Manchus to Han Chinese.

Even without the new threat from regional strongmen that it stimulated, the Taiping Rebellion would have had a profound and enduring impact on subsequent Chinese history. A series of other rebellions erupted once the dynasty was forced to concentrate its energies and resources on the Taipings. In the south, Gold Coin rebels routed government troops; an infamous secret society known as the Triads overran Xiamen and Shanghai in 1853; Red Turbans attacked Guangzhou in 1854; a bloody miners' rebellion broke out in Yunnan; Panthay Muslims established a separatist government in Dali, a city in Yunnan, that lasted from 1853 to 1873 and claimed 300,000 lives before it fell; and in central China armies of separatist Nian horsemen proved even more difficult to suppress than the Taipings. The Nian were gangs of thugs and bandits who, like the Mongols, sustained themselves through pillage. These gangs were not put down by the Qing until 1868.

The human suffering and destruction of the Taiping Rebellion staggers the imagination. One could travel for miles along the Yangzi River and see nothing but deserted villages where packs of wild dogs tore at rotting corpses. The historian Frederic Wakeman, Jr., gives us a glimpse of the horror of it all in his description of Ningbo. Here, he writes, was a "city of the dead," with no sign of its previous half a million inhabitants, "save for canals, 'filled with dead bodies and stagnant filth.'"[7] From Guangdi County in Anhui Province came reports that no food could be grown for 5 years. After all the grass, roots, herbs, and trees had been consumed, the survivors resorted to cannibalism. Fifteen years of war and famine cost China between 20 and 40 million dead.

The single most important of the gentry strongmen who rose to prominence during the Taiping Rebellion was Zeng Guofan, a former high official who had distinguished himself by organizing a unique local militia in his home district in Hunan Province. In the beginning Zeng's army was very small and led by upstanding scholar-gentry who recruited peasants from their own communities into its ranks. The army was organized around what amounted to the "old boy" network; officers were personally familiar with each soldier they recruited, and strong personal loyalties stressing Confucian notions of proper conduct and moral rectitude prevailed between leaders and their troops. In order to counteract the religious élan of the Taiping soldiers, Zeng inculcated Confucian ideology in his troops, each being taught that he was defending China's cultural heritage. Discipline and training were rigid, and the soldiers received roughly double the pay of the government's regular troops. Zeng hoped to build on this type of army, emphasizing interpersonal obligations based on community ties between the rank-and-file and the gentry, so the force could be employed for longer periods of time in areas outside the home districts.

In order to create such a fighting force, Zeng needed a regular source of revenue. If armies travel on their stomachs, they are sustained and made ready for combat by their treasury. Thus it was necessary for Zeng to control the provincial administrations of the areas in which they fought. Such a prerogative, however, would have signaled the breakdown of the Qing's centralized system of control. By 1860, with their own armies routed and collapse imminent, the Manchus reluctantly yielded and appointed Zeng as the regular administrative head of the provinces that his troops were to defend. Once given the right to oversee provincial administration, Zeng sought new revenues for his military machine. For this he turned to the use of what was called the *lijin*. First introduced in 1853, this was a levy on inland trade and business. The *lijin* ultimately became a major source of revenue for regional gentry leaders. The imperial government never knew exactly how much money it generated because its collection was difficult to centralize (perhaps only about 20–25 percent of this tax was ever reported to Beijing), and it became a means of provincial fiscal autonomy for those who might desire a certain degree of independence from the central government. It was said, with justification, that the *lijin* gave "wings to the tiger."[8] The working principle behind Zeng's military force, which came to be called the Hunan Army, was directly at odds with Qing bureaucratic practice: the dynasty utilized a functionally divided administrative organization, and it strictly forbade officials of any kind to develop personal relationships with men in their home districts. It was only Zeng's unassailable reputation as a metropolitan official, his firm loyalty to both Confucian tradition and the Qing dynasty, and, of course, the virulence of the Taiping menace that convinced the throne to accept the services of the Hunan Army. Because Zeng's experiment was so successful, a small number of carefully selected regional gentry were given permission to raise similar forces following the Hunan Army model. Thenceforth, regional military, fiscal, and administrative authority was combined in the hands of a number of strongmen who were semi-independent of Beijing. Thus, in order to assure its own survival, the Manchu dynasty was forced to permit the germination of rival sources of power (in effect, private armies), which became even stronger after the Taipings were defeated. In this fashion the waning of Qing authority led to the development of regionalism, a lethal phenomenon that had occurred repeatedly throughout Chinese history when a dynasty was about to collapse.

The Elite's Response to the Western Impact and Imperial Breakdown

Ultimately, it was Zeng Guofan's protégé, the regional strongman Li Hong-zhang, who became the most important leader in China after the demise of the Taipings. Li controlled the Huai Army of Anhui Province. What made this institution unique was its financial base. Having been appointed governor of Jiangsu Province, Li was able to utilize the revenues from Shanghai's foreign trade. By collaborating with treaty port capitalists, Li gained access to Western technological, scientific, and commercial knowledge, which he quickly used to construct an industrial empire. Because the maritime customs ultimately was under Beijing's auspices, however, Li had to secure imperial approval to use this important revenue source for the expansion of his forces. He managed to gain access to these important resources only after convincing the court that this wealth would not be used to enlarge his own army exclusively but would be devoted to the "self-strengthening" of the entire nation.

By using the slogan "self-strengthening," Li was deliberately appealing to tradition. "Self-strengthening" was an expression used to describe the nature of heaven as being enduring and strong. It was considered necessary, on certain occasions, for mankind to strengthen itself so as to maintain harmony with celestial rhythms. After 1860, in memorials and edicts to the throne, numerous scholars began to refer to "a changed situation," recognizing the necessity of strengthening oneself to meet the changed disposition of the heavens, in this case the problems created by foreigners and dynastic enervation. Such circumstances allowed the utilization of barbarian strengths (Western technology) to build up the wealth and power of the state so it could protect itself. Yet it was important not to alter the basic framework of Chinese culture. The ideological sanction for self-strengthening ultimately was summed up in the slogan "Chinese learning for essential principles, Western learning for practical application." In other words, practical Western knowledge could be used as a "means" to reach Chinese "ends," namely to conserve Confucian tradition. Unfortunately, such officials naïvely believed that the secrets of Western technology could be learned quickly. In the words of the Manchu reformer Prince Gong: "If we can strengthen ourselves, we [and the Europeans] can live with each other in peace and we can quietly subdue their ambitious schemes against us."[9] By employing Western knowledge and weaponry, by constructing arsenals, shipyards, and factories, Li would strengthen the empire against rebellions and external enemies. Thus from the beginning the inspiration for and leadership of China's modernization was not the central government but a regional strongman whose subsequent enterprises were always subject to Beijing's approval and intense scrutiny.

This arrangement was fraught with dangers and difficulties. Li, of course, was seen to be a serious threat to other regional leaders, to say nothing of conservative mandarins and Manchu aristocrats, all of whom at one time or another tried to undermine his modernization projects.

Fortunately for Li, his efforts at self-strengthening corresponded with an

era of cooperation between China and the West after the Treaties of Tianjin
and Beijing (1858 and 1860). The foreign occupation of Beijing appears to
have shocked the Manchus into appreciating the necessity of accommodating Western diplomatic procedures. After a brief inner-court power struggle
in the autumn of 1861, a new, apparently less xenophobic leadership came
into prominence. The result was the initiation of a new period of reform and
revitalization which, according to all the astrological and political signs,
seemed to conform to the traditional pattern of "restoration" that occurred
periodically throughout imperial history when the decline of a dynasty was
temporarily arrested and then reversed, giving the imperial government a period of grace during which it could get its house in order before the onslaught
of further decline. With the inauguration of this era, which was called the
"Tongzhi Restoration" after the reigning emperor, the West's bare tolerance
of the Qing dynasty quickly shifted to a policy of enthusiastic support, with
most of the powers now recognizing that without a strong central government
China would collapse into chaos and therefore threaten their own gains made
under the new treaty system.

It was under the philosophical stimulus of the Tongzhi Restoration that
the Manchus finally consented to establish an official ministry to deal exclusively with foreign affairs. This was the Zongli Yamen, imperial China's
equivalent of a Western-style foreign office. Several Manchu court notables
realized that China could benefit through careful diplomacy, and a period
of cordiality developed between the government and the foreign powers.
The Zongli Yamen also worked closely with Li Hongzhang to strengthen
China's industrial base and defense systems. And it was under the slogan
of restoration that the regional armies of Zeng Guofan, Li Hongzhang, and
others ultimately defeated the Taipings. Hence during the 1860s and 1870s it
seemed that the dynastic decline had been reversed and that China might hold
her own in a world dominated by aggressive, imperialist powers. Under the
tutelage of regional self-strengtheners China seemed to be moving into the
modern world by building railroads, textile factories, arsenals, and a modern
army and navy.

Despite the trappings of modernization, however, it is important to understand that the main intent of the court-sanctioned Restoration, which Li
could use to legitimize his own self-strengthening projects, was not to create
a new order but was rather an intrinsically conservative response to dynastic
decline. Fundamental to the thinking of the older men behind the Restoration,
in particular Zeng Guofan, was the Confucian premise that a ruling dynasty's
fall was directly related to its inability to rule well, a task that required "good
men" of outstanding moral character. Never was it assumed that dynastic
demise was caused by inadequate institutions. Instead, imperial decline was

believed to be triggered by the leadership's failure to discharge its proper functions as "the father and mother of the people." Throughout China's history issues of social, economic, and political structure were overlooked as sources of dysfunction; in fact, it was assumed that each new dynasty had to continue the institutions of its predecessor. Thus a government's decline could only be reversed by a new release of the dynasty's moral vigor. Of course all of this was in keeping with the Confucian tradition.

The inherent conservatism of the Restoration movement was most clearly revealed in its economic policies. Encouraged by the court, the thrust of Restoration economic reform was to revive the vitality of the old order, namely self-sufficiency in agriculture based on small peasant holdings, to the point where peasant life would reach the subsistence level and the state would be provided with adequate revenues from land taxes. The nonagricultural constituents of the economy were largely ignored. For example, there was no government plan for improving banking, communications, industry, or trade. Above all, foreign trade was considered parasitic and of no great significance as a source of wealth. In fact, the court obstructed those who were involved in foreign commerce (Li Hongzhang was singled out for much criticism on these grounds). Enlarged appetites for material goods, increased commercial and industrial productivity, and expansion of consumerism in any form were considered evil omens, harbingers of trouble that might upset social harmony by unleashing greed and avarice. The ethos of the Restoration discouraged self-enhancement, a principle dear to the heart of a market economy. All manifestations of individual greed were condemned in praise of thrift. In the words of one of the leading figures of the Restoration, the Manchu Prince Gong: "Teach the people frugality so that their incomes will suffice."[10] This official policy of dampening demand and stressing local self-reliance retarded economic growth. Economic expansion was never the intention of the Restoration. Its economic thinking was fundamentally Confucian, and Confucianism was essentially mercantilist in its view of wealth: the riches of the world were believed to be finite, hence an increase of wealth would occur at the expense of someone else and thus be socially disruptive.

These conservative sentiments associated with the Restoration, however, were not shared by China's greatest self-strengthener, Li Hongzhang. Li moved well beyond such limited thinking, but he frequently got into trouble with his more inflexible colleagues who denounced his policies to court reactionaries. Thus his ambitious programs were frequently undermined by Confucian conservatives. Li was in a difficult position, being open to criticism by those who saw his clever utilization of power to be "un-Confucian," on the one hand, and stymied by the limitations of imperial bureaucratic traditions, on the other. He had little choice but to use his official power to amass personal wealth, which was needed to implement modernization reforms. Yet Li's power and fortune were deeply resented by court officials who feared his strength, and they gave rise to a proverb that circulated widely at the time: "Every dog that barks for Li is fat."[11]

Perhaps the most virulent attack on Li Hongzhang resulted from his criticism of the conservative literary and philosophical biases of the official examinations. The content of the exams was not conducive to the kind of learning Li needed to further his industrialization programs and military reforms. He called the entrenched "eight-legged" essay used in the testing and the infatuation with calligraphy "hollow and ornamental." It was said that only the personal intervention of the most powerful person in Beijing, the Empress Dowager Cixi, saved Li from losing his head. If the self-strengthening efforts of China's single most powerful official were thwarted by the heavy hands of entrenched reactionaries, what possible success could lesser progressive-minded reformers have?

The pervasive antiforeign and reactionary sentiments at the highest levels of Qing officialdom found popular support among the common people. This is reflected in the popular attack on China's first ambassador to Great Britain, who took up his post in 1876. The ambassador was not only the subject of official-literati derision; his fellow townsmen were so ashamed of his journey to the citadel of barbarianism that they tried to destroy his house. When he finally published his memoirs in 1877, which had positive things to say about the West, there was so much public outrage that the government was obliged to destroy the printing blocks. This behavior is in marked contrast to that of the Japanese at this time, who were eager to send students and diplomats abroad and devoured books on the West faster than either government or private presses could print them.

The years of relative peace and diplomatic cooperation with the West that coincided with the Restoration gave China the time to build up her defenses and revitalize the economic and political order. The self-strengthening programs of Li Hongzhang seemed to have made notable progress by the 1880s, and Western powers were particularly impressed with China's efforts to build a navy. But appearance was not reality. The shortcomings of self-strengthening were exposed in 1894–95 when the imperial forces under Li were humiliated in a short war with Japan over the control of Korea, a traditional mainstay of China's tribute system.

The Sino-Japanese War

By the 1880s Japan, well along the path of modernization, was bent on extending its influence into the Korean peninsula. For more than two decades the

Japanese and Chinese governments had intrigued with Korean court factions in a covert attempt to control political developments. A rebel uprising in 1894 provided a pretext for Japanese military intervention, and by August China and Japan had declared war on each other. Although China's navy looked more impressive on paper, the smaller Japanese ships, better commanded and staffed, newer in construction and much faster, wreaked horrible destruction on Li Hongzhang's Northern Fleet. Japan's modern army was equally effective. Within a few months it had pushed China's armies completely out of Korea. Japan's peace terms were harsh: the territorial cession of Taiwan and the Liaodong Peninsula and a large war indemnity of 200 million taels, a staggering sum of money more than double the annual revenues of the imperial government.

Japan's decisive victory was a great blow to Chinese national pride. It was bad enough that the emperor had to give way to Europeans. Being crushed by the "dwarf bandits" of Japan, inhabitants of an island backwater that had always sat in the celestial shadow of the Peacock Throne and had borrowed heavily from Chinese civilization, was a humiliation beyond endurance.

Of more significance, Japan's victory seemed to portend the demise of the Qing dynasty. Out of fear that chaos might ensue at its collapse, Western powers began the dreaded scramble for concessions and special "spheres of influence" to safeguard their interests. In particular, Japan's foothold on the Asian mainland frightened Russia, which coveted the ice-free port of Dalian at the southern tip of the Liaodong Peninsula. The Russians convinced the French and Germans to join them in forcing Japan to remove herself from the peninsula on the grounds that such foreign presence threatened the integrity of Beijing. This so-called Triple Intervention sufficed to push an angry Japan off the mainland. But the European tigers turned out to be more dangerous and territorially ravenous than the Japanese wolf they had chased away. As compensation for its part in the Triple Intervention, in 1898 Germany asked for and, after a show of force, received a naval base along with mining and railroad rights on the Shandong Peninsula. Ostensibly to protect China from both the German and Japanese menace (and after a sizable bribe to the Chinese negotiators),[12] the Russians signed a military agreement with the emperor and in return were given a 25-year lease on the southern tip of the Liaodong Peninsula, including the port of Dalian and the Port Arthur naval base. Russia was also allowed to link these ports with a rail connection to the Chinese Eastern Railway. Such concessions unleashed a torrent of demands by other states: to keep pace with archrival Germany, Britain extorted a territorial lease on Weihaiwei and Kowloon and a sphere of influence over the Yangzi valley. France leased Guangzhou Bay and received a sphere of influence in three southern provinces. Only the demands of Italy, the weakest would-be

European imperialist, were rejected successfully after a show of force by a provincial governor. The Italians had to settle for part of the North African lands of the Ottoman Empire, a state that was even "sicker" than the ailing Manchu dynasty.

Although most European leases in China were granted for 99 years, it was generally recognized at the time that the concessions really were steps toward the ultimate annexation of Chinese territory. In an expression that gained fashion at the time, the great Qing empire indeed was being "carved up like a melon."

The harsh terms of the Treaty of Shimonoseki (1895), which concluded the Sino-Japanese War, and Germany's demands in Shandong were sufficiently shocking to convince the imperial government that more far-reaching reforms were required to preserve China's territorial integrity. Meanwhile, these foreign policy humiliations had also inspired a variety of reform movements within gentry circles. By the 1880s open talk of political and educational reform had become widespread among the elite, much of it being promoted by scholar-gentry who were not in office. This in itself was a dangerous omen for the Manchus, for Qing political regulations strictly forbad discussions or writings on such matters among those outside the government.

The Hundred Days Reform of 1898

The most influential reformer to step forward during this time of need was a young philosopher by the name of Kang Youwei. Along with his brilliant protégé, Liang Qichao, Kang advocated dramatic institutional changes, a sort of "revolution from above," following the models developed by Peter the Great of Russia and the Meiji Emperor of Japan, all this somehow to be accommodated within China's Confucian ideological heritage. Kang appears to have been one of the Confucian tradition's truly creative thinkers, and one of its most radical as well, for he attempted to modify that legacy into a system that was not only not inherently conservative, but progressive. Through a skillful analysis of ancient sources, Kang tried to show that Confucius and other great sages were innovators who had actually championed institutional change. By so arguing, Kang could use Confucius as a shield against the criticisms of conservatives. The thrust of his arguments was to integrate modern political and technological theories with Chinese civilization by demonstrating (always citing the appropriate text) that Western ideas and institutions had already been practiced in the Confucian tradition.

In the general atmosphere of alarm resulting from the disasters of 1894–95, Kang was called to Beijing where he was given an unprecedented five-hour audience with the young emperor, Guangxu. The result was the spectacular

Hundred Days Reform, in which the imperial government, following Kang Youwei's advice, initiated a series of acts designed to bring about a revolution from above. Kang's reform proposals were ambitious. He called for a reorganization of the entire administrative system so as to centralize imperial control; a general liberalization of laws in order to give all subjects the right to petition the throne (Kang revealed his sensitivities to democracy here); and vast educational changes, including a national university and technical, military, and medical schools. The traditional examination system based on the arcane eight-legged essay was to be abolished in favor of a modern civil service exam, and a new educational program would be set up in which Western liberal arts and sciences could be studied alongside the Confucian classics. Kang had outlined all of this in a memorial to the emperor and warned that if his suggestions were not followed, foreign intervention would continue unabated, ultimately leading to the demise of the dynasty itself. Politically, Kang hoped that his reforms would lead to the creation of a constitutional monarchy. The new education system, aside from training bureaucrats and encouraging a modern national press, was intended to pave the way for genuine representative government through the creation of a national assembly. In order to stimulate economic development, the Hundred Days Reform laid plans for the construction of modern banks, railways, and steam shipping. To implement this ambitious program, Kang convinced the emperor to weed out of the Manchu government the thousands of corrupt and incompetent officials, the sycophants and ciphers.

Kang's program failed for a variety of reasons. Its radicalism represented an acute departure from the gradualism of self-strengthening, and its directives were issued too quickly. The reforms were a clear threat not only to entrenched bureaucrats but also to aspiring scholars who already had an immense investment in mastery of the classics. In fact, the imperial edicts were so repellent that they spawned the slogan "eat Kang" among students studying for the state exam. Nor could the regional strongmen be expected to support Kang's proposals because they were designed to limit local autonomy and corruption by concentrating the emperor's power. The military reforms directly challenged the privileges of the army's elite, and Kang's recommendations to weed out corruption would have broken the very wheels by which Chinese officialdom moved.

If these formidable interests were not enough to sabotage the Hundred Days Reform, there was the final, most galvanizing obstacle of all: the wily empress dowager, Cixi. This extraordinary woman had illegally installed her nephew on the throne and served as the real power in China, acting as *de facto* ruler behind a bamboo screen. It was this political reality that Kang Youwei had overlooked when he convinced the emperor to promulgate the Hundred Days Reform.

When Kang and the emperor heard of the reactionary plot to disrupt their reforms, they turned to Yuan Shikai, the most powerful military figure in China, Li Hongzhang's successor, and a general known to be sympathetic to reform. When Yuan betrayed the emperor, the reform movement came to an abrupt end. Kang and his aide, Liang Qichao, fled for their lives, eventually finding asylum in Japan. Within a few days an Abdication Decree declared that the emperor was incapacitated owing to serious illness, making it necessary for Cixi to assume the regency.

The chief significance of the 1898 reforms was that the radicals' attempt at reform from above, a pattern of change similar to that used in Japan, could not work in China. Moreover, by strengthening the position of the conservative parties at court, the failure of the reform contributed to the acceleration of xenophobia, thus sowing the seeds for the Boxer Rebellion of 1900. Although Cixi continued to champion some reforms (mostly military), the pace of change was gradual, not at all satisfactory to the growing number of progressive elements within China's elite.

In a sense, it was the reaction rather than the reform that had failed. The forces unleashed by Kang, joined as they were by the continued influx of Western ideas, produced among the sons of the gentry a groundswell of political discussion and ferment that could no longer be contained. Most importantly, these groups were attracted to a number of "study societies," which produced a sizable volume of publications championing Western ideas. These organizations amounted to a political revolution of sorts, for they encouraged the growth of voluntary associations outside kinship bonds and the traditional bureaucratic network. The societies and their newspapers and journals focused their energies on concrete political, social, and cultural objectives, thus preparing their membership and readers for greater political participation. This type of activity also contributed to the growth of a genuine national consciousness among China's upper classes, many of whom came to see that their interests were different from those of a regime that was increasingly ineffectual and of course, significantly, not Chinese. Finally, the reform era witnessed the emergence of a new kind of intelligentsia. Men like Kang Youwei and Liang Qichao were outside the state bureaucracy, that is, not employed in any government office and unattached to any particular local or public agency. Their relationship to the political establishment was one of tension and conflict, not empathetic symbiosis as was the case with China's traditional scholar-gentry. One can clearly discern among this new intelligentsia a growing sense of alienation and critical consciousness, psychological characteristics that have spawned modern revolutionary movements.

The Boxers

Meanwhile, other developments were creating another source of trouble for the Manchus. By the late 1890s the steady intrusions of traders, diplomats, and missionaries had stimulated deep and widespread antiforeign sentiment throughout China. Of particular vexation to the Chinese was the behavior of Christian proselytizers who, through the Treaty of Tianjin, were given the right to travel freely in China, independent of the encumbrance of local laws and customs. Missionaries had difficulty winning converts, and eventually some resorted to monetary bribes and the offer of legal protection from official interference to those who embraced the faith. All this enraged the gentry, as legions of Bible peddlers smashed ancestral tablets, tore down temples, and built churches. Christianity was seen to be a threat to the traditional order, and before long rumors circulated about nuns and priests who raped and devoured children behind convent walls, grinding their remains into medicine or selling into slavery those who escaped the torture.

This increasing tension between the Chinese and the Christian missionaries was exacerbated by severe economic dislocations. The penetration of Western industrial products raised havoc with China's domestic manufacturing. A growing trade deficit, the chronic hardships that persisted after the devastation of the Taipings, and serious imperial budgetary imbalances forced the government to search for additional revenues. The result was a massive increase in tax levies, the full weight of which fell most heavily on the peasant masses, those who could least afford the new exactions. As life became increasingly burdensome, the downtrodden turned to banditry or sought reprieve through secret societies. It was in the midst of such woe that a major antiforeign riot broke out in 1900.

The moving force behind this event was a secret society called the "Righteous and Harmonious Fists," the name referring to the use of the fighting stance and the military calisthenics that were an integral part of their exercises. Foreigners inaccurately called them "Boxers." There were a number of disparate Boxer associations, all of which claimed special magical formulas to harmonize the mind and body for extraordinary feats in battle.

At first Beijing put down Boxer activities with force because they were an anti-Manchu secret society. But when they arose again in 1899 it became increasingly clear that certain reactionary interests at court, realizing that their anti-Christian, xenophobic vitriol could be used as a weapon against the West, were encouraging the uprisings. In June 1900 Boxers by the thousands descended on Beijing, burning churches and foreign residences. Chinese converts were killed on sight; some were even buried alive. With the support of the court the insurgents took control of the city and besieged the foreign legations in the hope of destroying the very roots of Western influence in China.

The major regional strongmen refused to support the court's encouragement of the Boxers. But the throne was not dissuaded. When the Westerners formed a relief expedition to rescue the legations, the government, under the sway of reactionaries, declared war on the foreign powers. Li Hongzhang and other regional leaders claimed that the imperial edict was an illegitimate order given without proper authorization from the throne. By this stratagem they helped perpetrate the notion that it was simply the Boxers in rebellion, thus hoping both to save their own hides and to mitigate the consequences of the court's actions. As the allied foreign armies advanced toward Beijing, the empress dowager, the emperor, and a small contingency of advisers fled to the imperial summer residence in Xi'an. Once the foreigners lifted the siege, Beijing—its palaces and its private homes—was thoroughly plundered. Out of utter fear of ravagement, hundreds of Chinese women and girls committed suicide by throwing themselves down wells.

The Boxer Rebellion was an ill-conceived, impassioned uprising against Western imperialism. On one level it can be described as the last desperate attempt of reactionaries to save a diseased dynasty. Yet there also was an unprecedented patriotic dimension to the rebellion. It was a popular direct-action response to a deep economic and political crisis that affected the entire nation. Those involved came from constituencies that cut through the Chinese social strata from top to bottom. The rank-and-file were mostly peasants, and, like traditional secret society rebellions, this one was led by frustrated monks, tradesmen, peddlers, and unemployed laborers.

The Boxer Rebellion proved to be a turning point in Chinese imperial history. Because of widespread fears concerning the collapse of the Qing and a wholesale partitioning of the empire, which financially and politically would have been too costly for Western interests, the foreign powers concluded that Chinese territorial integrity must be maintained so as to ensure the principle of free trade. Consequently, the occupation powers refrained from seizing any additional Chinese territory. Despite this respite from further imperialist aggression, China's international reputation was sullied, greatly embarrassing the elites, which had begun to savor patriotism. An even greater blow to national pride and sovereignty was the harsh peace settlement, the so-called Boxer Protocol. Among other things, the Protocol restricted the importation of military hardware, required the dismantlement of the forts used to protect the avenues to Beijing, and granted foreign nations the privilege of stationing troops in the legations and the right to deploy their soldiers from Beijing to the sea. China's war indemnity was set at a stunning $330,900,000, which, when factoring in the interest rate over four decades, amounted to more than a doubling of the original settlement. The huge outflow of capital required to finance the debt seriously weakened China's economic growth. Finally, as punishment for conservative scholar-gentry who encouraged the Boxers, examinations were suspended for five years in forty-five cities.

Thus ended the last phase of China's attempts to strengthen itself within the confines of tradition. The forced abolition of the examination system proved to be the death knell of the Confucian scholar. By 1905 the court had formally abolished the ancient system, and new schools and new academic programs were introduced to take its place. With the demise of the examination system the formal distinction that had determined membership in the scholar-gentry elite disappeared.

The Boxer episode, in the long term, proved to be a lethal blow to the Qing dynasty. For purposes of political stability, the empress dowager was allowed to return to power behind her bamboo screen. The court also initiated an extensive reform program that might have succeeded in meeting twentieth-century demands for modernization. However, the imperial reformist impulse came too late. By 1900 the patriotic consciousness of China's gentry and other new social forces (namely the compradores, a Portuguese term meaning "general manager" who represented foreign firms doing business in China, and military men) had been aroused. Being sensitive about a regime that was Manchu, and having tired of half-hearted attempts at reform, China's elites became infatuated with revolution along Western lines. By 1911, in the midst of massive popular demands for revolutionary change, the fall of the Qing, when compared to the world's other major historical upheavals, amounted to little more than the proverbial whimper.

An Analysis of Imperial Decline

The ways in which the Manchus tried to deal with the problems of dynastic decline, cultural deterioration, and foreign invasion created the framework for radical Chinese who wanted to fashion a nation that could play a more formidable role in the expanding international state system. In this, China was not as successful as two other latecomers to the ranks of international power brokers, Russia and Japan. Why was China less able to pass through the social, political, and economic structural transformations requisite for playing such a role? The factors that conditioned the course of imperial Chinese history were both indigenous, that is, specific to China and wholly unrelated to the Western presence, and external, in the form of expanding capitalist-driven nations. Which of these two forces was more important?

Some historians argue that China's failure to modernize effectively was caused primarily by foreign aggression. This view asserts that bourgeois capitalism, which would have strengthened the state and allowed it to compete with the West, might have developed out of traditional Chinese society had it not been weakened fatally by imperialism. The normal evolution of Chinese capitalism, it has been argued, was short-circuited by the military and economic power of foreigners. The plethora of industrial goods, special privileges, and huge foreign investments that were forced on China via the unequal treaties destroyed the traditional domestic industries and the Chinese variant of the putting-out system (a transitional stage to industrial-capitalism in which the entrepreneur furnishes the craftsman with raw materials and pays him a fee to work the materials into finished products), rendering both ineffective as crucial intermediary forces in the maturation of a truly capitalist society. These intrusions also contributed to unemployment and further impoverished the peasants, thus encouraging rebellions and riots. Marxists, following a line of argument developed by Lenin in his classic study of imperialism, *Imperialism, the Highest Stage of Capitalism* (1916), believed that large-scale Western investment in China distorted native economic development. It absorbed the little internal entrepreneurial talent and capital that could have been used to support domestic industries and thereby prevented China from developing what the economist Gunnar Myrdal has called "growing points," which could have stimulated sustained economic growth. Consequently, the combined forces of extraterritoriality, the privileged positions of foreigners in the treaty ports, large investments, usurious loans, low tariffs, and constant territorial encroachment had the overall effect of distorting normal political and economic evolution in China. It thwarted the emergence of a bourgeoisie that might have challenged the feudal landlord class and so weakened the state that it was unable to respond to the demands of modernization.

It is too simplistic, however, to blame China's problems on imperialism alone. Certainly the unequal treaties gave foreigners advantages relative to their Chinese competitors. Western access to superior technology and capital, and immunity from imperial taxes, laws, and official interference, allowed them to dominate a large part of China's modern economic sector. And the social and economic dislocations caused by this "semicolonial" situation contributed to the myriad of rebellions in the late Qing. Yet Western control of the modern sector of China's economy was not enough to cripple Qing social, economic, and political life.

Foreign investment in China was never large enough to destroy the domestic economic system; nor was it of sufficient volume to undermine the traditional handicraft industries beyond the reach of the treaty ports. In fact, the native putting-out system, unlike its European counterpart, did not make a substantial appearance until after the introduction of modern industries, and then it provided ancillary functions for factories. Great Britain, the world's foremost imperialist power and the dominant presence in China, invested a mere 4 percent of its national income overseas, and 75 percent of that amount went to the so-called "regions of recent settlement": the United States, Canada, Argentina, and Australia. Only 25 percent of British overseas investments went into what were known as "colonial" type enterprises (India getting the lion's share), this being capital for encouraging the exportation of raw materials to the mother country. On the whole, comparatively little foreign capital went to China, and that which did was channeled into enterprises directly related to treaty port activities. These sums were never large because the volume of trade in the treaty ports was relatively small. The vast majority of Chinese, far removed from the modern economy of the treaty ports, did not have the income to purchase capital-intensive industrial goods and instead relied on cheaper, more durable native commodities.

In addition, the Western-dominated treaty ports, the beachheads of foreign capitalism, were not of sufficient strength to destroy the Chinese economy, the center of which lay deep in the interior. China's self-sufficient economic system was too large to be swayed by marginal sea-frontier contact with Western ideas and trade, and true economic change got underway only when inland China began to stir. In fact, China's indigenous marketing and labor-intensive production systems predominated well into the 1930s. As of 1933, for instance, handicraft production accounted for 68 percent of China's total industrial output.

Although imperialism seriously weakened an already sick China, there is evidence that it also may have provided strong medicine for moderniza-tion by creating an environment conducive to entrepreneurial growth and technological development. For example, the treaty ports functioned as bas-tions of freedom in an otherwise stifling Confucian environment, providing refuge and nourishment to fledgling entrepreneurial and intellectual groups that ultimately could transform Chinese society so it might hold its own in an aggressive, imperialist world. The enterprising, experimental environment of Chinese cooperation with foreigners in the treaty ports attracted Chinese capital and talent that might have stagnated within the confines of the Confu-cian order. Chinese businessmen, learning their trade from the Western-trained compradores, clearly could benefit from the security and facilities of the treaty system once they learned to use them. Moreover, Chinese entrepreneurs in the treaty ports were free from the enervating grip of Chinese officialdom. Those who took advantage of the system by imitating Western capitalists had no need to fear governmental exactions and did not have to fight for commercial liberty. After the defeat of the Taipings, economic activity in the treaty ports was generating significant pools of investment capital and techni-cal and business talent that, in favorable circumstances, might have provided the means to bring China through the critical early stage of industrialization to self-sustained growth.

The treaty ports failed in this capacity primarily because they were only one small sector of the Chinese economy. The Japanese and Russian experiences demonstrate that industrial modernization demands a great deal of central direction and support. This was absent in China outside the treaty ports. Even Li Hongzhang, the most powerful leader in China and the major impetus for economic reform, had to admit as early as 1877 that institutional bias was too difficult to overcome: "My official duty is to command the military. . . . Even if I wish to go beyond this and take up the more important and fundamental reforms, it is certain that I shall never be allowed to carry out my wishes."[13] The industrialization of China would have required a more stable framework of law and monetary practice, a more independent style of entrepreneurship, more clearly defined national goals, and most significantly, strong leadership at the top committed to modernization. All this was lacking, and to understand why, we must turn to the singularities of China's traditions, for the key to its initial failure to modernize can be found not in the West, but in China itself.

The most serious problems facing the Qing dynasty in the nineteenth and twentieth centuries were internal and had little to do with foreigners. Unprecedented population growth between 1750 and 1850 severely limited China's economic strength and at the same time spawned conditions for social unrest. This single demographic fact might have sealed the fate of any program for modernization. Both Russia and Japan also experienced rapid population expansion at this time, but these were offset by substantial growth in per capita income from improvements in industry, trade, and agriculture. The grinding poverty of interior China, made worse by crushing numbers of people, floods, droughts, and other natural disasters, was unparalleled anywhere else in the world. The Abbé Huc, a seasoned traveler with great personal knowledge of nineteenth-century China, noted that scarcely a year went by without terrible numbers of people perishing from famine. A quirk of nature could cripple the crops of an entire province, producing armies of starving beggars sweeping the countryside for sustenance.

> The multitude of those who live merely from day to day is incalculable. . . . Many fall down fainting by the wayside, and die before they can reach the place where they had hoped to find help. You see their bodies lying in the fields, and at the roadside, and you pass without taking much notice of them—so familiar is the horrid spectacle.[14]

This kind of suffering fueled the many savage uprisings against the Qing that began at the end of the eighteenth century and became chronic by the

1840s. The regularity and viciousness of such occurrences were without prec-edent in Chinese history and were indicators of general and endemic structural weaknesses in China's political and economic systems. Beijing's failure to assume a more constructive role in combating these problems was rooted in its rigid adherence to traditional attitudes and institutions. The Manchu leadership did not recognize the need for genuine, full-scale reform until the catastrophic Boxer Protocol, a curse it brought on its own house. Centuries of successful conservatism had now come home to roost. Nowhere was this more apparent than in the dynasty's economic policies.

China's economic problems, many of which were the inescapable result of severe national poverty, were never addressed adequately by Manchu financial institutions to the point where the state could generate revenues necessary for industrial growth. In other so-called "underdeveloped" countries with deficient consumer demand and capital supply, notably Russia and Japan, the state produced the required revenues for industrialization. This did not hap-pen in China. The efforts at restoration and self-strengthening were informed by the desire to achieve self-sufficiency, not economic expansion, and even during the high tide of emulating the West, the Mandarinate never attempted to create a modern banking system (as had the Russians and Japanese) that might have supplied capital for industrial investment.

Centuries of cultural prejudice against mercantile activity also made it difficult for a native merchant class to serve as a catalyst for capital growth. Those few who had capitalist ambitions found very little institutional support or protection for their activities. Because there were no commercial laws or legal guarantees to safeguard merchant rights and properties, Chinese en-trepreneurs were necessarily cautious with their finances and investments. Large profits would generally attract the attention of government officials who claimed the right to confiscate such wealth for state interests. Consequently, those who were successful businessmen hid their gains in a safe place (usu-ally in land, which meant that they ultimately became part of the "system" as merchant-gentry) because reinvestment would signal a new pool of wealth that a capital-starved government could extort.

Finally, there were a number of social factors that worked against China's potential for modernization. Unlike Russia or Japan, the state's ability to command the allegiance of the elites was compromised by their strong sense of family solidarity and overriding loyalty to lineage. In Russia, the court's power had been assured by its complete success in breaking the powers of the landed elite. In Japan, the Tokugawa Shogunate wielded unparalleled control over the powerful Japanese provincial clans by demanding unquestioned political, ideological, and economic loyalty. In China, on the other hand, the individual's close association with the family unit, coupled with the absence of primogeniture and the relatively open social mobility via the examination system, meant that loyalties frequently cut across social stratification lines. This not only reduced the court's ability to dominate the gentry, it also had the effect of reducing class consciousness in favor of family solidarity, thereby eliminating another major catalyst for social change.

Because of the centrality of family life in Chinese culture, the state's ability to control the elite was limited. Yet the gentry itself was not inclined to expand its powers and thereby serve as a vehicle for change, nor did it have the means to do so if it had so wished. Unlike its European and Japanese aristocratic counterparts, the Chinese gentry was of such fluidity that no single interest group was ever able to monopolize positions of power for extended periods of time. For one thing, the scholar-official class could not perpetuate itself. Its status was achieved through excellence in education, and this alone guaranteed it rights of political participation. Even the wealthiest landowners had difficulty ensuring that at least one of their own secured an advanced degree through the examination system. Without a constituency or familial protégés to follow him, the scholar-official's political power was restricted to his tenure in office. Moreover, there were few ways in which the elites could accumulate personal wealth. Business investments were not legally protected, and it always was difficult for families to build a power base through concentrated landholding. All this militated against the development of a corporate consciousness among the Qing elites. Without the necessity of guarding the privileges and wealth of estate, or the need to aggrandize them, there was not much that could move the gentry to take action in defense of its special interests. As opposed to the European and Japanese aristocracies, who took revolutionary action to safeguard their privileged status and economic well-being in the midst of social change, the Chinese elites never had many reasons to feel dispossessed. Consequently, they felt no need to buttress their positions by investing in commercial, industrial, or agricultural enterprises, and they also put little pressure on the state to change the course of affairs.

In almost every respect, unlike similar latecomers to modernization, China's society was not poised for change. Her inability to react more forcefully to outside aggression and the corresponding failure to build a viable industrial base to buttress the strength of the dynasty and move the state into the twentieth century had relatively little to do with the ravages of Western imperialism. Instead, late imperial China experienced a profound structural breakdown brought on by traditional forces that propelled dynastic cycles. At this unfortunate juncture between dynastic breakdown and foreign intrusion, the leadership simply lacked the internal resources to protect China from other expansive nations in search of wealth and glory.

4

The New Chinese Republic

Front center: Dr. Sun Yatsen (1866–1925).

Although the 1911 Revolution brought an end to the Qing dynasty, it was nearly bloodless when compared with other violent revolutions that overthrew inept monarchies; for example, the French monarchy in 1789. By the turn of the twentieth century the demand for change permeated Chinese society. During the previous decades a deep cleavage had developed between the Han Chinese majority and the alien Manchus because of the dynasty's inability to protect its people from foreign encroachment. Every class with any political clout had significant complaints. The scholars and the gentry were alienated by the dynasty's reform efforts. Merchants and treaty port Chinese bitterly opposed preferential treatment accorded to foreigners in China. Students were disgusted at the obvious backwardness of Manchu rule, especially when compared to Japan, the young imperialist power and model for many Chinese revolutionaries. These groups, after years without cooperating, came together briefly in 1911 to force the abdication of the Qing emperor.

The Groundwork for Revolution

In 1902 the Empress Dowager Cixi returned with her entourage from the western provinces where she had been hiding during the foreign siege of Beijing, claimed responsibility for the Boxer uprising, and declared that a long-awaited reform program would begin. Ironically, many of the proposals made in 1898 by reformers Kang Youwei and Liang Qichao were adopted, at least on paper. But these efforts came too late to satisfy those Chinese who wanted real change, and furthermore had the effect of continuing to undermine Manchu control. In 1905 the Manchus, after years of foreign insistence, terminated the centuries-old civil service examination system. Their attempt to "modernize" China's educational system with the creation of new schools and curricula alienated the gentry; in other words, Han Chinese who had succeeded in the exams or whose sons would eventually rise to the top of the existing Confucian hierarchy. Now years of study and the prestige associated with passing the difficult examinations were virtually worthless. The class that had an interest in preserving the status quo was now no longer its supporter. Thousands of students were sent abroad and thus had to learn foreign languages; their careers were forced to take new directions. The Han gentry resented this affront to their status by the alien Manchus. Many of their sons who studied in the West and Japan became revolutionaries.

In 1905 there were about 5,000 Chinese students in Japan; by the following year there were 13,000. Japan was a logical choice for many Chinese seeking an education abroad because of its proximity, but the huge increase in the number of Chinese students studying in Japan was not only the result of ending the examinations but also reflected the pride Asians felt after Japan astounded the world with its crushing defeat of Russia in 1905. Japan's development became a model for many Chinese. In Japan at this time Chinese students encountered scores of Chinese revolutionaries exiled because of their anti-Manchu activities. One such revolutionary-in-exile was Sun Yatsen, the man who later became known as the "Father of the Chinese Revolution." During the first decade of the twentieth century, there were no fewer than sixteen attempts to overthrow the Qing dynasty. Sun Yatsen orchestrated at least ten of those. Sun was from a Guangdong peasant family. In 1878, at 12 years of age, Sun left China for Honolulu with an elder brother and studied for several years at an Anglican missionary school, where he learned English. After a brief visit home, Sun left again for Hong Kong, converted to Christianity, and embarked on a career in medicine. In 1893 he began a practice in medicine on the Portuguese island of Macao, just outside of Hong Kong. It was in Macao that Sun organized his first secret society, the Xing Zhonghui (Revive China Society), with several like-minded iconoclastic Chinese. Initially, he and his colleagues proposed the establishment of a constitutional monarchy for China, but as time passed they increasingly came to view the Manchus as the primary obstacle to progress. The slogan of the Revive China Society was "Expel the Manchus, restore Chinese rule, and establish a federal republic." Sun claimed that it was difficult during the 1890s to gain sympathy and financial support for his organization among many Chinese because there were on the scene at the time other societies and apparently more effective leaders, such as Kang Youwei and Liang Qichao, who competed for the reformers' support. Nevertheless, in March 1895, Sun and his colleagues organized a plot to capture Guangzhou. Approximately 3,000 armed men planned to march on the city in October, but their plan was discovered, and Sun was forced to flee to Hong Kong and then to Japan. From then on, Sun was branded a revolutionary and was pursued by agents of the dynasty.

In 1905 members of several antidynastic organizations exiled in Japan allied with Chinese students in Tokyo to form the Tongmenghui (Alliance Society), an antidynastic, anti-imperialist revolutionary group. Sun was chosen to head the organization, whose goals were similar to those of the defunct Revive China Society. Many Chinese students blamed the Western imperialists for the Qing dynasty's problems. Thus one of the goals of this new group was to free China from Western encroachment, a goal the Japanese supported wholeheartedly. Chinese revolutionaries received both protection and encouragement in Japan at a time when Japan itself was expanding its empire into China, competing with the West for Chinese territory. The Tongmenghui also called for the "equalization of land rights," a proposal that profits made from landownership should benefit all Chinese.

By this time Sun had developed the "Three Principles of the People," his own program for creating a modern China. The three principles were nationalism, democracy, and social well-being. His goal with respect to nationalism was the creation of a strong Chinese state by expelling, for example, the Japanese, who controlled Manchuria; the Russians, who held Mongolia; and the British, whose booty was Tibet. The United States and several Western European countries whose ethnic and cultural diversity had not hindered the development of nationalism were cited as models of nation-building for modern China to emulate. Sun hoped that the second principle, that of democracy, would be the final outcome of the gradual enfranchisement of all citizens. In order to achieve this goal, he proposed the adoption of four electoral rights: universal suffrage, referendum, initiative, and recall. However, Sun did not feel that the Chinese people were ready for democracy, so he proposed a period of "tutelage," a time of transition during which citizens would be educated in the ways of participatory government. Sun's concept of democracy bore little resemblance to what Westerners consider "liberal" democracy or participatory democracy in which, in theory, the individual is sovereign and seeks freedom for self-enhancement. Instead, Sun stressed that the individual should be liberated so as to better serve the state, and he believed that the right to rule should belong to an elite group of the best-qualified officials. This can be seen in his "five powers" of government, which included the executive, legislative, and judicial branches, as well as a censorate and a civil service examination system—the latter two having been part of the traditional Chinese political structure. As Sun himself explained, "If we now want to combine the best from China and the best from other countries and guard against all kinds of abuse, we must take the three Western governmental powers . . . add to them the Chinese powers of examination and censorate and make a perfect government of five powers."[1] Sun claimed that the third principle, which he referred to as the people's livelihood, would solve the problems of land and capital. He called for the revaluation of private property, which would then be purchased by the government and given to landless people. His method for dealing with China's lack of capital, the fuel required to drive the modernization process, was to borrow from foreigners, particularly British and Americans, employing outside capital to build up Chinese industry and transportation.

Sun's other major contribution to the course of the revolution was his ability to raise money from Chinese living overseas. His talent for finding the necessary funding was one of the main reasons Sun earned the title "Father of the Revolution," because he was actually in the United States when the revolution finally occurred in October 1911. Chinese capitalists, many of whom lived abroad, supported Sun because of their increasing dissatisfaction with the Manchus' concessions to foreign business interests, which kept the Chinese comparatively disadvantaged. The unequal treaties allowed foreign goods to enter China with tariffs too low to prevent damage to many indigenous businesses. On the other hand, the government raised internal taxes to acquire capital while exempting foreign businesses from such taxes. Many Chinese found it more profitable to reside abroad where, despite discrimination, the economic climate was relatively more stable. As a result, overseas capitalists were the source of substantial funding for the revolution.

The 1911 Revolution

The Qing dynasty had begun reforms designed to establish a constitutional monarchy in China. These changes, like those in education, led to unrest and increased dissatisfaction with Manchu rule. In 1905 an imperial commission traveled to Japan to study the Japanese constitution and, on its return, outlined a timetable for the creation of a constitutional government for China within a decade. One of the first steps was the establishment of provincial assemblies in 1909. As assemblymen met throughout China, they focused their complaints on the ailing dynasty, particularly because their efforts at governing were merely advisory to the Manchu throne. Moreover, provincial leaders from Guangdong, Hunan, Hubei, and Sichuan were outraged at the throne's plan in the spring of 1911 to nationalize railroads owned by gentry from those provinces. In a move that helped fuel revolutionary fervor, the Qing government determined that railway owners from Guangdong, Hunan, and Hubei would be compensated for full market value, but those from Sichuan would be paid significantly less as a result of alleged embezzlement by the various Sichuanese owners. In response, Sichuanese gentry established the Railway Protection League in June 1911 in an attempt to halt nationalization, but within weeks, merchants' strikes, rural rebellions, and other antigovernment activity spread throughout south China. To add to China's misery, the lower Yangzi overflowed its course in September, drowning at least 100,000 and causing the starvation of many more.

The Chinese revolution that created the new Chinese Republic began on October 10, 1911 ("Double Ten," since then a Taiwanese national holiday), in Wuchang, the capital of Hubei Province. Hours after three local revolutionaries were executed, anti-Qing troops seized Wuchang's arsenal and secured most of the city, causing the officials to flee the following day. The incident signaled the beginning of the revolution. Members of the Tongmenghui and other antidynastic societies throughout China attacked Manchu garrisons in dozens of major cities. Within two months, fifteen provincial assemblies, many of whose members were associated with the Tongmenghui, declared their independence from the dynasty. On February 12, 1912, the Manchu regents for the 6-year-old Emperor Puyi abdicated, and the 268 years of Manchu rule came to an end.

The 1911 Revolution did not produce either a genuine republic or a unified China. One of the results of overthrowing the dynasty was a strengthening of the positions of provincial and local elites, many of whom were social and political conservatives who had been among the most vocal critics of Manchu rule. They supported the 1911 revolt in order to control it and thereby prevent any revolution in the social order. On the other hand, Western-influenced radicals and followers of Sun Yatsen demanded real social and political change. The Manchu dynasty was replaced formally by a republican form of government in March 1912. The new Chinese Republic was a feeble attempt to bring political order to a fractured empire. The new government lacked a strong political organization and military structure, producing what Lucian Pye has called a "phantom republic."

Provisional President Sun Yatsen, who had provided both inspiration and financial backing for the revolution, found the task of creating a viable government impossible. After the fall of the dynasty, the single unifying goal of his Tongmenghui had been accomplished. Once this occurred, internal factionalism, often spawned by opportunistic new members, weakened the party, which was renamed the Guomindang (Nationalist Party), the organization identified with Sun until his death in 1925.

Sun wanted to implement his Three Principles of the People in order to unify China, eventually create a democracy, and provide for the people's livelihood, but his proposals angered many Chinese leaders who wanted to retain their traditional authority and privilege, not to mention land. Moreover, Sun stood apart from other revolutionary figures because of his southern peasant background and missionary school education. He had never been a classical scholar, and he was closely associated with foreigners and overseas Chinese, especially because he spent most of his youth in foreign countries. For many Chinese, including his Guomindang colleagues, Sun was not suited to be the new president. He did not enjoy credibility among those leaders who actually participated in the revolution. Many looked toward the leadership of Song Jiaoren, a gifted and industrious politician from Hunan. Some members of Sun Yatsen's own party also distrusted his program, particularly the policy of inviting foreign investment, a plan that they believed would only increase foreign control of China. Sun reflected on his problems in Shanghai in 1918 when he wrote, "The Chinese people [are] becoming more and more unhappy. To a considerable extent this results from my inability to influence my party comrades and, apparently, my incapacity to guide them."[2] But Sun also blamed his colleagues, particularly those in the newly created Nanjing Assembly, established by representatives in the provincial assemblies after the revolution began, for failing to carry out his revolutionary program. Shortly after the revolution, Sun became merely the titular head of the Guomindang. Real power within the Assembly fell into the hands of other Guomindang reformers, including Song Jiaoren, whose more radical ideas called for the immediate smashing of traditional power structures. Moreover, the Nanjing Assembly elected General Yuan Shikai, then in Beijing, and not Sun to be the first president of the Chinese Republic. This was done with Sun's blessing because Yuan appeared to be the one leader who could unify the disparate groups of reformers.

Yuan's election by the Nanjing Assembly was not surprising. He had his own military force, the Beiyang Army, which, though too weak to unify China, was the strongest in the land. The last of the generation of nineteenth-century self-strengtheners, Yuan was also well known to the Chinese people for his career in government service. He had gained the respect of many Western and Japanese leaders for taking independent stands against the dynasty. For example, he had helped undermine the Hundred Days Reform Program in 1898 and later, in 1900, refused to comply with the Empress Dowager Cixi's orders to aid the Boxers in Beijing. Moreover, Yuan's base of power was in the capital, where he had been prime minister since November 1911, after the revolution began, but before the Qing abdication. The Nanjing Assembly had wanted the capital moved to the south, forcing Yuan away from his power base, but Yuan refused when his men staged an allegedly spontaneous mutiny after hearing of the impending move. Because Yuan also had foreign support to keep the capital at Beijing, the pro-Nanjing forces collapsed.

Yuan Shikai as President

Yuan's rise to power as China's first president was the result of social and political forces largely beyond his control. During his 4-year term, Yuan continued to face problems over which he had little influence. The failure of democracy, the growth of Japanese territorial encroachment, and increased regionalism all debilitated the new Chinese Republic.

By 1913, provincial leaders who had joined the 1911 Revolution gave support to a dictatorship headed by Yuan in order to avert domination by Guomindang radicals in the Parliament, who demanded the establishment of a cabinet as a check on presidential power. The radicals threatened the conservatives, whose interests remained in preserving traditional power structures. Yuan allegedly was responsible for the assassination of newly elected premier Song Jiaoren, the popular Guomindang radical who was to head the cabinet. When Yuan negotiated a 25-million-pound loan from a group of nations including Britain, Japan, France, Germany, and Russia without consulting Parliament, some Guomindang members called for armed resistance. During the summer of 1913, seven southern provinces declared their independence from Yuan's government, initiating a so-called "Second Revolution," but Yuan successfully put down the revolt and replaced the rebellious governors with his own men. Yuan dissolved the Guomindang for reasons of national security in November 1913 and forced its members underground. Thus the Guomindang became an antigovernment secret society based in the south, led again by Sun Yatsen, while Yuan began a campaign to make himself emperor.

Yuan Shikai was concerned with China's fate and not just personal aggrandizement when he decided to restore the monarchy in December 1915. Yuan not only lacked experience with democratic government, but within China there were no democratic models to emulate. The imperial model was appropriate to this old self-strengthener's background. The problem of succession was particularly vexing because China was so weak in 1915 that its future as an independent nation would be seriously jeopardized if chaos ensued after his death. Moreover, Yuan was nearly as powerful as an emperor already; his critics in Parliament had been effectively silenced, his army remained among the strongest in China, and he had placed loyal men in the governorships of all but four provinces. Yuan's American adviser, Dr. Frank J. Goodnow, agreed that a monarchy might be more suited to the conditions of China. He believed that the creation of a monarchy, for example, would perhaps give the fledgling regime an appearance of stability.

By 1915, Yuan and Goodnow realized that China was teetering on the brink of disaster. On January 1, 1915, the Japanese presented "Twenty-one Demands" to the Chinese government with the goal of making China a virtual Japanese colony. The Japanese wanted the Chinese government to cede Shandong to Japan, an area that it had just taken from Germany at the start of World War I; allow Japanese investments and troops in Manchuria and Inner Mongolia; give up partial control of several Chinese-owned iron and steel industries; refuse to give other foreign nations additional coastal territory; and allow Japanese advisers to run the Chinese government. Yuan was in no position to block the demands, given Japanese military strength, but when he leaked them to the press, the public outcry made it possible for him to negotiate. The European powers, embroiled in World War I, could not help him. The British, then allies of Japan, said Yuan had no choice but to give in. Yuan met most of the demands, but the growing Chinese resentment convinced the Japanese to give up the goal of running the Chinese government. China had avoided becoming a Japanese colony, but the groundwork was laid for future problems with Japan.

Yuan's short-lived dynasty was anything but stable. Soon after hearing the news of Yuan's claim to the throne, provincial leaders in the south once again declared their independence from the empire. Even Yuan's own generals urged him to annul the dynasty. In March 1916, he vacated the position of emperor and returned to the presidency. This experiment with imperial rule was a fiasco, and in the months before he died in 1916, Yuan was ridiculed as an incompetent fool. The anger and frustration provoked by Yuan aided in his demise. After he died in June 1916, Yuan was succeeded by his vice-president, who reconvened Parliament. Theoretically, power was once again based in the cabinet, but in reality it was held by the new premier, Duan Qirui, former commander-in-chief of Yuan's army. Duan, like his predecessor, Yuan Shikai, had military control over China's capital, but unlike Yuan, he did not have the prestige to control the leaders of other regional armies. It was clear by the time Yuan died that the strength of powerful regional authorities had grown during his years in power. As a result, for the next decade Chinese politics became chaotic, with dozens of military commanders competing for territory and power. They were known as warlords.

Warlords, 1917–1927

Warlords controlled personal armies that owed their allegiance to their commanders instead of to the state. They dominated most of China from 1917 to 1927, but were certainly not unique to that decade. Warlords have appeared throughout China's long history, especially during the chaotic years between dynasties. Antecedents of the twentieth-century warlords can be seen in Zeng Guofan and Li Hongzhang, who created regional armies during the late nineteenth century to defeat the Taiping rebels. Although these leaders maintained their ties to the Qing dynasty and supported the prodynasty self-strengthening movement during the Taiping Rebellion in the nineteenth century, their armies were not disbanded after the Taiping defeat, and so they continued to wield considerable power over their territories. While Zeng and Li, at least theoretically, were subservient to the monarchy, the warlords of the 1910s and 1920s answered to no national authority. They alone governed the peasants, institutions, organizations, and financial resources within their domains. Moreover, they represented a new generation of generals who, unlike their predecessors, did not have a Confucian education. Many of them began their careers as soldiers and rose through the ranks because of cunning or luck. As a result, their behavior was not governed by the traditional system of ethics.

Military rule was one of the few shared characteristics of the Chinese warlords. Individual traits, such as strength, rank, background, education, religion, interests, and personality, often determined the kind of rule imposed on their subjects. There were, for example, "reforming" warlords noted for the educational programs, public projects, and other progressive innovations they instituted. Others were known for the rapacity and unrestrained brutality of their rule as they extracted as much wealth as they could from the population. Warlords also could be subordinate to other warlords, forming a pyramidal hierarchy that controlled large areas of the country. Through subordinates, warlords maintained control over vast territories and were therefore important figures in the political struggles that plagued China. One was Premier Duan Qirui, the warlord who controlled the area that included Beijing. Competition among warlords was disastrous for China. Because warlords controlled the collection of taxes within their domains, the national government in Beijing was deprived of the resources necessary to function effectively. The warlords sought every opportunity for their own advantage, and several even attempted to negotiate loans from foreign powers in return for territorial or other concessions. For example, in 1917 Duan Qirui obtained a loan from Japan, an unpopular move with Chinese patriots and jealous warlords, but one that strengthened his hand against his enemies. The warlord decade was characterized by incessant fighting and intrigue among various warlord coalitions. No alliance was permanent. Once a common enemy was defeated and his army disbanded, allies often turned on each other. During this period, more than one million marauding soldiers marched over China, brutalizing the population. In 1920 an English diplomat residing in a town in Hunan described the arrival of a warlord army.

> The arrival of Chang [Zhang] [Warlord Zhang Jingyao] himself . . . was the signal for a general looting of the city. I have never seen more thorough work. Every shop, every house in this beautiful and prosperous city has been literally stripped. There is not a vestige of any usable commodity from one end of the city to the other. . . . The place is furnished only by troops, who lie disconsolate, dirty, hungry and demoralized on the floors and the counters of the shops and on every flat surface that is shaded from the sun. Most of the population has fled, but some 10,000 remain all crowded into the American Mission Hospital.[3]

World War I in China

Foreign powers, which had extended diplomatic recognition to the Republic of China in October 1913, recognized the warlord Duan Qirui's regime as the government of China, primarily because he was in Beijing and therefore controlled the machinery of national government. As a result, Duan was courted by both the Japanese and the Americans in their quest to draw China into World War I. China's role in the war was less important than Japan's and hardly worth mentioning compared to the Western powers', but the war profoundly influenced political developments in China. From the initial declaration of war to the postwar settlement, the events of World War I contributed to the turmoil in China.

The declaration of war against the Central Powers by Duan Qirui in August 1917 created an uproar among the leaders of China's feeble national government because it was done without parliamentary ratification. Since the beginning of the conflict in 1914, the British and French wanted China in the war to deal with the German concessions in China. They hinted at China's chance to recover German holdings in Shandong but also signed secret treaties with Japan promising the Japanese this Chinese province. In fact, the Japanese had already taken that territory from the Germans in 1915. The Americans, on the other hand, did not know of the secret agreements and openly petitioned the Beijing government to support the Allies with the promise of Shandong's return to Chinese sovereignty. The Japanese also supported China's entry into the war, although it would seem contrary to their interests. Japan had already signed the secret agreements with Britain, France, and Russia for Shandong and also took the opportunity to sign several secret deals with Duan Qirui to obtain additional concessions in areas that belonged to other warlords. In return, Duan received financial aid from Japan. Despite a great deal of nationalistic rhetoric, China's entry into World War I was less a national effort than an example of warlord politics. For a time, Duan, who became increasingly viewed as a tool of Japanese imperialism, was able to manipulate international events to his own advantage. Of course, he was not alone in such efforts. Other warlords sought and received foreign aid, and the foreign powers selected favorites with whom to deal. The Russians, British, Americans, and Japanese all loaned money or transacted business with one or more of the warlords. The Japanese alone supported several, mostly in north China, in order to gain a stronghold there, while the British and Americans looked to southern warlords whom they saw as potential threats to northern coalitions supported by Japan. Meanwhile, Sun Yatsen, who considered himself the one true patriot because he demanded the unification of China by defeating the warlords and kicking out the foreigners, failed to procure any help whatsoever from the foreign powers.

Sun and dozens of Guomindang politicians, who had lost their positions in Parliament when Duan Qirui returned to power, expressed disgust at Duan's riding roughshod over Parliament and his deals with Japan. In August 1917, with the patronage of several southern warlords, they set up a rival government in the southern city of Guangzhou (Canton) with Sun at its head. While they claimed to be the true nationalists, they found it impossible to win the support of foreign powers that continued to recognize Duan's government. Sun was frustrated over his inability to convince the Americans and Japanese, in particular, that he had enough power to grant concessions in return for financial aid. In short, during World War I, China was the scene of competition not only among the various warlords, but also between the northern and southern governments and even among the Allies.

After World War I ended, conditions in China continued to deteriorate as civil war persisted. In December 1918 representatives of the Beijing and Guangzhou governments met at a conference after a series of inconclusive battles. Fighting most likely would have resumed had it not been for an event that changed the course of twentieth-century Chinese history. This was the May Fourth Movement of 1919, which marked the Chinese reaction to the post–World War I agreements at Versailles. During the negotiations, the Chinese people found out about the secret deals between Japan and the Allies that gave away Chinese territory. The reaction was swift, violent, antigovernment, and antiforeign. It started with a demonstration of more than 3,000 college students from institutions in Beijing and quickly spread to other urban centers throughout China. Police repression by Duan's government merely fueled the outrage. Chinese nationalism had come of age.

The May Fourth Era

The May Fourth Movement was the result of decades of humiliation suffered by Chinese at the hands of foreign imperialists, but its importance goes far beyond the protests against the Treaty of Versailles. The movement had its roots in an urban intellectual renaissance that had begun about 4 years earlier. It closed with the birth of the Chinese Communist Party in 1921. Historians refer to the years 1915 to 1922 as the May Fourth era because of the far-reaching changes brought about by the complete rejection of Confucian beliefs and the substitution of a variety of Western ideas, such as democracy, egalitarianism, nationalism, republicanism, and eventually, Marxism. Many Chinese intellectuals had become enamored of Western society; they believed in Western models, particularly democratic models, for change in China. But, for many, belief in Western ideals was shattered by the Allies' rejection of Chinese nationalism and sovereignty. Many Chinese had believed, perhaps naïvely, in the goals for which the Allies claimed they were fighting, in particular the Fourteen Points of American President Woodrow Wilson, an idealist who wanted to establish an international system to abolish war for all time. One of Wilson's points was "national self-determination," whereby the people of a state could determine their own political future free from foreign influence. It was not clear during the war, however, that the imperialist European powers, such as Britain and France, had any intention of relinquishing control over their colonies and protectorates. As it turned out, at the Versailles peace talks, national self-determination was a principle to be applied only to Europe, particularly to those parts of Europe dominated by the defeated Central Powers of Germany, Austria-Hungary, and the Ottoman Empire. The two Chinese delegations at Versailles, one each from the Beijing and Guangzhou governments, were not the only ones who had their claims to self-determination rebuffed. Delegations from African colonies, India, and other Asian colonies all were incensed by the hypocrisy of the settlement. The wartime deals with Japan were enforced despite Chinese protests. Although the Japanese outmaneuvered the Chinese, even they were not fully satisfied with the postwar settlement. Their proposal to include a racial equality clause as part of the postwar treaty was not approved by the Western delegates.

Meanwhile, World War I had served as a catalyst for the Russian Bolshevik Revolution of November 1917. The Bolshevik leader, V. I. Lenin, soon pulled Russia out of the war, denouncing it as a symbol of the madness of capitalism, and declared that his new government was anti-imperialist. As proof, he publicized the terms of the secret treaties with Japan signed by Tsar Nicholas II, promising the Bolsheviks would not adhere to them and would return Russian holdings in China to the Chinese. Although such promises were never kept, they were precisely what patriotic Chinese wanted to hear. Lenin's revolution and his adherence to Marxism captured the imagination of many Chinese intellectuals and therefore had a profound effect on China's future.

Among the leaders who emerged during the May Fourth era were several pro-Western intellectuals, including Chen Duxiu, Li Dazhao, and Hu Shi, all of whom made significant contributions to developments in China. The causes they supported represented the options available to Chinese intellectuals who, by the 1920s, found themselves with two very different programs for China's future offered by two political parties: a revitalized Guomindang and a nascent Communist Party. No longer did Chinese reformers look to Confucianism or self-strengthening as inspirations for development. The careers of these Westernized men are representative of the forces that were bringing vast changes to China.

Chen Duxiu is considered one of the most important May Fourth leaders because he influenced a generation of Chinese thinkers through his provocative *New Youth* magazine, founded in 1915. He was later a co-founder of the Chinese Communist Party. In his youth, like other Chinese intellectuals of his generation, Chen prepared for the civil service examinations by studying the Confucian classics, but soon became disgusted with the highly competitive, extraordinarily stressful system. Taking the exams, said Chen, had the feel of a circus performance: "It was just like an animal exhibition of monkeys and bears performing every few years."[4] In 1902 Chen went to Japan after being expelled from school, allegedly for speaking out against the dynasty. There Chen's budding radicalism was nurtured. Japan was rapidly changing at this time, and the liberal democratic and scientific ideas that pervaded its schools had an indelible influence on students' minds. Chen helped establish a Chinese student Youth Society in Japan whose members believed that they had the answers to China's ills. They were willing, moreover, to do whatever was necessary, including organizing an army to fight injustice. Chen was soon expelled yet again, however, this time for assaulting a Qing government student adviser in Japan. Chen and two friends subdued the man, cut off his long braided hair, the symbol of Manchu pride, and displayed the trophy in the student union. Chen later returned to study in Japan from 1907 to 1909, but he spent much of his early career nearer home, taking advantage of his family's wealth and influence, studying, translating, writing, and speaking out in the iconoclastic fashion for which he had become famous.

The aftermath of the 1911 Revolution left Chen and others who had worked against the Manchus deeply disappointed. The corrupt and tyrannical behavior of Yuan Shikai and later Duan Qirui became targets for Chen's criticism. More importantly, Chen was now in a position to develop a significant following. In 1915, while dean at Beijing University, he established *New Youth*, which found a ready audience among his students. Articles that appeared in *New Youth*, often written by Chen and his colleagues, challenged Chinese tradition. The ideas and policies set out in its pages formed the basis of the New Culture Movement, which was associated with the May Fourth era.

Chen assaulted Confucian values in his "Call to Youth," the first article in the premier issue of *New Youth*. The respect he accorded to youth was, in itself, iconoclastic, because age was equated with wisdom and power in Confucian society. He attacked the patriarchalism of the Chinese family and condemned the practices of arranged marriages and subservience to the extended family. In an essay that appeared in *New Youth* in December 1916, Chen explained,

> In today's civilized society, social intercourse between men and women is a common practice. Some even say that because women have a tender nature and can temper the crudeness of man, they are necessary in public or private gatherings. It is not considered improper even for strangers to sit or dance together once they have been introduced by the host. In the way of Confucian teaching, however, "Men and women do not sit on the same mat," "Brothers- and sisters-in-law do not exchange inquiries about each other," "Married sisters do not sit on the same mat with brothers or eat from the same dish," "Men and women do not know each other's name except through a matchmaker and should have no social relations or show affection until after marriage presents have been exchanged," "Women must cover their faces when they go out," "Boys and girls seven years or older do not sit or eat together," "Men and women have no social relations except through a matchmaker and do not meet until after marriage presents have been exchanged," and "Except in religious sacrifices, men and women do not exchange wine cups." Such rules of decorum are not only inconsistent with the mode of life in Western society; they cannot even be observed in today's China.[5]

Chen asked young men and women to rebel, not only in their personal lives but also against corrupt government officials and warlords who represented parochialism and the privilege of the old nobility. He believed that China's problems could be solved only by radical youthful intellectuals who would reject Confucianism and revolt against the government. Only they would implement democracy, utilize scientific knowledge, and strengthen China's international position.

Chinese students enthusiastically embraced Chen Duxiu's ideas. Many, like Chen, were quick to blame China's ills on their elders who had allegedly sold out to foreigners. Moreover, they relished the new freedom, living away from parental control, and were encouraged by those they respected to abandon traditions. The New Culture of the 1920s was characterized by optimism, patriotism, demand for change, readiness to accept Western ideas, freer life-styles, imitation of Western culture and fashions, and sexual freedom for both men and women. This generation eagerly studied Western subjects, dressed in European-style clothing, and abandoned spouses to whom they had been betrothed as children for partners of their own choosing.

They also embraced another of Chen's innovations—the use of vernacular language for writing. Many students who had studied Western subjects also were deficient in the difficult classical literary form of Chinese, a totally different language from that which is commonly spoken and not the language in which Western subjects were taught. Chen made *New Youth* a vernacular journal. The vernacular literature campaign, espoused by other outstanding reformers such as Hu Shi, had the goal of reaching greater numbers of readers. Hu Shi was a student in the United States when he first made contact with Chen. He sent a vernacular translation of the Russian short story "The Duel," by Nikolai Teleshov, to *New Youth* for publication. In his letter to Chen, Hu called for literary reform and criticized Chinese writers for being old-fashioned because they did not write about contemporary Chinese society and the issues Chen believed were significant for young Chinese. Chen encouraged Hu and in January 1917 published his suggestions for the reform of Chinese literature. Hu wanted writers to create a "living literature" that would be realistic and use the vernacular. Several early issues of *New Youth* were devoted to vernacular translations of European and American fiction, ostensibly to serve as models for Chinese writers. Chen attacked the intellectual conservatives, scholars whose power was based on their mastery of the old literary language. He prodded his fellow writers "to overthrow the pedantic, unintelligible, and obscurantist literature of the hermit and recluse, and to create the plain-speaking and popular literature of society in general."[6] In response to his critics, Chen commented in the May 1917 issue of *New Youth*:

> Those who oppose literature in the "national language" and uphold the classical are similar to the Chinese in the eighteenth century who opposed Western astronomy and the theory of the rotation of the earth around the sun. We really do not have the leisure to argue with them over such a meaningless question.[7]

As time passed, fewer of the younger generation had the ability to read the more obscure language form used by Chen's opponents. Thus the vernacular literature movement effectively silenced the old guard. Moreover, the use of the vernacular was, in itself, part of the social revolution Chen proposed because it allowed those traditionally outside of the scholar-gentry classes to participate in political and intellectual debates. *New Youth* soon became a major vehicle for the dissemination of new ideas. After the May Fourth demonstrations, the journal became the forum for discussions on Marxism. Chen, like many other Chinese intellectuals, became disenchanted with Western democracy after Versailles. He spent several years searching for alternatives before adopting the model of the Bolshevik Revolution.

In 1921 Chen Duxiu co-founded the Chinese Communist Party with a colleague from Beijing University, Li Dazhao. Li was China's first Marxist. Like Chen, Li studied in Japan, where he became a staunch advocate of democracy. In 1916 he returned to China and became associated with a clique of relatively conservative intellectuals who resisted the trend to replace traditional Chinese values with Western ideas. They believed that Western democracies were on the decline and that the devastation of World War I would mark the end of the most powerful democracies, such as Britain and France, so that they were no longer useful models. As Li became dissatisfied with a democratic model for China, he was encouraged by events in Russia. In 1917 he formed a Marxist study group in Beijing to investigate the writings of leading Marxists. During the next 3 years, Li wrote numerous articles on Marxism. He focused on the peasants as the potentially revolutionary class in China and told his students to go and work in the countryside. Li was an activist who believed that the Chinese people, particularly Chinese youth, could remold reality. In an essay entitled "Spring" published in *New Youth* in 1916, Li envisioned a China that was reborn from within the old decaying former nation as a result of the actions of dedicated youth. Li consistently demonstrated an optimism for China's future based on his belief in the ability of patriotic Chinese to mobilize to effect the necessary changes. Such ideas would have a profound impact on China's future, not the least because a young man who worked for Li at the Beijing University Library was Mao Zedong, future head of the Chinese Communist Party and an architect of peasant mobilization.

Li Dazhao grappled with the task of adapting Marxism and Leninism to a precapitalist China. In the 1920s China had an urban proletariat that comprised a tiny portion of the total population. Moreover, many within this group were members of guilds and therefore were considered preindustrial, hardly the potentially revolutionary proletariat on which Marxist revolution depends. But Li was impressed that revolution had occurred in Russia, another preindustrial society. He found in Lenin's *Imperialism* (1916) some possible explanations for China's predicament. Lenin wrote that the capitalist powers temporarily solved their internal problems and postponed the inevitable proletarian revolution through profit-seeking overseas. Colonies were both markets and places to dump surplus labor through emigration. Therefore, the way to defeat capitalism in Europe would be to cut off its colonies and semicolonies.

Li's primary concern was not for revolution in Europe; he wanted change for China. He refocused Lenin's theory and portrayed an international "class structure," comprised of bourgeois (colonizer) nations and proletarian (colonized) nations. Within this scheme, China was a proletarian nation because it was exploited by Western and Japanese capitalists, much as workers are exploited by factory owners in Marxist theory. Therefore, China could have a "proletarian" revolution when the Chinese people united to overthrow the imperialist powers that controlled China.

The terms of the Treaty of Versailles confirmed for Li the desperately exploitative nature of the Western powers, which insisted on holding onto their colonies despite the promises of Wilson's Fourteen Points. Now, many of those intellectuals who had been Anglophiles or Francophiles, like Chen Duxiu, as well as those who had never been entirely enamored of the West, like Li Dazhao, gravitated to Marxism as the answer for China. In 1921 they formed the Chinese Communist Party (CCP).

The Development of the CCP

In March 1919 Lenin established the Comintern (Communist International), an organization whose job was to spread revolution worldwide. Even before the founding of the CCP in 1921, a Comintern representative, Gregory Voitinsky, met with Chinese Marxists to help organize the party. Two Comintern members were present at the CCP's first secret meeting in Shanghai where Chen Duxiu was elected secretary-general, despite his inability to attend. The CCP started out with just over fifty members.

Chen soon traveled to Shanghai to launch party activities, including organizing more than 100 workers' strikes during the following several years. In 1922 a second congress approved a manifesto calling for democratic revolution against imperialism and feudalism, the latter referring to the warlords. The membership agreed that the revolution needed the support, if not the unity, of workers, peasants, and petty bourgeoisie. The CCP's interest in organizing these three "classes" also coincided with Comintern goals.

The Comintern followed Lenin's view of imperialism. Revolution in China would weaken the Western imperialist nations, thus hastening the proletarian revolution in those countries as well. Therefore, the Comintern was more interested in supporting successful revolution than building up a nascent communist party. To that end, at the Third CCP Congress in June 1923, Comintern representatives suggested that CCP members also join Sun Yatsen's Guomindang in Guangzhou. As a result, CCP development from 1923 to 1927 was tied to Guomindang growth.

In 1923 the First United Front agreement was negotiated by Sun Yatsen and the Comintern. The Comintern representative, Adolf Joffe, suggested that the Chinese Communists be included in the final deal. Because Sun insisted that CCP members join his party as individuals, the CCP was reduced to a "bloc within" the Guomindang. The Comintern's goal was to aid the CCP in the eventual subversion of Sun's party, but the new constitution of the Guomindang, drawn up by Comintern agent Mikhail Borodin, established a highly centralized network of party cells, an executive committee, and a politburo—an organization that would prove difficult to undermine.

The First United Front agreement, with its promise of Soviet aid, was a major accomplishment for Sun Yatsen. Sun had already spent several years unsuccessfully seeking foreign aid to build up an army. By 1923, Sun's and Lenin's goals for China had much in common. The Bolsheviks were searching for Chinese leaders who could unite China and kick out the Western imperialists. In 1921 a Comintern agent had even interviewed a warlord in south China who had been accepting loans from the Europeans, but he was deemed unacceptable as a potential ally because he had too little political clout. Because the CCP was too weak, the older Guomindang, although in political disarray, appeared to be the only organization with the potential to carry out an independence movement. Most Chinese Communists agreed with the Comintern assessment; they had little choice to do otherwise. Sun's agreement with Moscow called for Chinese independence and national unity. CCP/Guomindang cooperation was seen as a first step toward those goals. Soon, CCP members, headed by Li Dazhao, joined the Guomindang while continuing to maintain their allegiance to the Communist Party. The Communists therefore would aid in securing an independent China and only after that carry out a revolution against the ruling classes. Li, whom Sun appointed as one of a five-member Guomindang presidium, explained at the First National Party Congress in January 1924 that Communists would participate in the Nationalist revolution and would not try to convert Guomindang members to communism. This marked the establishment of the First United Front of the Communist and Nationalist parties.

During the years of the First United Front from 1924 to 1927, several future leaders of both the Communist and the Nationalist parties emerged. These were the years when a young Mao Zedong (born in 1893), who within a decade would head the CCP, learned firsthand of the revolutionary potential of the Chinese peasants as he worked with the Guomindang's Peasant Movement

Training Institute in his home province of Hunan. He followed the lead of a talented fellow Communist, Peng Pai, who had organized the Institute in 1924 and who, within 3 years, had mobilized peasants in two counties to form a soviet, a cooperative government that temporarily replaced landlord control and redistributed land. Mao succeeded Peng as the Institute's director in 1926 and taught that year's class of more than 300 students about class structure in the countryside. By this time Mao apparently had accepted the Leninist concept of a world movement against capitalist imperialism, but he also felt that a Chinese revolution could succeed if the CCP guided class struggle by uniting large numbers to attack the smallest target. In other words, during the 1920s Mao was a quasi-Leninist because he did not believe that a small professional revolutionary organization like the Bolsheviks who carried out the November 1917 Bolshevik coup in Russia was an appropriate model for China.

Mao's 1927 report to the Guomindang hierarchy on his experiences as director of the Peasant Institute outlined the nature of peasant exploitation in the countryside. More importantly, he also wrote of peasant initiatives for change. Mao, like Li Dazhao and Peng Pai, had discovered a powerful force for change in the peasants. But such ideas were a challenge to Marxist-Leninist doctrines, which stressed the importance of the working class as the revolutionary force, as well as to the tactics of the United Front. CCP members remained loyal to the United Front and to the Comintern policy to carry out first a "bourgeois" revolution against imperialists in China. Therefore, the Communists were to wait for the social revolution in the countryside. Meanwhile, the real power behind the revolution, the military, fell squarely into the hands of an anti-Communist Guomindang leader, Chiang Kai-shek. By 1927 this would prove disastrous for the CCP.

Chiang Kai-shek, whose name would later become synonymous with the Guomindang, was a follower of Sun Yatsen in his youth. At the age of twenty, while a military cadet studying in Japan, he joined Sun's antidynastic secret organization in Tokyo. He later participated in the 1911 Revolution. In 1923 he was appointed head of the army created by the United Front with Soviet aid. That summer he was sent to Russia to study military science, and it was there that he allegedly acquired his distaste for the Communists, particularly the young Chinese Marxists who looked on this military man with disdain. Chiang returned home to head the Whampoa Military Academy, which trained many of the future commanders of both the Guomindang and the CCP. The Academy became especially significant for Chiang's future; from its graduates he developed a corps of loyal followers who played a crucial role in his rise to power.

Chiang Kai-shek's chance at leadership came sooner than expected with

Sun Yatsen's untimely death from cancer in 1925. Sun was clearly the mastermind behind Guomindang/CCP cooperation, and his death led to a power struggle within the Guomindang between Chiang and Sun's heir apparent, Wang Jingwei. Sun Yatsen had been the unifying force within a party of disparate views. His death revealed a cleavage between two major factions that was never overcome. Chiang Kai-shek headed a group known as the Guomindang Right because of its strong anticommunist views and a preponderance of military men in top positions, while Wang Jingwei's coalition, the Guomindang Left, was made up mostly of civilians and those who saw advantages to continued cooperation with the CCP. The CCP had demonstrated its organizational strength and popular support earlier in 1925 during the May Thirtieth Incident, a massive protest against foreigners in south China. The incident was sparked by a Japanese killing of a Chinese union leader and member of the Communist Party who worked in a Japanese-owned factory. On May 30, hundreds of students demonstrated in Shanghai. After their arrest, thousands of sympathizers took to the streets in protest. A British police officer, unnerved by their great numbers, ordered his troops to fire on the crowd. Ten were killed. In response, the Communists in Shanghai organized a workers' strike, backed by shop owners and students. Within a month, strikes, which were to last more than a year, had spread throughout south China, crippling Shanghai, Hong Kong, and Guangzhou. Despite retaliation by British, French, and Portuguese police, the strikers continued to be effective. Because of the May Thirtieth Incident, Wang Jingwei wanted to tap CCP strength for the Guomindang, while Chiang Kai-shek feared the CCP as a potential enemy.

Chiang's rise to the Guomindang's top post in 1926 came as a result of skillful maneuvering. Outwardly, he talked of cooperation with the Communists in order to maintain financial ties with the Soviets through the Comintern adviser in China at the time, Mikhail Borodin. Chiang reinforced the view that he was a United Front supporter by publicly denouncing Guomindang conservatives who, soon after Sun's death, declared their intention to expel the Communists and send Borodin home. A confrontation between the Guomindang conservatives and the pro–United Front group took place at the Second Party Congress in January 1926, which proved to be an overwhelming success for the Communists and their supporters in the Guomindang Left. Communists or their allies were elected to top posts in nearly half of the party's departments. Moreover, support for Sun Yatsen's policy of cooperation with the Soviets was renewed. Borodin saw the election results as a positive sign, a reaffirmation of the Comintern's goals. But Chinese leaders in both parties were concerned. Chiang's group, the Guomindang Right, felt threatened, while some CCP members were worried that their success would provoke a purge. Their fears were justified. As soon as Borodin left south China, Chiang, with the help of the Whampoa Military Academy, arrested Chinese and Russian Communists throughout the Guangzhou area and sent the Russian military advisers home. Chiang let it be known that he was now in charge of the Guomindang and that he would cooperate with foreigners and capitalists in the treaty ports, supporting their business interests in China. The head of the Guomindang Left, Wang Jingwei, left for France. This did not spell the end of the United Front, however. Borodin's return to south China prompted the Guomindang's Central Committee to reconvene. Chiang reiterated his support for the alliance, but the Communists were denied the victories they had won in the earlier election. No Communist could head a department. Chiang announced that he now controlled the administration of the Nationalist government as well as the entire armed forces. Borodin did nothing to stop Chiang and his associates.

The Northern Expedition

The next step for the United Front involved securing the territory over which the Nationalist government would preside. In 1926 the Guomindang's base was in Guangzhou, while the rest of China was still controlled by warlords or foreigners. The "bourgeois revolution" planned by the Guomindang and the Comintern was to take the form of a military campaign to capture warlord-held areas to the north. The Northern Expedition, as the plan was called, was originally Sun Yatsen's dream to restore China's sovereignty to a Chinese central government.

During the summer of 1926, Chiang Kai-shek and other Guomindang leaders thought that the time had come to move against the warlords. Neither the Communists, represented by Chen Duxiu, nor Borodin agreed. They believed that the Nationalist army was headed for defeat. But Chiang prevailed, and his assessment of the fragility of warlord alliances proved correct. Approximately 50,000 Nationalist troops left Guangzhou and headed north in three columns, one of which was led by Chiang Kai-shek, commander-in-chief of the overall operation. Warlord territory in central China was the first major target. Strong resistance was anticipated, but Communist efforts, notably those of Mao Zedong, in organizing the peasants in Hunan Province paid off. The countryside came to the aid of the Nationalist soldiers and, as a result, the provincial capital was taken by August. The two other columns, including Chiang's, although somewhat slower, were also successful, so that by January 1927 the Guomindang Central Committee wanted to move its capital farther north, into the interior of the Nationalist government's newly acquired territory.

This suggestion reopened the conflict between Chiang and the Guomindang

Right, on the one hand, and the Communists and their supporters, on the other. Chiang insisted that the new capital be at Nanchang in Jiangxi Province, the city where he was wintering with his soldiers, while the others had chosen Hankou on the Yangzi River in Hubei Province. The Communists and their allies defied Chiang's demands and moved to Hankou on their own. Moreover, their move into Hankou culminated in an attack by workers directed by the CCP's Liu Shaoqi on the British concession. As a result, the British were forced out of that interior city, an event whose repercussions were felt throughout the foreign communities. This marked a turning point for Chiang Kai-shek. As commander-in-chief of the Nationalist forces, Chiang now represented an apparently formidable force. Although warlord propaganda during the Northern Expedition portrayed Chiang as just another tool of the Russian Communists, numerous wealthy Chinese and even some warlords were willing to take their chances and approach Chiang in the spirit of accommodation. During the first few months of 1927, Shanghai businessmen, allegedly bearing gifts, paid tribute to the commander whose headquarters was now in their vicinity.

Meanwhile, Shanghai was the site of intensive efforts on the part of the CCP to organize unions in support of the impending invasion. Several of the Communist Party's most talented leaders, including Zhou Enlai, who had earlier served under Chiang as deputy director of the Whampoa Military Academy's political department, were in Shanghai working among the masses. In February, when one of the Northern Expedition's columns was just over 100 miles outside the city, the CCP called for a general strike, which paralyzed Shanghai. They expected reinforcement from their comrades in the Northern Expeditionary forces, but instead the troops waited outside the city while warlord armies massacred strikers and publicly displayed their severed heads. Communist historians blame Chiang Kai-shek for intentionally condoning the massacre. Undaunted, the unions tried again several weeks later as the Nationalist soldiers marched closer. This time they took over the city, handing it over to Chiang, who "liberated" Shanghai from warlord control in late March 1927.

During that same week, China's southern capital, Nanjing, also was captured by Nationalist troops. Several foreigners there were killed during the fighting, which led to retaliation by foreign warships. Reports out of Nanjing blamed Communist officers. Chen Duxiu, apparently aware that these actions met with disapproval, published a joint statement with Wang Jingwei, who had recently returned from France at the request of his anti-Chiang friends, claiming that the Communists had no intention of supporting workers' attacks on foreign settlements. They believed, like Chiang, that a war with the foreigners would signal the death of the Nationalist revolution. Although Wang backed Chen's views at a meeting with Chiang in Shanghai, soon after Wang left the city, Chiang turned against the Communists and the unions they had organized in Shanghai. On April 12, 1927, he initiated the White Terror, a day still commemorated in the People's Republic of China. Communist headquarters, the Workers' General Union, and other union organizations were raided and their members executed. Crowds of demonstrators who protested were met with gunfire. A reign of terror continued for weeks in Shanghai, while Chiang, with the help of urban gangsters, notably the notorious "Green Gang," recruited for the Guomindang cause, ordered additional executions carried out in Guangzhou and Nanjing. On April 18 the new Nationalist government, firmly under Chiang's control, was established in Nanjing.

Chiang had not yet eliminated all of his opposition, however. Wang Jingwei had gone to Hankou, where the Communists and their supporters had set up an administration the year before. That group protested Chiang's actions and actually ordered his arrest. But as time passed, and Hankou was subjected to an economic blockade by Chiang's troops, morale deteriorated. Furthermore, Chiang reached an agreement with two powerful northern warlords for a joint attack on China's capital, Beijing. Chiang clearly had covered all the bases: he pledged protection for the foreigners and Chinese business communities, and he either defeated warlords or incorporated them into his forces as allies. Meanwhile, Chen Duxiu continued to adhere to the Comintern's policy of cooperation with the Guomindang while depending on Wang Jingwei and his friends in the Guomindang Left for political survival. By mid-1927 this last thread of support for the CCP within the Guomindang was cut after a Comintern representative from India, M.N. Roy, purportedly convinced Stalin that the workers and peasants in China should be armed and mobilized immediately to complete the revolutionary process. Stalin sent Roy to China, where he ran into opposition from Borodin, who advocated caution. When Roy went ahead nonetheless and informed Wang Jingwei of Stalin's desire to arm the lower classes, Wang and his Guomindang Left associates were horrified at what they interpreted as Soviet designs on China. They broke with the CCP, leaving it even more vulnerable. Simultaneously, with the cooperation of the local warlord, Chiang organized the capture of Beijing. The takeover of the capital also was an attack on CCP pockets of strength. During the fighting, Beijing University's Li Dazhao, co-founder of the CCP and Mao's former mentor, was arrested and executed. On July 15, 1927, the Guomindang leadership formally expelled the Communists from the Nationalist Party. Borodin, M. N. Roy, and Soong Qingling (Sun Yatsen's widow and a CCP supporter) all fled to the Soviet Union.

The First United Front ended with the near annihilation of the CCP. During the next decade, although the foreign imperialists and several warlords remained unsubdued, Chiang Kai-shek and his party would dominate China.

5

Nationalists and Communists

Chiang Kai-shek (1887–1975) in March 1945.

Just as the cycle of birth, life, death, and rebirth occurs at many different speeds in varying parts of the natural world, with some organisms racing through it in days and others meandering along its course over centuries, this sequence can move at radically different paces in the political world. This was certainly true in China, where over the millennia some dynasties lasted only a generation while others endured for centuries. The decade after 1928 was one where the pace was exceptionally fast, as two political movements—Nationalist and

Communist—raced through their respective life cycles in different parts of their mutual habitat, the Nationalists in the lush river valleys and teeming urban centers of China's heartland and the Communists in scrubby mountain regions at the nation's fringes.

Chiang Kai-shek followed his successful Northern Expedition by selecting the city of Nanjing on the Yangzi River to be the capital of the new Guomindang (GMD) government. While Chiang's new government had many problems, it also had formidable assets. The GMD was the party of the revered Sun Yatsen, and Chiang was in a position to claim the role of Sun's successor. He commanded the most powerful army in China, had shattered the power of the Communist Party, controlled a substantial part of the country, and had considerable support among the most progressive and educated elements of Chinese society. Yet at first glance what looked like the rebirth of a new nation turned out to be nothing more than a political movement that aged and deteriorated so quickly in the harsh East Asian political environment that by 1937, the year Japan launched its invasion of China, the GMD was showing clear signs of decrepitude and terminal illness.

While the GMD was settling into Nanjing, remnants of the shattered Communist Party, in the wake of the 1927 Shanghai debacle, were taking shelter in desolate mountain nooks and crannies, like wounded animals about to die. Yet some of them managed to recover and breathe new life into their party, especially a group located in Jiangxi Province in southeast China. The life span of that effort proved to be short, and by 1934 the Communist Party was again close to death's door and in headlong flight from Chiang's legions. But what in 1934 looked like a mortally wounded political organism was instead a movement in the throes of a painful rebirth that, as it turned out, would become the seed of a new incarnation for all of China.

The Guomindang Regime

Whatever the faults of the GMD and Chiang, there was considerable optimism and good will for the new government as it set to work in Nanjing in 1928. The upbeat atmosphere was reflected on October 10 of that year, the anniversary of the 1911 "Double Ten" uprising that ended the Qing dynasty, when the new government proclaimed the end of the warlords and civil war and the victory of the new order. It did not take long before the realization set in that these grandiose claims were premature. As Chiang himself put it in 1932:

> The revolution has failed. My only desire is to restore the revolutionary spirit that the Chinese Guomindang had in 1924.[1]

Chiang's pessimism in 1932, like the general optimism of 1928, was overdrawn, but the fact is that too much began to go wrong for the Guomindang from the beginning. Some of the blame belongs to Chiang himself, some to shortcomings of the party as a whole. At the same time, Chiang's and the GMD's failings took place within a larger and extremely unforgiving context: on the one hand the unfavorable relationship between the limited resources and the time they had to rebuild a battered China, and on the other the almost cosmic size of their task, which was made even more imposing by the hostile forces that seemed to ambush the Nanjing regime at every turn.

The Nanjing government's first challenge was to assert its control over the country. While it is true that by 1928 it controlled more of China than any entity since the death of Yuan Shikai, that control was limited to only parts of China and was often tenuous where it did exist. This was in part owing to Chiang's failure to defeat many of the warlords he encountered during the Northern Expedition. Instead of fighting and destroying their armies, he negotiated agreements whereby the warlords pledged to support him and put their armies at the service of the GMD. In other words, Chiang absorbed, rather than eliminated, many warlords and their armies, in effect swallowing but not digesting them. Although this enabled Chiang to continue his northward crusade with greater strength, it left large parts of China under the control of allies of dubious loyalty and the GMD armed forces composed of units of equally uncertain reliability. This became all too clear almost immediately. Between 1929 and 1931 Chiang faced several revolts by a variety of presumed warlord allies; by 1936 there had been more than twenty uprisings against the fledgling Nanjing regime. With so many uprisings squeezed into such a short period, some inevitably overlapped. This prevented Chiang from decisively defeating enemies he might have had on the ropes. For example, in 1931, as he was pressing an offensive against the Communists, whom he considered the GMD's most dangerous enemy, Chiang had to cut short his campaign to face not one but two crises, one caused by Japanese aggression in the north and the other by dissident GMD factions in the south. So harassed was Chiang that twice he was compelled to resign his leadership position, once in 1927 and again in 1931, only to have his party recall him both times.

Along with its domestic opponents, the GMD in Nanjing also had to contend with foreign interference in Chinese affairs. Although the Western powers had yielded some rights in their various concessions, and the number of foreign concessions was gradually reduced, the Western powers still exercised varying if declining degrees of control over parts of China. Meanwhile, an eastern power was increasing its influence in China. In 1931 the Japanese invaded Manchuria, detached it from China, and the next year set up the puppet state of Manchukuo, officially ruled by Puyi, the last Manchu emperor, who had abdicated and thereby officially ended the Qing dynasty back in 1912. Japanese pressure on China continued until they launched a full-scale invasion of China proper in 1937, beginning a struggle that lasted until Japan's ultimate defeat in World War II in 1945.

Through it all, between 1928 and 1936 Chiang managed to extend and strengthen his government's control over China. By 1936 the greater part of the country, all or part of eleven of China's eighteen provinces, was ruled with greatly varying degrees of effectiveness from Nanjing. The Nationalist government had recovered control of twenty of the thirty-three foreign concessions in China, as well as the nation's customs and postal service. Given the staggering obstacles involved, this was an impressive achievement and represented the closest China had been to unity since Manchu days. Still, as with almost everything else associated with Nanjing, it was not enough.

Another hobble on the GMD regime was the nature of the party itself, which remained faction-ridden into the 1930s. Meanwhile, Chiang alienated the GMD from China's masses with his purge of the Communist Party. By the end of 1927 he had killed thousands of its members and scattered most of the rest to remote, forsaken sanctuaries in the countryside. Chiang's purge continued for several more years and engulfed other leftists and reformists, as well as many others unfortunate enough to be labeled opponents of Chiang's regime. The obvious result was that those people who would reach out to the Chinese masses, for whom the GMD under Sun had promised a program of "People's Livelihood," were eliminated from the party by 1930, and with them much of the GMD's ability to build a broad base of support for its regime disappeared.

In effect, Chiang's rise to power was symbolic of the conservative path the Guomindang had taken, and this was reflected in governmental policy. After 1930, landlord interests took primacy over peasant ones. A 1930 law limiting the amount of a peasant's crop that could be taken as rent to 37.5 percent was never enforced. Instead, rent levels generally ran well beyond half—and sometimes more than two-thirds—of what the impoverished, debt-ridden peasants produced. When government forces were able to drive Communists out of areas they controlled, land reform, which had benefited the peasantry at the expense of landlords, was often reversed. In the cities, trade unions and other worker organizations were suppressed; the only unions permitted were those controlled by the government, and union officials had to belong to the Guomindang. This situation obviously benefited the merchants and industrialists in urban areas, but the real beneficiaries of GMD largess were the country's large bankers, who provided much of the funding that kept the government afloat and received commensurate favors in return.

The severing of Nationalist ties with China's masses was reinforced by other factors. As already mentioned, the Guomindang did not always defeat the warlords, but instead absorbed them into the fold. Along with the warlords and their armies came warlord officials and administrators, who now staffed parts of the Nanjing bureaucracy. These people brought with them their old interests and governing habits, which basically consisted of using their posts to squeeze as much out of the people as possible. Some of this bounty went to the government, but a great deal of it, in the old imperial tradition, benefited the officials themselves. This corruption became even more pervasive because the Nanjing regime lacked the resources to supervise properly its far-flung network of officials. Corruption reached epidemic proportions, so that the advice "become an official and get rich" was increasingly heard. Added to all this was the corruption and demoralization that resulted from the ties of Chiang and his regime to underworld gangs, including the notorious Green Gang of Shanghai. These elements siphoned off their fat share of the nation's meager resources, further undermining social reform as well as efforts to promote economic development along capitalist lines.

Corruption was just one aspect of the Guomindang's failure to govern China effectively. There were more than 2,000 districts in China, and the GMD lacked the manpower, whether honest or corrupt, to administer them. Many of its most highly skilled people, those trained abroad in a variety of technical areas, tended to crowd into the coastal cities where the rewards for their skills were the greatest and where they felt the most comfortable. The training and foreign experiences of the GMD elites in effect alienated them from the majority of the nation that so desperately needed their help. The Nanjing government also lacked the resources to attack China's enormous problems. The vast bulk of its income went to repay its huge debt and to support its overblown army and military establishment. Military outlays, in fact, were never less than one-half of the total budget, and in later years, as war engulfed China, swelled to more than 80 percent of total expenditures. It is therefore not surprising that it was common for the bulk of a local region's meager budget to be eaten up by salaries and administrative costs, with precious little left over for improving local conditions. The frustrating result was that even when there were good intentions, whether in the form of programs or committed people, these intentions remained plans and promises that left necessary reforms or improvements unfulfilled.

A dialectical twist had taken place. Prior to coming to power, the Guomindang had stood for change. The degree of change advocated varied, depending on which wing of the party one looked at. Once in power, however, that quickly changed. It was not only that the personnel of the party had changed over time, tipping the balance of power from the GMD's radical to its conservative wing, or that the Nanjing regime lacked the resources to do its job, but that once the GMD was in power its primary goal became to maintain that power and the comfortable and profitable positions that went with it. In other words, once in power the GMD repudiated the very reasons it presumably had for seeking that power in the first place. In terms of the crucial question of social reform, the Nanjing regime stood for the status quo.

The methods the Guomindang used to maintain itself were harsh. Repression was the rule. People were arrested without cause and sometimes disappeared without a trace. Organizations that attempted to safeguard political rights, such as the Chinese League for the Protection of Civil Rights, lived precarious and often short lives. Dissident students expressed their views at the risk of their lives. Censorship, while not applied with notable consistency or efficiency, still made expressing one's views in print or trying to publish controversial writers an uncertain business. During most of the 1930s Chiang and the GMD had a strike force against any person or group designated as an enemy, the Blue Shirts, which allegedly was the embodiment of Guomindang ideals. Modeled on Hitler's Brown Shirts and Mussolini's Black Shirts, Chiang's Blue Shirts functioned as an intimidating cross between a street gang and the secret police.

The ultimate guarantor of the Nanjing regime was the army, the strongest in China and the means by which the Guomindang had come to power. Once the regime came to power, the army in effect became its social base; that is, the part of the population on whom it could rely to maintain its position. Already by 1929 military personnel accounted for more than one-half of the party's membership; by the mid-1930s more than 40 percent of its governing body—the Central Executive Committee—were military officers. The preponderance of the military, whose officers generally came from China's upper classes, was yet another weight pulling the Guomindang toward conservatism and against real reform.

At the top, of course, there also was a military man, Chiang Kai-shek. Chiang certainly had his talents. He was an expert at intrigue and at maneuvering his enemies both within and outside of the party so he could pick them off one at a time. He was able to build coalitions and alliances, often with rather unsavory elements such as powerful gangs in the Chinese underworld or unscrupulous financial and banking circles, which allowed him to get out of many tight corners and survive. And he demonstrated some military ability, at least during the years prior to the civil war with the Communists.

Overall, however, Chiang's faults outweighed his attributes. One of his failings was his view of where and how to lead China. Chiang certainly was an advocate of modernization. He was well aware that China's economy, social order, and political institutions were unsuited to achieving national security in a dangerous international environment filled with powerful and predatory nations. Like his mentor, Sun Yatsen, Chiang drew some of his ideas for modernization from the West. But in Chiang's case the model that provided inspiration was fascism, and the two most powerful countries guided by that ideology, the Italy of Benito Mussolini and the Germany of Adolf Hitler.

The New Life Movement

Chiang's ideas were embodied in what he called the New Life Movement. First proclaimed in 1934, it was Chiang's alternative to Marxism, which he considered China's number-one enemy. The general, whose main successes had come as a commander of armies, was convinced that only the militarism of the fascist state could pull his country together and inspire the populace as a whole to the discipline and sacrifices necessary to move the country forward. As he put it:

> In fascism, the organization, the spirit, and the activities must all be militarized. . . . In the home, the factory, the government office, everyone's activities must be the same as in the army. . . . In other words, there must be obedience, sacrifice, strictness, cleanliness, accuracy, diligence, secrecy. . . . And everyone together must firmly and bravely sacrifice for the group and nation.[2]

The New Life Movement was a clarion call to adopt new personal habits to revitalize the nation. Every effort was made to enforce the fifty-five sections on conduct and forty-one on hygiene in the widely distributed pamphlet called "On the New Life." It commanded all of China to stand up straight; to button its suits properly; and not to spit, drink, dance, gamble, or eat noisily. Intellectuals and other educated people frequently laughed at Chiang and his exhortations, but defying them was best done in private, as the police and the Guomindang's 10,000 Blue Shirts made a point of harassing people who publicly violated its dictums. As for the masses, as the historian Lucien Bianco has observed, "they would gladly have forgone the new life being urged upon them in return for some assurance that the only life they had would not be snuffed out."[3]

While extolling the virtues of modern Western European fascism, the New Life Movement drew from ancient Chinese tradition, especially Confucianism. Confucian texts were read with renewed enthusiasm by GMD adherents. Confucianism became the official state religion, and the sage's birthday returned as a national holiday. What this all added up to as a theory is difficult to define; historian John K. Fairbank called it "anti-

Marxist Confucian totalitarianism."[4] In practice, since the Nanjing regime never wielded the power to approach anything resembling totalitarianism, the Guomindang with its New Life doctrine really was offering the Chinese people its version of conservative nationalism. It was supposed to be a viable substitute for solving the pressing social problems that Chiang and the GMD leadership chose to place on the back burner as they first put their country back together again.

In 1943 Chiang summed up his ideas in a book called *China's Destiny*. That it was dedicated to the nineteenth-century Confucian scholar and soldier Zeng Guofan gave little comfort to those in the Guomindang who still advocated social reform and who, like Sun Yatsen, believed the Guomindang should draw its inspiration from the revolutionary Taipings, not from the man who had defeated them and rescued the Manchu dynasty. *China's Destiny* was even a greater problem outside of China. This ode to fascism Chinese-style came at an inconvenient time: in the middle of the great Allied struggle, of which Nationalist China was officially a part, to defeat German fascism, which was threatening to engulf the Western world, and, simultaneously, Japanese fascism, which was attempting to do the same to China and the rest of eastern Asia. Although some of the more embarrassing passages of *China's Destiny* were cleaned up in translation, this sanitizing did not prevent the book from becoming known as "China's *Mein Kampf*."

Nationalist Reforms

In spite of all of its difficulties and disadvantages, the Nanjing government succeeded at modernizing segments of Chinese society. Railroad mileage increased by almost 50 percent, to 11,000 miles. About 60,000 miles of new roads were built, and improvements were made in postal and telegraph services. During the mid-1930s, industry grew at about 6.7 percent per year, and some industries did significantly better for the decade as a whole: cotton cloth output grew by 16.5 percent and electric power by 9.4 percent. Increased tariff protection helped industry grow, while the abolition of the internal *lijin* tax as well as currency reform helped expand the internal market for local manufactures. But all of this put only a dent in the overall problem. As the 1930s drew to a close, industry as a whole remained only a tiny part of the Chinese economy, and modern industry a smaller fraction still. China remained hopelessly backward compared with modern industrial powers, and much of what was modern in China remained in foreign hands, including a large part of the nation's factories, railroads, and mines.

One of the reasons for the lack of real progress is that far too great a percentage of China's resources was directed into economic sectors that did not contribute to economic growth. The most important of these in what may be considered China's modern economy was a corrupt banking establishment. Chiang was connected by marriage to the important Soong banking family; in 1928 he married the American-educated Meiling Soong, sister of Sun Yatsen's widow and sister of prominent banker T.V. Soong. Although the government, working with the banking community of the treaty ports, contributed to economic stability by promoting currency reform to restructure China's foreign debt, the banks mostly contributed to the enrichment of a small number of financiers and speculators. The bankers connected to the regime and its four government banks were not above using extortion to raise funds from Chinese industrialists and businessmen, something that obviously drained away funds which might have been used for investment in productive enterprises. Beyond that, those bankers connected to the regime in one way or another helped finance the government by buying its bonds. The government then used a large part of its tax revenue, much of it extracted from overtaxed and impoverished peasants, to pay its creditors, in effect draining money from millions of poor taxpayers to inflate the overblown wealth of the banking community. Because so much of what the bankers collected went back to finance the government and its army and not into commercial and industrial enterprises that might have contributed to real economic growth, precious resources were wasted.

Meanwhile, China's agricultural sector, which employed more than 80 percent of her people and produced about two-thirds of her wealth, suffered and stagnated. Land reform, an essential condition of modernization, was ignored, a development consistent with the Guomindang's growing conservatism. After a period of good weather in the late 1920s, unfavorable weather conditions—which produced, among other tragedies, disastrous floods in 1931 that claimed millions of lives—combined with governmental inaction to drive farmers deeper into debt. Many lost their land and were forced to become tenants. Most government projects meant to help improve agricultural productivity, such as irrigation schemes, never got out of the planning stage. During the early 1930s the share of the national budget devoted to improving agriculture did not reach 1 percent; it went up during the next few years, but still only got as high as 3.7 percent. The result was that during this period agricultural production grew at a slower rate than the population, leaving the peasantry as a whole worse off with each passing year. The general economic malaise hurt not only farmers but rural handicraft industries as well, among them the important silk industry. The mid-1930s were particularly hard in many parts of China. Good weather produced decent harvests again in 1936 and 1937, but the basic problem of grinding poverty, backwardness, and low productivity had not been touched.

Chiang Attacks the Communists Again

Most of Chiang's vigor, in fact, seemed to be directed at destroying the Chinese Communist Party. After the disasters of 1927, the CCP had managed to establish a number of rural bases of operation, the most important of which was in Jiangxi Province. While generally ignoring the Japanese threat in the north, Chiang undertook a number of "extermination" campaigns against the Communist bases in the south. The first, launched late in 1930, quickly came to grief in the face of skillful Communist guerrilla warfare. It was followed by another failure early the next year, and by yet another toward the end of 1931. The third extermination campaign was interrupted by the so-called Mukden (Shenyang) Incident of September 18, 1931. Responding to a fabricated Chinese bombing of a railroad, the Japanese began their occupation of Manchuria, which ended in 1932 with the establishment of the puppet state of Manchukuo. Unable to arouse foreign pressure to force the Japanese out, Chiang did not oppose the Japanese aggression, preferring first to try again to dispose of the Communists.

While the Japanese increased their pressure on Nanjing, including the occupation of additional territory in north China, Chiang once again attacked the Communists. His fourth campaign ended in March of 1933 like the three before it—a failure. Undaunted, he tried again that same fall. But this time he had foreign help in the form of advisers from Nazi Germany. Now Chiang's armies, trained to an unaccustomed degree of discipline and efficiency by the Germans, closed in on the Communists behind an ever-shrinking ring of fortified blockhouses. By the spring of 1934 it was over; the Communists had been defeated and were fleeing for their lives.

Chiang's victory was not final. The Communists managed to escape his clutches and find refuge in north China after their now legendary 6,000-mile "Long March." But Chiang and the Guomindang had cause for satisfaction during 1935 and 1936, the last 2 years before the whole country was engulfed by war. Nanjing's physical control over China had increased to the point where it was possible to claim the country was unified, Japanese activities in the north notwithstanding. The economy had improved considerably during 1935 and 1936. And Chiang's personal prestige had grown, helped by rising anti-Japanese feelings in China.

At this point even Chiang's mistakes helped him. In December 1936, angered when one of his generals refused to attack local Communists because he wanted to oppose Japanese aggression, Chiang went personally to speak to his recalcitrant subordinate. Instead of submitting, the general took Chiang prisoner in the city of Xi'an in Shaanxi Province. Now it was the general's turn to make demands. After complex and somewhat bizarre negotiations, during which Chiang's Communist enemies interceded on his behalf, in return for his freedom he agreed to halt the war with the Communists and focus all his energies on opposing the Japanese. The Xi'an Incident galvanized additional support behind Chiang, and produced an agreement between the Nationalists and the Communists that bore the optimistic and exaggerated title of the Second United Front. This union in reality was an uneasy truce during which both partners, while moderating their mutual hostility, never ceased to scheme against each other as they put forward the best possible face against Japan.

As 1937 began, Chiang Kai-shek was the recognized leader of China, the man everybody looked toward to deliver the country from the Japanese. The problem was that his regime rested on a narrow and porous social base. Most of its support was concentrated in China's coastal cities. The bureaucratic apparatus through which it tried to govern was corrupt and inefficient. While some of its programs had begun to modernize parts of Chinese society, their effects, again, were concentrated almost exclusively in the coastal cities. The villages where the peasantry lived remained virtually untouched by any GMD activities other than tax collection and the recruitment of unwilling soldiers. The army, despite its victory over the Communists, was ill-equipped to defend China against a technologically advanced enemy. The government was burdened by a massive debt and inadequate resources. And total war, that most pitiless test of a regime's viability, was only months away.

The Chinese Communist Party

If the Nationalist Party in Nanjing had a formidable task after 1928, the challenge facing the Chinese Communist Party (CCP) was staggering. Although the party had survived the White Terror of 1927, it was decimated physically, scattered geographically, and divided politically. The next several years would be a relentless struggle on several fronts. The Communists had to find a physical refuge and defend themselves against almost constant attack from Nationalist armies. In addition, the party had to find itself politically, to come up with an overall strategy for dealing with the revolution in the wake of the 1927 disaster and the implications that the multiple defeats of that year had for the party's theory and practice of revolution. And it had to heal the deep and bitter divisions among its various leaders and factions. It should not be surprising that in the period following 1927—which is usually bracketed by the years 1928 and 1934 and identified by the rural bases established first in the remote, desolate mountain district of Jinggangshan and then, more importantly, in the equally remote but somewhat less desolate province of Jiangxi, where the party proclaimed the founding of the Chinese Soviet Republic—the party was unable to accomplish any of these tasks completely. The remarkable thing is that the

CCP achieved some partial successes, and so enabled itself to absorb even more defeats and hardship, and survived to fight yet another day.

If the CCP's first imperative was to elude the physical grasp and murderous assaults of the Nationalists, its main enemy, in order to recuperate and regain strength, China's Communist movement also had to escape the organizational restraints and ideological clutches of what were presumably its two main friends: the Communist International (Comintern) and the Marxist conception of how to make revolution. The problem with the Comintern was its relationship to Moscow; it was, in reality, not a voluntary organization of independent Communist movements, but a creature of the Soviet Communist Party and, as such, the puppet of men who knew little of Chinese conditions and who used the organization strictly as their tool. Since the mid-1920s the Comintern had been in Stalin's hands. His orders to Communists on the front line in China reflected his struggle against Leon Trotsky, his main rival for party leadership, rather than conditions in China itself. The results were disastrous. After 1927 the orders from Moscow were determined by formulas for revolution crafted in a European rather than a Chinese reality or by the crude needs of Soviet statecraft. Thus the Comintern never abandoned its insistence that the urban working class had to lead a Marxist revolution, even though in China the proletariat was a minuscule percentage of the population. When Soviet foreign policy came into play, the problem could become downright embarrassing, such as in the fall of 1929 when the CCP found itself compelled to "defend the Soviet Union" as the Russians invaded Manchuria and retook control of the China Eastern Railroad, which had fallen into Chinese, albeit Nationalist, hands earlier in the year.

Marxism itself, at least certain central aspects of Marxist theory, was another burden on revolutionaries in China. The product of German minds living in an industrial Europe, Marxism assumed that the peasantry's isolated and narrow world made it incapable of carrying out a socialist revolution. Marx himself was deeply hostile toward the peasantry as a class, and Lenin's modifications of Marxism—he postulated that the peasantry at least could play a *junior* role to the proletariat in the revolution—did little to make the overall doctrine more applicable to a society in which the urban working class was less than 1 percent of the population and the peasantry well over 90 percent.

The CCP's effort to sort out its relationship with the Comintern and to formulate an overall revolutionary strategy that had a chance of success in China was complicated by a leadership struggle that lasted for the entire period under consideration here. There were three generally recognized party leaders who held varying, and sometimes rather limited, degrees of authority between 1927 and 1935: Qu Qiubai (1927–1928), Li Lisan (1928–1930), and a group of Moscow-trained activists known as the Twenty-eight Bolsheviks

(1931–1935). They struggled over a bewildering array of issues and strategies as they fought, denounced, and deposed each other. However, these leaders did have one thing in common: they believed that the urban proletariat had to have the leading and central role in a Chinese socialist revolution. This did not mean, especially in the case of Li Lisan and the Twenty-eight Bolsheviks, that the CCP leadership during those years was blind to the Chinese peasantry as a revolutionary class that could play a supporting role in the movement; but, as Marxists, they could not bring themselves to give up on the proletariat as the leading revolutionary class and cede primacy in the socialist movement to the peasantry.

The various CCP leaders who continued the urban/proletarian revolutionary strategy after 1927 had more than Marxist theory to back up their arguments. Despite Guomindang repression, factory worker despair and militancy produced several waves of strikes between 1928 and 1930. In addition, the Great Depression, which began in 1929 with the New York stock market crash and spread across the capitalist world, increased the confidence among Communists all over the globe that the time had come for a decisive blow to the class enemy; as they put it, a new "revolutionary wave" was rising. But no existing revolutionary wave could cover the deadly political shoals on which the urban/proletarian strategy inevitably ran aground in China: the relative size and weakness of the Chinese working class, and the GMD's strength in the cities that enabled it to bring its military and police forces to bear on CCP activists who had conveniently put themselves within its reach. Qu Qiubai came to grief during the urban uprisings of late 1927. Li Lisan, while willing to pay considerable attention to organizing in the countryside, ultimately worried lest the peasantry come to dominate the Communist movement as a whole and insisted that the party attempt to take over several cities in 1930. The resulting defeats ended Li's tenure as party leader. He was replaced by the Twenty-eight Bolsheviks, who had just returned from the Soviet Union with the Comintern's backing to take over the party leadership. Following recent Comintern resolutions, the Twenty-eight Bolsheviks endorsed work among the peasantry. Still, they kept CCP headquarters in Shanghai, China's largest and most economically advanced city, and refused to abandon the urban/proletarian–centered strategy even after they were forced to abandon Shanghai and relocate their headquarters in the countryside in 1932.

The Emergence of Mao Zedong

Meanwhile, a number of CCP leaders were already in the countryside. They were concentrated in remote and therefore relatively safe mountain regions, where they had managed to establish organizations that, whatever their considerable limitations, at least seemed to have the ability to survive. Despite this undeniable virtue, these rural-based movements were viewed with suspicion, mainly because they violated Marxist doctrine by focusing on the peasantry, who, after all, made up the population living in these areas. The most successful and ultimately most important of these "mountain Communists," as they were disparagingly called by the conventional Communists in urban China and Moscow, was a peasant-born intellectual from Hunan Province named Mao Zedong.

Mao was born in 1893 into a relatively wealthy peasant family. According to Mao, there were "two parties" in his family, the "Ruling Party" of his hard-working, stern, and hot-tempered father, who often administered beatings to Mao and his brothers, and the "Opposition" made up of young Mao, his "kind, generous, and sympathetic" mother, a brother, and occasionally a laborer who worked on the Mao family farm. Despite the misgivings of the "Ruling Party," Mao attended a local primary school between the ages of eight and thirteen, although to his dismay he found his teacher belonged to the "stern-treatment school" and often beat his students. Primary school, which Mao's father thought should suffice as his son's education, was followed by an unpleasant stint working on the family farm and intensive late-night reading that provoked constant fights between father and son. Young Mao preferred books about modern technology or Chinese literature—although he noticed with disapproval that the heroes of the stories were always "warriors, officials, or scholars," but never peasants—while the elder Mao thought his son should focus on Chinese classical works, which in the Chinese legal system of the day apparently were useful, if a litigant knew an appropriate quote or two, for winning lawsuits.

Mao ultimately defied his father's wishes, left home, and attended several middle schools while considering a number of professions, including a police career. In 1911 he participated in uprisings that helped topple the Qing dynasty. In 1913 Mao was admitted to the First Normal College in Changsha to train for a career as a schoolteacher. When he graduated in 1918 Mao found a job as an assistant to the librarian at Beijing University, the Marxist thinker Li Dazhao.

Along with being influenced by Li, Mao was swept up by the turbulence of the May Fourth Movement that erupted in 1919. It was back in Changsha that he established a reputation as an activist and skilled political writer. Mao's first direct encounters with a few of the basic works of Marx, Engels, and Lenin occurred in 1920, the same year (having read a bare minimum) that he began considering himself a Marxist. But he had read and done enough to get in on the ground floor of a new movement; in 1921 Mao attended the founding meeting of the Chinese Communist Party. After 1923, he worked for the

Guomindang as a loyal CCP member participating in the United Front. After the United Front was shattered by Chiang Kai-shek's White Terror, Mao, on party orders, led the quixotic Autumn Harvest Uprising. He was lucky to get out of it with his life. Captured, he managed to bribe his way out of captivity. He then beat a quick retreat to one of the most wretchedly poor and forsaken regions of China, Jinggangshan, a mountainous territory on the border between Jiangxi and Hunan provinces.

On these desolate rocks, where barely 2,500 peasants scratched out a living, Mao began to build his Communist church. He soon received some help when he was joined by a small band of soldiers led by Zhu De, whose military talents would make him the father of the Red Army and its commander in the victorious civil war against the Nationalists in the 1940s. Mao and Zhu quickly built up a small army, which was vital to defend their tiny enterprise against constant GMD attack. They began a land reform program and made some efforts to educate the local inhabitants. An unexpected and most welcome bonus was the defection to their side of an entire GMD military unit led by an officer named Peng Dehuai, a man destined to play major roles both as a military commander and a political figure in the party. But none of this was enough to keep the Jinggangshan project alive. The Guomindang's military pressure was too much, and at the end of 1928 Mao and Zhu moved eastward to another part of Jiangxi, this time on the border with Fujian Province, there to begin again.

The experiences and lessons learned first at Jinggangshan and then in Jiangxi provided the basis for what turned out to be a successful blueprint for revolution in China. Mao now took the lead in introducing several crucial innovations in Marxist revolutionary strategy. It was nothing new for a disciple to introduce changes in the prophet's teachings. One inescapable truth about Marxism as it spread from its German birthplace is that it was changed by practitioners in other countries as they struggled to cope with local conditions. This occurred in Russia, where the main architect of change was Lenin, and it occurred in China as well, where Mao was the major innovator. Mao was a product of Chinese culture, a Chinese patriot, and a revolutionary before he became a Marxist, and all of these things shaped—some would say warped—his Marxism.

The first and most fundamental of Mao's principles, which at once was the most crucial to success in China, radically changed the Marxist doctrine, and therefore met with intense resistance from the party leadership, was the idea that the peasantry, not the proletariat, was the class that would make socialist revolution in China. Mao's ideas on the peasantry grew out of two observations: that the peasantry was the overwhelming majority in China and that its suffering had driven it to the point of rebellion against the established order. Chinese peasants, of course, had rebelled many times in the country's history; the problem for Mao and his fellow Marxists was how to win the peasantry to their particular cause: the struggle for a socialist revolution. It was good politics to use the peasants to make the socialist revolution in China. After all, as the overwhelming majority of the population, the peasantry could, if organized, potentially become the irresistible force Mao had been trying to build since the mid-1920s. The problem was that it was bad Marxism. Marxism required the proletariat to play the central revolutionary role, and to claim otherwise was ideological heresy. To what extent Mao realized that he was flirting with heresy is uncertain, although there is no doubt that in internal party debates, for example with Li Lisan, he was accused of overemphasizing the peasantry at the expense of the proletariat. In any case, Mao and his colleagues in Jiangxi made sure to genuflect to Marxist dogma. In 1931, when they were strong enough to proclaim the independence of what they called the Chinese Soviet Republic, they wrote laws favorable to what in fact was the nonexistent proletariat of their newborn republic. These included laws regulating working conditions and, more importantly from an ideological point of view, laws that favored the phantom Jiangxi proletariat in local governing councils known as soviets.

Mao did not arrive at his view of the Chinese peasantry on his own, easily, or in one stroke. Many of his thoughts on the peasant base of the Chinese revolution, as well as related ideas on China's position in the world and on the role of human consciousness in making a revolution, can be traced to Li Dazhao, Mao's mentor at Beijing University. Nor were Mao's post-1928 efforts at organizing the peasants for social change the CCP's first such attempt. That began in 1922 in Guangdong Province, led by an upper-class youth turned Communist named Peng Pai, whose pioneering work proceeded under GMD auspices after 1923. Several years later Mao in effect became one of Peng's students when he came to work at a Guomindang-sponsored school Peng headed—the Peasant Movement Training Institute, or, as this radical stronghold sometimes was called, "Little Moscow." Peng's efforts temporarily survived the debacles of 1927, as he managed to maintain control over parts of two populous counties while his ex-student Mao Zedong was fleeing for his life into the mountains. Student soon would outdo teacher, however, as Peng was captured and murdered by the Guomindang in 1929, just as Mao was getting a new start in Jiangxi.

Another source of peasant revolutionary activity from which Mao drew inspiration was in his native province of Hunan. More than a million peasants had risen in protest and insurrection there late in 1926, and it was this movement that Mao witnessed and wrote about in his famous "Report on an Investigation of the Peasant Movement in Hunan." In this report, written in early 1927, Mao predicted that "in a very short time . . . several hundred million peasants will rise like a mighty storm, like a hurricane, a force so swift and violent that no power, however great, will be able to hold it back." He warned his fellow Communists who considered themselves to be the leaders of a new China that all "revolutionary parties and comrades will stand before them to be tested and either accepted or rejected as they [the peasants] decide." Mao then asked: "To march at their head and lead them? Or trail behind them, gesticulating and criticizing? Or stand in their way and oppose them?"⁵

Mao's optimism was premature. A storm did indeed rise in 1927, but it was Chiang Kai-shek's White Terror which swept with such murderous violence over Mao and his CCP comrades. And Mao himself was less than a full convert to the idea of a peasant-based socialist revolution; it would take several more years, perhaps as late as 1930, for him to turn his back completely on the city for the countryside. In the meantime, Mao and his comrades were studying the practical aspects of making a peasant revolution in the best, if also most unforgiving, school of all: the real world school of hard knocks. The result was a multifaceted strategy and set of principles formulated and revised over time during the late 1920s and early and mid-1930s. Since there could be no revolution unless the movement could ensure its physical survival, a crucial corollary of the new strategy was that the revolution had to have a secure physical base. Given the Guomindang's strengths, this meant that the Communists had to set themselves up in remote rural areas, often in the mountains, beyond the Nationalists' deadly reach. Mao, of course, was not alone in recognizing this. Between 1928 and 1934 there were about fifteen Communist bases scattered across China, although the one that Mao headed became the strongest and most successful.

A second essential principle of Mao's thinking was that the party and its revolutionary base had to be protected by an armed force. That force would begin in the late 1920s as a ragged band made up of whoever was willing to join—initially a motley crew including urban intellectuals, peasants, and outright bandits. It would grow by the mid-1940s into a disciplined, well-equipped force of millions. The key ingredient in the fledgling Red Army was its relationship to the people. Chinese peasants dreaded their country's armies. To them the army, whether under the command of warlords or the Guomindang, meant pillage, looting, murder, and rape if it passed through their village; and meant brutal, inhuman treatment if one were impressed to serve in its ranks. The army that Mao and his lieutenant Zhu De began to build was radically different. Red Army soldiers were treated with respect by officers, who shared their hardships. Equally important, everyone in the army was governed by the "three rules and eight points." The three rules— prompt obedience to orders, no confiscations of any kind from poor peasants, and the immediate turning over to the government of all goods seized from landlords—provided a general framework that made it clear that this was a new kind of army for China. The eight points, which were added somewhat later, filled in the gaps. Designed to win the support of the poor peasantry, they specified scrupulous honesty and courtesy when dealing with civilians, to the point of making sure that soldiers were "sanitary" and dug latrines "at a safe distance from people's houses" and that they made sure to "replace all doors when you leave a house."[6]

While this concern for the people certainly reflected the party's commitment to public welfare, it was not entirely altruistic. To survive against the far stronger Guomindang armies, Mao and his colleagues had to fight with methods that made the most of their very limited strength. This meant stressing mobility and hit-and-run tactics against isolated Nationalist units whenever possible. Red Army units therefore often adopted the tactics of guerrilla warfare, and these methods depended on support from the local population, which provided invaluable shelter and supplies, information on the movements of the enemy, and, in certain instances, additional men to fight alongside the regular Red Army troops.

The Red Army's main job, of course, was not to promote public welfare but to destroy the Nationalist regime. It reflected the central role of violence in Mao's theory and practice of revolution. Mao's emphasis on violence was a product of the reality that the Chinese revolution took place not only in a rural environment, but also in a violent and martial one. Marxists had always been aware that as revolutionaries they were in a violent business, something that Marxism's basic primer, *The Communist Manifesto*, makes clear. The upheavals of 1848–49 in Europe, which ended in bitter defeat for the revolutionaries, affirmed the importance of force in overthrowing the old order. Events in Russia in 1905 and after 1917 further underscored how violent the profession revolutionaries had chosen was. But nowhere in Europe, at least before they came to power, did Marxist revolutionaries experience the sustained, long-term violence that they did in China.

The impact of this violence on party life as well as on Mao was clear and unmistakable. He knew well the extraordinary violence of Chinese peasant life, where grudges and conflicts were often settled with unspeakable torture as well as murder. He had served in the army at eighteen, and as a civilian a decade later received an unforgettable lesson on the uses of military force and violence during the disasters of 1927. The next quarter century of his life was then spent in chronic, if not constant, warfare. What this all meant was that violence became an accepted and routine method of carrying out policy. Mao summed up his attitude more than once. Perhaps his most famous statement on the subject was that a revolution is not the same as inviting people to dinner, or writing an essay, or painting a picture, or doing fancy needlework; it cannot be anything so refined, so calm and gentle, or so mild, kind, courteous, restrained, and magnanimous. A revolution is an uprising, an act of violence whereby one class overthrows another.[7]

A key agent in the application of this violence, inevitably, was the army. As the role of the army in carrying out party policy became more important over the years, its role in party life evolved into more than simply an agent of policy. The Red Army, as it participated in all sorts of civilian endeavors— for example, helping with planting or harvesting—became in Mao's eyes a model for the party and the people to follow. Although Mao insisted that the party must have primacy and control over the army, in practice he often relied quite heavily on the Red Army, and men who made their initial contributions to the revolution as its leaders, such as Lin Biao and Peng Dehuai, eventually were found at the very top ranks of the party.

Meanwhile, violence came to be routinely used not only against the party's enemies but also against one's enemies within the party. A case in point is how Mao dealt with a rival faction in 1931. Mao used brute military force as a weapon against the dissidents. Once they were defeated, thousands of arrests and mass trials followed. Five of the defeated leaders were then paraded around Communist-controlled areas, and three of them were executed. Years later, two decades after the party came to power, many party members and outside observers were shocked at Mao's use of the army as a power base and his willingness to unleash mob violence against his long-time colleagues, to the point of seeing some of them murdered and the country thrown into turmoil. Had those same observers studied the history of the party's revolutionary struggle and factional fighting more carefully, they might have been more prepared for what Mao did during the notorious Cultural Revolution when, as an old man, he employed, albeit with greater intensity, the same methods he used as a young man.

The factor that probably is most vital to understanding the real essence and core of Mao Zedong as a revolutionary thinker and practitioner is a third principle he infused into his Marxism: the role of human will in the revolutionary process. Traditional Marxism stressed what Marx called objective historical conditions. It was axiomatic to Marx that individuals could act only if historical development had paved the way first. The essence of what Marx called "scientific socialism" was his claim that he had deciphered the laws of history and had built his theories, including the presumed inevitability of socialism, on what he had discovered. Thus Marx had insisted that socialism could become possible only after capitalism had done its job, both in creating an industrial society and a class inevitably associated with it, the class that in fact would make the socialist revolution: the proletariat. Mao, of course, violated this dictum by transferring the revolutionary role to the peasantry, but as a Marxist he felt compelled to explain why. In doing so, he violated yet another fundamental Marxist tenet: the idea that objective historical developments, not what revolutionaries might want, governed when socialism could be realized.

Mao's thinking on this issue boiled down to the belief that human will could overcome virtually any temporal obstacle. His ideas on the primacy of human will were partially derived from Chinese philosophic traditions. He was also influenced by Li Dazhao, one of the two founders of the CCP, who also had stressed the historical role of human will. To solve the problem of not having a proletariat, Mao used human will, what he called "conscious activity," by turning it into the key catalyst in a grand experiment in intellectual alchemy. Back in the cities of Germany and England in the mid-nineteenth century, Karl Marx had insisted that it was the objective conditions under which people lived that turned them into proletarians and gave them the insight to select socialism as the solution to their problems. This was not necessarily so, Mao insisted in the mountains of China in the early twentieth century. If peasants could not become proletarians, they could at least function like proletarians. The key was to make them think like proletarians, something that the party could accomplish through education and propaganda. If this seemed impossible to some Marxists, Mao was unwilling to heed their objections. And, in fact, Mao would have more to say about human will after the Communist victory in China, again despite the objections of some of his more scrupulously Marxist colleagues, when he insisted will could be mobilized to overcome the "objective" economic and political problems the CCP faced in the 1950s and 1960s.

Disputes Within the CCP

Although there were many factions in the CCP between 1928 and 1934, there was one overriding division in the party: the cleavage between the official leadership (whether Li Lisan or the Twenty-eight Bolsheviks) which had the imprimatur of Moscow and the Communist International and controlled the central party machinery, and the "mountain Communists," the most important of whom was Mao. The pivotal date for the official party leadership during this period was 1930, when Li Lisan fell and was replaced by the Twenty-eight Bolsheviks; for Mao and the "mountain Communists," the key date was 1931, when in their Jiangxi redoubt they proclaimed a supposedly independent "Chinese Soviet Republic." But regardless of who was at the helm or where the mountain Communists were holed up, the disagreements between the two branches fell under three broad categories: to what degree the party would follow an urban/proletarian or rural/peasant strategy, how to handle the problem of land reform in rural areas, and what military strategy to follow in battling the powerful Nationalist armies.

Some of these issues arose at the party's Sixth Congress, which met in Moscow (there was no place in China deemed safe enough) during mid-1928. In the absence of Mao and other rural leaders, the congress reaffirmed the primacy of the urban strategy. It also stressed that any land reform had to deal harshly with those peasants who were somewhat better off than the average (labeled the "middle" and "rich" peasants) as well as landlords, the most natural target of peasant discontent, something that some rural cadres felt was counterproductive to their efforts to build a wide base of support in the rural areas. Disagreements surfaced in more dangerous form in 1930, when Li Lisan, whose recklessness was of concern even in Moscow, ordered his rural-based colleagues to mass their forces for attacks on the cities. Apparently with some reluctance, Mao and Zhu De followed their orders to attack the city of Changsha, one of the three major urban targets on Li Lisan's list. But when the odds against them proved too great, Mao and Zhu broke off the fighting and retreated into the mountains. This event was significant, not just because it marked yet another Communist defeat in the cities in the face of superior Nationalist power but also because, as Zhu later commented, "For the first time we openly disobeyed the orders of the Central Committee."[8] In the wake of this disaster Li Lisan was removed from power. The Communist International dispatched to the scene their top China expert, Professor Pavel Mif. Mif brought with him twenty-eight of his Chinese protégés who, while living in Moscow, had been studying how to make a revolution in China. These "Twenty-eight Bolsheviks," under Mif's patronage, were now installed as the party leaders. Their dogmatic commitment to a proletarian/urban–based revolution and their ignorance of the realities of power politics in China were manifest when they set up shop, under the nose of the GMD police, in Shanghai.

A more decisive step in asserting the influence of the rural cadres on party policy came with the establishment of the presumably independent "Chinese Soviet Republic" in the Jiangxi mountains on November 7, 1931. Its president was Mao Zedong. While Mao, of course, was the outstanding advocate of a peasant-based revolutionary strategy, the Chinese Soviet Republic suffered from the start from the party's ideological schizophrenia. For example, it adopted a rather elaborate law mandating working conditions for factory proletarians, and another favoring them in elections to local soviets—one worker's vote was worth four peasant votes—all without any factories or proletarians anywhere within the "republic's" borders. Its land law, adopted in 1931 and reflecting the views of the urban party leadership, was radical and harsh, not only in its treatment of landlords, but also in the severe treatment of so-called "rich" peasants. In practice, Mao and his rural colleagues operated quite differently. While they seized landlord property, they did not deal as harshly with the landlords as the law provided. Mao and his colleagues also were circumspect in redistributing land between richer and poorer peasants. They in fact permitted disparities in wealth to continue, which ran counter to Communist ideology. But in practice these moderate practices had enormous value, first by allowing the party to broaden its support among all segments of the peasantry; and second, by minimizing interference in the peasantry's work and the production of food, on which not only the peasants, but the party cadres, were dependent for survival.

Military policy, too, was a source of dispute. Mao generally favored a strategy based on small, mobile units. Larger units would not take on Nationalist troops until they had been lured deep into Communist territory, far from reinforcements and their base of supplies, where the Communists could defeat them. The central party leadership favored classic positional warfare, under which large Communist units would confront Nationalist armies head-on as they began their attacks on Communist territory. One of the strongest advocates of this approach was Zhou Enlai, who after 1935 would be won over by Mao and go on to serve as Mao's right hand and also as an indispensable mediator among party factions until his death, just nine months before Mao's, in 1976.

So while they fought the established order and the Nationalists, the Communists continued to fight among themselves. In 1932 the Twenty-eight Bolsheviks were forced to move party headquarters from Shanghai to Mao's mountain stronghold in Jiangxi in order to survive. While this move helped them, it was not good for Mao, who now had his freedom of action limited by the presence on the spot of ranking party leaders who disagreed with him. At the beginning of 1934, in fact, Mao was demoted and deprived of most of his posts and authority, although he retained the presidency of the Chinese Soviet Republic.

The Destruction of the Chinese Soviet Republic and the Long March

The Nationalists soon rudely interrupted these disputes. After four failures, by the fall of 1933 Chiang Kai-shek with his new German-led forces and military strategy was ready for his fifth extermination campaign. Chiang threw 900,000 troops into the fray, as well as an array of modern weapons that included almost 400 airplanes. The Red Army, following the strategy of its Comintern adviser, a German named Otto Braun, fought the Nationalists with a positional strategy that included digging trenches, thereby totally forfeiting the mobility that had served it so well in resisting Chiang's previous campaigns. The results were disastrous, as the Red Army in effect had made itself a stationary target. At this point, in the spring of 1934, Mao emerged again with an alternative to the leadership's strategy, urging a mobile, guerrilla strategy. For his efforts he was placed under house arrest. But as the Nationalist forces pressed on, and the combined civilian and military death toll reached one million, the Communist position rapidly became hopeless. The stage had been set for a dramatic and desperate act, one that would carry the center of party activity from southern to northern China, while it carried Mao from his personal political nadir to the top position in the party.

The Long March, as it is known, was really a desperate flight. The Communists zigged and zagged; clambered over mountains; crossed nearly unpassable swamplands, raging rivers, and searing deserts; and fought hostile populations, all the while engaging in constant fighting with pursuing Nationalist troops. During a trek of more than 6,000 miles lasting 368 days, the Red Army crossed twelve provinces, eighteen mountain ranges, and twenty-four rivers.

The expedition began without sufficient preparation, with the result that whatever plans existed soon had to be abandoned, along with most of the party's and army's records and equipment and, worst of all, many of their personnel. Somehow in the middle of it all, in January 1935 the party managed to pause for a conference—the seminal Zunyi Conference—where the old leadership was deposed and Mao emerged as the new leader. Meanwhile the Communists survived virtual certain defeat more than once. They also survived their political infighting, which did not end with the Zunyi Conference despite the victories Mao had won there. In October 1935, with fewer than one out of ten of those who had begun the Long March, Mao arrived in Shaanxi Province in north China, a desolate area whose main virtue was a remoteness that offered sanctuary from the relentless Guomindang.

The Long March became the stuff of legends. Mao, who had led the party to safety, emerged as its new dynamic leader. His collaboration with his former critic Zhou Enlai, which would be part of the bedrock of the CCP for the next 40 years, was established. Many of the Long March commanders, among them Lin Biao, Liu Shaoqi, and Deng Xiaoping, became the party's top leaders for decades to come, while lesser luminaries who survived the ordeal made up the elite who served just under them, in effect the party's aristocracy. All the survivors emerged from their ordeal with a new sense of mission and even of destiny, convinced that they had met the supreme test and conquered it. But, as Mao himself pointed out, at that time the Long March was really a drawn-out defeat from which the party and he had to recover and rebuild. In 1936, a year after arriving in Shaanxi, the party relocated about 60 miles to the walled town of Yan'an, where they proceeded to do just that.

6

China at War

Mao Zedong (1893–1976) as a young man.

It is fair to say that nobody was ready for the long, grinding war that began when Japan launched its full-scale invasion of China in July 1937. Although the Guomindang had officially made its peace with the Chinese Communist Party and the two rival parties had formed the Second United Front, it was a cold peace that produced no viable cooperation. The Nationalist army, while equipped with some modern equipment, was hopelessly unprepared to take on the modern Japanese war machine. The CCP was just beginning its recovery from the defeats of 1934–35 and, while more united than in the past, was still plagued by political infighting. There is no way the Chinese people could have been prepared for what awaited them as the Japanese poured into China. The Japanese brought terror to China on a horrendous scale. Indiscriminate bombing, the wholesale slaughter of civilians, the use of poisonous gas, and rampant rape and torture all became the lot of those Chinese unable to escape from the invader. During the 8 years of total war it is estimated at least 15 million, and perhaps as many as 20 million, died. It is for good reason that not only in China, but in all of eastern Asia from Korea to the Philippines, the passage of more than 60 years has not erased the memory of wartime Japanese atrocities.

Nor, ironically, were the Japanese themselves prepared for what was about to happen. They expected that a quick three-month campaign would enable them to conquer China and reduce it to a pliant client state. They were mistaken; the war against China dragged on until it was subsumed by World War II, and Japan found itself fighting a host of formidable enemies, including the United States. Meanwhile, the Chinese government escaped to the vastness of the country's interior, the CCP reorganized and fought the Japanese from its remote strongholds, and the Chinese people as a whole resisted the invader. Within a few months the Japanese were able to occupy most of China's coastal areas and key industrial centers. But Japan's army was far too small to occupy all of China, and therefore as it moved into the countryside it was in effect stalemated, swallowed up by the beast it was able to penetrate and brutalize, but never to possess or kill.

The Guomindang at War

World War II was a crushing blow to the Guomindang. At the very start of the war, Chiang Kai-shek and the party benefited from the Japanese onslaught as the country responded with patriotic enthusiasm to its government and to Chiang himself, who quite suddenly gained tremendous prestige and long-sought recognition as the legitimate successor to Sun Yatsen. His personal power within the Guomindang increased, and he basked in the glory of being the "Generalissimo," one of the growing number of titles he took for himself. But the glow soon wore off under the pressure of defeat and manifest incompetence. In the months after July 1937, the Japanese inexorably swept to the south and west. The Nationalist government was driven from China's major cities, which until 1937 had provided it with its financial and social base. The loss of Shanghai, the country's financial and industrial center, cost the regime customs and tax revenues, as well as illicit funds derived from the local opium trade. The Japanese soon drove Chiang's government from its capital of Nanjing, and then celebrated their victory in the infamous "rape of Nanjing," an orgy of murder, rape, and looting that took tens of thousands of lives (perhaps as many as 300,000) and laid waste to the city. The invaders then set up a puppet Chinese regime in Chiang's former capital to help them manage the huge areas they had occupied.

The situation quickly went from bad to worse. The government retreated into the country's interior, making its new capital in Chongqing, in landlocked Sichuan Province. Along with the paraphernalia of government went China's intellectual elite, the students and professors of entire universities, as well as hundreds of China's invaluable factories, which were literally disassembled and carted piece by piece to the interior out of Japanese reach. But Chiang's strategy of "trading space for time," while physically saving his government in the short term, created dangerous problems in the long term. In effect, what Chiang did was to hole up in the mountains and wait for outside help, enduring intense Japanese air raids on his wartime capital and conserving what strength he had for what he considered his primary battle, an eventual showdown with the Communists. As he put it, the Japanese were a "disease of the skin," while the Communists were a "disease of the heart." The problem was that by surviving, while at the same time failing to successfully resist the Japanese, Chiang and the Guomindang abdicated their roles as national leaders. That in itself might not have been fatal had others not been able to assume that role. But as Chiang waited in his southwestern mountain redoubt, Mao and the Communists, far away in the northwest, placed by fate almost cheek to jowl with the Japanese invaders, began to do precisely that.

The Communists got their chance because the Nationalists failed so completely. As war swept the country, in its wake came food shortages and starvation. Conditions would have been serious enough had the government made a serious and honest attempt to distribute what food there was, but its notorious corruption resulted in hoarding and profiteering while millions of peasants starved. The following eyewitness account of the situation in Henan Province was typical of conditions in Nationalist-controlled areas:

> The peasants . . . were dying. They were dying on the roads, in the mountains, by the railway station, in their mud huts, in the fields. And as they died, the government continued to wring from them the last possible ounce of tax. . . . The government in county after county was demanding of the peasant more actual poundage of grain than he had raised on his acres. No excuses were allowed; peasants who were eating elm bark and dried leaves had to haul their last sack of seed grain to the tax collector's office. Peasants who were so weak they could barely walk had to collect fodder for the army's horses, fodder that was more nourishing than the filth they were cramming

into their own mouths. Peasants who could not pay were forced to the wall; they sold their cattle, their furniture, and even their land to buy grain to meet the tax quotas. . . . One of the most macabre touches of all was the flurry of land speculation. Merchants . . . , small government officials, army officials, and rich landlords who still had food were engaged in purchasing the peasants' ancestral areas for criminally low figures. Concentration and dispossession were proceeding hand in hand, in direct proportion to the intensity of the hunger. . . . [1]

The Nationalist army was a scandal. It was largely led by incompetent generals who owed their positions to cronyism. Officers stole funds intended for supplying the troops, leaving them to plunder and loot to avoid starvation. Soldiers died more from lack of food or medicine than from battlefield wounds; 10 percent of the army probably had tuberculosis. The army made enemies instead of friends out of the people. Peasants were conscripted into the ranks by force—that is, when they did not flee their villages or mutilate themselves to avoid conscription—while their families mourned them as dead as they were led away, often shackled to one another. The demoralized Nationalist army often lurched out of control and pillaged and raped; it was so hated that peasants frequently killed Nationalist soldiers who fell into their hands. Nor were things better when it followed orders. In 1943 in Henan Province, for example, Chiang's troops took all the local peasantry's grain for taxes. The result was a famine so horrible that it drove the people to cannibalism.

Not even what are considered Nationalist victories did much good in the war against Japan. One of the few occurred in June 1938 when Chiang ordered the Yellow River dikes opened to slow the Japanese advance. Chiang was successful, but only at the cost of creating a flood that killed thousands of peasants and left an estimated 2 million homeless.

Things were not much better on the financial front, a vital part of any government's ability to conduct a war. The government's financial situation deteriorated without the taxes and fees it had drawn from the cities. Chiang's response was to print the money his regime needed; the inevitable result was a disastrous inflation that undermined and demoralized both the middle class and even government workers who provided a large part of the regime's support.

Perhaps worst of all, the Nationalist government was unable to tap into China's greatest untapped potential reservoir of political support: the peasantry. Although Japanese atrocities created an unprecedented wave of nationalist sentiment among the peasantry, the Guomindang was unable to mobilize it against the invaders. The problem ran deeper than the regime's failure to provide even the most rudimentary services, or the bad reputation of its army, although these factors certainly made the job more difficult. What crippled the Guomindang's ability to reach out to the peasantry was its own base of support. In retreating to the countryside, Chiang's regime became increasingly dependent on the landlords who dominated the rural areas. But organizing the peasantry into a force capable of effectively resisting the Japanese, through guerrilla war in occupied areas, for example, would have made them capable of resisting and even overthrowing the landlords as well. Therefore the Nationalist regime was not simply handicapped with regard to organizing peasant resistance but unable even to consider this strategy as an option because organized peasant action was as much a threat to the Nationalists as it was to the Japanese.

Chiang's policies hurt him in yet another way. For several years he had to get by on limited foreign assistance. Not until the Japanese bombed Pearl Harbor and brought the United States into the war did significant foreign material assistance become available. But Chiang squandered much of that aid and the good will that went with it because his regime was so corrupt and because he fought the Japanese only when it was unavoidable. The Americans were further angered by Chiang's constant demands for more aid and his threats to make a separate peace with Japan when he did not get what he wanted. The first American coordinator of military aid, General Joseph Stilwell, wondered aloud, "Why can't sudden death for once strike in the proper place." Stilwell became so exasperated with Chiang that President Roosevelt, at Chiang's insistence, had to replace him with General Albert Wedemeyer. Wedemeyer got along better with Chiang, but was unable to do much to improve the Generalissimo's performance against the Japanese or change the general impression of many American military experts on the scene that, as one general put it, "We are allied to a corpse."

The role of World War II in the subsequent defeat and collapse of the Nationalists in the civil war of 1946–49 is still a matter of debate. The war struck direct blows at the Nationalist regime. The Guomindang army suffered by far the lion's share of the losses in the fighting against the Japanese. More than 3 million soldiers died and were wounded versus Communist losses of perhaps 45,000.[2] Modern armies and foreigners with new ideas penetrated China's countryside as never before and broke traditional bonds that held the Chinese peasantry in place, creating new opportunities for those who wanted to overthrow the Guomindang. That alone, however, while probably a necessary cause, was not sufficient to destroy Chiang's regime. For that to happen, Chiang and the Guomindang had to fail as leaders, and that is precisely what they did. Meanwhile, the Communists led by Mao Zedong were filling the leadership vacuum and thereby strengthening their movement. All this makes it reasonable to agree with historian Lucien Bianco that "it was during the Second World War that the Kuomintang [Guomindang] lost the civil war."[3]

The Communist Party at War

It was in the midst of a national struggle for survival, which in turn was part of a larger world war—and only after much trial, error, and agony—that the CCP in Yan'an found the wherewithal to survive and become the most powerful political force in China, one that was capable of winning a civil war and, more importantly, carrying out a social revolution once it came to power.

A brief statistical comparison between the CCP's condition in 1937 and in 1945 indicates the scope of how its fortunes changed during the war. In 1937 the CCP controlled a small rural backwater inhabited by about 1.5 million poverty-stricken peasants, its battered army numbered 80,000, and party membership stood at 40,000. In 1945 more than 90 million Chinese lived under Communist control (the population of the United States at the time was 140 million) in territories scattered across north China whose total area was twice the size of France; the Red Army numbered 900,000 and was supported by more than 2 million militia troops, while the CCP had more than 1.2 million members. No wonder that in later years as the party struggled with the problems of governing and its own internal disputes the call was heard for renewal under the slogan "Return to Yan'an."

During the early wartime years Mao cited what he called the party's "three magic weapons" for the struggle at hand: the United Front, party-building, and armed struggle. The United Front was never more than an uneasy truce with the Guomindang in the face of the Japanese invader; often it was even less than that. In return for the breathing space from Nationalist attacks, the CCP officially put its troops at Chiang's disposal, although the Red Army remained intact and under party control. The party also moderated its social policies to make them more consistent with Nationalist laws. For example, it limited land rents instead of confiscating large landholdings. It instituted the so-called "three-thirds" system of government in CCP-controlled regions. Instead of establishing a CCP political monopoly, positions in local governments were apportioned by thirds: one each for the CCP, for the GMD, and for independent people. Actual control behind the scenes remained with the CCP, but this system allowed the party to meet its obligations to its United Front partner and, equally significant, to increase its support beyond its peasant base to intellectuals and even some propertied classes who were enlisted in the common struggle against Japan. Mao justified all this in a 1940 essay called "On New Democracy," in which he proclaimed that the current fight against imperialism was a struggle of a "bloc of four classes": the proletariat, the poor and middle peasants, the petty bourgeoisie, and the "national capitalists," that is, those capitalists who had not compromised themselves by collaborating with foreign powers. The United Front provided the opportunity to infiltrate both the Nationalist government and army by specially selected CCP personnel called, respectively, "United Front cadres" and "friendly armies." In a literal sense the United Front was very much a front, behind which the GMD prepared one day to destroy the CCP, while the CCP built its power and undermined the GMD, notwithstanding effusive Communist rhetoric that, among other things, endorsed Chiang's leadership and proclaimed the CCP's belief that the GMD held "first place" in the struggle against Japan and could look forward to a "brilliant future."

Party-building, Mao's second "magic weapon," was a recruitment and indoctrination program. It stressed not only building strength by enlarging party membership but also avoiding past defeats by reformulating party doctrine and improving training and discipline to meet new and growing challenges. Armed struggle, the last weapon, dealt mainly with how to confront the Japanese. In practice, the Communists, like the Nationalists, had little interest in confronting the Japanese war machine head on. Like Chiang, Mao focused mainly on building his party's strength for the anticipated postwar struggle to control China. While CCP guerrilla units fought the Japanese over most of north China throughout the war, the Communists mounted only one conventional campaign against the invaders, the "Hundred Regiments" offensive of the summer of 1940. The Japanese response, the murderous "three alls"—burn all, kill all, loot all—campaign, largely put an end to this type of strategy. Armed struggle thereafter was confined mainly to guerrilla warfare, as CCP cadres moved into villages from which the Japanese had chased the Nationalists and often the local landlords.

Although Mao did not mention it as such, the Japanese put a fourth and extremely powerful weapon in the party arsenal: nationalism. One of the CCP's major problems prior to 1934 was that despite its efforts at social reform, it was unable to build a mass base of sufficient size and constancy to withstand the Guomindang. Now the Japanese did the CCP two favors: they drove the GMD from large parts of China, and they treated the population so brutally that they aroused a potent hatred and national feeling ripe for mobilization and direction. The GMD was incapable of doing this. Given the dangers involved, it is to the credit of the CCP that it was. Thus the CCP was able to gain popularity not only among the groups it considered its natural allies, the peasantry and working classes, but also among Chinese of all classes who wanted to see the invader expelled. By the end of the war more Chinese looked to the CCP, the rebel group that had organized resistance in the cities and villages behind Japanese lines and built an efficient administration in the areas it controlled, than to the GMD, the government that had first fled to the hills and then sank into corruption and demoralization as the war dragged on.

The CCP had another asset that Mao avoided mentioning in his weapons list, what he called the "Sinification of Marxism." By *sinification* Mao meant freeing the CCP from strategies mandated by Marxist ideology that had no application to Chinese reality and often, as in 1927, led the party to disaster. Mao denounced what he called "abstract Marxism," as opposed to the "concrete Marxism" he and others were developing in response to Chinese conditions. He urged ending reliance on "eight-legged essays on foreign models" in favor of strategies that fit China's "national peculiarities." Or, as Mao bluntly put it in 1942:

> We must tell [our comrades] honestly, "Your dogma is useless," or, to use an impolite phrase, it is less useful than shit. Now, dogshit can fertilize a field, and man's can feed a dog, but dogma? It can't fertilize a field or feed a dog. What use is it?[4]

The sinification of Marxism originated in theory with Li Dazhao even before the CCP's official founding, and in practice with the activities of Peng Pai and Mao in the mid-1920s. Now in the 1940s it was openly acknowledged and elevated to a doctrine, one that permitted a variety of new or modified strategies at a time when survival depended so much on the ability to adapt to a harsh and rapidly changing environment.

The need for new strategies arose rather suddenly in 1940 and 1941 in the wake of several shattering defeats. The first 3 years of the war had been relatively good to the party. While the Japanese tore through China's cities and central agricultural areas and dealt blow after blow to the Nationalists, the CCP, only the secondary target, expanded its power in north China, both behind Japanese lines and in unoccupied territory. Beginning in the summer of 1940, both the Japanese and the Nationalists turned on the growing and menacing third force in the north. After the "Hundred Regiments" campaign, the Japanese directed more firepower at the Communists. Meanwhile, the GMD openly turned on its presumed United Front partner, which had taken advantage of the prevailing chaos to establish a military presence south of the Yangzi River. Although GMD and CCP forces had clashed earlier, the GMD drastically upped the ante in January 1941 as Communist military strength increased in the Yangzi delta region, a vital agricultural and industrial center. Over the course of a week, GMD forces attacked and decimated the CCP's New Fourth Army. This was followed by a blockade of Communist territory. Together, these events were a severe blow that recalled some of the party's earlier defeats in 1927 and 1934. It also marked the effective end of the Second United Front, although the fiction of its existence was maintained until the end of the war. It was in reaction to this defeat that under Mao's leadership the CCP developed a series of responses that were remarkably successful;

having been conceived in the party's remote Yan'an headquarters, they came to be known as the "Yan'an Way."

The Yan'an Way

Because the Nationalist blockade and Japanese pressure cut the Communists off from most outside supplies, economic self-sufficiency became the order of the day. Everybody, not only farmers, pitched in by growing food; Mao's contribution was to raise lettuce on a small plot of land. Meanwhile the "battle for production" saw grain harvests increase dramatically after 1940. Cotton, hardly produced at all before the war, became a major and vital crop in north China during the Yan'an years. The peasantry did not achieve these impressive results working alone; when necessary, Red Army troops, intellectuals, and anyone else, even government officials, were sent to pitch in. Small factories, often located in caves, produced everything from agricultural equipment to weapons for war. Often the party's ability to mobilize the population's enthusiasm was enough to get results, but when all else failed, other methods were used. Taxes were increased to keep the Communist government financially afloat, while forced labor was conscripted for vital public works projects, such as irrigation works.

Education was a crucial part of the Yan'an Way. Literacy campaigns were used not only to teach people to read but also as effective indoctrination tools. Traditional peasant folkways served this purpose as well because ancient tales and songs could be fused with modern Communist ideology to spread the party's version of the truth. New mass organizations served a similar purpose, some of the most important of these being organizations that mobilized women, at once increasing the supply of labor available to the party and undermining the traditional social structures the Communists wanted to destroy.

The idea of having everybody pitch in was more than a matter of practical need. Mao was convinced that a real Communist revolution required that the leadership never become isolated from the masses it was leading. If this were to happen, he believed, a class structure, albeit in another form, would reassert itself and the concept of equality, the fundamental ideal of a Communist revolution, would be lost. Mao's remedy for this was called the "mass line." Mao's concern with the subject went back to the Jiangxi days, but it was in Yan'an that it received its fullest formulation. According to the mass line ideology, it was fatal for revolutionaries to come to a village and simply tell the peasantry what to do, even if in fact what the revolutionaries were suggesting was for the peasants' own good. It was not even enough to confiscate the landlords' land and turn it over to the peasantry. Instead, the mass line required that revolutionaries come to a village and *listen* as well as talk. Nor was learning about peasant problems enough. Revolutionaries literally had to *share* peasant hardships so that they genuinely understood and felt the peasant experience. This was not easy. Mao pointed out that even though he was of peasant origin, when he returned to the countryside in the 1920s after years in the cities, he had developed elitist attitudes toward what was admittedly an uneducated and narrow-minded peasant mass. He was repulsed by the filth, crudeness, and brutality he found in the countryside and had to force himself to shed his urban-centered elitism and reforge real human ties with the population from which he had sprung. And what Mao found difficult to do himself was much more difficult for those who lacked his insight, determination, and ability to be, at least in this case, self-critical.

But the mass line approach did not mean letting peasants determine party policy or, for that matter, even decide what was best for them. Mao was, after all, both a Marxist and a Leninist, that is, a member of an elite whose self-proclaimed historic role was to lead society through the revolution to socialism. Mao might insist that understanding the living conditions of the masses and listening to them was essential, but there were clear limits to what the peasants could do. Alone, the peasantry lacked the insights, what Marxists call "consciousness," to make a genuinely socialist revolution. To provide it with that consciousness, in fact, was precisely why the Communist Party existed. Therefore, while it was the job of party cadres to listen to the peasants and to understand their grievances, the purpose of having that information was to be able to mobilize the peasantry to support the party's goals. In Russia a generation earlier, Lenin and his Bolshevik Party demonstrated their conviction that they alone had the right to determine the interests of the proletariat, the class they claimed to represent, and the path of development all of Russian society should take. Likewise in China, the Marxist-Leninist CCP, even though it focused its attention on a different social class than did the Bolsheviks, insisted on being the arbiter not only of what revolutionary goals should be pursued and what means should be employed to reach those goals but of what the peasantry's interests were. The CCP leadership developed several methods for enforcing its mass line. Probably the most important was a policy called "to the villages," under which intellectuals, party cadres, and others were sent to live and work directly with the peasants for lengthy periods. This campaign served two purposes: to break down the cultural snobbery these people often held for the peasants, and to help the party penetrate the villages and broaden its power base. Another program, "crack troops and simple administration," was designed to combat impersonal, bureaucratic methods of administration in favor of more personal and direct involvement between administrators and the people at large.

Equally important to the Yan'an Way was the *Zhengfeng*, the so-called "rectification," or thought reform, campaign of 1942 to 1944. On one level, *Zhengfeng*, "to change the direction of the wind, to change one's style," was the party leadership's response to the difficulties it faced in controlling its cadres. Party membership had expanded dramatically during the war, and many of the new recruits, at least from Mao's unforgiving perspective, were of questionable quality or simply unreliable. They included people from various classes, among them independent-minded intellectuals, whose personal agendas often extended beyond narrow Communist or even narrower Maoist goals and objectives. At the same time, Mao had not completely disposed of all his former rivals for leadership, most notably Wang Ming, the most prominent of the Twenty-eight Bolsheviks. Having reached Yan'an in the fall of 1937 after another sojourn in Moscow, Wang had unsuccessfully challenged Mao's primacy, but still held a seat on the party's governing Politburo. *Zhengfeng* was an all-purpose tool Mao could use for fixing his problems with both wayward cadres in general and his remaining rivals in particular.

Zhengfeng was an innovative and brutally harsh process of indoctrination supplemented by frenzied mass rallies, detention, torture, and incarceration under terrible conditions. Its core was "criticism and self-criticism," as cadres spent months on end in a variety of intensive group sessions in which individuals were expected to admit their sins, whether in thought or deed, and submit to unrelenting interrogation and denunciation from their peers. They were required to study and master twenty-two key texts, a reading list that left no doubt about which of their leaders mattered most. Six of the texts were by Mao himself, five were partially authored by him, and a few others were by his closest associates. Of the remainder, only three were by Stalin, supposedly the leader of the world Communist movement. The intent of the campaign, according to Mao, was not to destroy but to heal the "sick" and thereby make them better able to carry out party work. Significantly, one of that infected group, and rectification's first notable target, was the popular writer Wang Shiwei, who had manifested his ideological illness by criticizing the considerable material inequalities prevailing in Yan'an—the "three classes of clothing and five grades of food"—that benefited the party leadership at the expense of ordinary cadres. For pointing out this inconsistency between what the party leadership preached and what it practiced, Wang Shiwei was denounced in the most vicious terms and subjected to a brutal show trial, after which he was held in solitary confinement under conditions that left him a broken man.[5]

The *Zhengfeng* campaign was the final bulldozer that cleared the way for Mao to become the CCP's unquestioned leader. In March 1943, when the party announced a revised leadership team, Mao was named chairman of its

Politburo and newly formed Secretariat. Wang Ming, although still officially in the Politburo, had been rendered powerless and was no longer a top leader. The year 1943 also witnessed the debut of a new party orthodoxy based exclusively on Mao's ideas called "Mao Zedong Thought." Two years later, at the Seventh Party Congress, "Mao Zedong Thought" was incorporated into the CCP's new constitution, and Mao himself became the party's "Chairman," a post, it turned out, that would be reserved for him alone in the history of the CCP. By then, every other party leader had pledged his loyalty to Mao. The Chairman's top aide in bringing about his ascendancy was Liu Shaoqi, who had arrived in Yan'an in 1937 after several years of highly successful work in Shanghai and was the only party leader Mao spared the ordeal of repenting for alleged past errors. That turned out to be only a temporary respite from Mao's totalitarian rage. Although Liu and Mao would work together for more than a quarter of a century, tensions between them began to surface in the mid-1950s. Their final break culminated with Liu's imprisonment and death from maltreatment during the Cultural Revolution.

As the war continued, the growing strength of the Communists in north China, which stood in such contrast to the continued deterioration of the Nationalist government, did not escape the notice of others fighting Japan, including the United States. This was one reason why an American mission (called the "Dixie Mission" because it was visiting the Chinese "rebels") came to Yan'an in the summer of 1944 to investigate the possibility of aiding the Communists. Mao and the CCP leadership were anxious to reach a working arrangement with the Americans, but Chiang, fearing his domestic enemy would gain strength for the struggle he expected after the Japanese were defeated, opposed the project and it was abandoned.

In August 1945, the American atomic bombs dropped on Hiroshima and Nagasaki forced the surrender of the Japanese Empire and ended World War II. On paper, the Nationalist Party, despite its problems, still looked strong. It possessed China's largest and best-equipped army and a leader whose international reputation, especially in the United States, dwarfed that of any other Chinese political figure. Chiang was confident that he could now complete what his extermination campaigns had left undone back in the 1930s.

Mao and the CCP, however, had come through the war in excellent shape and were no less confident than Chiang. In its barren Yan'an cocoon, the party had been transformed. By 1945 it had developed the strategy and tactics to mobilize nationalist feeling, draft social and economic policies that were winning widespread support, maintain discipline and enthusiasm among a growing party membership, and wage effective guerrilla and conventional war. The stage was set, despite American efforts to prevent it, for the final struggle between the two would-be modernizers of ancient China.

Prelude to Civil War

Instead of bringing peace to China, the defeat of Japan intensified tensions between the Nationalists and Communists, which in turn led to civil war within a year. In 1945 the issue of immediate concern was to whom the Japanese should surrender. The Communist presence was strong in the north, where the bulk of Japan's troops were situated. This provided the Communists with an edge in securing valuable military supplies and strategic geographic positions. Chiang Kai-shek, however, insisted that the Japanese surrender only to Nationalist forces. With the help of American air and sea lifts and diplomatic support, Chiang moved his troops quickly into the major cities and rail and communication centers of the north. Thanks to U.S. assistance, which deeply angered the Communists, Chiang won the first round in the new GMD/CCP struggle.

The Nationalists had a more difficult struggle in Manchuria, China's most valuable industrial area, which had been occupied by Soviet troops just prior to Japan's surrender as a result of agreements reached by the Allies earlier in 1945. The CCP, hoping for support from the Soviets, was determined to prevent this rich region from falling into the hands of Chiang's government.

To settle these thorny problems, Chiang and Mao agreed to meet in the Nationalist capital of Chongqing in January 1946. These claimants to the Mandate of Heaven were joined by General George C. Marshall, America's most distinguished soldier, who had been sent to China as President Harry Truman's special ambassador. Marshall's objective was to help bring unity to China without civil war while assuring that the country remained free of Communist control. It seemed clear to most observers that Chiang would inherit the Mandate of Heaven; his apparently unassailable position was even appreciated by Stalin, who urged Mao to accept it. Marshall's job was to assist the Nationalists' efforts to reestablish authority but without involving the United States militarily in any fashion. From the outset, he made it clear to Chiang that large-scale American aid would depend on the cessation of hostilities and the creation of nationwide political stability.

At Chongqing, Marshall persuaded the two parties to work toward three objectives: an immediate cease-fire, negotiations to establish a coalition government, and the integration of Nationalist and Communist forces into a national army. Both adversaries had little choice but to appear reasonable because American support was crucial, and a war-weary Chinese public would have turned against the party seen responsible for the prolongation of civil strife.

Talks continued throughout the first few months of 1946. Mao was willing to accept a coalition government in order to break the GMD political monopoly, but Chiang feared sharing political power with the Communists unless they first gave up their army. Mao refused; he had no intention of putting his party in the same position it had been in during the disastrous 1920s. The few tentative agreements arrived at soon collapsed in March, when both armies were drawn into Manchuria to fill the vacuum created by the withdrawal of Soviet forces. Although the Russians had literally dismantled factories and removed industrial components worth $900 million to the Soviet Union, the value of Manchuria remained such that Chiang made it his primary strategic objective. It was his refusal to accept "nothing less than complete Nationalist government sovereignty in Manchuria" and his insistence on gaining it at any cost that propelled China once again into bloody war.

The Nationalists had far greater resources than the Communists. Chiang's military received enormous amounts of aid and extensive training from the United States throughout the war with Japan, and America continued to pump large sums of money into China after the war. Little wonder, indeed, that some observers referred to Chiang Kai-shek as "General Cash My Check." The Guomindang regime also inherited substantial war booty from the puppet government that the Japanese had set up during the war after seizing Nanjing. In addition, there was a vast pool of wealth in the hands of the Nationalist ruling clique, including the property of T.V. Soong who, thanks to his theft of American Lend-Lease funds and reputed heroin trafficking in the United States, was thought to be the world's richest man.

On paper, the Nationalists' armed forces seemed far more formidable than those of the Communists. In mid-1946, the government's armed forces consisted of roughly 3 million men. It also had China's only air force and a navy. The Communists could field only about 600,000 regular and 400,000 irregular troops, although a successful recruitment drive was expanding those numbers rapidly.

Yet the Nationalists faced daunting political, social, and economic problems that drastically compromised their efforts to unify China. Given the rampant graft, corruption, and political repression that marred their government, drastic reforms were essential to stabilize it. Instead, Chiang's regime systematically alienated nearly every section of its constituency. The slide toward disaster accelerated with the retreat of Japan. At this juncture, the Nationalist government was in a position to reestablish its authority over an area that contained more than three-quarters of the nation's population. Instead of renewing its political mandate by initiating programs that would win the support of the people, however, the government used the opportunity to plunder the territories it was reoccupying. This included running gambling, prostitution, and extortion rackets, often in collaboration with underworld mobs such as the Green Gang. When newly liberated areas were turned over to the Guomindang, its officials seized the larger and more profitable businesses and industrial enterprises, and ran them as private monopolies. This systematic looting, which an American observer called one of the biggest carpetbagging operations in history, took the name "bureaucratic capitalism," initiated ostensibly for the good of the state. No attempt was made to curb the rapacity of Guomindang officials as they descended like famished locusts on liberated cities and towns. A correspondent for a Chinese newspaper filed a story on what he had seen in the Manchurian city of Shenyang in 1946:

> . . . First there was a scramble for industrial equipment, and then for public buildings and real estate, and now government officials are competing for furniture . . . the local populace was surprised by the fact that the "central government men" are no better than the others.[6]

The Nationalists also mismanaged the treatment of those who collaborated with the Japanese. Despite the widespread popular demand that the Guomindang remove these people from positions of responsibility and punish them, the government was slow to do either, partly because of the necessity of maintaining public order but mostly because of its fear of the Communists. Instead of putting the collaborators on trial, the government employed Chinese troops that had served the Japanese, granting their leaders a "clean bill of health" to oust the Communists from north China. Instead of reestablishing its own authority in the recovered areas as soon as possible, the GMD delegated authority to discredited collaborationist leaders. Many of these notorious officials were welcomed back into the Guomindang fold, their acts of treason conveniently overlooked for the more pressing task of defeating the Communists.

The Nationalist government forfeited public confidence further when it failed to undertake meaningful economic reform. In the countryside, Nationalist officials returned land titles to the wealthy landlords who had fled the Japanese and permitted them to collect back rents as well as interest on taxes for the years of Japanese occupation. The government's fiscal policies also created havoc for those who lived in urban areas. Flagrant currency manipulation and the enormous costs of maintaining a garrison state that devoted 87 percent of its revenues to the military helped produce skyrocketing inflation. To meet these expenses, the government simply printed money. The Chinese dollar once had near-parity with the American dollar; during World War II, the official exchange rate between the Chinese and American dollars was roughly twenty to one; by late 1948, it took 12 million Chinese dollars to purchase one American dollar. The most seriously affected by this phantasmagoric currency collapse were those on fixed incomes: schoolteachers, professional soldiers, students, and civil servants—precisely those elements on whom the

Guomindang depended in its struggles with the rural-based Communists. Inflation also put great burdens on small- and medium-sized capitalists as organized labor, freed from 8 years of war controls, demanded wage adjustments to rising costs of living. Inflation brought on a tremendous boom in speculation and corruption. The purchasing power of Nationalist officials fell so far behind the devaluation of the currency that they had little choice but to increase their squeeze on the public. It is not surprising that many Chinese came to believe that life under the Communists could hardly be worse than this. The overall effect of the inflationary spiral was to undermine middle-class faith in the Nationalist regime, blurring the notion that a Communist victory would be a disaster because much of the middle class had already been ruined. An association of university professors observed, for instance, that they were now being paid less than coolies or the men who shoveled manure in the countryside.[7]

This rot within the Guomindang prompted a number of Chinese intellectuals to initiate a movement with a reformist and democratic political focus. The China Democratic League grew out of this concern. Formed in October 1944, the League aimed to call public attention to the need to expand civil liberties, avoid civil war, and bring together a National Assembly to establish a constitutional government for China. The China Democratic League was an umbrella organization encompassing those liberal voices that America's envoy, General George Marshall, hoped might exercise a "controlling influence" on the "irreconcilable" reactionaries within the Nationalist government. Instead, the liberals associated with the League were censored, harassed, and finally hunted down by the regime's secret police. After the Guomindang rigged the elections to the National Assembly in 1947, the Democratic League went over to the Communists and was outlawed. The GMD was equally brutal toward dissident students. Police and army units were sent to campuses where protests occurred. Students were arrested and sometimes shot, numerous faculty were dismissed, and, crowning the government's reign of terror, two leading professors were assassinated.

Repression proved to be a poor substitute for sound government. An American military adviser sent by President Truman in 1947 to advise the Generalissimo on an "informal and confidential basis" captured the essence of the Guomindang's problems in his final report to Washington in November 1948 when he wrote that the Nationalists' military debacles had less to do with lack of ammunition or equipment than

> to the world's worst leadership and many other morale destroying factors that can lead to a complete loss of will to fight. The complete ineptness of high military leaders and the widespread corruption and dishonesty

throughout the armed forces, could, in some measure, have been controlled and directed had . . . authority and facilities been available. Chinese leaders lack the moral courage to issue and enforce an unpopular decision.[8]

Conditions were starkly different in Communist territory, where joining the army was a badge of pride. In fact, large numbers of young people undertook long arduous treks to Communist headquarters in Yan'an, which for them had become a symbol of China's resistance to Japan as well as a model for a new society. Whereas the war with Japan exposed Chiang Kai-shek as an emperor without clothes, the conflict was a veritable fashion show for the Communists, allowing them the opportunity to mobilize the peasant masses through an artful combination of nationalism and sociopolitical revolution.

During the anti-Japanese war, in order to win the support of the small land-holders who constituted the majority of the peasantry, the Communists had abandoned radical schemes for land confiscation in favor of rent and interest reductions. After the defeat of Japan, more far-reaching policies were initiated. In October 1947, for example, the CCP passed legislation that abolished the landowning privileges of the wealthy and authorized village peasant organizations to redistribute the properties of wealthy landlords. Animals and equipment also were subjected to confiscation and redistribution, and the law canceled all debts. Such dynamic agrarian reform, carried out during the heat of civil war, generated much peasant enthusiasm for the Communist cause, which they soon came to identify with their own. The result was electrifying. One military commander could say with considerable truth that "land reform supports the war and the war is basically for land reform." In the autumn of 1948 Mao reported that some 1.6 million peasants who had received land had joined the Red Army.

The Civil War

In 1946 Chiang Kai-shek moved against the Communists. With a military superiority of five to one, and convinced that the United States would aid him in taking Manchuria, Chiang was confident that victory would come quickly. He claimed that the Communists would have been crushed with ease if Marshall had only "unleashed" the Nationalist armies. Throughout the summer and autumn of 1946, Nationalist troops won victories in Manchuria, giving credence to Chiang's claims that Marshall had been holding back the tiger. Chiang boasted that he would wipe out the Communists in eight to ten months, a claim that seemed credible when his soldiers occupied Yan'an in February 1947. Meanwhile, finding the GMD and CCP unprepared for compromise, Marshall was called home in January 1947—his mission was a failure and a deep personal disappointment.

Although the Nationalists had early successes in Manchuria, they were able to seize only major urban centers. The Communists retreated into the countryside, taking up positions along the lengthy communication lines that the Nationalists required to supply their troops. This was an extremely dangerous situation for the Nationalists. Chiang had been warned against committing so many troops to Manchuria: supply lines were perilously long, manpower was widely distributed in a few central locations, and Chiang needed to protect his northern flank against Communist moves to the south. Undaunted by such advice, Chiang continued to move his best troops and equipment farther into Manchuria. In the winter of 1948 the Communists struck, cutting Nationalist supply lines and denying the Nationalist-dominated cities all links to the south. By mid-1948, the Communist General Lin Biao, fortified with valuable American weapons either captured from the Nationalists or, in many cases, sold by Nationalist officers, had destroyed more than 250,000 of Chiang's best troops. When the Manchurian campaign ended, the Nationalists had lost almost half a million of their best soldiers.

After throwing the Nationalists out of the northern provinces, the People's Liberation Army, as the Red Army was called after 1946, moved into China's heartland. The final confrontation was the Battle of Huaihai, in which two entire Nationalist divisions defected to the Communists. When it became clear that the battle was lost, Chiang ordered the air force, which had hardly been used throughout the Japanese or civil wars, to bomb his own troops to prevent weapons from falling into Communist hands. When the smoke finally cleared in January 1949, after sixty-five days of fighting, the Nationalists had lost 500,000 soldiers, including 327,000 taken prisoner.

After the disaster at Huaihai, and ten days before the fall of Beijing, Chiang resigned as president of China. He officially left the presidency of China in the hands of one of his best generals, Vice-President Li Zongren, although Chiang in fact remained in charge. Chiang already was preparing for a retreat, if necessary, to the island of Taiwan. Meanwhile, Mao and the Communists crossed the Yangzi in April 1949. They took Chiang's capital of Nanjing before the end of the month and Shanghai by the end of May. Contrary to conventional assumptions, recent research indicates that during much of the civil war the successful CCP war effort was reinforced by significant aid from the Soviet Union. Soviet aid had been flowing since late 1947, when Stalin apparently became convinced that the Communists in China had a good chance of success and that the United States was unlikely to intervene directly in the fighting.[9] In any event, by October the PLA had driven all the way south to the sea and taken Guangzhou, completing a conquering march of nearly 2,000 miles in less than a year.

In the final analysis, it was social and economic issues, along with military force, that decided China's civil war. The Communists used a combination of social revolution and nationalism to win the support of China's rural masses. The Nationalists not only failed to attract this constituency but also forfeited the support of China's urban classes. This occurred because the Guomindang was not really procapitalist, at least as that term is understood in the West, but simply pro-Guomindang, a clique that controlled the government for its own selfish purposes. Still, despite economic mismanagement and hyperinflation, the majority of China's intellectuals, students, and entrepreneurial groups continued to prefer the Guomindang to Communist rule. But what they had in mind was a reformed Guomindang, one that was willing to venture a coalition with the Communists. The Nationalists' insistence on sacrificing all economic, social, and political reform to mount a military campaign that would eliminate the Communists as a political force was a price too high for China's nascent bourgeoisie to pay. As the civil war struggles dragged on and the peasantry rallied to the CCP, China's urban classes withheld support and cooperation from the GMD, thereby driving the last nails into its coffin.

During 1949, Chiang and the Nationalists took refuge from the unstoppable Communist storm on Taiwan, 110 miles off China's coast, carrying along as baggage the nation's $330 million in gold reserves and additional uncounted millions in art treasures. There they used brute force to maintain control of the island, which they had occupied after the Japanese surrender in 1945, and establish a government that they continued to claim was the legitimate government of all of China. Meanwhile, the Communists completed their conquest of the rest of China in late 1949 and 1950.

Mao returned to Beijing in March 1949, entering the city in an American jeep captured from the Nationalists. On October 1, 1949, in front of a huge crowd in Tiananmen Square, he proclaimed the establishment of the People's Republic of China. Starting from a rag-tag band of struggling revolutionaries and poverty-stricken peasants, overcoming the most fearsome obstacles with essentially no outside help, Mao and his followers had endured and triumphed. An even greater challenge now loomed before them.

7

Creating the New Order

1949–1957

The cover picture of the first issue of *China Reconstructs* in 1952 shows emancipated farmers in high spirits as they anticipate the bright future of new China.

> *The Chinese revolution is great, but the road after the*
> *revolution will be longer, the work greater and more arduous.*
> *This must be made clear now in the Party. The comrades must*
> *be taught to remain modest, prudent, and free from arrogance*
> *and rashness in their style of work. The comrades must be*
> *taught to preserve the style of plain living and hard*
> *struggle. . . . Not only can the Chinese people live without*
> *begging alms from the imperialists, they will live a*
> *better life than that in the imperialist countries.*

—Mao Zedong[1]

Much like their Bolshevik predecessors in Russia, the victorious Chinese Communists inherited a bruised and battered nation when they assumed the reins of political power in 1949. Twelve years of war had shattered the economy. Rampant inflation ravaged the urban classes, agricultural production was 25 percent lower than in the closing years of the Qing dynasty, and the fledgling industrial centers were in ruins, with factory production being 53 percent below prewar years. There was a shortage of managers, skilled workers, technicians, and capital. In many respects, the CCP was ill-equipped to deal with such daunting problems. It was a rural-oriented party with no experience managing urban areas or large-scale industrial programs. Yet rapid industrial development was imperative. Socialism could be built only on an industrial substructure that would establish the social and economic conditions for the powerful proletariat, whose mission it would be to push the historical dialectic toward communism.

Nevertheless, despite the herculean task of overcoming the nation's poverty and backwardness, the Chinese Communists were in a much stronger position to meet these challenges than their Russian counterparts had been in 1917. Unlike what happened to the Russian Communists, who had virtually no training in the arts of government and statecraft when they came to power in the November Revolution, and whose authority was soon challenged by civil war, the prolonged character of the revolutionary struggle in China had given the Communists time to develop their own unique administrative structures and organizational techniques. The party was large, was highly disciplined, and enjoyed a unity of leadership—a solidarity of elites—unprecedented in previous revolutions. By 1949 the traditional imperial order had been thoroughly discredited; the civil war had been fought and won. In contrast to Lenin and the Bolsheviks, the CCP had deep popular support in the rural areas, and even in the cities, where it had no significant political roots; the intelligentsia and professional classes, exhausted from the crime and anarchy of Guomindang rule, were favorably disposed to cooperate with the Communists. Nationalism, a force of little significance in the Bolshevik victory, also played an important role in helping the CCP legitimize its authority. Mao's legions had emerged from the anti-Japanese war as heroes of the national resistance to imperialist aggression. Last, as opposed to Lenin's precarious revolutionary government in 1917, Mao's state was neither threatened by foreign intervention nor would it be isolated diplomatically from the international community. Although there were serious "family" differences between the two Communist states, the Chinese could rely on their Soviet elders as allies in the international arena and could draw on Soviet experience to guide them through the perilous paths of industrial development.

The "New Democracy"

All these advantages were of little solace to Mao when in the autumn of 1949, as the Nationalist government collapsed and fled to Taiwan, the population under his control suddenly jumped from 200 million to over 600 million. Although the Communists had wide popular support, they did not possess the manpower, the time, or the experience to consolidate their rule and restructure the state. A particularly troubling specter were the towns and cities that were largely under the control of the professional classes and industrial and financial bourgeoisie, social elements about whom the Communist cadres knew little. Yet these were the progressive classes whose urban modes of thinking and technical skills were needed to guide the Communists as party cadres blazed the trail to modernization.

The task of consolidating power obliged the Communists to foster wide cooperation among all the disparate social elements in China because without such a policy the varied geographical regions, urban areas, and social groups could not be brought into the new political order. The ideological groundwork for consolidating power and creating the new state was provided by Mao Zedong. In July 1949, on the threshold of victory, he issued "On the People's Democratic Dictatorship." This document explained the form and programs of the new Communist state, which was to repose on the basis of what Mao termed the "New Democracy." Mao made it clear that the Chinese People's Republic would not be a "dictatorship of the proletariat," which prevailed in Moscow, but rather a "democratic dictatorship," a class alliance of workers, peasants, "petty" bourgeoisie, and "national" bourgeoisie led by the proletariat and the Communist Party. The latter two groups would have the task of constructing the new governing institutions. The dominating figure who loomed large behind all the state's ruling bodies was Mao, who monopolized power as chairman of the Central People's Government, chairman of the party, and chairman of the Revolutionary Military Council. The existence of this four-class united front provided the regime with the appearance of democracy, while the proletariat/party leadership would serve as a dictator over those reactionary elements outside the new order. These ideas, essentially a continuation of the pragmatic united front policies used so skillfully throughout the anti-Japanese war years, became part of the so-called "Common Program" adopted by the party in September 1949.

Instead of highlighting class war, the emphasis in the early years of consolidation was on understanding and persuasion because, as Mao insisted, China had much to learn from the superior economic, financial, and cultural experiences of the urban classes. This approach was necessary to complete a bourgeois democratic revolution, without which the transition to the higher socialist phase of the Marxian dialectic was impossible.

The New Democracy revealed a practical Mao. At this juncture we find no windows to Utopia, no fiery rhetoric about a revolution to shake the world. Instead, Mao articulated a candid appreciation of the arduous struggles ahead. "Our triumph," he wrote in 1949, "is only the first step in a long march of ten thousand *li*."

This initial period of relative political moderation, designed to encourage the cooperation of bourgeois social elements whose skills were needed to revive the economy and political order, lasted about one year. Under the formula of the four-class alliance, large businesses and industrial enterprises—those of the Guomindang elites, the so-called "bureaucratic capitalists" who were not invited into the class alliance—were taken over and managed by the state; but the smaller businesses belonging to those in the coalition, the so-called "national" and "petty" bourgeoisie, were allowed to remain in private hands. However, Mao never disguised the fact that this particular stage of the New Democracy was not intended to be permanent but rather an interlude of recovery, preparing the ground for the transition to socialism.

Another important feature of the period of consolidation was *Zhengfeng*, or thought reform. This particular dimension of Chinese communism sets it off from the Soviet system and also reveals how the Chinese revolution, under helmsman Mao, steered against the tide of orthodox Marxism.

Mao's emphasis on peasants as the vanguard of revolution was in itself a revolutionary departure from Marxism-Leninism. Of equal significance was his modification of Marxian dialectics as the fuel of revolution. From his early days as a revolutionary in Jiangxi, Mao disparaged the elevation of Marxist ideology to that of the sacred. Although Marxism was international, he believed it could never develop in a vacuum, but, as in the case of Russia, must be shaped by the cultural environment in which it contended. "Straw sandals have no pattern," Mao said, but "shape themselves in the making." Marxism-Leninism, Mao told party intellectuals in 1942, had no particular mystical quality or religious truth but had considerable "use value"—as a hammer to pound at one's enemies—and was essentially a guide to action. Notions about the mythical value of pristine Marxist ideology would have to make way for the Chinese style and spirit, which, Mao declared, were concerned with results. Mao's use of the standard communist lexicons was highly selective and superficial. A careful reading of his *Selected Works*, for example, reveals that half the quotations were drawn from classical Chinese sources and no more than 4 percent from Marx and Engels.[2] Indeed, one of Mao's pro-Russian colleagues claimed that his dialectics were flawed, so "subjective" and "voluntarist" that anyone with a sound grounding in Marxism would "laugh till his teeth fell out."[3]

A fundamental premise of Mao's thought was the startlingly non-Marxian idea that the key to revolutionizing society was to reshape the individual, not the class to which he belonged. This could be accomplished by restructuring a person's consciousness through thought reform. As was revealed in the Yan'an years, Mao differed from Marx and Lenin in his belief that human consciousness—individual will—had an objective reality of its own. Marx had asserted that ideas were derivative of objective class conditions, a mere reflection of society's material forces. Mao, on the other hand, had insisted that proper ideas, adequate will, and "right thinking," could advance the revolutionary dialectic:

> But everything must be done by man; the protracted war and final victory will not take place without human action. And action presupposes ideas, arguments, plans, directives, policies, strategies and tactics.[4]

Mao argued that only the peasants, who in China bore accumulated centuries of landlord exploitation and were armed with the requisite will to make revolution, could breathe life into socialism.

These beliefs were the product of Mao's revolutionary experiences in the Chinese countryside. Mao himself conceded that when he first became a revolutionary he did not possess a modicum of Marxism but that he came to discover Marx in the field, not the classroom. During the Yan'an interlude he came to realize that reforming one's ideas, restructuring thought, was a more effective way of altering behavior than conventional Marxist-Leninist means. Marx believed that fundamental intellectual change came about as a result of economic alterations. But Mao discovered that psychological conditioning through ideological discussion, a form of group therapy, could accomplish this irrespective of economic conditions. In other words, thought reform—*Zhengfeng*—could create revolutionary socialist consciousness prior to the establishment of a socialist economy. Proper revolutionary consciousness itself could create socialism. Thought reform also had an important side benefit: it gave those who profited from it a new sense of group identity and common purpose, a feeling of being part of a crusade to reshape the social order.

The special techniques of *Zhengfeng* had been developed during the Yan'an era to combat the intellectual autonomy of writers so as to harness them to party-controlled culture. It was a three-stage process designed to break the individual's sense of self following a group assault on his personal opinions, the incessant tensions of which broke the person's inner will. The only way to resolve such powerful value-stripping was for the victim to atone for his sins by submitting totally to the will of the party. On a broader societal level, the techniques of *Zhengfeng* were to be carried out by cadres who applied the process at the village levels through group discussions.

Another method of social control, closely related to *Zhengfeng* but more effective at quickly reaching the population at large, was the use of mass campaigns. This practice grew out of Mao's recognition of the need for rectifying the behavior of party members and maintaining loyalty among the public at large, the key to this technique being the so-called "mass line." Following the principle "from the masses to the masses," the party would solicit the views of the general public, analyze them in terms of what the leadership wanted, and then deliver back to the masses the correct "party line" in such a way that the people would believe the commands to be their own. The role of the cadre, who had a close link to both the public and the party leadership, was to mobilize the masses and manage these issues according to the purposes of the party. This assured that the leadership and the masses would have an open line of communication that served to keep the party close to the thoughts of the people and in a good position to implement the necessary techniques to arouse the public to achieve certain goals. This was to be the dynamic process by which Mao would give shape to his new society:

> We must go among the masses; arouse them to activity, concern ourselves with their weal and woe; and work earnestly and sincerely in their interests. . . . If we do so the broad masses will certainly give us support and regard the revolution as their very life and their most glorious banner. . . . The masses, millions upon millions . . . are a wall of bronze and iron which no force can break down.[5]

Under the rubric of the "New Democracy," thought reform was carried out through a series of mass movements organized by the party to politicize people and get them individually involved in various projects and campaigns. Women, for instance, were organized into groups to agitate for social equality. The family was singled out for attack, and attempts were made to break it down so that the old sentiments of filial piety could be redirected toward the state. Considerable progress was made in this regard with the passage of the Marriage Law of 1950. This law gave women full equality with men in rights of marriage, divorce, and property ownership. But the state's real objective was to replace the patrilineal, extended family with the nuclear model that gave the party greater opportunity to tighten its social controls with fewer kin and lineage ties.

Another feature of thought reform was to penalize those who did not go along with party-mandated policies. Those who made "mistakes" had to make public confessions, go through the obligatory therapy ("struggle sessions"), and accept the new ideology. This was not achieved without violence, though it was far less extreme than that which occurred in the Soviet Union under Stalin, and it pales in comparison to the later "killing fields" of Mao's imitator, the murderous Pol Pot in Cambodia. Instead of shooting class enemies, as was both Stalin and Pol Pot's style, the Chinese Communists first tried rectifying their thought. Sometimes this required the truncheon and forced labor, but, as one historian has noted, the CCP learned that it was more efficacious to have the damned serve socialism through compulsory labor than as fertilizer. Those who were at least ready to work should be spared, said Mao, "so that rubbish can be transformed into something useful."[6] By recycling human garbage—by extending the group therapy and forced labor to deviants—the state could create "new men."

Although the CCP was striking out on its own, crafting a uniquely Chinese socialist revolution, the Russian influence during these crucial years was significant. Soviet theorists, for instance, were widely studied in CCP circles, and the New Economic Policy, a program that had been carefully designed by Lenin to breathe life into the faltering Soviet transition to socialism in 1921 and carefully sculpted to fit acceptable Marxist thinking, served as an important guide for the gradualism that Mao wanted to prevail in the Chinese advancement toward his version of a democratic economy. Although the Chinese highlighted the "democratic" aspects of the consolidation of power, such notions were window dressing, a veneer to gloss over the hard edges of the rock on which the regime was being built, a structure identical with that of the Soviet Union: a Leninist-style party dictatorship that would never tolerate equality or independent sources of power and opinion. The point was reflected in the four-class alliance, which was never an alliance of equals but one spearheaded by the working class and led by the party vanguard.

Agrarian Reform

The caution with which the party went about its business of consolidating power in the cities was not replicated in the countryside. Because CCP cadres were experienced in the ways of rural life, the party was poised to take a bolder approach to solidify its programs in the countryside. The methods employed for this presaged the extremism in store for China within the next few years. For the time being, however, Mao held back, fearing that changes too rapid and drastic might frighten the national bourgeoisie, with whom the regime was trying to collaborate. Yet he realized that the task of mobilizing the peasantry for reform would be far more difficult than it had been in north China, where the party had its greatest success before coming to power. Conditions were now different because earlier Communist agrarian reform in the north was carried out in wartime, spurred on by an atmosphere of struggle and anger. Now with the fighting largely over, Mao warned that the "shock to society will be particularly great."

The Agrarian Reform Law introduced in June 1950 was aimed primarily at the peaceful redistribution of holdings, transforming ownership from rich landlords to so-called "middle" and poor peasants. Unfortunately, the regime underestimated the strength of recalcitrant landlords and the reluctance of poorer peasants to take an active role in pushing for the redistribution of property because the latter feared a vengeful counterreaction, something that always occurred in the past when the wealthy inevitably returned to power. Landlords also were able to mitigate the potentially revolutionary behavior of poor peasants by highlighting the complex ties of clan and kin that had long served to integrate rural communities. Traditional attitudes concerning local residence, family obligations, and even secret societies were deftly manipulated by the gentry to conceal their wealth and sustain the existing power structures. All this was beyond the understanding of the hastily created peasant associations, which the party had designated to spearhead land reform. In their rush to change the structures of rural China, the Communists had neglected to appoint a sufficient number of experienced cadres to these peasant associations. This partly accounted for the lack of success in the initial stages of land reform. Conflicts naturally occurred between enthusiastic cadres, many of whom were students and urban intellectuals, and the peasants whom they were to lead. In fact, more than 3,000 cadres were reported killed in the first year after liberation in their attempts to collect the grain tax.

The leadership soon concluded that harsher measures were in order. Although Mao at this point was still in his moderate mode, he had long appreciated that revolution was not a dinner party and that violence had the sanguinary effect of raising political awareness. "The masses would be unhappy," said

Mao, "if we did not kill some tyrants in a revolution of six hundred million people." With this new, more hard-headed approach, consciousness-raising cadres were quickly dispatched to the countryside to "purify" the peasant associations. After careful reprogramming, appropriately trained cadres, drawn mostly from the ranks of poor peasants and schooled in Marxist revolutionary thought, now encouraged the rural masses to "speak bitterness" in public trials where the gentry could be unmasked as feudal exploiters.

Up to this point, the party had been able to push its reforms without resorting to a reign of terror, owing partly to the fact that the compradore bourgeoisie and landlords who had not fled the country were politically weak, lacked self-confidence, and had not yet coalesced into a coherent social class. These people disliked the revolution, but without an alternative political group to which they might rally there was little likelihood that they would openly resist the government. Consequently, within the first few months of coming to power, the CCP did not feel threatened by counterrevolution. The situation changed, raising fears of a counterstrike against the revolution, with the outbreak of the Korean War in June 1950. Now the party decided to tighten its control over society, taking off the velvet gloves for the iron fist, both to protect the reforms made so far and to assure that the next more radical steps toward socialism could be manipulated more effectively.

The Korean War began in June 1950 when North Korean troops invaded South Korea. After United Nations troops (most of which were American, but also included contingents from several U.S. allies) under the command of U.S. General Douglas MacArthur began to push Kim Il-sung's forces back into the north in what seemed to be an effort to reunite the two Koreas under American auspices, Mao Zedong warned the United States through Beijing's ambassador in India that the Chinese would not tolerate American-led troops close to their borders. The notice went unheeded. In October, when MacArthur bombed bridges on the Yalu River, which separates China from North Korea, Mao sent 250,000 People's Liberation Army (PLA) troops storming over the border to aid Kim Il-sung.

The war with the United States created severe economic and political tensions within China. The initial effect was to encourage some landlords that the CCP had bitten off more than it could chew and that the Americans would smash the Communists in Korea and possibly overthrow the regime in China itself. In expectation of such an event, many began actively to resist Mao's agrarian reforms. The Communists, fearing counterrevolution, decided to turn up the pressure on the remaining gentry (many of whom, it was believed, were hiding either in the countryside or with compradore bourgeoisie in the cities) and on all those who had been involved with Americans at one time or another.

The threat of a United States invasion and the fear of the "enemy within" became a justification for increasing the coercive powers of the party, producing a sharp increase in terror against those suspected of being disloyal to the revolution. A law against "counterrevolutionaries," promulgated in July 1950, led to a succession of mass demonstrations in major cities. Thousands were accused of treason and sentenced to death after a public denunciation of their crimes. In Shanghai, for example, trials were held at a former race track where large audience participation was made possible by radio transmission. This terror, combined with the war in Korea, served to mesh loyalty to the party with patriotism, and many who had appeared lukewarm to the Communists quickly recognized the wisdom of offering whatever they could as financial gifts to the regime. By late 1950 directives from Beijing called for more radical land reform and an intensification of class struggle in the countryside in order to break the back of gentry resistance once and for all.

In rural areas the zealous sloganeering and hate campaigns targeted at so-called feudal overlords became part of the "settling accounts movement," which not only confiscated property from wealthy landlords but also bloodied them in the process. Under the direction of Mao's orders of "not correcting excesses prematurely," the behavior of zealous cadres generated an atmosphere of rural terrorism. Many who found themselves targeted as exploiters of the people were stoned to death, others were rounded up in batches and shot, while not a few chose suicide.

All this marked a sharp increase in violence, the likes of which China under the Communists had never yet experienced. It is difficult to determine the exact numbers of victims of the campaign against counterrevolutionaries. Government figures cite 800,000 counterrevolutionary trials and 135,000 official executions for the first six months of 1951 alone. Actual executions were certainly far greater than this, some unofficial estimates ranging as high as 10 or 15 million. One well-known and impartial historian with access to key government documents believes the actual toll was between 1 and 3 million victims.[7] The effect of the campaign went beyond the elimination of the gentry: it struck fear into the hearts of the urban bourgeoisie, smothering any potential resistance to the sweeping economic reforms that the party was preparing to implement.

The iron-fisted land reform, coinciding with the patriotic drive against counterrevolutionaries, yielded a significant harvest for the Communists. For them it had the economic virtue of destroying the wealth of the rich peasants and landlords, shattering the socio-political foundation on which a privileged gentry had for centuries commanded the heights of Chinese history. Proprietorship was now transferred to the less advantaged. Roughly

43 percent of China's cultivated land was redistributed to 60 percent of the rural population. By 1953, 90 percent of the agricultural holdings in China had changed hands. Many of the poorest peasants were encouraged to join agricultural cooperatives, containing what Mao called "seeds of socialism," whose sprouts would prepare the garden for the next stage of agricultural development.

More important were the political and social consequences of land reform. The successful assault on the gentry was a convincing demonstration to the rural masses that the party was the new source of political authority and that they could safely throw in their lot with the new regime. The destruction of the solidarity of the wealthy clans, the traditional source of power, finance, and local socio-political unity, emancipated the individual from family and village authority and created a new elite of small landowners. Yet this also had the effect of removing the traditional screens that shielded the rural populations from the coercive powers of the state, and this was precisely what the land reform was intended to accomplish. Finally, the reforms sowed the seeds of future discord, because the new landowning peasantry saw the changes in proprietorship as an end in itself, whereas the party encouraged it as a means, indeed as a beginning, to a higher end.

Mao's success in preventing MacArthur's advance to the Yalu River raised the prestige of the CCP throughout the Communist world. The Chinese reaped an enormous propaganda windfall from having stopped the world's most powerful military machine, bringing sweet revenge for 100 years of defeat and humiliation. The commander of the PLA troops in the Korean campaign, General Peng Dehuai, offered this message to the struggling underdeveloped nations of the world:

> It is a lesson whose international meaning is of supreme importance. It proves beyond all doubt that the time when a Western aggressor could occupy a country by placing a few guns along the shore—and that time lasted for several centuries—has gone for ever. . . . It proves that a nation, once aroused, which dares to rise and fight for its glory, its independence, and the safety of the fatherland, is invincible.[8]

During the Korean War even the Soviets began to realize that China's revolution might be the real thing. But if the Chinese gained respect in Moscow's eyes, the appreciation was not reciprocated. Mao knew that China paid the price of thwarting American expansion with the currency of blood and tears. The cost was high, undoubtedly setting back the party's economic reconstruction, and it touched Mao personally because he lost his son in an American air raid. China did the actual fighting and absorbed the battlefield casualties while Stalin chose the easier path of talking, undertaking the verbal defense of North Korea at the United Nations. Moreover, Mao was beginning to recognize a stingy pattern to Soviet friendship: the Chinese paid full market price for Soviet weapons and ammunition supplied to the PLA during the Korean War and even were obliged to underwrite the living and travel expenses of journalists sent from Moscow to cover the conflict.

After the great patriotic campaign that grew out of the Korean War and helped bring about a revolution in landownership in the countryside, the party was prepared to move into the next stages of consolidation with considerably less fear of counterreaction.

The "Antis-Movement"

The next two campaigns caused less bloodshed but were equally significant in what they accomplished. The "Three Antis-Movement" began at the end of 1951 when Mao called on his minions to "wave banners and beat drums" in a mighty struggle against corruption, waste, and bureaucracy. This campaign was aimed at politically unreliable officials, many of whom were not party members, but whose service had been badly needed to bring order in 1949, and older cadres who had allegedly separated themselves from the masses by falling prey to the charms of power and bourgeois influences. The latter evil was particularly vexing to Mao, who believed that urban life was morally suspect, posing a major threat to the purity of his revolution. The Three Antis-Movement was but the first of many official rectification efforts designed to revive the party's ethics and move it closer to the masses.

In the spring of 1952 the state launched the "Five Antis-Movement," a political drive against those who had corrupted the targets of the Three Antis-Movement with their bourgeois "sugarcoated bullets." The ostensible purpose of this drive was to eradicate the "five poisons" of bribery, tax evasion, fraud, and theft of government property and state secrets. This campaign focused on urban centers, especially Shanghai, where dope dealing, gambling, and prostitution had still been running rampant since the Guomindang days. It was during the Five Antis-Movement that the notorious Green Gang was finally put out of business; Shanghai itself soon became unrecognizable from its former days as fleshpot of the China coast. The real objective of this campaign, however, was to phase out the bourgeois industrial and commercial elements that had been invited to join the four-class alliance in 1949. These groups provided the skilled factory managers and technicians required to get China's economy moving again after years of debilitating war. Their expertise had been indispensable in the early stages of consolidation in order to prevent the breakdown of the urban sector. But they were seen as temporary crutches to be discarded once socialist networks could take over the organization of work. That time had now arrived. These obsolete social elements were not to be liquidated as a class, however, but rather "reprogrammed" to accept state ownership of their enterprises and to take on future roles as salaried managers. Instead of seizing bourgeois property outright, with the attendant inconvenient violence and disruptiveness, the state levied huge fines designed to crush their operations; it then quickly offered a reprieve by proposing to rescue the enterprises from bankruptcy through usurious loans, the calculated effect of which was to make the bourgeoisie permanently dependent on the government. By steadily harassing businessmen with confiscatory fines and taxes, Mao hoped to alert the doomed to what was in the wind so they would bow to the inevitable. The ploy succeeded, as one businessman after another rushed to request that his firm be nationalized so as to be relieved of massive taxes imposed by the state. Mao was pleased and later told his colleagues that nationalizing the private sector was like getting the cat to eat chili. How so? "Rub the chili into the cat's ass," said Mao, "and when it begins to burn, the cat will lick it off, and be glad of it."[9]

The drive was not without violence. By using the criteria of the "five poisons" the government could accuse practically any business or entrepreneur of tax evasion, cheating, bribery, and the like. Because few could have functioned in the midst of civil war and reconstruction without having flirted with at least one of the five sins, anyone who ever was involved in any kind of entrepreneurial activity recognized that he could be a target of party terror. In public radio announcements businessmen as a class and even specific individuals were singled out for condemnation and invited to police headquarters to confess their crimes. As in other campaigns, Mao established a set quota of "criminals" who were to be guilty from a broad category of suspects, and in this case 90 percent was the designated target.

In what was known as the "tiger hunt," thousands of businessmen were put through humiliating public trials. The flood of secret denunciations, accusations, and condemnations, compounded by the psychological threat of professional ruin, drove many to suicide. But the considerable sums collected through fines and confiscations proved to be a bonanza for the regime: the revenues generated from this legalized robbery were used to finance the next important stage of development, the state's industrialization drive.

The physical and psychological terror associated with the mass campaigns had the cumulative effect of destroying the spontaneity and spiritual independence of China's exhausted social classes as well as enhancing the party's control over private enterprises, thus refining the mechanisms of political control required for implementing the first Soviet-style five-year plan.

The First Five-Year Plan

The First Five-Year Plan was launched in 1953. As in the Soviet Union, the program stressed large-scale heavy industry at the expense of lighter consumer industry and agriculture. Although rapid industrialization was imperative, from the outset Mao Zedong was not comfortable with the way in which the regime was obliged to go about the task. There were at least three problems. First, the model required a heavy reliance on Soviet aid. China's brand of socialism never was fully welcomed in Moscow, Stalin having accused Mao of being a "radish communist": red on the surface, white on the inside. Stalin also detested Mao's independent behavior during the years of struggle with the Guomindang. In Mao's view, on the other hand, Stalin had provided considerable support to Chiang Kai-shek's efforts to unite China, and, in the end, slapped his so-called comrades in the face by removing state-of-the-art industrial equipment from Manchuria worth some $900 million as war booty after the Japanese surrender.

According to Zhou Enlai, a high-ranking party member and Mao's close confidant, Mao initially would have preferred to receive U.S. aid and technical assistance. But American intervention in the civil war and its hostile response to the Communist victory precluded this possibility. The outbreak of the Cold War convinced Mao that it was necessary to "lean to one side" in the international arena, and at the end of 1949 he traveled to Moscow for his first official meeting with Stalin. Mao was given a reception matching the cold Russian winter and negotiations were long and arduous, but by February 1950 a treaty of "Friendship, Alliance, and Mutual Assistance" was finally hammered out. This eventually led to Soviet extension of short-term credits to the People's Republic of China of some $300 million, ironically, a third of the value of the factory equipment the Soviets had stolen from Manchuria. The Soviets also sent technical advisers, accepted Chinese factory trainees and students for advanced study, supplied sophisticated industrial equipment, and contributed to the construction of some 350 large projects. However, none of these were outright grants-in-aid, but instead had to be paid for by the Chinese in agricultural exports.

In addition to industrial and educational aid, the Treaty of Friendship also was designed to help the Chinese modernize their military. New Soviet weaponry and large numbers of military advisers were sent to China. This material assistance, in conjunction with fighting the Americans in Korea, helped transform the PLA from a guerrilla army into a more professional fighting force equipped with modern weaponry provided by the Soviet Union.

Besides making the Chinese too dependent on the Russians, the second problem with the Soviet model from Mao's point of view was the nature of the system itself. The Soviets had developed a highly centralized, bureaucratic-driven program for modernization, one that required the fuel of technology and expertise. The drawback was that for the sake of rapid industrialization the Chinese were obliged to draw on a system that conflicted with Mao's "Yan'an style" of communism, an informal, highly personalized approach to development emphasizing one-to-one relationships, self-reliance, diversification of labor, and a strong sense of community. The Soviet approach, with its dependence on specialists and bureaucracies, had the potential to drive the party farther from the masses in whose interest it was supposed to serve. By rationalizing industrial development on a large scale, the PRC had to encourage the development of a professional managerial class as well as skilled technicians, an elite coterie of experts who could orchestrate this revolution from above.

Finally, the First Five-Year Plan would be a colossal undertaking. A major question for the Chinese leadership, as it was for the Soviets a generation earlier, concerned how such large capital investments could be made without squeezing consumers to the point where they might threaten the stability of the regime. The costs, as in the Soviet Union, would have to be borne by the agricultural sector of the economy. The kind of central planning necessary to make the plan operable also demanded the complete elimination of private enterprise, though this sector had been largely bludgeoned into submission by the Five Antis-Movement.

The capital designated for heavy industry in the First Five-Year Plan was a staggering 58 percent of total investment. Agriculture was given lower priority, receiving less than 8 percent of the total. The rate of industrial growth from 1953 to 1957 was spectacular. Production rose 128 percent, national income increased 9 percent per year, and per capita growth averaged about 2.5 percent per year throughout the 1950s. This compares favorably with other developing countries and is even more impressive considering that it was achieved with comparatively modest foreign financial assistance (from 1953 to 1957 the Soviet Union contributed a mere 3 percent of the total investment).

The Socialist Transformation

The First Five-Year Plan marked the official transition from the "bourgeois-democratic" stage of the revolution to the beginning of the socialist phase, a higher stage of development that required a solid industrial base. By 1956, as the pace of industrial growth accelerated, the party had completely nationalized the private sector with relatively little resistance.

Bringing socialism to the countryside, on the other hand, was a more complicated task. In many respects the Land Reform Law of 1950 had created a nation of small peasant proprietors. The Five-Year Plan set in motion the mechanisms for phasing out this populist arcadia because it was believed that the widely dispersed small units of cultivation would make it difficult to introduce more efficient work methods and modern agricultural technology. This was imperative because increased agricultural productivity was to provide the lion's share of capital investment for industry. Socializing the relations of rural production through the creation of large, mechanized collective farms also had the advantage of concentrating labor, rendering it more amenable to management techniques of the factory and thereby allowing the state to control peasant behavior more easily than would be the case at the family farm level. Finally, it was important to move out of the stage of private ownership quickly so as to prevent the emergence of a rich class of peasants who, like the kulaks (wealthy peasants) in Russia, might rekindle the capitalist temperament.

The shift from private proprietorship to state ownership of land and its corollary of transforming labor from the family to the production team were profoundly revolutionary, and there was the potential for severe culture shock in the countryside. There were few places in the world, for example, where the principle of private ownership of land was more deeply entrenched than in China. The state's claim to a monopoly of landownership, with all its legal distinctions between the private and public domains, had been dead for well over a millennia. The village and family farm long had been the cornerstone of Chinese economic and social life.

The relatively easy and rapid transition from private proprietorship to socialized agriculture in China was the result of special rural circumstances and wise party planning. The chaos and violence that accompanied the Soviet collectivization drive served as a grim reminder of what could occur without careful preparation. Despite the CCP's agrarian reforms, the persistence of rural poverty, exacerbated by a ballooning population and scarcity of land, had made it very difficult for individual farmers to survive economically. Probably 60 to 70 percent of China's rural population were "poor" peasants, defined by the party as those who were nearly destitute. This constituted a powerful special interest group for change. In addition, the collectivization process was facilitated by zealous cadres, most of whom had been recruited from the ranks of poorer peasants. These elements had emerged as a dominant political force in the countryside after the agrarian reforms of 1950. A final ameliorative factor in the transition to socialized agriculture was that the collective farms, underwritten and managed by the state, could offer a broader kind of mutual insurance that was difficult for marginal farmers to resist.

The party moved the peasants toward collectivization in stages, avoiding the impetuous, headlong leap that so disrupted rural life in the Soviet Union.

The first elementary stage of collectivization was initiated in 1953. By this point many peasants were convinced that China simply did not possess enough quality farmland to make agriculture based on private ownership profitable. In order to remedy the situation, the party announced the creation of "voluntary" Mutual Aid Teams. These consisted of four to ten families who would pool their limited resources in the interests of more efficient farming. Peasant families in this arrangement would share their tools and participate in the cooperative planting and harvesting of crops. This prepared the way for the next step toward collectivization, the so-called "lower" Agricultural Producers' Cooperatives (APCs). In this stage, sections of villages with increasingly large households (from twenty to forty) consolidated their land and tools. Higher levels of cooperation were called on here; farming implements were jointly owned or used, seeds and fertilizers were purchased cooperatively, and the designated farming unit administered the land and marketed the produce. Harvests were shared according to how much labor and capital each family invested.

A final and third stage, the "higher" APC, was to emerge out of the groundwork laid down by these "lower" cooperatives. The higher stage was designed to create full collectivization. In these arrangements families now gave up their land to the collective. Private property was abolished and peasants were paid according to how much work was contributed. Initially, entrance into the APCs was "voluntary" (in a short while force would be applied in generous doses), but once a peasant entered he was forbidden to leave. At first, incentives instead of terror tactics were employed to attract families into the APCs. The government guaranteed that the advanced cooperatives would have access to the best fertilizers, seeds, credit, and equipment; and the state made it illegal to purchase or sell anything in the countryside except through official APC organizations. Those few peasants who desired to stay in private farming encountered an offer from the party that was impossible to refuse if they preferred survival to starvation.

The changes fashioned by collectivization were intended to be far more than purely economic. As was the case in the various mass campaigns and with the new marriage law, a major objective was to weaken the one serious rival to the party, the Chinese family. With the dissolution of the ancient custom of private proprietorship, the party-controlled APCs replaced the family as the core economic and social unit of the village. This loosened family control over individual members and thus facilitated vertical social mobility; more deliberately, however, by integrating the cooperatives into a national economy, the party vastly increased its power to control social and political life.

The transformation from private farming to collectivization did not go as smoothly as Mao had wished. The debates it ignited, coinciding as they did with preparations for drafting a national constitution and a codified legal system for China, created serious tensions within the party. Hidden at the time to all outside the elite ranks, these debates marked the beginning of a split in the leadership that would manifest itself to the outside world in more turbulent fashion in the 1960s. At issue was a question of methodology. The years of mass movements (1949–53) had consolidated party rule, but now many leaders believed it was time to formalize the administration of the state through the rule of law. A constitution could institutionalize the new order, regulating social behavior by legal codes, not mass drives. Mao, however, was not disposed to accept formal governing methods because they would severely limit his ability to manipulate the revolution, to prevent it, in particular, from settling into enervating routines. In addition, Mao feared that legal codes would cramp his special style of leadership, which was bolder, less restrained, and, in his view, more creative than anything offered by his colleagues.

Mao's struggle against the party's efforts to establish a system of laws codified by a constitution revealed a significant departure from the Chinese political tradition, one that always recognized a set of values above the state (Confucianism), and highlighted the most fundamental characteristic of Mao's emerging regime: kinship with the central principle of totalitarian political practice, namely, the refusal to accept legal boundaries with clearly defined limitations to the use of power beyond which no act has legitimacy. Establishing this quintessential feature of totalitarianism was a key moment in the revolution because it would institutionalize illegality, making any notion of human rights meaningless, and thereby remove any possible shield behind which the people might protect themselves from the raw power of the state. The totalitarian implications of Mao's intentions may not have been obvious to those who expressed their methodological differences in party debates concerning how to bring socialism to the countryside. But Mao's ultimate victory in such matters further solidified the revolution's totalitarian tendencies.

It was assumed by all Chinese Communists that socialized agriculture would be far more productive than that based on capitalist methods. The logic seemed clear: vast numbers of small plots of marginally useful land could be farmed more efficiently when merged collectively on a larger scale; labor on collectives could be ordered more rationally, making it possible to create work battalions to maintain canals, undertake irrigation projects, and reclaim forests; and scarce capital equipment could be shared more effectively in larger collective farming enterprises.

Unfortunately, such clear logic escaped those who were obliged to perform the labor: many peasants resisted the transition from Mutual Aid Teams to APCs. Several factors contributed to the disruption of the process. The first was the reluctance of wealthier households to join the APCs because they recognized that they had little to gain in the more advanced stages of collectivization. Such resistance was exacerbated by the inability of party functionaries to assume leadership of the program, their incompetence compounded by the widespread illiteracy of many cadres. Inadequate leadership at the grass-roots level, combined with poor weather conditions, resulted in disappointingly low harvests in 1953 and 1954.

This lackluster agricultural performance posed serious difficulties for the party. Not only did China have to feed a rapidly expanding population, but the capital for underwriting the industrial component of the First Five-Year Plan had to come from agricultural sales to the Soviet Union.

The party now faced a dilemma: Should it cut back on the drive toward collectivization, thereby mitigating rural resistance, or was it better to overcome the roadblocks by rapidly accelerating the drive toward the socialist ideal? The more moderate party members, led by Liu Shaoqi and Gao Gang (the latter of whom Mao soon purged), believed that the disappointing harvests were encouraged by the very pace at which peasants were being forced onto the collectives. The big push toward APCs came too quickly, they asserted, producing inefficiencies, widespread dissatisfaction, and general mismanagement. Liu and his associates were more pragmatic, therefore more gradualist, in their approach to the farm problem and argued that the agricultural sector needed fuller mechanization and better supplies of chemical fertilizers before the collectivization drive was accelerated. They also appreciated that the Chinese peasants' attachment to private ownership still ran deep and that more trained cadres were required in the countryside in order to facilitate the transition to collectivization. These moderates lobbied hard for the dissolution of large numbers of APCs and supported the retention of private plots and a limited number of markets to provide incentives for increasing low productivity. For a brief time, Liu and the moderates prevailed, and the collectivization drive was moderated and private plots were reintroduced. Their victory was short-lived, however, as Mao outflanked his colleagues in a surprising move around the central party apparatus.

Mao had strongly condemned the timidity of the gradualists' views, noting with sarcasm that some of his comrades were "tottering like women with bound feet, constantly complaining that others are going too fast." The hardliners who supported Mao feared that rural capitalism would take root if socialism were not grafted onto the countryside quickly. Rather than "get off the horse," said Mao, the party leadership must drive its mount boldly "and not fear dragons ahead and tigers behind."[10]

Mao resolved the collectivist dilemma by climbing on his own horse, as it were, and, in a style that foreshadowed behavior for which he would later become notorious, bypassed his timid Politburo colleagues with bound feet.

Mao went directly to the provincial party leadership, urging them to bring a "high tide" of socialist transformation to the countryside. The response to Mao's end run was electrifying. With the traumatic rectification campaigns fresh in their minds and fearing they would fall victim to the label of "right-wing deviationist," thousands of provincial officials rallied to the call with unbridled enthusiasm. By the end of 1956 significant numbers of "higher" APCs had been put into place, and two-thirds of all peasant households in China could claim membership in an agricultural collective of some kind. Still, the vast majority were in "lower" collectives, and despite the enthusiasm of local cadres, reports of a "spring famine" in March and April of that year and signs of peasant unrest required the party to scale down the pace of collectivization. Regulations governing private production and marketing were eased; pigs, chickens, fruits, and vegetables were peddled on local markets, and corveé labor for the state was cut back. Yet, Mao was pleased at the numbers of those who joined collectives and spoke with zeal about a "leap forward" in agricultural output.

The success in carrying collectivization forward helped Mao maintain his hold on the party's leadership. He was able to thwart efforts to draft legal codes during the constitutional deliberations, and his "high tide" was given formal approval at the Supreme State Conference that met in January 1956. The mechanisms for collectivizing agriculture were officially put in place, and full collectivization was achieved by 1957, far sooner than even the more optimistic party leaders had imagined possible. This achievement vindicated Mao's position and served to dampen the split within the regime, seeming to assure continued party unity for the immediate future.

China and Khrushchev

Suddenly, however, a dark shadow emerged over Mao's inner-party maneuverings concerning collectivization and the whole socialist transformation. In February 1956 the new leader of the Soviet Union, Nikita Khrushchev, delivered a speech at the Twentieth Party Congress in Moscow that sent shock waves through the entire Communist world. He condemned Joseph Stalin for crimes against the party. Specifically, he singled out Stalin for the sin of placing himself above the party and beyond criticism by fostering a cult of personality. This provided the platform from which Stalin unleashed a reign of terror against the Soviet Communist Party, resulting in serious economic setbacks for the Soviet revolution.

The ideological thaw that followed Khrushchev's speech had profound repercussions. The most serious were in Hungary. Workers in that country rose up against their Communist-imposed regime, and the Soviets saw fit to respond in recently vilified Stalinist fashion by using tanks to crush the rebellion. Khrushchev's de-Stalinization campaign raised similarly embarrassing issues for the Chinese Communist Party. Mao himself was vulnerable to the charge of building his own "cult of personality," and his penchant for mass campaigns certainly had terrorized party and country. In addition, despite his own personal loathing for Stalin, Mao had frequently publicly heaped lavish praise on the Soviet dictator: Stalin, he announced on the leader's death in 1953, was "the greatest genius of the present age."

These awkward issues loomed ominously over the Chinese Communists' Eighth Party Congress. This important gathering met in two sessions, the first in September 1956, and the second in May 1958. Even at the first session the de-Stalinization drive had begun to work its way into the CCP. The collectivization struggles had taken their toll on Mao's energies, and many within higher party circles seemed to have grown weary of his radicalism. The delegates from the fifty-six foreign Communist parties present at the conference paid their respects to China's international achievements, but the applause was less vigorous for the party's domestic programs. It soon became obvious that a move to nudge Mao gently to the sidelines was under way, and that certain elements within the party were resisting his "leaps" and "waves" of economic management. There also was an attempt to rein in the cult tendencies associated with Mao's rule because the principle of collective leadership instead of one-man rule became the theme of the conference. If one man stood out from the rest, it was Liu Shaoqi, who seemed to be assuming the position of heir apparent to Mao's revolution. Mao did not address the congress, and there were no discussions of his ideas.

The congress gave the party an opportunity to present a general and positive picture of its accomplishments and to target areas requiring more attention. Although there was a sense that the Communists were on the threshold of completing the transition to socialism, the successes had produced some troublesome contradictions that needed immediate resolution. The issues that enveloped this conference proved to be a turning point in the revolution because they led to a split in the leadership and sketched out the battle lines for struggles that were to tear China asunder in the next decade.

Mao had been shocked by Khrushchev's revelations and, perhaps to avoid Stalin's errors, resolved to keep an open line between himself and the masses. Stalin's mistake was to have alienated his office and person from the people, directing the revolution from above, behind the masks of party bureaucrats. Mao recognized the importance of closing the widening gap between leaders and followers. By this time he also was aware of the party's problems with intellectuals, many of whom had come to see the hollowness of Marxism. For example, in 1956 it was claimed that in Beijing only four out of every ten educated Chinese supported the regime, one out of ten actively hated the party, and the rest could very easily disengage from it altogether.[11]

The Intellectuals' Critique

China's intellectuals had good reasons for not warmly embracing the CCP. In the beginning, the educated classes had welcomed the Communists, partly out of their loathing for the Guomindang and because, as patriots, they recognized that the party could bring monetary order and political unity to the nation. The honeymoon with communism was a short one, however. By 1951 the regime had mounted a tough thought reform campaign to wean China's intellectuals from the Western liberal traditions of the May Fourth experience—which had given shape and direction to their formative years—to Soviet-style Marxism-Leninism. The new party policy was orchestrated to impose intellectual conformity, encouraging writers and artists to employ their talents to serve the cause of socialist realism and Mao Zedong Thought. Those who pursued an independent line were silenced, finding no forum in which to publish their views, or, in many cases, they were terrorized by stalwart cadres into accepting party orthodoxy. The more tenacious who refused to swallow the party line were driven to suicide or sent packing to mental institutions. The party's campaign against independent thought stretched well beyond the intellectual community, pushing outward into the rural hamlets, embracing the humblest of peasants. Writers of national stature who asserted their autonomy became popular symbols of evil, targets of a struggle against bourgeois selfishness for the higher good of serving the needs of the people.

One of the most notorious of these smear campaigns centered on the writer Hu Feng, the best-known disciple of the party's literary hero, Lu Xun. Hu had founded the journal *Hope* in order to attack those who, like the corrupt literati of the previous Qing dynasty, were deceiving the new regime, in this case undermining the true principles of Mao and the party. Hu sought to liberate intellectuals from the deadening hand of the bureaucrats by recharging the critical spirit of early communism that had grown out of the May Fourth experience. Hu Feng was not trying to undermine the established order but only desired to reform the intellectual environment through the kind of critical thinking that he assumed informed the founding of the CCP in 1921. This independent mind-set, however, ran contrary to the system of controls that the party was attempting to set up.

The real purpose behind the campaign unleashed against Hu Feng in 1955 was not simply to punish freedom of thought but to create an environment of terror conducive to the completion of agrarian collectivization and the nationalization of industry. As an official party pronouncement put it: "Our

First Five-Year Plan cannot be brought into realization in a calm, placid way. It demands a class struggle, an acute, complicated struggle."[12] Hu Feng was kindling for the fires of class struggle. By the summer of 1955 the assault on "Hu Fengism," meaning independent thought and behavior, had reached such heights of madness that several writers associated with literary journals took their own lives. Hu's followers were purged from professional positions and "sent down" to the countryside for rectification, and their wives and children were denounced. Hu himself was imprisoned; after considerable resistance against the thought control of the party, he succumbed to a mental breakdown.

The Hundred Flowers Movement

The unrelenting campaign against Hu Fengism and all similar manifestations of independent thought severely strained the party's relations with intellectuals, many of whom had become completely alienated from communism. Mao had determined prior to the Eighth Party Congress, however, that the regime's feud with intellectuals officially had to be ended. The new push to higher stages of industrial and agrarian development would require the full support of China's educated and professional classes. As early as May 1956, in an effort to win back the loyalty of intellectuals, Mao proposed to allow free discussion and debate "in order to break down contradictions" between the government and the masses. Letting "a hundred flowers bloom and a hundred schools of thought contend," asserted the Chairman, would be the best means of resolving such misunderstandings. Mao claimed that Marxism-Leninism was a superior social system grounded in scientific truth and had nothing to fear from open criticism and debate.

In a major speech to the Supreme Soviet Conference in February 1957, Mao outlined how contradictions between the proletariat and the remaining vestiges of the bourgeoisie could be resolved by persuasion and discussion, without recourse to the kind of government violence that so marked the case in Hungary. Mao seemed to be laying down the framework for a new, more humane version of communism, one that could avoid the brutality of Stalinism and where everyone would work together for the good of the community. The old face of China had already been transformed by the civil war and the party's drive to revolution and socialist construction. Now China was finally united, and this suggested that the next stage of rectification could be carried out in a more enlightened spirit.

The next higher stage of rectification would come more easily, Mao insisted, because the socialist system had been firmly established. There were, however, certain contradictions remaining between the relations of production and the productive forces of China. These, said Mao, were due to bourgeois holdovers from the old order and weak linkages in state institutions. Yet the following transition to a higher stage of socialism would not require turbulent class struggle because "the people" were well on the way toward consolidating their rule. The next battle would not be class-driven but mandated by a unified Chinese people and designed to overcome scarcities in nature. In short, this would be an economic struggle to increase productivity.

One month later, in an address to the CCP's national propaganda conference, which included an audience of both party and nonparty cadres, Mao admitted Communist errors and encouraged the party to accept greater freedom of expression in order to correct past mistakes. Such openness was not to be seen as dangerous but actually desirable:

> Will it undermine our Party's prestige if we criticize our own subjectivism, bureaucracy and sectarianism? I think not. On the contrary, it will serve to enhance our Party's prestige. The rectification movement during the anti-Japanese war proved this.[13]

The central purpose of this speech was to underscore the importance of winning nonparty support for China's economic development and the corresponding necessity for the party to improve its relations with the people.

Although China's leaders recognized the need for party rectification, there was disagreement about both the timing and form the campaign should take. Peng Zhen, the tough party veteran now in a key position as mayor of Beijing, and several others on the Politburo, for example, wanted to delay rectification, convinced that the political environment was still too charged by Khrushchev's anti-Stalinization speech and the ensuing Hungarian uprising. A liberal policy at this juncture would be politically destabilizing. Mao, however, was determined to start the campaign quickly and, over the opposition of many of his colleagues, open the process to all people, not simply party members.

Many CCP leaders, on the other hand, had a different view of the rectification process. They saw it as a device created primarily for intra-party contradictions and, only after success in that realm, should it be gradually and very carefully extended to the larger public. Mao, however, seems to have rejected the notion that rectification needed to be a two-stage process. For him, rectification of the party and people was to be accomplished in one fell swoop.

Mao's decision to open the floodgates of criticism had the support of two key allies, Zhou Enlai and Deng Xiaoping. Many others in the elite, however, had strong reservations about inviting outsiders to participate in what previously had been exclusively a party affair. Among these were Liu Shaoqi, the persuasive Lu Dingyi, who had been one of Mao's chief *mishu* (secretaries who were personally close to the top leaders but not part of the open bureaucratic system—and thereby capable of exercising considerable power behind the scenes) and had been promoted to head of the propaganda bureau, and Mayor Peng. Peng Zhen, whose position gave him control of the main official newspapers and journals published in the capital, had been given charge of the party's first rectification campaign in Yan'an. But he had a deep distrust of intellectuals and feared giving them the power of criticism.

Mao clearly felt isolated in Beijing. He realized that the cards were stacked against him, admitting that as many as 90 percent of the higher echelons were opposed to his ideas. It is noteworthy that the party's chief propaganda organ, the *People's Daily*, was also slow to back Mao at this juncture and delayed for some time a discussion of his ideas on rectification. Mao was deeply annoyed: "We used to say that the papers were run by pedants, now we should say they are being run by the dead."[14]

Mao had to move away from an inhospitable Beijing to Shanghai, where he found a more sympathetic group of officials willing to publish his ideas. By April 1957 the *People's Daily* finally came around, publishing some five editorials that explained the themes of Mao's views on rectification. Other recalcitrant officials soon fell into line, but only after Mao pulled out all the stops, assuring them that there would be no disruptive class struggle. "I am not encouraging the people to make disturbances; I am not holding riot-promoting conferences," he told supporters in Hangzhou, hoping to neutralize the growing complaints of party hardliners.[15] In May 1957 what came to be known as the "Hundred Flowers Movement" was launched. Mao, however, was not pleased with those who resisted his plans. Later events reveal that Mao would never forget what he considered a betrayal; nor would he forgive.

There appear to have been at least three purposes behind the Hundred Flowers Movement. One objective was to grant intellectuals more freedom to gain their cooperation in building the next stage of socialism. The second was to foster a more critical analysis of the officials within the CCP in order to improve the efficiency of the government and party bureaucracy, in short, to follow the advice of the previously vilified Hu Feng. What was needed was a low-keyed criticism like "a gentle wind and fine rain," as Mao put it. Mao feared that officials were drifting away from the masses (and his own personal control), developing elitist habits and superior airs. Criticisms led by the intellectuals and echoed by the public could be used as a means of rectifying such behavior. Third, Mao hoped that by lifting the party's heavy lid on free discussion he might ease the kinds of tensions that could produce an anti-Communist rebellion like that which engulfed Hungary.

Many intellectuals, however, impressed by the fate of Hu Feng, were chary of engaging in a little "blooming and contending" because for the past 6 years such behavior had brought nothing but repression and punishment. The party cadres were also only paying lip service to the campaign's flower slogans, making it seem that the spring season was experiencing an early drought. The thunderclap might be loud, it was said, but the raindrops were small.

This initial apprehension, however, soon dissipated as loyal cadres, whipped into high spiritedness by Mao, cajoled the justifiably pusillanimous intellectuals to venture forth into the sunlight of open debate. The cool early spring weather soon gave way to the heat of summer, but the anticipated mild winds of criticism blew into a violent thunderstorm that washed over the land.

The gusts of criticism went beyond Mao's wildest imagination. Scientists objected to benighted cadres determining the direction of their research. Economists questioned the relevancy of Marxist-Leninist economic theories for China. Philosophers pointed out that the CCP had ignored the humanitarian ideals of Marx. The outpouring of criticism spread to the universities, sparking student demonstrations and wall poster campaigns. Several magazines even recommended the overthrow of the party, one well-known scholar publicly calling for the killing of thousands of Communists "for the good of the people." Student criticisms were particularly disturbing because their call for independence from meddlesome cadres and demands for legal protection of basic civil liberties revealed that the party, despite years of indoctrination, had failed to expunge the liberal legacies of the May Fourth era.

The experience horrified Mao and did little to improve his standing with the party leadership. The embarrassing consequences of his campaign validated the misgivings of Liu Shaoqi and Peng Zhen. Instead of simply exposing the failings of a system that could be mended quickly, doubts were raised about the very nature of communism itself. It seems that the intelligentsia's repressed hostility to party dictatorship with its legions of obstreperous cadres was too great to be confined to the gentle rain of mild criticism. Instead of fragrant flowers, the spring sunshine of criticism had brought forth "poisonous weeds."

Repression and Reeducation

The party's reaction, under the direction of General Secretary Deng Xiaoping, came swiftly in what was called the antirightist campaign. The assault began in June 1957 in an editorial in the *People's Daily* accusing "rightist elements" of waging a war against party rule in order to foist a "bourgeois dictatorship" on China. The general public was invited to participate in a patriotic crusade to ferret out rightists who were bent on destroying the nation. It did not take much prodding to incite the masses to action. Traditionally, the average Chinese had never shown an appreciation for political dissent, and there always had been widespread resentment of intellectuals, who seemed aloof and arrogant. People who were the most vociferous in fingering culprits were rewarded with promotions and new jobs, in many instances taking over from those whom they denounced. The antirightist hysteria had the effect of turning over a good portion of the middle-ranking elite, thereby opening doors to upward mobility for those who were considered politically reliable.

The official repression was ruthless. Three leaders of a protest in Wuhan were executed. Although the most openly critical were purged, the attacks spread far beyond hard-core dissidents. What made the campaign so terrifying was the policy of setting arbitrary quotas for how many were to be given the "rightist cap." Some 550,000 people were so tagged, a mark of infamy that in most cases had the effect of ruining a person's life. Zhou Enlai later admitted that as many as 98 percent of these accusations may have been applied incorrectly. For the most part the rectification of rightists involved ideological struggle and the loss of jobs, not lives, because, as Mao opined, it was important to "treat the illness to save the patient" so the regime could at least get labor power for its continuing economic drives. The actual violence that did occur during the antirightist campaign was not at the hands of party officials who loomed in the background, but was carried out by young activists who simply followed party orders. When activist behavior became excessive, resulting in deaths, the officials could disclaim responsibility for what they called "accidents" resulting from understandable "mass enthusiasm."[16]

The administrative policies of the antirightist campaign that anathematized whole categories of people labeled "bad" (i.e., counterrevolutionary) prepared the ground for a massive outpouring of violence that would later mature in the Great Proletarian Cultural Revolution of 1966. As the work of Lynn T. White has shown, after the antirightist rectification drive, individual Chinese saw the efficacy of acquiring politically correct labels ("proletarians" and "cadres" vs. "revisionists" and "intellectuals") to secure personal gains and protection. This led to a wide-scale emergence of "status groups," the membership of which provided access to jobs, school placement, housing, and so forth. Within a short while, conflicts developed between these various groups with their bosses and monitors over spoils of patronage. The squabbles and resentments of clients betrayed by their status group leaders who could not deliver on promises, combined with legitimating violence through mass campaigns ("killing chickens to scare monkeys," as Mao put it) designed to frighten people to support party goals, were crucial factors contributing to the political frustrations and unprecedented furies that defined the Cultural Revolution.[17]

Yet another practice that the struggle against rightists helped institutionalize and also became a key feature in the later Cultural Revolution was *xiafang*, meaning to send one "down to the countryside." *Xiafang* was designed to bring the urban classes closer to the peasants, who supposedly represented the true spirit of revolution. It consisted of a process of "reeducation" through manual labor, where allegedly haughty urbanites with superior airs were forced to rub shoulders with the peasant masses by wallowing in pig dung. Such rural experiences were brutal to the extreme for those unaccustomed to the rigors of peasant life, the test of acculturation usually consisting of sharing greasy blankets, black from use with one's peasant hosts, or drinking from cups that had touched the filthy lips of the communal household.

The grinding poverty of the Chinese countryside could easily shock an urban intellectual. One unfortunate deportee, "sent down" in later years, wrote that the peasant couple with whom his family took residence was so poor that they had one pair of pants between them. These were shared and worn only when one of them went to market in the commune center. The food in these quarters was such that the couple consumed at their table the fodder the government provided as pig feed and gave their animals the sweet potato leaves that they would have liked to eat themselves. Still, the government complained that the man's pigs were underweight. Thus "every time Old Guo took a pig to market, he fed it watered-down slop to bloat its belly and plugged his anus with a cloth to keep it from losing precious poundage. Even so, officials usually sent it back again."[18]

All this was hard to endure for those accustomed to the rhythms of urban existence. Out of sheer desperation and horror many tried to flee the countryside; others committed suicide. Instead of reeducating the urban classes, *xiafang* soon became institutionalized as a mechanism for rectification, resulting in the alienation of a sizable number of the younger generation and promising serious trouble for the party in years to come.

The failure of the Hundred Flowers Movement was embarrassing to Mao and weakened his already precarious position on the Politburo. Mao attempted to justify his apparent carelessness by arguing that his real objective had been to smoke out the true enemies of the revolution:

> The purpose was to let demons and devils, ghosts and monsters "air views freely" and let poisonous weeds sprout and grow in profusion so that people, now shocked to find these ugly things still existing in the world, would take action to wipe them out.[19]

Unfortunately, these ugly weeds proliferating from the storm of intellectual protest simply added to Mao's burdens as he frantically maneuvered to keep control of the revolution.

The Second Five-Year Plan

Another nettlesome problem that dominated the Eighth Party Congress concerned the implementation of a Second Five-Year Plan. This issue was taken up by the second session of the congress in May 1958. The tone of this meeting was more menacing than that of the first session in 1956, owing largely to Mao's resolve to impose his line following the purges of the antirightist campaign.

A central question was whether the Second Five-Year Plan, scheduled for 1958, should follow the model of the first. Although the First Five-Year Plan yielded substantial increases in industrial production, overall economic growth was highly skewed. Heavy industrial goods had expanded five times more rapidly than agriculture. In fact, the collectivization drives had resulted in a decrease in production of foodstuffs. Productivity in the farm sector barely kept pace with the requirements of an expanding population. Grain output increased only between 1 and 2 percent during 1953–54. Other industrial crops such as cotton, soybeans, and oil seeds increased at even smaller levels. By 1956 it had become clear that such inadequate production was seriously limiting the expansion of manufactured consumer goods that were dependent on raw materials from agriculture.

A related problem with the Soviet-style First Five-Year Plan was that it demanded the exploitation of agriculture for large investments in the heavy industrial sector. Agriculture had been the fuel for Moscow's modernization drive. The farm sector provided food staples at low prices for the country's urban work force, and its surpluses were sold abroad to earn capital for the construction of industrial plants. This approach was not easily replicated in China. Where the Soviets could expect surpluses from the farms, Chinese agriculture never was able to increase production for sales abroad. The country was very poor: at this time per capita agricultural output was roughly half that of the Soviet Union in 1928, and the population was far larger. The Soviets too were prepared to use brute force to command tribute from the peasants and, in so doing, exterminated millions. The CCP was less willing to extract such a toll from the rural populations. The fact that its membership was at least 70 percent rural in composition militated against pillaging the countryside as the Soviets had done.[20]

Finally, the central planning that was so much a part of the Soviet model for development generated a technical and managerial elite, the concept of which flew in the face of Mao's Yan'an-style communism. It was precisely the elitism and bureaucratism of the First Five-Year Plan that was so savagely criticized in the Hundred Flowers Movement.

Leaders at the 1958 party congress debated strategies to increase agricultural productivity to provide high capital investments for continued rapid industrial growth. These economic discussions were remarkably similar to those that took place in Moscow during the late 1920s when the Soviets were faced with the same problems. The Chinese Communist Party's leading economist, Chen Yun, proposed a policy that paralleled the strategy developed by Nikolai Bukharin, a leader of the so-called Bolshevik Right Opposition, who had a falling out with Stalin. Chen appreciated the virtues of more balanced economic growth and the need to maintain social stability in the countryside. Consequently, he recommended that peasants be provided with material incentives to increase productivity, primarily through higher prices for foodstuffs. This policy would require the state to invest more capital in light industry so it could satisfy higher rural consumer demands fueled by the improved pricing policy. Increased sales of consumer goods would stimulate the expansion of light industry, enhance profits, and build up a pool of capital which could be tapped for heavy industrial investment.

From Mao's perspective, however, there were several drawbacks to Chen Yun's strategy. First, although Chen's balanced approach had the advantage of maintaining rural stability, it would not work developmental miracles. China's economy might grow steadily, but not in any great sudden leaps. Because the plan relied on material incentives, it had the potential for creating a rural bourgeoisie, a social configuration that would work against the ultimate goal of collectivizing agriculture. Second, Chen's strategy, much like the First Five-Year Plan, required the continued strong leadership of the government ministries, with their various managers, statisticians, and assorted technocrats, many of whom were not party members. In short, it would increase the role of the urban intelligentsia, the specialists who were already pulling the regime farther away from the peasant masses.

Finally, it appears that by 1957 Mao Zedong had decided to terminate any policies that continued along lines set down by the Soviet-style First Five-Year Plan. Mao's relationship with Moscow had deteriorated steadily since the anti-Stalin campaign. Khrushchev had refused to give Mao the recognition and power-sharing that Mao believed he deserved as a senior Communist statesman, yet he continued to pressure the Chinese into supporting Soviet positions in international relations. Beijing's continued reliance on the Soviet development model, requiring large infusions of technical and financial assistance, could be used by Khrushchev as economic leverage to coerce China into following Moscow's line. If Mao were to survive Khrushchev's assault on personality cults and Moscow's emphasis on collective leadership, he would have to liberate China from economic dependence on the Soviet Union.

As a consequence of all these considerations, Chen Yun's development strategy was deemed unacceptable. It was politically and sociologically dangerous, yet it also was overly cautious, in Mao's opinion. Mao believed that his collectivization drive had disappointing results because of the constraints of officials who were supposed to be taking the lead. Instead of rejecting such projects, he was convinced that organizational changes and massive resource mobilization could provide the dramatic breakthroughs necessary for rapid growth, which, in turn, would free China from the apron strings of Moscow and also from other "objective" constraints.

There was much sentimental appeal to Mao's mass mobilization strategy as a means of breaking the agricultural bottleneck, as opposed to Chen's emphasis on "material incentives," because it harked back to the halcyon days of the Yan'an years, when the party, not yet tarnished by the self-serving hands of bureaucrats, had overcome adversity through self-reliance and close working relationships with the masses. Moreover, the anti-intellectualism that swept the country in the wake of the antirightist campaign had discredited the urban intelligentsia and generally undermined those who took issue with social radicalism. This, in conjunction with the purge of government officials who had fallen prey to "careerism," had reduced the pool of critical alternatives to mass mobilization tactics, creating a temporary power vacuum open to the enthusiasm of pro-Maoist party cadres. All these factors made it possible for Mao to win support for his solution to China's retarded economic development.

Mao and the Socialist Transformation

Despite Mao's frustrations about not yet achieving economic miracles, an overview of the period from 1949 to 1957 reveals that the CCP had notable success when it followed the kind of nonideological, pragmatic policies similar to those set down during the anti-Japanese war. In 1949 the Communists had inherited a country that was physically and spiritually devastated by more than three decades of almost unrelenting military conflict. The party's Common Program, drawn up in the year of victory, successfully brought together China's fractured social classes in an alliance designed to mend a shattered economy and political structure to consolidate the nation's energies for constructing socialism. This early stage of the building process was marked by gradualism and party consensus, even though the regime was willing to issue carefully calculated doses of violence when it encountered resistance.

While agricultural reform was not brought about without a certain degree of bloodshed (estimates of deaths varied from one to three million), the party managed to avoid the enormous human devastation that was so much a part of Stalin's drive to do the same. By 1953 the regime had eliminated the power bases of the gentry, effectively reversing landownership patterns of millennia through programs that redistributed property to the peasant masses. This was accompanied by a social revolution that subordinated family to state and redefined gender roles. These carefully prepared reform drives set the stage for the next level of agrarian change, bringing socialism to the countryside. By the end of 1957 the party could claim to have completed the collectivization of agriculture, and there is good reason to believe that there was considerable support for these changes among the rural masses.

China's efforts at industrialization were even more remarkable. The first industrialization drive was spectacularly successful, achieving levels of productivity, without sizable foreign assistance, that quickly became a model for the underdeveloped nations of the world. And in the midst of undertaking such breathtaking projects, the Chinese Communists made the world take notice of China's arrival as a world power. The People's Liberation Army restored China's cultural pride and earned the country international respect as a great military power by successfully standing up to the Americans in Korea.

Yet, throughout these years of consolidation there lurked beneath the surface of China's great reform drives an impulse to extremism and violence that was not always kept in check by the consensus within the party to pursue a gradual, carefully planned journey to socialism. By 1957 the charismatic leader of China's revolution was showing signs of impatience after these early accomplishments and becoming obsessed about the usual problems that confront all revolutionaries as their revolutions settle into the more rational, bureaucratic channels that are part of the task of creating a new social order. The Hundred Flowers Movement was a turning point in Mao's career. It was his first major mistake since coming to power. And the campaign was a costly one because it exposed the party to public criticism and ridicule, opened serious rifts in the Communist leadership, and called into question Mao's own leadership ability. As the historian Roderick MacFarquhar has pointed out, there is an easy explanation for Mao's miscalculation: Up to this point in the revolution there had been no open discussion of views, and Mao had no way of knowing how the people really felt.[21]

Mao learned something from the experience, though not the virtues of open discussion. The poisonous weeds of dissident voices showed him that the intelligentsia, for whom Mao had long harbored deep contempt, were antisocialist and therefore could not be relied on to help the party accelerate the drive toward socialist industrialization. At this juncture Mao concluded that it would be necessary to "go down to the masses" in the struggle against bourgeois backsliding. He was now convinced that the energies unleashed by rekindling class warfare could provide the impetus to carry the revolution to a higher level.

The mass campaign was to become the defining feature of Mao's politics.

Indeed, the country experienced a major campaign almost every year up to Mao's death in 1976. The physical and psychological tolls were such that many Chinese subsequently came to date their life's experiences more in terms of political mobilizations ("just after the Three-Antis, Five-Antis," "just before the Four Cleanups," etc.) than by days and months of the calendar.[22]

Mao's decision to rekindle the dynamics of struggle brought both disorder and disaster. His "leaps" and "waves" managerial techniques served to open up divisions within the old Yan'an leadership, and after 1957 the Communist revolution would become increasingly extreme and unbalanced as Mao impetuously moved outside the formal party structure to bring his version of revolution directly to the masses. The reverberations of Mao's relentless efforts at what could be called permanent revolution through his revered "mass line" were to wreak worse destruction in the 1960s.

By 1957, however, it seemed to Mao that the disposition of the heavens was such that he could call on his cosmic powers to make the final push for creating his new society. The taste of success would not linger on Mao's palate for long. With unchallenged command of the machinery of the state, he now prepared to begin the final phase of construction of his socialist utopia.

8

The Great Leap and the Bad Fall

Chinese farmers toiling in the fields amidst CCP propaganda.

The springboard for what would be called the Great Leap Forward was the second session of the Eighth Party Congress, which met in May 1958. In effect it marked a victory for Mao after a struggle that he had been waging since at least late 1957 to get the party to change its economic policies. Nor did that struggle end once the Great Leap was announced, as was made clear by the continuing purge of recalcitrant mid- and lower-level party officials during the start-up period of the new campaign. At any rate, Liu Shaoqi, Mao's designated successor, recognizing the wisdom of falling in line with the Great Helmsman's wishes, formally announced the Great Leap during that May meeting. It was the most far-reaching and radical program to be unleashed in China since 1949. The goal was nothing less than to mobilize China's entire 600-million-plus population in military-like fashion to overcome the limitations of economic scarcity by "leaping" over the mountain of physical constraints, and striding forward from there along the high road to a Communist utopia.

The Great Leap Forward

Nothing better illustrates Mao's fundamental rupture from Marxism-Leninism than the Great Leap Forward. Its basic premise was that the key to revolution was political rather than economic, as one of the Great Leap slogans—"Put politics in command"—made clear. That premise rested on Mao's passionately held belief that human will was capable of overcoming even the most adverse material conditions. Inadequate agricultural production, Mao asserted, could only be partly blamed on inefficient tools, shortages of fertilizers, poor weather, and exhausted soil. The more fundamental obstacle to advancement was the tendency for some peasants to lapse into sloth or capitalist modes of thought. Equally at fault was the lack of vision of party cadres, who were more concerned with personal advancement than with advancing the revolution. Economic backwardness, Mao claimed, could be overcome by focusing the political effort, heightening class consciousness, and undertaking unyielding class struggle against bourgeois influences.

Mao's refusal to be bound by objective conditions went beyond the specific problems of how agriculture was managed to the very nature of China's overall predicament. Instead of accepting the notion that China was handicapped by poverty and underdevelopment, Mao announced his discovery of certain hitherto unappreciated "advantages to backwardness." He postulated that the wretched of the earth had accumulated generations of suffering that with proper guidance could be put to good use in the release of tremendous pent-up energy that had incalculable advantages for revolution:

> Apart from their other characteristics, China's 600 million people have two remarkable peculiarities; they are, first of all, poor, and secondly blank. That may seem like a bad thing, but it is really a good thing. Poor people want change, want to do things, want revolution. A clean sheet of paper has no blotches, and so the newest and most beautiful words can be written on it, the newest and most beautiful pictures can be painted on it.[1]

All China was to be his canvas. Mao, the self-designated Picasso of revolution, was primed to produce his masterpiece. He urged his minions to do everything "faster, better, more economically" and promised that in one sudden burst of revolutionary energy, they could turn their poor backward country into a prosperous industrialized society. That energy, Mao maintained, now delving into the realm of physics to back up his social and economic theories, was readily available in China:

> . . . our nation is like an atom. . . . When this atom's nucleus is smashed the thermal energy released will have really tremendous power. We will be able to do things we could not do before.[2]

Mao admitted that even with the release of this previously untapped energy there would be difficulties and sacrifices, but the short-term sacrifice involved would be worth it; there would be "hard work for three years, happiness for a thousand."

The aura surrounding the start of the Great Leap Forward bathed it in a messianic glow. To make Mao's promises more believable, Great Leap propaganda was accompanied by an unprecedented campaign of adulation for its chief inspirer, who was likened to "the sun giving light wherever it shines." And if Mao's simply being like a heavenly body were not enough for some, they could take comfort that in "the era of Mao Zedong, heaven is here on earth."[3] Once China's emperors had claimed the Mandate of Heaven; now the party's Chairman apparently was able to manipulate heaven itself.

The Great Leap was to be all the more spectacular because it would go in several directions at once. One aspect of this involved changing the direction of economic development. Under the First Five-Year Plan of 1953 to 1957, the Chinese followed the Soviet model of stressing industry at the expense of agriculture. Central planning had been the crucial conduit for funneling resources from agriculture to industry. This always bothered Mao and many of his supporters, as did the excessive reliance on Soviet technology. They now backed the slogan of "walking on two legs," which, together with the idea that the nation should make use of both modern technology and traditional methods for promoting economic development, meant that industry and agriculture should be developed together. It also meant that industry would not be concentrated exclusively in urban centers but scattered throughout the countryside, where it would serve peasant and agricultural needs more directly and effectively than before.

The Great Leap also rejected centralized planning under the control of government bureaucrats. Those bureaucrats, after all, were an important source of the problem Mao was trying to solve: the passivity of the mass of the Chinese people. The CCP now encouraged people to become self-reliant and take the initiative to build small-scale manufacturing facilities in their own villages and neighborhoods. The most celebrated of such enterprises were the so-called backyard steel furnaces that appeared all over China. These were built and worked by peasants, students, physicians, clerical employees, and others during lunch breaks, after regular work hours, and on weekends. The goal, said Mao, was to catch up with Britain in steel production within 15 years. Mao's exhortation to "go all out and aim high" was answered by tens of millions of Chinese. By October 1958, it was reported that 600,000 backyard "Bethlehems" (the town of Bethlehem, Pennsylvania, was a leading American steel center) had been built and were being operated by 90 million people. Some were built and operated by schools, including primary schools. Even hospitals closed down when doctors and nurses left their patients and went into the courtyards to build their mini blast furnaces. When massed together, they were a remarkable sight in a land so long dominated by agriculture; perhaps that is why Mao and his comrades never paused to notice how well they worked:

> Furnace fields were everywhere in Lushan county. . . . From a distance the leaping flames and columns of smoke look like some new construction site accidentally ablaze. On the scene the atmosphere is like a fairground, with scores of people bustling in and out of the rows of furnaces. . . . Small red flags fly overhead indicating the sections belonging to the various companies and squads of farmer-steelworkers who are organized like militia units. The air is filled with the high-pitched melodies of local operas pouring through an amplifier above the site and accompanied by the hum of blowers, the panting of gasoline engines, the honking of heavily-laden lorries, and the bellowing of oxen hauling ore and coal.[4]

The frantic pace of the work on these furnaces was matched in regular factories, where machines ran night and day as some workers vacated their homes and simply moved into the plants so they could labor around the clock.

Along with its feverish enthusiasm, the Great Leap was driven by a fierce anti-intellectualism; ideological correctness was deemed superior to technical expertise in all endeavors, from tilling the soil to writing poetry. Peasants and urban workers who had just emerged from illiteracy were heralded as a new breed of scientists, engineers, and philosophers capable of all kinds of achievements because they possessed pure revolutionary consciousness, which was considered vastly superior to the decadent bourgeois ideas of the intelligentsia. The intellectuals may have studied more science than the masses, said Mao, but they did not necessarily know more about the science of society. Intellectuals read more Marx and Lenin than ordinary people, but they were incapable of "entering into the spirit of it, or really understanding it." Nor was an advanced education necessarily the route toward progress, Mao insisted:

> Ever since ancient times the people who founded new schools of thought were all young people without too much learning. They had the ability to recognize new things at a glance and, having grasped them, they opened fire on the old fogeys. The old fogeys with learning always opposed them. When Martin Luther founded the Reformation, and Darwin's theories appeared, many people opposed them. The inventor of sleeping pills was not even a doctor . . . he was only a pharmacist. . . . I am told that penicillin was invented by a man who worked as a laundryman in a dyers and cleaners. . . . Of course some things can be learned at school; I don't propose to close down all schools. What I mean is that it is not absolutely necessary to attend school.[5]

The Great Leap ideal, as one historian put it, was to marry mental with manual labor and thereby create the "new man," the complete Communist, a worker-soldier-poet who could write, weed, and fight: a "jack of all trades but master of only one thought."[6]

The People's Communes

The seedbed for this new man, the soil from which the Communist consciousness would bloom and pollinate the land, was the people's commune—the central institution of the Great Leap. The communes were designed to be the nation's basic social unit, organizations of agricultural and industrial production as well as incubators of revolutionary Communist behavior. They were to be, as well, the Chinese alternative to the Western route to modernization that Mao so fervently rejected. The process of modernization in the West had moved the social order in the direction of increased urbanization, reliance on bureaucracies, large-scale production, social stratification, specialization of labor, and domination of elites. The communes were intended to break up this lock-step process by bringing industry to the countryside, thereby avoiding the assorted social and political ills that accompanied urbanization.

There were several unique aspects to the communes. They were gigantic, suitable at least in sheer mass for the mammoth job assigned them. In a land where for centuries individual families farmed plots measured in a few acres or even fractions of acres and raised possibly a dozen farm animals, a typical commune contained 25,000 people—although they were as "small" as 5,000 and as large as 100,000 people—farmed an average of 10,000 acres, and had 100,000 or more cows, pigs, chickens, goats, and sheep. Along with perhaps a dozen primary and middle schools and several times that many infant nurseries, many communes acquired dozens of pieces of heavy farm machinery such as combines and harvesters for their sprawling fields. Altogether, by the fall of 1958 China's 750,000 collective farms, containing more than 500 million inhabitants, had been combined into 26,000 rural communes. The party also created urban communes, although these were on a smaller scale and were abandoned as ineffectual after a short time.

Administratively, the commune was designed to assume some important government functions by providing for tax collection, policing, education, and health services. The most important features were economic and social. Private household plots and family ownership of animals, along with all vestiges of rural marketing, were abolished. For the most part, the commune assumed ownership of all personal property, and, as the hallmark of a true Communist society, workers were paid in kind according to their needs. Such activities as cooking, washing, and raising children were removed from households and turned over to the commune. Instead of in individual homes, meals were provided in giant canteens that fed hundreds of people at a time. This was done, in part, to release female labor, which could then join a "work army" that undertook the diverse labor requirements of the self-sufficient commune. In place of the "specialists" who reigned supreme in the capitalist nations and in the "phony" socialist world of the Soviet Union and Eastern Bloc countries, the communes would rely on the all-around person, one who could on one day harvest the crops and build dikes, and on the next day repair machinery and manufacture steel. Workers were to be paid according to need rather than in proportion to what their labor actually produced. This innovation was consistent with the desire to move beyond the old capitalist environment dominated by greed to a Communist world where altruism would motivate everyone to work unselfishly for the common good.

In addition, the communes were to become the instruments with which Mao could regain control over the administrative system he helped create but could no longer dominate. They would allow Mao to bypass the officials who controlled the party, state, and military institutions by establishing a direct bond between himself and the people, thus regaining his grip on a revolution gone astray.

The Great Leap Forward triggered a brief national euphoria concerning what was possible given the proper spirit. Initially it appeared that the Leap was a tremendous success as many of China's 600 million people responded with devotional fervor to Mao's exhortations. Reports came from all over the land of families donating their cooking pots, stoves, and even iron beds and the hinges of their doors to the state for the production of steel. From Hebei Province came word that its "Little Bethlehems" in one twenty-four-hour day produced as much steel as was produced in that same period by the entire industry of the United States. Agricultural productivity figures from the communes allegedly were no less impressive. It was announced that wheat production rose nearly 70 percent in just six months, so that by year's end China's crop was proclaimed to be larger than that of the United States.

Such claims sounded incredible, and they were. These production figures were the fantasies of star-struck cadres. Accountants, state planners, and other traditional record-keepers had been purged by the antirightist campaign of 1957, a struggle that had altogether decimated the manpower of the state statistical bureau. The motley entourage that advanced their careers on the ruins of those who had been charged with elitism were not especially professional in their duties. Many commune accountants, for example, dispensed with bookkeeping altogether as something "bourgeois" and a mere waste of time. Pressures from party zealots had mobilized mass labor efforts and inspired optimistic pledges of production expansion, but the reported increases were built on nothing but hope and enthusiasm, and, all too frequently, on fear of being labeled a slacker. Even the party's leaders were deceived. Basing their projected performance quotas on inflated reporting and themselves becoming intoxicated by the fervor of the moment, they exacerbated the situation by further increasing production demands.

The figures did not add up because the methods with which they were calculated were faulty. One of the major reasons for forming huge communes was to make possible the mobilization of vast labor armies of tens of thousands to undertake the construction projects, such as building dams and irrigation canals, which had been beyond the capacity of the old collective farms. Mao was convinced that this technique had been underutilized in labor-rich China, especially because there were slack periods—such as the time between planting and harvesting—when peasants did relatively little work. Mass mobilization of labor, of course, was nothing new in China; it had gone on since ancient times. Just prior to the announcement of the Great Leap, there had been the highly publicized success of the Ming Tombs Reservoir, which had been constructed near Beijing in only six months. During the Great Leap, however, mass mobilization was both overdone and used on projects for which it was not suited, with disastrous results. Millions of peasants were rounded up after planting and sent to labor on enormously ambitious projects, often a long distance from their homes and fields. All too frequently, they were not returned to their fields in time for harvesting. Thus Mao and the CCP did accomplish a miracle of sorts, but hardly the one they wanted: in a matter of months they turned a labor surplus into a disruptive labor shortage.

Another problem often arose with these mobilizations. Great Leap ideology assumed that it was inefficient for peasants to be rooted to one field, where they did all the work from preparing the soil and maintaining the irrigation network to planting and harvesting. Millions of them therefore were massed into huge mobile work gangs that moved from field to field, performing a specific task at every stop, much like a factory assembly line. This succeeded mainly in removing farmers from the fields they knew and cared about and putting them in situations where they neither knew the terrain nor cared about a harvest they would never see. The result was that the roving labor gangs often did low-quality work. Sometimes the problem was that nobody present knew what was best suited for a given field—for example, soil conditions could vary from place to place—and therefore the proper agricultural methods were not employed. Peasants laboring in someone else's field might rush a particular job in order to return home more quickly, or because they were being pushed by a party cadre anxious to meet or possibly exceed an arbitrary quota imposed from above. These problems, as well as many others, cut into the harvest.

In some instances, poor harvests resulted when Great Leap policies replaced time-tested peasant folkways in the fields. For example, the logic that informed the Great Leap Forward dictated that if the distance between individual plants was halved, twice as much could be planted and the harvest doubled. But this logic contradicted the stubborn ways of nature, for many crops do not thrive without adequate space. Another Great Leap policy compelled peasants to "deep plow," on the assumption that soil deeper down had not been exhausted like the topsoil that had been used for centuries. But the subsoil that deep plowing turned up was infertile—not having benefited from centuries of backbreaking effort to make it fertile by generations of peasants—and, again, the crops did not thrive. Deep plowing also exposed subsoil moisture to the air, causing it to evaporate and the soil to dry out.

Great Leap policies to increase the supply of water were equally misconceived. Sinking new wells in semi-arid regions without proper planning tended to lower the water table or, quite often, produced no water after considerable effort and expense. Irrigation projects, again undertaken with ample enthusiasm but inadequate planning, helped certain areas, but only while simultaneously depriving other fields farther downstream of essential water. And dams built without proper engineering quickly collapsed, causing losses of both human life and crops.

Meanwhile, the policy of paying peasants on the communes according to need irrespective of work performed more often brought out the worst in people and reduced productivity. The lazy got away with shirking their obligations while the industrious were demoralized. Many peasants were further demoralized by being required to eat in dining halls, which often wasted more time than they saved when poor coordination resulted in enormous lines and hours of waiting for food. They were infuriated when, as occurred in many areas, their houses were destroyed and replaced by dormitories—when the necessary building materials were available, that is—as party cadres strove to break down family ties that allegedly interfered with devotion to the cause and the effort to intensify the level of regimentation that presumably would lead to increased production. And peasants were exasperated when they followed the CCP's call to kill millions of sparrows because the little birds ate the grain in the fields. A din of banging pots and pans and frenzied shouting engulfed the countryside, as millions followed a strategy of keeping the sparrows aloft until they collapsed of exhaustion and could be finished off. But sparrows had consumed insects as well as grain, and once the sparrows were gone China found itself infested with insects that created much more damage than the late, and by then lamented, sparrows ever had.

Peasants also resisted the elimination of their tiny private plots and the seizure of their few farm animals, somehow failing to see the benefit to their survival of giving up these essentials, even if they went to what the party called the "ownership of the whole people." Generally, peasant resistance to these policies was passive; for example, they would kill household animals and eat them rather than give them up to the state. Sometimes, however, the protests took more assertive forms, as peasant discontent eventually swelled to open rebellion in several provinces.

The Great Leap Forward also caused problems in the industrial sector. The industrial infrastructure incurred serious damage as machines were run around the clock without being shut down for proper maintenance. Steel from the backyard furnaces was largely useless, which should not have surprised anyone because high-quality steel is mass-produced in modern factories using sophisticated technologies, not in homemade forges. This ill-conceived project wasted resources on a vast scale, not only the iron ore and household pots and pans and other iron implements gathered in the exhaustive search for raw materials but also the trees that were cut down to fuel what turned out to be useless contraptions. This was a tragedy in a country already almost totally denuded of its natural forests over the millennia. It was now clear that the "new" Communist man simply lacked the managerial skills and technical expertise to do Mao's bidding. Neither physicians and professors nor peasants and students built serviceable blast furnaces.

Once the Great Leap was in full swing, the one thing that almost all Chinese people lacked, wherever they lived, was energy. People were worked to exhaustion. In the countryside, mobilized peasants often did not get enough time to sleep, despite the rigor of their work. To keep them from fretting about weariness, great publicity was given to workers who remained at their posts for twenty-four or even forty-eight consecutive hours. When the Great

Leap's crop failures caused food shortages, the combination of overwork and inadequate food produced its own bumper crop of disease and desperation.

The Great Leap Forward in Crisis

By the fall of 1958, following a number of inspection tours to the country-side, it was becoming painfully clear to the party leadership that the Leap was failing, that the extravagant production figures were nothing more than the echoes of Mao's exhortations. In November and December of 1958, Mao himself publicly recognized the need for adjustments. At a meeting in December 1958, the Central Committee authorized a reversal of many of the Great Leap policies. Neither the Central Committee nor its leading member, Mao Zedong, accepted any blame for the problems that had developed as a result of policies that now were being modified. Instead, the hapless cadres below were found to have become "dizzy with success" and raced ahead too fast in policies that according to the Central Committee were basically correct and simply required refining. At the same time, again without assigning blame, the Central Committee announced that Mao would step down as president of the People's Republic when his term expired early in 1959. His successor in that post would be the pragmatic Liu Shaoqi, who the party continued to insist, despite increasing evidence to the contrary, was Chairman Mao's "closest comrade-in-arms." If this were not technically a demotion—Mao remained as chairman of the CCP, the country's most powerful post—it still was a diminution of Mao's standing because it removed him from the day-to-day running of the country while he supposedly concentrated his thought on long-term and ideological problems. At any rate, by February 1959 even Mao admitted that the people needed a rest. Yet he refused to acknowledge that the Great Leap had been a failure. After a brief period of relaxation, a respite for consolidation, the struggle would have to be renewed.

Meanwhile, Liu Shaoqi, assuming a more dynamic role, had recognized that the rapid agro-industrial drives were moving China to the brink of disaster, and he took official steps to slow down and reverse the process. In the spring of 1959, consistent with the December 1958 decisions and discussions at additional meetings during the next several months, the households were reinstated as the basic social unit of rural society. Peasants were given permission to have individual garden plots and to raise their own animals. Free market conditions were returned to the countryside on a small scale because without them it was obvious that the rural economy would not function.

Other reforms allowed peasants once again to retain their housing, furniture, and bank deposits as their own property, as well as to cook at home and remove their children from communal nurseries. At the same time, the

Central Committee reminded zealous party cadres that people needed time for sleep, and even for recreation.

With his image slightly tarnished and perhaps feeling somewhat like the "old galosh" that Khrushchev derisively called him, Mao retreated into semi-retirement. At this point the debate over the Great Leap merged with another policy dispute, this one involving Mao in a conflict with an important interest group whose concerns ranged beyond China's borders. The People's Liberation Army (PLA) stood to lose a great deal if Mao's ideological differences with Moscow jeopardized overall relations with the Soviet Union, as cuts in Soviet aid had already placed the military's modernization program in jeopardy. Mao's plans for the PLA ran contrary to the high hopes of many top echelon officers who eagerly awaited the arrival of advanced Soviet weapons systems. The leading opponent of Mao's ideas was the Minister of Defense Marshal Peng Dehuai. Peng, whose association with Mao dated from the late 1920s in the Jinggangshan mountains, was a Long March hero, a man of extraordinary valor, and a forceful proponent of the army's modernization strategy. He firmly opposed Mao's plans for reviving traditional guerrilla tactics, which emphasized self-sufficiency and political indoctrination. Nor was Peng pleased with programs that diverted soldiers from their military training and had them instead build factories and work on agricultural projects. Peng was part of the moderate faction in the party: he was convinced that if China's military were to provide viable national defense it must be poised to utilize the latest in engineering, high technology, and modern management techniques. Such a defense system required a rational domestic economic program as well as continued close ties with the Soviet Union, both of which had been undermined by the Great Leap Forward. Finally, Peng recognized the threat to his professional army posed by Mao's plan for the creation of a popular militia, a defense force that was supposed to emerge out of the self-sufficient communes, independent of the regular army and answerable to and controlled by the party.

The apparent failure of the Leap and Mao's resulting loss of influence afforded Peng, who had clashed with Mao many times on other issues over the years, an opportunity to discredit the Chairman's military plans. He did so in a dramatic style at a party meeting gathered at the mountain resort of Lushan in July 1959 by critiquing the Great Leap Forward. His "Letter of Opinion" was restrained in tone and avoided attacking Mao directly, mentioning him only twice in passing. Nonetheless, Peng was attacking policies that first and foremost were identified with Mao. Peng blamed the failures of the Leap and the communization drive on "dizzy" comrades who had lapsed into "petty bourgeois fanaticism." He attacked what he felt was the misguided formula of "putting politics in command" without giving adequate consideration to "economic principles" and "concrete measures in economic work." The Great Leap Forward, lamented Peng, like a rush of blood to the head, totally ignored the "socialist laws of planned and proportionate development."[7]

Peng mounted his attack against Mao after returning from a trip to the Soviet Union and Eastern Europe, during which he had met with Khrushchev to discuss the situation in China, about which both he and the Soviet leader had serious misgivings. Peng's attack on Mao could have been arranged in advance with Khrushchev as a move to reduce Mao's influence and to repair Sino-Soviet relations. In any event, four days after Peng's critique, Khrushchev made a speech of his own lambasting the Great Leap and its communes.

Mao may have been injured by the unsuccessful leap to utopia, but he was far from being on his political deathbed and still possessed enormous charismatic power. His counterattack was a potent blend of fury, eloquence, and biting humor. He admitted that the Leap had produced "grand chaos" and accepted *some* of the responsibility for the problems, but certainly not all of it. The Chairman reminded party leaders that they had supported him and that "if you agreed with this you should take some of the blame." He also pointed out to his fellow Marxists that "Marx also made many mistakes."[8]

Mao's heated reaction to Peng's charges caught Peng off-guard and stunned the party. The fact that Khrushchev had just publicly criticized the commune movement played directly into Mao's hands; he charged that Peng was in outright collusion with the Soviets and thus a traitor. He promised to go to the countryside himself to lead the peasants to overthrow the government if the Great Leap and the communes were allowed to perish. Mao left no doubt about what he thought the outcome of such a confrontation would be:

> If those of you in the Liberation Army won't follow me, then I will go and find a Red Army, and organize another Liberation Army. But I think the Liberation Army will follow me.[9]

The choices were very simple: either the party accepted Mao's leadership or he would make another revolution. Although Peng Dehuai may have had the backing of Liu Shaoqi and the party moderates, as proponents of order they were unwilling to follow their colleague into civil war. They yielded to Mao's wishes and rejected Peng's views. Several months later Peng and his associates were purged, Peng himself losing his position of defense minister to Mao's avid supporter Lin Biao. Meanwhile, the party endorsed a renewal of the Great Leap, which led to further disastrous economic consequences.

The results of the struggles at Lushan proved to be a watershed in the history of both the CCP and the People's Republic of China. No one suffered more from Mao's political follies than the masses of China. With the return of "leaping," hardship was transformed into terrible famine. The renewed Great Leap was an unmitigated disaster. In 1960 the communes were reestablished and the rural markets abolished. Agricultural output quickly and dramatically declined, and this soon affected light industry, which decreased by 9.8 percent in 1960, by 21.6 percent in 1961, and by another 8.4 percent in 1962. The result was a serious goods shortage that matched the precipitous decline in foodstuffs. Heavy industry followed a similar disastrous pattern: production declined 68.8 percent between 1960 and 1962. Bad weather in 1960 and the withdrawal of the Soviets in the summer of that year, whose assistance was key to several industrial schemes, compounded these difficulties.

As famine ravaged a countryside whose people were too hungry to work and pigs too hungry to stand, Mao voiced nothing but scorn for all the fussing about shortages of vegetables, pork, grain, and even umbrellas. In his eyes the much-revered masses had fallen from grace, had become "soft" in those 3 years of struggle that promised a millennium of happiness. The renewed Leap of 1959–60 triggered a famine in which some 25 million and perhaps even 50 million people starved to death. It seemed that the long-suffering Chinese had lost their nerve, having dared to whimper in the face of what was probably the most devastating famine in world history.

Divisiveness in the CCP

Besides bringing misery to those whom the revolution was supposed to serve, the decisions made at the Lushan Conference also tore gaping holes in the fabric of party consensus. The inner-party unity that had served the Chinese revolution so well since the Yan'an years were now gone. And after the Great Leap Forward, Chinese politics became increasingly polarized. Mao's purge of Peng seems to have overturned a long-standing, informal party practice governing debate among the top leadership. Following the tradition of Leninist-style democratic centralism, the party customarily allowed critical discussion, provided there was universal support of policy once a decision was rendered. Mao challenged this procedure by demanding total support for his positions and warning that he would split the party if he could not command a majority. This meant that future problems could not easily be brought to the Central Committee for discussion. Considering the bitterness that Mao's behavior undoubtedly caused, it was to be expected that the true feelings of party members would stay beneath the surface. Certainly, top-ranking leaders would not want to bring up controversial issues for party discussion, and after Lushan there is no record of any party leader challenging Mao openly and publicly until after his death.

The attack on Peng Dehuai and his so-called "right-opportunist anti-party clique" allowed Mao to make a strategically important appointment at the Ministry of Defense, which in case of future troubles would secure him a bridgehead at the summits of power. Peng did not lose his head in the purge that followed. Instead, Mao showed some nasty humor in his mercy by having the ex-marshal assigned the task of running a "Sino-Soviet Friendship Farm" in remote northeastern Manchuria, in effect relegating him to political oblivion. Peng attempted a political comeback in the early 1960s, but without success. In 1966 he was arrested and endured brutal interrogation. He died in 1974, a prisoner of the revolution he had served so loyally.

Peng's position was given to a man Mao believed he could manipulate, Lin Biao. Once in his new position as minister of defense, Lin proceeded to forge the PLA into the instrument Mao could call on to cleanse the revolution should it go soft once again. Within the PLA the philosophy of the Great Leap was applied whole hog. Revolutionary virtue was substituted for professional expertise, spiritual factors took priority over material and technical concerns, and there was a shift away from Soviet techniques to the older principles of the peasant guerrilla.

In the end, the prestige of the party took a terrible beating because of the fateful decisions taken at the Lushan Conference. Mao's reputation was also sullied by these events. The terrific aftershocks of famine and wholesale death were kept from the outside world, but within the party Mao's prestige was tarnished. As the scale of the disaster became more obvious, Mao found himself increasingly relegated to the sidelines, where he complained of being treated like a "dead ancestor."

Mao's complaint was not entirely valid. While the collapse of the Great Leap Forward was a catastrophe for China, which endured enormous suffering, disorder, and demoralization, and a grave debacle for the Chinese Communist Party, which had led the country into the quagmire and now had to find a way out of it, for Mao himself it was a setback, nothing more, albeit a serious one. This was in part because of the way Mao looked at the events of 1958–60. He obviously knew things had gone wrong, but he had not lost confidence in his conviction that his approach to revolution and building a socialist China was the correct one, in fact the only one. Equally important, while Mao's political standing was temporarily diminished and although he lost control over the day-to-day operations of the state, he remained the chairman of the party and a singular political figure whose revolutionary record and prestige still exceeded that of any single rival within the Communist leadership. To make sure that things stayed that way, his comrades were encouraged to refer to their leader as "Chairman Mao," a designation no other party member could claim and one that, if nothing else, demonstrated George Orwell's dictum that some members of a classless society inevitably end up more equal than others.

The Policies of Liu Shaoqi

Mao nonetheless found himself in a position he did not like and, in the long run, was unwilling to tolerate. The majority of the party elite that had followed his policies since the Long March now turned to alternative leadership. It was a collective leadership led by Liu Shaoqi, and included Deng Xiaoping, Chen Yun, and Zhou Enlai, although Zhou continued as always to serve as a bridge between Mao and the others. While none of these men could match Mao's stature, Liu had impressive credentials and was an excellent choice for the formidable task at hand. He was a brilliant organizer with a record of success dating back to the 1920s. Among his triumphs were his role in organizing coal miners during the 1920s and building and maintaining the party's apparatus behind enemy lines during the 1930s and 1940s. Liu was a workaholic whose long workdays lengthened to as much as eighteen hours when he became head of state. His reputation for honesty and frugal living was impeccable; nothing, not even his family, was allowed to interfere with his dedication to the revolution. A quiet, reserved man who was known to work at his desk for hours without saying a word, Liu Shaoqi did not see the world through the prism of a gargantuan ego, which probably enabled him to settle for goals that were more realistic than those of Mao Zedong.

Liu's approach to building socialism differed from Mao's, although how different would become clear only with the passage of time and the eruption of new disputes. Still, the reality was that party leaders had been divided since the 1950s over what aspects of development to emphasize first in order to reach socialism. Liu and his supporters, who eventually came to be called the "pragmatists" because they appeared to have a more practical approach to building the new society, took an orthodox Marxist-Leninist view on the subject. They insisted that society had to undergo specific modes of organization in order to reach the final stage of communism. Where Mao above all believed in mass mobilization and revolutionary enthusiasm, Liu, who had studied in the Soviet Union in the early 1920s and apparently absorbed much of the traditional Leninist view of revolution, placed greater emphasis on orderly centralized management carried out through the party organization. In economic matters, Liu was far more comfortable than Mao with the system of central planning that inevitably deprived both local cadres and the masses themselves of decision-making opportunities. Liu also was more tolerant than Mao of concessions to the material interests of the masses, even if they involved practices that catered to self-interest, such as allowing peasants on collective farms to cultivate private gardens, provided those concessions encouraged people to work harder and produce more. With the Communist Party in firm control of the state and almost all of the nation's productive resources, Liu, unlike Mao, was not concerned that such policies might foster the return of capitalism. In addition, Liu did not share Mao's faith in human will and its ability to overcome any and all material obstacles. That was one of the reasons Liu had argued for a slower pace of collectivization during the mid-1950s. By 1960 Liu was completely disillusioned with Mao's utopian Great Leap techniques; early in 1962, after receiving a report on the grave conditions in his (and Mao's) native Hunan Province, Liu commented that the Great Leap disasters were 70 percent due to human errors and only 30 percent due to natural causes. There was no doubt whose human errors Liu had in mind when he assessed the Great Leap.

"Red Versus Expert" was the phrase used to describe the disagreement and conflict between the "Liuists" and the Maoists. Liu and his followers stressed the role that experts—scientists, technicians, teachers, university professors, managers, and even "expert" farmers—had to play in building a new China. Because their services were considered essential, they enjoyed privileges not accorded the masses of workers. Liu's experts not only earned the respect traditionally associated with the old Confucian elite, but they were provided with better wages and working conditions. In general, theirs was a significantly more comfortable life than that enjoyed by most Chinese. It was this group, as well as the equally privileged party bureaucrats, that later became the prime target of Mao, who demanded that a person's commitment to the goals of the revolution preempt all other considerations. Mao's concern was for ideological purity, "redness," over expertise. It was this philosophy that had led him to the Great Leap Forward in the 1950s; in the 1960s it would lead to the Cultural Revolution.

Despite his strong reservations regarding what Liu and his practical-minded colleagues did in the wake of the Great Leap crisis, there was little Mao could do to prevent the implementation of policies he did not like. He had to admit his own errors: the extent of the failure was too great for him to do otherwise, even while the Chairman did try to shift as much blame as he could to others. Mao even felt obliged to admit the time had come to "seek truth from facts," which in the early 1960s meant making unwelcome concessions to an unforgiving reality. Nor for several years—the "three bitter years" that followed the Great Leap—could Mao criticize those policies; after all, they worked relatively quickly and brought China from the abyss of chaos and mass starvation to a plateau of order and sufficient food by 1962.

Liu's policies were not without their own pitfalls, however, for they brought unanticipated hazards to the CCP. Because of their success, Liu's practical policies—his "expert" approach—provided the party with a model for building socialism that was different from Mao's idealistic "red" approach. This divergence had emerged even before the Great Leap over several issues, including how to implement collectivization. With Mao's Great Leap failure and Liu's post-Leap successes, this divergence began to widen as each side began to see less merit in the other's approach, but especially because of Mao's increasing fear that his revolution was being undone by erroneous policies. By late 1965 and early 1966, the party found itself at the edge of a new and yawning abyss, as what had begun as a difference of opinion over specific policies took on the shape and proportions of a party split.

The policies that Liu and his comrades used to forge China's economic recovery were based on the primary need of feeding the population and on the basic reality that China remained overwhelmingly an agricultural country. Agriculture thus was the "foundation" that was given priority, while industry was the "leading factor" whose role it was to supply agriculture with the materials and tools it needed, from irrigation equipment to farming machinery to fertilizer. In order to use better what industry supplied, Great Leap institutions and policies were largely abandoned. The massive, unwieldy communes were divided so that their number tripled. Production responsibility on each individual commune devolved further, eventually being vested in so-called "production teams," groups of twenty to forty households that often coincided with existing villages. Unpopular practices like communal dining halls were abolished, while peasants were paid for their labor in the collective farm fields according to their work via a system of work points. The party adopted a rule never to take more than 5 percent of farm labor out of those fields for special projects. Consistent with Liu's dictum that peasants should be given more responsibility for production and with Deng Xiaoping's favorable comment regarding peasant "individualism," peasant families once again were permitted to work tiny private plots, and to sell what they did not consume in rural markets where supply and demand rather than state-controlled directives and prices determined what goods were available and what they cost. By 1962 the priority of increased food production even led to individual families in some parts of China being permitted to "go it alone" in a range of farming and marketing activities. Talk was heard in some party circles about a return to private landownership, although this particular idea remained just talk. The peasants evidently liked these policies and considered them constructive, for they worked hard and efficiently and raised production impressively while they were in place, from a low of 150 million tons of grain in 1960 to 170 million tons in 1962 and steadily by about 5 percent yearly through the mid-1960s. In 1961, in order to stem the tide of famine while the new policies were being introduced, China imported 10 million tons of grain. For Liu, these policies were practical and reasonable, and, while involving free market forces and individual entrepreneurial activity, they hardly threatened the basic socialist structure of Chinese society. For Mao, however, they produced seeds of capitalism by the millions and therefore were a serious threat to be feared and warned against.

In industry, Liu, Deng, and their associates once again relied on Soviet practices, along with common sense dictates of efficiency. Central planning was restored. To increase worker productivity, individual incentives such as piece-rate payment methods were introduced in many factories. Factories that were hopelessly inefficient were simply shut down, and their former employees dispatched, or "sent down" (*xiafang*), to the countryside. Being "sent down" was an unwelcome fate because urban life in China was far preferable to the material deprivation and deadening isolation of rural life. Nonetheless, about 20 million people, including many party members, were "sent down" between 1960 and 1962, with the Liuist leadership applying the necessary pressure to achieve its goals. To make sure people stayed on the farms, a rigid system of residence permits made it extremely difficult for anyone to reside illegally in urban centers. Industrial recovery paralleled that of agriculture, despite a serious blow in 1960 when the Soviet Union abruptly withdrew its aid and advisers (along with their blueprints) from approximately 275 major industrial projects, leaving the Chinese to fend for themselves as best they could. Nonetheless, the new economic policy of "readjusting, consolidating, filling out, and raising standards," while not terribly inspiring from a revolutionary point of view, was effective from an economic one, and it accomplished the goals of Liu Shaoqi and the majority of the leadership.

At the same time, Liu was bringing his and party General Secretary Deng Xiaoping's organizational skills to bear on the CCP itself, again to Mao's chagrin. At the end of the Great Leap the party underwent a thorough purge that unseated thousands of cadres who had used the turmoil of the Leap to advance their careers. This was accompanied by a "reversal of verdicts" campaign in which cadres purged during the "antirightist" drive of the late 1950s were reinstated. All of this obviously increased the strength of Liu's supporters at Mao's expense. In 1960, six regional bureaus were established to improve central control. Perhaps mindful of China's traditional reverence for a larger than life leader, the normally modest Liu even poached a bit on Mao's turf by permitting huge posters of himself, equal in size to Mao's, to be hung in public places.

Mao's unhappiness with Liu's economic programs was compounded by Liu's policies regarding intellectual life. Liu relaxed the harsh policies on intellectuals in place since the late 1950s, and one of the results was the expression of opinions that were, at least indirectly, critical of Chairman Mao. One of the most infuriating was expressed in a play published in 1961 by the vice-mayor of Beijing, Wu Han, entitled *Hai Rui Dismissed from Office*.

Although the play was about a loyal servant of the Ming dynasty dismissed by an intolerant emperor centuries before, it reminded many, including Mao himself, of the Chairman's harsh persecution of Peng Dehuai that had culminated in Peng's dismissal from his post of defense minister in the not-so-distant year 1959. Satirical essays and articles in the press, often at the thin-skinned Mao's expense, did little to soothe the Chairman's anger or improve his opinion of his comrade Liu Shaoqi. Nor was Mao, who distrusted intellectuals for their independent thought as well as for their alleged elitism, pleased with new university regulations issued late in 1961, which he felt fostered that elitism. According to the new rules, universities were primarily places for research and teaching, while the specialization necessary for mastering complex modern courses of study was endorsed, as was the view that faculty should be able to do their work without excessive party interference. Mao was no happier with changes in primary and secondary education that undid his Great Leap reforms. Schools with inferior standards, many of which dated from the Great Leap, were closed. Talented students, rather than those with "correct" political attitudes or backgrounds, were given academic and professional encouragement. The CCP committees that had run the schools during the Great Leap Forward became merely advisory bodies. And the unpopular practice of requiring students to do manual labor as part of their course of study was dropped in many areas.

The Sino-Soviet Split

There was one thing that even Liu Shaoqi could not fix after 1960: the emerging split between the Soviet Union and the People's Republic of China, the world's two great Communist powers. Tension between Soviet and Chinese Communists was nothing new; it dated from the 1920s, when Soviet advice and strategy contributed to the disasters of that decade. Mao had risen to power in the CCP during the 1930s despite Stalin's support of other leaders, while during the 1940s Stalin had angered Mao and the CCP by his continued diplomatic recognition of Chiang Kai-shek's Guomindang government during the Chinese civil war. The Soviets had provided China with aid after 1949, but always in smaller amounts than the Chinese wanted and with strings attached that they resented. This tension, however, was obscured by fulsome expressions of international Communist solidarity, by a 30-year treaty of friendship signed by the two Communist giants in 1950, by the frigid Cold War atmosphere of the immediate postwar era, and by the outbreak of the Korean War and the United States' support of the Guomindang regime on the island of Taiwan, 110 miles off the China coast.

    If Mao did not particularly like Stalin, at least he appreciated the accomplishments of the man who had led the Soviet Union through industrialization and the trauma of World War II to superpower status in the postwar world. Mao did not accord the post-Stalin leadership the same respect, even when the new Soviet leaders under Nikita Khrushchev made significant concessions to Beijing that included abandoning Soviet rights to the ports of Dalian and Port Arthur in northeast China and other economic privileges that recalled the unequal treaty era. Mao, in fact, felt with Stalin's death that he, Mao, had become the world's foremost Communist leader, a claim that aroused no response in Moscow. Beijing meanwhile was distressed by both Khrushchev's domestic and foreign policies. Mao strongly disapproved of Khrushchev's de-Stalinization speech of 1956 and his subsequent continued debunking of Stalin, in part because Khrushchev had not consulted with Mao first on the issue and, probably more importantly, because Khrushchev's denunciation of what he called Stalin's "cult of personality" could easily be applied to Mao's own practices.

Mao also disapproved of Khrushchev's emphasis on improving the material welfare of the Soviet population, which Mao felt involved concessions to "capitalist" and "bourgeois" methods and desires. Equally serious from Mao's perspective was Soviet foreign policy. In 1956 Khrushchev announced the policy of "co-existence" with capitalism, in effect abandoning Lenin's dictum of the inevitability of war between the Communist and capitalist worlds. To Khrushchev this did not mean the end of the Communist/capitalist struggle for world preeminence. Far from it, in fact. But it did mean that the struggle could be waged largely on peaceful terms, that the system which produced the most for its people ultimately would be the winner. Khrushchev's reason for endorsing peaceful co-existence was clear: the advent of nuclear weapons meant that both capitalist and Communist societies would be destroyed in the event of a Soviet-American war and nuclear exchange. This did not impress Mao and his comrades, whose anti-Americanism in light of the Korean War and Washington's support for Chiang Kai-shek's regime on Taiwan burned intensely during the 1950s and 1960s. If Moscow's newfound conciliatory attitude toward the West angered the Chinese, the Soviets collectively and unanimously shuddered at the analysis of the nuclear threat Mao offered them in 1957:

> Let us imagine, how many people will die if war should break out? Out of the world's population of 2,700 million, one third—or, if more, half—may be lost . . . if the worst came to the worst and half of mankind died, the other half would remain while imperialism would be razed to the ground and the whole world would become socialist; in a number of years there would be 2,700 million people again.[10]

A number of events during the 1950s added to the tensions. The Hungarian Uprising of 1956 was proof to Mao that de-Stalinization was a disaster. In 1958 the Chinese were angered when the Soviets, who were trying to improve their relations with the United States, refused to support the PRC in its attempt to use force to drive the Nationalists from two small islands in the Taiwan Straits. The Soviets openly disapproved of the Great Leap Forward, in large part because this presumed direct leap to communism was part of Mao's attempt to claim world Communist leadership for himself and the People's Republic. In 1959 the Soviets, increasingly leery of their presumed comrades in Beijing, reneged on their agreement of 1957 to provide China with nuclear technology, while in 1960 almost all aid ceased with the sudden withdrawal of Soviet economic and technical advisers.

While Mao certainly was part of the problem, matters did not improve with the new decade or the new policies under Liu Shaoqi. Liu initially muted criticism of the Soviets and even paid tribute to them, in the hope that his words of comradeship might once again turn the Soviet Union into a viable source of aid that Liu believed China needed for its modernization. But the divergent positions and interests of the two countries—the Soviet Union two generations removed from its revolution and now a relatively developed country with a great deal to lose in a nuclear war, and China a wretchedly poor nation still led by the revolutionary generation—broadened the gap between them to the point where it soon was visible to the whole world. Open disputes over doctrine occurred in the wake of Khrushchev's intensified de-Stalinization efforts beginning with the Twenty-second Congress of the Communist Party of the Soviet Union in 1961. Zhou Enlai, who attended the congress, made Beijing's feelings clear when he laid a wreath in Stalin's honor at the mausoleum he shared with Lenin (just before Khrushchev had Stalin's body removed and reburied in a less honored place) and then proceeded to leave Moscow with the congress still in session. In 1962, when Khrushchev retreated in the face of superior American power in the Cuban Missile Crisis, and thereby avoided nuclear war, Beijing denounced him for being a coward.

Chinese anger increased shortly thereafter when the Soviets refused to support Beijing diplomatically during its border conflict with India. That conflict resulted from China's actions in Tibet (Xizang), the plateau and mountain region that for centuries was an effective buffer between India and China. Tibet, whose 469,000 square miles was home to only 3 million people, was, in 1950, the last major mainland area to fall under Communist control. According to a 1951 agreement, the Tibetans were to retain a large measure of local autonomy. But Tibetan Buddhism (Lamaism) and Chinese communism were incompatible, and in 1959 the Tibetans rose in rebellion against CCP attempts to tighten Beijing's control over the region and erode traditional Tibetan culture. The revolt was suppressed brutally and quickly, and followed by the destruction of local institutions, intensified forced assimilation of the Tibetans, and increased Chinese colonization of the region. Although these developments certainly suited the PRC leadership, they frightened India, which suddenly found itself geographically cheek by jowl with its northern neighbor. Beijing and New Delhi soon became involved in a border dispute that in 1962 resulted in a short but fierce border war. The Chinese won this fight handily, but they were disappointed and angered when the Soviet Union, which had signed a friendship treaty with India in 1960, officially remained neutral in the dispute and was, in fact, actually sympathetic to India.

The next year, Moscow signed a partial nuclear test ban treaty with the United States banning testing in the atmosphere, a pact the Chinese denounced and refused to be a party to as they continued their efforts to develop an atomic bomb. Not even Khrushchev's fall from power in 1964 helped, although the new Soviet leadership under Leonid Brezhnev briefly tried to patch up the rift with Beijing. Instead, the Chinese went from Mao's denunciation of Khrushchev's "phony communism" in the summer of 1964, months before his nemesis was deposed, to warning in 1965 that the Soviet Union was restoring capitalism, by which time it was Brezhnev and his colleagues who were the targets of Beijing's ire.

Mao Regroups His Forces

There was little Mao or any of his comrades could do about the Soviet Union. At home, however, although Mao had been pushed to the sidelines while others rebuilt the economy and reorganized the party, he was not totally inactive or without dedicated supporters. One of the most important was his fourth wife. A former actress of questionable talent from Shanghai, Jiang Qing had come to Yan'an in the late 1930s, charmed Chairman Mao, and ended up marrying him. She never had been popular with most of the Long March and Yan'an veterans, not the least because her arrival had contributed to Mao's divorcing of his third wife, one of the genuine heroines of the Long March and a widely respected comrade. After years in the background, Jiang Qing emerged after 1960 as a major activist in the revamping of Chinese culture. She proved to be an unrelenting and ruthless soldier in her husband's cause, motivated in part by her intense bitterness against those who had rejected her in the past, and in part by her determination to make her mark as a builder of a new and presumably authentic socialist culture. Other important supporters during this difficult time for Mao were Chen Boda, a skilled propagandist with a fanatical devotion to Mao, and the sinister Kang Sheng, whose specialty was security, a trade he had learned in the Soviet Union from two purge masters, Stalin's henchmen Henrikh Yagoda and Nikolai Yezhov.

Mao's most important ally was Lin Biao, an immensely talented soldier whose battlefield exploits marked the Long March, World War II, the civil war, and the Korean War. With Mao's support, Lin became defense minister in 1959 after the dismissal of Peng Dehuai and then turned his energies to making the PLA a Maoist political base. Lin's efforts were along several fronts. After the Korean War and the appalling losses the PLA had suffered at the hands of the technologically superior American army, many military men, led by Peng, had worked to modernize and professionalize China's armed forces. Peng's program included acquiring new weaponry, introducing a more stratified hierarchy of ranks, issuing officers distinguishing uniforms on the Soviet model, and increasing pay differentials between officers and enlisted men. All this disturbed Mao, who was concerned that Peng's policies were promoting the same elitism in the army, especially among its officers, that Mao saw among party cadres. Chairman Mao wanted the army to remain true to the tradition of Yan'an, where soldiers and officers had lived together and the army itself had worked with the people on everything from farming to industrial projects.

Once Lin Biao was in charge, he devoted himself to restoring Yan'an ideals and, most importantly, securing the PLA for Mao. Ideological campaigns stressed the virtues of the Great Leap Forward and commanded the soldiers to "read Chairman Mao's works, listen to his words, do as he instructs, and become a good soldier of Chairman Mao." To guarantee this, Lin planted carefully screened political operatives in his military units. To combat elitism, officers spent a month each year serving in the ranks. Lin's efforts were successful; Mao's prestige in the PLA was high to begin with, and by 1963 Mao was confident enough of Lin's work to urge the entire country to "learn from the PLA."

Mao's relative quiescence actually ended in 1962, the year the economic recovery was completed. Mao seems to have concluded by then that his revolution was in danger, not because the power of the CCP was threatened, but, ironically, because of what the party was doing and becoming. Using the Soviet Union as an example, Mao had become convinced that a once-revolutionary party could lapse into what he called "revisionism" and degenerate, undoing its own revolution and sliding back into what Mao called "capitalism." This was precisely what Mao felt had happened in the Soviet Union under Khrushchev, and it in turn explained for Mao why the Soviets had become so friendly with the United States (an assessment of their relationship that neither the Soviets nor the Americans shared) and had deserted the CCP and the cause of the international socialist revolution.

If the Soviet slide into capitalism was bad, and in fact already an accomplished fact, what disturbed Mao even more was that he saw the same thing happening in China under Liu Shaoqi. The process, Mao felt, had two major manifestations. First, Liu and his associates were far too tolerant of "capitalist" methods of promoting economic growth such as private plots, piecework, and other material incentives. These methods appealed to "bourgeois" tendencies and created class differences, which were essential to capitalism but antithetical to socialism. Mao was convinced that ends and means were inseparable, that socialism could only be built by socialist methods such as collectivized farming and the moral incentives of the Great Leap. "Capitalist" methods threatened to put the country on the "capitalist" road, and that could only lead to one place.

Second, and even worse, the CCP was rapidly becoming part of the problem. Mao was afraid that the party was changing, and in a sense this was undeniable. By the early 1960s, charged now with managing a huge country, it had grown into a vast apparatus of 18 million people, 80 percent of whom had become members since 1949 and who therefore had not experienced the halcyon days of the Long March, Yan'an, and the civil war. But Mao was concerned with something else. Whereas once the party had lived and worked with the people while it devoted itself to revolutionary social change—that was the essence of the Yan'an experience—now increasingly it was becoming an organization of people who enjoyed privileged positions and had exclusive access through those positions to the best material comforts China had to offer. The CCP membership was therefore separating itself from the masses and, in the process, becoming a new ruling class.

Mao called this phenomenon "bureaucratism" and railed against the many examples he saw of it. He was distressed by Soviet-style central planning, under which bureaucrats issued orders from their Beijing offices, transmitted them through the apparatus, and saw to it that the people passively carried them out. This was a disaster to Mao, who since the 1920s had stressed that the people had to participate actively in making their revolution. Mao also pointed to the elitist education system, which was becoming intensely competitive and only allowed those students with the best preparation or connections to advance to the university level. Overwhelmingly they were the children of urban-based cadres or, even worse, the offspring of intellectuals who often were not even Communists and therefore, Mao insisted, "bourgeois." A system of elite key primary and secondary schools, resentfully called "little treasure pagodas" by many, reinforced these tendencies. Because a university education was the key to advancement, this meant that party members were passing on their power to their children through education much as the old ruling classes did through their possession of private property; Mao went so far as to compare the CCP to the old Confucian gentry, which also had used education as the key to power.

In January 1962 Mao attempted to stop the slide. At a work conference of 7,000 cadres, he defended his Great Leap policies without noticeable success. Indeed, Liu's assertion that the Leap had been a failure was reaffirmed. The next month, to Mao's distress, Chen Yun, the party's leading economist, had the audacity to suggest returning the nation's farmland to individual households. At the same time, large numbers of purged "rightists" were rehabilitated, including Peng Dehuai. In July, Deng Xiaoping made his famous statement, "It doesn't matter if a cat is black or white, so long as it catches the mouse it's a good cat," which to Mao meant the door was open to yet more "capitalistic" policies. In August, Liu's essay "How to Be a Good Communist" was reissued with great fanfare, another sign that Chairman Mao's influence was dangerously on the wane.

As early as 1959 Mao had warned against "bourgeois elements" that were "infiltrating" the party. Now he began to fight back in earnest. The scene of his first major battle was the dramatic Tenth CCP Central Committee Plenum in September 1962. Mao strongly criticized the party's direction and issued his clarion call: "Never forget class struggle." Bringing to bear all his prestige, he got the party to agree to a campaign he called the "Socialist Education Movement." Its formidable goals were to clean up corruption in the party, which was widespread and recognized by Liu and his supporters no less than by Mao, and to restore the party's ideological purity.

The Socialist Education Movement lasted from 1962 to 1965 and included a number of rectification campaigns of criticism and self-criticism on the model that dated from Yan'an days. To overcome their alleged "divorce from production," in other words, their tendency to ensconce themselves in comfortable jobs far from factory floor and farm field, cadres were sent from their urban nests to labor in the country alongside the peasants. Peasants were organized into what were called "associations" to criticize cadres who were corrupt or elitist. Meanwhile, what were called "work teams" of higher-level cadres were sent to thousands of localities, where they "squatted" for a period of time and worked to eliminate abuses of power by cadres and "capitalist tendencies" among the peasantry.

The problem was that the Socialist Education Movement, at least from Mao's perspective, did not work. It was carried out by the party apparatus, which is not surprising because there was no organization other than the CCP able to do the job. Yet it was precisely the party apparatus, and Liu and the others who controlled it, who were Mao's problem. The work teams illustrated Mao's dilemma. In his view, work teams were to do their jobs primarily by setting an example: living and working alongside the peasantry and accepting criticism from them, something that local cadres increasingly were not doing, while at the same time rigorously combating the peasantry's "capitalistic" tendencies, such as spending too much time on their private plots or devoting their energies to other money-making sidelines. Under Liu's management, work teams did attack corruption and, in certain extreme cases, rural private enterprise. Some 2 million local cadres were purged for corruption or otherwise poor performance. But all this was done *from above*; work teams came to a locality and took over, issuing orders to local cadres and peasants alike, precisely what Mao opposed. In 1963 and again in 1964, Mao voiced his objections, but aside from cosmetic adjustments—Mao called Liu's response to his complaints "left in form but right in substance"—nothing was done to satisfy the Chairman's objections.

By 1964 Mao was rallying his forces outside the party apparatus. His main source of help was the PLA, which by then, thanks to Lin Biao, was the bastion of "Mao Zedong Thought." It was the PLA that first published *Quotations from Chairman Mao*—the so-called "little red book"—a pocketbook-sized volume with selections from the Chairman's writings and speeches that presumably provided the essential guidance one needed to lead a proper socialist and revolutionary life and that eventually would be found in the hands of almost every PRC citizen capable of reading it. By 1965 the PLA, setting an example according to Mao's instructions, abolished the ranks of the 1950s and discarded its old uniforms in favor of a simple distinction between officers and enlisted men and a common, simple uniform decorated only by a red badge and a star. Additional support came from Jiang Qing on the cultural front. She was busily gathering radical intellectuals together to create "revolutionary" theatrical productions and, more importantly, succeeding in getting some of them performed.

All this effort produced only a frustrating stalemate. In 1965, Mao got the party leadership to agree to form a five-man group to organize what Mao called a "cultural revolution," in other words another campaign to restore ideological purity to a party that had not responded properly to the Socialist Education Movement. The "Cultural Revolution Group," headed by Beijing's mayor and prominent Liu supporter, Peng Zhen, did little but mark time. Mao and his minions then intensified their pressure by openly attacking Wu Han for his play *Hai Rui Dismissed from Office* in November 1965. By attacking Wu Han, who had criticized the party Chairman by comparing him to, of all things, a Ming emperor, Mao in effect was attacking the party apparatus and the leadership that had permitted publication of the play and implemented many other policies that Mao opposed. Convinced that the conservative government and party bureaucracies again had sabotaged his efforts at radical social change, Mao made plans for yet another more spectacular assault on the establishment; this one truly would turn the Chinese world upside down.

9

The Cultural Revolution

"Long Live Revolutionary Mass Criticism"

Why a Cultural Revolution?

Mao's final effort to regain control over the progress of revolution came in the form of a power struggle against Liu Shaoqi and his supporters. Ever since Liu assumed power as head of state, Mao had continued to challenge his policies. Mao was not only angered by Liu's economic policies but the Chairman and many of his supporters also believed that revolutionary development of all aspects of Chinese society had stagnated. For them, China was still mired in enervating traditional cultural conventions—customs and habits that were millennia old. If Chinese society was to evolve from socialism to communism in accordance with Marxist theory, then drastic change was necessary. What was needed, according to Mao, was nothing less than a thorough revamping of Chinese culture. By culture Mao was referring not only to how people were educated, what they read, how they created their art and music—although these were important—but also to how people interrelated, what they thought, even how they amused themselves. All aspects of culture had to be changed so that working class values replaced traditional bourgeois customs because, according to Marxists, cultural consciousness reflects the economic values of the prevailing class. Mao Zedong explained to fellow revolutionaries in Yan'an:

> In the world today all culture, all literature and art belong to definite classes and are geared to definite political lines. There is in fact no such thing as art for art's sake, art that stands above classes or art that is detached from or independent of politics.[1]

When a society is in its feudal or capitalist stage, culture is identified with the values of the wealthy. Education, literature, and the arts all have their roots implanted deeply in this past and, more importantly, are often available only to the privileged. While scholars, writers, and artists can and do emerge from the working class as a result of exceptional talent or luck, the works they produce are understood only by those with an appropriate education. The knowledge they acquire through education or training sets them apart from the class from which they have emerged. Working class intellectuals may be able to join the elite, but they remain, as a group, relatively few in number.

A problem for Marxists is that the existence of an elite is not necessarily challenged by a socialist revolution. Although specific groups, such as the landowners and wealthy bourgeoisie, may be annihilated during the revolution, they are merely replaced by another elite, namely, party leaders and those whose talents are needed in the new society. Mao called this elite the new "bourgeois" class because it held fast to prerevolutionary values. The actual makers of revolution had not forsaken attitudes from the past because cultural values respected for centuries tend to pass into the new social order. Party leaders in the Soviet Union, for example, enjoyed many of the same dances performed by the Bolshoi Ballet for the tsars.

A similar situation of cultural atavism existed in China during the 1960s, and Mao and his followers perceived it as a serious threat to an all-out socialist revolution. In the new China, the dominant class was to be the proletariat, but a proletarian culture did not yet exist. Although the capitalist means of production were gone, many older institutions remained and continued to function as they had prior to the revolution. One such institution that became a target for change was the university. Faculty, curricula, and admissions procedures conformed to standards established in traditional China. The universities were obviously indispensable because they educated the new society's much-needed engineers, scientists, and technicians. Yet they also produced a new privileged class. Mao feared that this situation would perpetuate a schism within society based on the privilege and deference accorded to those who possessed knowledge instead of those who did manual labor. Such attitudes were deeply ingrained in Chinese society with its Confucian heritage, a tradition that revered the Mandarin scholar with his long fingernails, a symbol of life without physical labor. As a result, the status of the new intellectual class, many of whom were sons and daughters of the revolution, was challenged by the Maoists in order to produce a new Chinese culture: a proletarian culture. Mao also believed in the need for "permanent" revolution to keep revolutionary and proletarian values alive. The generation of students and young leaders coming of age during the 1960s was too young to have experienced the privations of civil war. They had little appreciation for the struggles undertaken by the older generations to produce the new society. Mao felt that Chinese youth should not be complacent; they should work vigilantly at improving society. He wanted to entrust China's future to its youth and not to those he charged with "taking the capitalist road." Moreover, Mao sought out the youth of the working class to lead the Cultural Revolution because his goal was to establish a proletarian culture, a culture defined by the masses. Such changes did not come easily. There were many within the CCP who did not agree with such ideas. These people not only presented serious obstacles to the Maoist strategy, but they were also the ones who held power during the mid-1960s.

Mao Regains Power

According to CCP historians, the cataclysm known as the Cultural Revolution began on November 10, 1965, when the Shanghai *Wenhui Bao* printed Yao Wenyuan's criticism of *Hai Rui Dismissed from Office*. It was no secret among China's leaders and intellectuals that those who had supported Mao during the Great Leap Forward were targets of this satire. Its hero, Hai Rui, was personified by Peng Dehuai, Mao's antagonist, who had been dismissed for his disagreements with the CCP chairman in 1959. The play satirized the plight of peasants who had lost control over their land. Those who tried to stop the process were depicted as heroes. At Mao's instigation, Shanghai journalist Yao Wenyuan attacked the play and its author, a move that was merely a thinly veiled attempt by Mao to lash out at his critics. In December 1965 Mao remarked:

> The crux of *Hai Jui [Rui] Dismissed from Office* was the question of dismissal from office. The Jia Qing Emperor [of the Ming dynasty, 1522–1566] dismissed Hai Jui from office. In 1959, we dismissed Peng Dehuai from office. And Peng Dehuai is "Hai Jui" too.[2]

While by no means an earth-shattering event in itself, this was a significant political tremor: a first step in Mao's road back to power.

Mao set up his strategic base in Shanghai, far from Beijing, the center of CCP power. When Mao felt he was losing ground in the struggle to stay in power, he retreated, turned his back on the party, and appealed directly to the masses. This had happened several times throughout his career—in Hunan during the late 1920s when he discovered the revolutionary potential of the peasants, in the anti-Japanese war when the CCP fought behind Japanese lines, and during the civil war when Mao earned popular support for his anti-Guomindang campaign. This strategy was hardly revolutionary. Its precedent was the recognition that from the people came the Mandate of Heaven, the authority to rule in Confucian China. Mao now needed popular support to regain power, so he tried to repeat the process during the Cultural Revolution. While Liu Shaoqi and Deng Xiaoping controlled the party Central Committee in the capital, Mao worked with a closely knit group of supporters in Shanghai away from the center of party power. The group included Yao Wenyuan, and Jiang Qing, Mao's wife, an enthusiastic force behind the Cultural Revolution.

During the first six months of the Cultural Revolution, from November 1965 to June 1966, the conflict centered on the debate over Wu Han's play. Although Liu Shaoqi, Mao's adversary, later became Mao's chief target, during this first phase Liu himself was not portrayed as a major opponent. Instead, one of Liu's supporters, the mayor of Beijing and Politburo member, Peng Zhen, became the scapegoat. Mao's plan was to pick away slowly at the Liuists, perhaps never making it clear that they were his targets and thereby avoiding or at least delaying a potential counterattack. Furthermore, Mao had several reasons to be especially annoyed with Peng Zhen. As Beijing's mayor and a CCP leader, Peng represented those in power in the capital, the vortex of CCP power. He also was a supporter and a friend of playwright Wu Han and had become increasingly bold in his attacks on Maoism by the mid-1960s. Peng became entangled in the debate over Wu Han's play in an attempt to defend his colleague. He collaborated with other friends in the CCP and successfully blocked the publication of Yao Wenyuan's article in many of China's newspapers. Peng's well-publicized opinion was that the entire debate was an academic issue with no political relevance. This particularly grated Mao because Peng and friends were openly dismissing the importance of his own attack on Wu

Han's play. On December 30, 1965, the Maoists were able to pressure Wu Han into admitting publicly that he had failed to use the leader's theory of class warfare in his play. Peng then announced that he would end the conflict soon, implying that the debate was trivial and that the argument would be settled in short order. Peng had Wu sent to a rural commune. To the Maoists, however, such lenient punishment was inadequate for the crime; indeed, Wu's visit to the countryside suggested that the party had exonerated him.

Meanwhile, Peng also became head of the "Group of Five in Charge of the Cultural Revolution," clearly a potentially powerful position for charting the subsequent course of events. Many historians have debated whether this appointment signaled Mao's total loss of power in the early months of 1966. Others suggest that because it was Mao who contrived the Cultural Revolution, Peng's appointment as group head was, in reality, a calculated step in the fulfillment of Mao's long-term goals. Mao could now wait for the inevitable failure of Peng and his followers to implement the changes the Maoists demanded, because a Maoist program would run counter to Peng's philosophy. By April, Peng was referred to by Mao's supporters as the "representative of the bourgeoisie," and Mao's friends formed a second Cultural Revolution Group. Their initial intentions were to eradicate the "bourgeois mentality" that had permeated China during the previous 4 years. The five original members were deliberately selected for their support of Maoist policies. They included Jiang Qing, by this time Lin Biao's appointee as cultural adviser to the army; Chen Boda, Mao's long-time secretary and supporter; Zhang Chunqiao, controller of the secret police and the only holdover from Peng's committee; and Yao Wenyuan, the Shanghai journalist who wrote the critique of Wu Han's play. At one of the new committee's first meetings, some members of Peng's old group made an abortive attempt to assassinate Mao. Several years later, Jiang Qing told American historian Roxane Witke that Peng's supporters actually burst into the room where Mao's allies were meeting and started shooting, but no one was injured. The group was immediately arrested.[3] Peng quickly became a victim of the new committee. On March 26, the day on which his supporter President Liu Shaoqi left for an official visit to Afghanistan and Pakistan, Mayor Peng was purged from the party. Jiang Qing launched an offensive against the remainder of Peng's supporters for what she claimed was their evil influence in the fields of art and literature. According to Jiang, the group had openly supported "bourgeois" artists and intellectuals, thereby assuring that Chinese culture would not reflect proletarian values. For the next few weeks, a series of accusations against the "Black Gang" penned by Mao's supporters appeared in the *Liberation Army Daily*, the journal controlled by Lin Biao. On April 30, Premier Zhou Enlai outlined the goals of the Cultural Revolution:

A socialist cultural revolution with a significant historical meaning is now rising in our country. This is a fierce and long-term struggle in the ideological sphere between the proletariat and the bourgeoisie. We have vigorously to promote proletarian thoughts and smash bourgeois thoughts in all the academic, education, journalistic, art, literary and other cultural circles. This is a crucial problem concerning the country as a whole, a problem of development in the socialist revolution in the present stage. It is of the utmost importance, involving the fate and future of our Party and our country.[4]

Simultaneously, there was a revival of an old Chinese custom, the use of wall posters to allow the expression of opinion to a large, if local, audience. The first poster appeared May 25 at Beijing University, often the site of political unrest. A philosophy instructor, Nie Yuanzi, with several of her colleagues, criticized the administration of the conservative university president, Lu Ping, who also happened to be a longtime friend of the purged Peng Zhen. Nie called on Mao and the Central Committee to "break down all the various controls and plots of the revisionists" and "wipe out all ghosts and monsters and all Khrushchev-type counterrevolutionary revisionists, and carry the socialist revolution through to the end." Mao supported the poster campaign and asked a member of the Cultural Revolution Group to publicize it nationally. In fact, Mao and Lin Biao had approved earlier of Nie's year-long criticisms of the Beijing University administration. Some weeks later, Mao produced his own poster. Its message was unmistakable: "Bombard the Headquarters!" The posters and the editorials had two purposes: first, to get the public involved in the debate and, second, to gain support for the eventual elimination of the Liuists.

During the first week of June 1966, Mao's allies went on the offensive. Many of Peng's and Liu's supporters in CCP organizations were replaced with Maoists. Much of the Beijing press was restaffed. Lu Ping, president of Beijing University, was dismissed, and a pro-Mao group arrived there to run the school's Cultural Revolution. By this time campuses throughout Beijing were being torn apart by strikes, protests, murders, and suicides. Ironically, many of the suicide victims were students of working class and peasant families who were unfairly branded as counterrevolutionaries by their peers. Alliances changed daily; those who were revolutionary one day were branded by other Red Guards as revisionists the next. On June 24, Mao's young followers in Beijing made their intentions clear:

You say we are too rude? We should be rude. How can we be soft and clinging towards revisionism or go in for moderation in a big way? To be moderate towards the enemy is to be cruel to the revolution!

You say we are going too far? To put it bluntly, your "avoid going too far" is reformism; it is "peaceful transition." You are day-dreaming! We are going to strike you down to the dust and keep you there![5]

Meanwhile, in mid-July, Marshal Lin Biao marched into Beijing with the People's Liberation Army. On July 18, during the height of violence in Beijing, Mao returned to the capital. The PLA had paved the way for Mao's safe arrival and for a series of purges in the political and educational leadership. Mao was forcefully demonstrating his own belief that "political power comes from the barrel of a gun." Mao was soon followed by the members of the Shanghai Cultural Revolution Group who visited the universities in a vain attempt to quell the violence. By now a turning point had been reached in the Cultural Revolution. Mao's decision to take up residency in Beijing signaled that he was closer to regaining full power. Any questions the opposition may have had about Mao's ability to retake control owing to reputed illnesses or the fact that he was now 73 years old were dispelled soon after he demonstrated his "youthful vigor" by swimming for an hour in the Yangzi River. This much-publicized event helped solidify his support among enthusiastic revolutionary youth. But there remained several formidable obstacles to his complete political recovery, most notably President Liu Shaoqi and party General Secretary Deng Xiaoping.

Throughout the summer of 1966, Liu and Deng attempted unsuccessfully to control the Cultural Revolution. A crucial issue was that the CCP leadership, including Peng Zhen before his purge, insisted that Cultural Revolution activities be monitored by party directors. This meant, of course, that the direction of the revolution would be dominated by those in control of Beijing, the Liuists. Mao's group, on the other hand, demanded that the Cultural Revolution Group from Shanghai have equal status among party committees in charge. In this way, Mao would be at the helm. The conflict was settled on August 1 when Mao named Marshal Lin Biao first vice-chairman of the Central Committee in a reshuffle that made him second in command in the CCP hierarchy while Liu Shaoqi fell to number eight. More importantly, the military became even more powerful because Lin Biao was also PLA commander.

On August 8 the Central Committee, now in Maoist hands, published a Sixteen-Point Directive on the aims of the Cultural Revolution. In the directive, Mao insisted on the necessity of molding public opinion and gave the party's blessing to a movement led by youth. He wanted the masses to be "liberated" and united against the 5 percent of the population that was antiparty and antisocialist and, in particular, against CCP leaders who had taken the "capitalist road." Cultural Revolution committees were established in schools, factories, mines, and neighborhoods throughout the country. Furthermore, those committees made it clear that those young people who followed their directives would be excused for any excesses or mistakes they might make. As he stirred up youth to "seize power," Mao relaxed police controls, thereby creating conditions for anarchy. This was the most important specific spark for the Cultural Revolution because it forbade the public security forces from suppressing the emergence of new political groups seemingly carrying out Mao's designs. Almost everyone now became involved in political organizing either to defend themselves or to make new power claims. Certainly thousands who had been discriminated against saw this as an opportunity to vent their frustrations and seek revenge. Mao, for his part, seems to have been positively charged by the chaos he initiated. After a violent struggle at a school in the summer of 1966 he announced, "There is one good thing about our era: the left-wingers get beaten up by the right-wingers, and this toughens up the left-wingers."[6]

The Sixteen-Point Directive on the aims of the Cultural Revolution unleashed a reign of terror against the Chinese population carried out by Mao's newly created youthful revolutionaries, the Red Guards. In August, an official radio broadcast defined the Red Guards as "an organization set up by middle-school pupils from families of workers, poor and lower-middle peasants, revolutionary cadres and revolutionary soldiers." As it turned out, the Red Guards or "little revolutionary generals" as they were sometimes called—a term of flattery that Mao's followers coined to encourage zealousness—were students of all ages. They came from schools throughout China that had closed during the summer of 1966 as a result of the mayhem caused by the Cultural Revolution. The Central Committee invited the youths to leave their homes and schools and come to Beijing where they would be greeted by Chairman Mao. Approximately 11 million young radicals arrived to join the ranks of the Red Guards. On August 18, Mao, Jiang Qing, Zhou Enlai, and Lin Biao reviewed their young followers. One million appeared at a rally that afternoon at the Beijing Workers' Stadium, where they wore the red armbands that were the hallmark of several peasant armies during the civil war. Some boys arrived in their fathers' old Red Army uniforms. It was a highly emotional meeting, with the members of the Cultural Revolution Group accompanying Mao on stage in rallying the youth to action. Liu Shaoqi and Deng Xiaoping were verbally abused before the millions. The New China News Agency (Xinhua) summarized the event:

> A great proletarian cultural revolution without parallel in history is being carried out in our country under the leadership of our great leader Chairman Mao. This is a revolution of world significance. We will smash the old world to smithereens, create a new world and carry the great proletarian cultural revolution through to the end.

Sailing the seas depends on the helmsman, the growth of everything depends on the sun, and making revolution depends on Mao Zedong's thought. . . . Chairman Mao is the reddest sun of our hearts. . . . [7]

The Red Guards then turned to rectifying the "ills" of Chinese society. Among their first targets were the schools from which they came. Curricula, admissions procedures, books, testing, and teaching methods were attacked. Professors became the victims of humiliating accusations. Mao's own visceral hatred for intellectuals certainly aided and abetted the Red Guards' violent campaigns against their teachers and professors. As early as May 1958, for example, Mao had boasted that he had already outdone the notoriously cruel first emperor of the Qin dynasty in his policy against intellectuals:

He buried only 460 scholars alive; we have buried forty-six thousand scholars alive. . . . You [intellectuals] revile us for being Qin Shi Huangs. You are wrong. We have surpassed Qin Shi Huang a hundredfold. [8]

In August the press announced that schools at all levels would remain closed for at least six months until a new system could be created that would meet the demands of the Red Guards. Considerable controversy, both inside and outside China, resulted from the zeal with which the youth attacked what they considered to be reactionary elements in society. With the support of the Cultural Revolution Group and with free access to public transportation, and liberated from academic obligations, the gangs of youths rampaged through Beijing and its suburbs changing street and store names, burning foreign books, defacing buildings constructed during the imperialist era, vandalizing homes of formerly wealthy families, lashing out at "bourgeois" vendors, humiliating and beating older citizens, destroying priceless art and artifacts in many of China's best museums, fighting with police, and attacking soldiers. As one Western eyewitness to these events reported:

The slogan on everyone's lips was "Smash the old; build the new!" . . . The smashing was selective and symbolic: We saw stone lions broken with sledge hammers, wooden motifs chiseled off and carted away in trucks, statues of the Buddha replaced by red flags. [9]

The fury continued from August to January when a new phase began, an even more virulent campaign directed against Liu and Deng, even though they had remained virtually powerless since Mao's return in July. It started with a rally on December 12, 1966, where the Liuist Peng Zhen and some of his supporters were publicly degraded. Under military escort, the hapless offenders were brought to Beijing's Workers' Stadium where 10,000 Red Guards waited. There the "enemies of the masses" were forced to wear heavy wooden placards around their necks on which their names were first printed then crossed out with huge X's. As party leaders looked on, Peng and his associates were "tried" and condemned. They were later sent to prison. Liu and Deng remained out of sight. Meanwhile, the Red Guards stampeded across the countryside wreaking havoc on the most remote provinces. There the going became tougher; they met with sharp resistance from conservative peasants and national minorities who looked on the urban youth with contempt. The American agronomist William Hinton, who lived and worked in Long Bow Village, 400 miles southwest of Beijing, described great outbursts of fighting, the reasons for which "no one could really explain." A young villager was employed in a local mine in 1967 as the Cultural Revolution began to heat up. During this time he "learned very little about mining but a great deal about political agitation, debating, poster writing, and, finally, street fighting." As the miner explained it:

> Fighting began early in the year. In those days we fought with fists and sticks. If we began debating, we ended up fighting. If we put up posters, we fought over their content. Once I spoke at a meeting and they beat me up. Sometimes, when we sat down to eat in the dining room, we began to argue. The arguments led to brawls. We threw stools at each other and smashed all the lights. Nobody got killed, but a lot of people got hurt.
>
> One night two or three of us were eating in the dining room along with four or five opponents. They began to talk about how good their faction [revolutionary group] was. When we disagreed they grabbed our bowls and smashed them on the floor. Then we all took hold of stools and went after each other. I got whacked twice on the back. Since we were outnumbered, we already had a plan. We would knock out the lights, then skip out, leaving the opposition to fight among themselves. As soon as the fracas began I got it on the back, but when the lights went out I managed to sneak to the far end of the hall and escape. I hid among the crops in the fields until I found my companions. Then, at 2:00 A.M., I ran back to Long Bow.[10]

The Red Guards also attempted to take over whole administrative areas in the hope of establishing a revolutionary collective modeled on the Paris Commune of 1871. Until December 1966, Jiang Qing had pressed the Red Guards under her leadership to take such action. She retreated only when Mao expressed his disapproval. Another member of the Cultural Revolution Group, Chen Boda, called for the establishment of "Paris Communes," and as a result Red Guards attempted to seize control of cities throughout China. Their one success was in Shanghai. Two members of the Cultural Revolution Group, Zhang Chunqiao and Yao Wenyuan, were overseeing events in Shanghai at the time. They did nothing when a group of student leaders from Beijing took over several Shanghai newspapers and radio and television stations, and called for the workers to overthrow the existing city government and seize power. Soon all normal urban activities ground to a halt. The rebels gloated over the terrible disorder they caused. A Red Guard newspaper reported:

> In the brief time of a few days, Shanghai, with its population of 10 million, has been turned upside down! . . . This is wonderful! There will be no stopping the movement now! . . .
> We rebels have been trying for six months to get this kind of chaos. We'd had little success up to this, but now at last we've made it! Rebellion needs disorder. Without revolutionary disorder, there cannot be broad democracy for the working class.[11]

On February 5, 1967, Yao and Zhang proclaimed the establishment of the Shanghai Commune, with more than 1 million demonstrating in celebration. But both Mao and Lin Biao, who regarded the behavior as tantamount to secession, quickly disapproved. The two Shanghai leaders were recalled to Beijing, and within a few weeks Mao set up a new government in Shanghai incorporating members of the CCP and the PLA over whom he had control.

By the spring of 1967 the number of clashes involving the Red Guards began to escalate. In Beijing alone there were 133 incidents of violence reported between April 30 and May 10, involving some 60,000 people.[12] Beijing was not the only scene of fighting. Violence continued in most major cities and throughout the countryside. Mao had made a move to defuse the fury of the Red Guards by reopening many of the secondary schools and universities on March 1, but this did not stop the fighting or settle the real issue, namely what to do about Liu, Deng, and the remainder of their followers still holding important party positions. Red Guards continued to denounce Liu and those surrounding him. Liu's wife, Wang Guangmei, also became one of their prime targets. Wang was characterized as an "enemy of the people" for numerous reasons. She had been a forceful and articulate supporter of her husband and his views, having directed programs under his guidance. In her own right, Wang was a talented and respected intellectual. Born in Beijing, she attended Fu Jen University. She served as translator for Americans in Yan'an during the 1940s and traveled on state visits with her husband. Wang often wore stylish clothes instead of plainer working class dress and occasionally danced socially. Such "bourgeois" habits were sufficient to unleash against her the wrath of the Red Guards.

On April 10, 1967, a student leader of one of the Red Guard groups organized a rally at Qinghua University in Beijing. More than 3,000 people attended. Despite protests by Liu, the campus and a special kangaroo court were plastered with anti-Liu posters. The unfortunate Wang Guangmei was marched before the students. She had been dressed by some of the Red Guards in a tight evening gown, spiked heeled shoes, "an English aristocrat's" straw hat, and a necklace of ping pong balls on which skulls had been painted. Presented as such, Wang Guangmei became an unwitting caricature of her despicable "bourgeois" days. As the crowd jeered and chanted, Wang Guangmei was forced to reap the scorn directed against her hated husband.

Protests continued to focus on Liu Shaoqi, Deng Xiaoping, and their families. Thousands of Red Guards marched by Liu's house daily demanding his dismissal. His famous pamphlet "How to Be a Good Communist" was publicly denounced. Subsequent editions made the grievous error, according to the Maoists, of having failed to include the ideas of their "Great Helmsman." Liu and his wife were pressured into public self-criticism. Liu confessed to the charges of having right-wing ideas, possessing a bourgeois class outlook, and failing to appreciate the true meaning of Mao's thought. He was put under house arrest, but not officially dismissed from his post as state president because such action would have required a vote of the National People's Congress. Despite Mao's apparent control over the progress of the Cultural Revolution, a victory among his party colleagues in the Congress was not necessarily assured. But Mao managed to reorganize the entire government in April, replacing the Liuists with his supporters. The Politburo then voted by a close margin to condemn Liu; Premier Zhou Enlai cast the deciding vote. Liu was accused of following an antiparty policy for more than two decades. His and Deng's subsequent exile signaled Mao's return to power; but it was not until October 1968 that the CCP Central Committee announced that the Liuists had been ousted from their party and governmental positions. On October 13, a plenary session of the Central Committee ratified the "Report on the Examination of the Crimes of the Renegade, Traitor, and Scab Liu Shaoqi" and resolved to dismiss him from all posts inside and outside of the CCP. They also called on all Chinese to carry on "deep-going revolutionary mass criticism" to eradicate Liu's counterrevolutionary revisionist ideas.

The Cultural Revolution is replete with tragic stories of families turning against each other, students attacking their teachers, and friends denouncing friends. This was the ugly legacy of a society in full-scale rebellion against its cultural heritage. The humiliation and suffering of "struggle sessions" touched nearly everyone, but few more tellingly than that visited on Liu Shaoqi and his wife. The sad tale of their end has been described by the historian Anne Thurston. After severe beatings Liu, who had lost his shoes, limped toward his wife, Wang Guangmei. As they were taken by the Red Guards back to captivity,

> . . . Wang Guangmei stopped only a few paces from where their children were watching. She broke loose from her captors, turned and faced her husband, her hands reaching out. Husband and wife grabbed each other's hands and held on, a circle of two. Hands in each other's hands, they looked into each other's eyes, trying to straighten their bent and broken bodies. Liu Shaoqi was kicked and beaten, but still husband and wife clung to each other, hand in hand. Rudely, they were pulled apart. Wang Guangmei struggled loose from her captors again, grabbed on to her husband, and refused to let go. Only by violence were they separated.
> It was their final farewell.[13]

The purge of Liu Shaoqi and Deng Xiaoping and their followers cleared the way for Mao to retake control and also to end the Cultural Revolution. The Ninth Party Congress, held in April 1969, officially marked the end of the Cultural Revolution and Mao's return to power. There were some pressing issues, neglected during the power struggle, which now demanded attention. Order had been restored, for the most part, by the PLA, which used force when necessary to stop Red Guard violence. China's economy was in shambles as a result of the pervasive violence. Mao and his followers had been surprised by the resistance to the Cultural Revolution among the "masses" and peasants—the very groups that were to be the beneficiaries of its policies. Industrial laborers, police, soldiers, and other workers often would not submit to Red Guard authority. National minorities, bent on preserving their own culture and traditions, also joined the battle against Red Guard zealots. The resistance of such disparate groups damaged the economy in many parts of China. A retreat was necessary.

Moreover, many CCP leaders, especially Premier Zhou Enlai, had begun to feel that China had become vulnerable to superpower aggression because of its isolation from world affairs. Ending the Cultural Revolution and restoring a Chinese presence in the diplomatic community was necessary before relations with foreign nations could improve. This was particularly important because China's dispute with the Soviets had intensified while the United States had increased its commitment to Southeast Asia. The United States had stationed more than one-half million troops in Vietnam by 1968 and unleashed a fury of bombing attacks in North Vietnam, dreadfully close to China's southern border. The vitriolic criticism of the two superpowers by the Chinese press and the Red Guards portrayed China as the enemy of the powers to its north and south. With the end of the Cultural Revolution, Zhou pursued avenues to return

China to the international community, softening the rhetoric, and eventually winning China's seat in the United Nations from Taiwan in 1971.

The Impact of the Cultural Revolution

The Cultural Revolution was an attempt to transform Chinese society in a more profound way than the reform programs of the 1950s. Chinese culture would undergo a genuine metamorphosis and everyone would be called on to play a role in the drama. Confucian tradition, residual bourgeois materialism, and capitalism were to be completely erased. These millenarian goals were never realized, but the Cultural Revolution dramatically and often painfully changed many people's lives. Society was rearranged at all levels when the Maoists consistently enforced the "downward transfer" (*xiafang*). Officials, intellectuals, and the "upper crust" who survived the violence were routinely sent to rural areas to labor and live among the peasants. By 1967 at least 400,000 "enemies of the people" were forced to leave the cities for rural villages. Urban high school students worked in factories or on farms for 2 or more years before going on to college. Managers did laborers' jobs, and laborers participated in decision-making and management. This role-swapping was to encourage mutual respect for the other's position, but there was also a disruptive side to the process. Careers were postponed for years; many were ruined. The teenagers sent to factories and farms far from home and family were often more of a problem than a help for local management. Efficiency was sacrificed for the spirit of revolution. Moreover, the well-being of millions of young Chinese was abandoned for the revolution.

The cost in terms of human suffering is hard for the mind to grasp. Hu Yaobang, general secretary of the Communist Party, estimated that between the antirightist campaign of 1957, which prepared the ground for the Cultural Revolution, and the conclusion of the upheaval, 100 million people became victims of its violence (this is roughly one-tenth of China's population).[14]

The rapid economic and industrial development characteristic of the first half of the 1960s was also sacrificed in the Cultural Revolution, not so much by the restructuring of management practices but by the rampages of the Red Guards. In 1966 the Red Guards began a 2-year campaign during which productivity fell sharply. Industrial output decreased 15 to 20 percent in 1967 when, according to economic predictors, it should have increased by about 5 percent. It was not until 1969 that industrial productivity rose to a level above that of 1966. One of the few areas that did not experience setbacks was nuclear weapons development. In August 1966 a Central Committee communiqué backed by Zhou Enlai, who often tried in vain to moderate Red Guard actions, announced that scientists would not be targets of the Cultural

Revolution. Like other sites untouched by the Red Guards, China's nuclear research facilities carried on with the momentum of the pre–Cultural Revolution period. During the most violent years of the Cultural Revolution, 1966 and 1967, there were four successful nuclear tests.

One sector profoundly affected by the Cultural Revolution was education. The closing of schools disrupted educational continuity, but that in itself created fewer problems than the new system adopted when the schools reopened. The Maoists attacked the educational system as it existed in the mid-1960s because it was considered a remnant of the past. Education was viewed as a class-based institution, in this case, catering to the new Chinese "bourgeoisie." In general, children born to educated parents with good vocabularies, an interest in reading, and access to educational and cultural facilities fared better in school. Universities were filled with the offspring of the urban middle class, party cadres, and formerly wealthy families. Absent were significant numbers of peasant children and national minorities. The Cultural Revolution changed this. As part of the Red Guards' assault on bourgeois values, better students were ridiculed for good study habits. Those who studied the liberal arts or foreign languages were condemned because the Red Guards apparently understood Mao's point when he said, "The capitalist class is the skin; the intellectuals are the hairs that grow on the skin. When the skin dies, there will be no hair."[15] Many of the best students, who allegedly revealed traces of their bourgeois education, were sent to remote areas to labor for years, interrupting if not destroying promising careers.

An entirely new group of students entered the universities once they were reopened. Cultural Revolution admissions committees allowed only those with "correct" backgrounds to study beyond high school level. The sons and daughters of peasants and workers now had new opportunities. But if the educationally disadvantaged were to enter universities, standards had to be drastically lowered; in order for many of them to succeed at performing college-level work, academic and scientific standards had to be dropped altogether. Shorter courses and less rigid testing replaced older teaching methods. Curricula were changed to satisfy the Maoists. Political education, the thought of Mao, became as important, if not more important, than more traditional subjects. The humanities, classics, even the study of some scientific principles were now banned. Many of the best professors and teachers, particularly those with a foreign education or travel experience who might have been "contaminated" by the taint of foreign bourgeois cultures, were removed from their positions and sent to the countryside. Often they were replaced by supporters of Mao, Cultural Revolution zealots, whose academic credentials under normal circumstances hardly would have qualified them for their new positions. As a result, a generation of relatively incompetent professionals and leaders was promoted because of their experiences in the Cultural Revolution. But this group was able to bask in their success only temporarily. By the early 1980s they had become the target of hostility from a younger, better educated generation. They became a "lost generation," without skills or education, who watched their younger brothers and sisters leapfrog over them to the top.

Along with education, the arts and literature also came under heavy fire during the Cultural Revolution. Even before the Cultural Revolution had begun, Mao criticized the Ministry of Culture as a haven for revisionists who promoted "bourgeois" and "feudal" values. Mao often quipped that if the Ministry did not change, it should be renamed "the Ministry of Emperors, Kings, Generals, and Monsters, the Ministry of Talents and Beauties, or the Ministry of Foreign Mummies." In 1964 Jiang Qing declared the arts in China to be anachronistic; an entirely new art form was needed in order to reflect China's socialist economy. Condemning the state of China's arts, Jiang estimated:

> there were 3,000 theatrical companies in the country. . . . Of these, around 90 are professional modern drama companies, 80-odd are cultural troupes, and the rest, over 2,800, are companies staging various kinds of operas and balladry. Our operatic stage is occupied by emperors, princes, generals, ministers, scholars and beauties, and on top of these, ghosts and monsters. As for those 90 modern drama companies, they don't necessarily all depict the workers, peasants, and soldiers in our country, whereas there is only a handful of landlords, rich peasants, counterrevolutionaries, bad elements, Rightists, and bourgeois elements. Shall we serve this handful, or the 600 million?[16]

In order to serve the bulk of the population, socialist art had to be produced. "Model" operas and ballets and plays were written, such as *The Red Lantern, Spark Among the Reeds, Raid on White Tiger Regiment, Taking Tiger Mountain by Strategy,* and *The Red Detachment of Women,* all depicting peasants, workers, or poor young women as heroes and model citizens. Writers, directors, and performers came under the close scrutiny of Jiang. The performances of "feudal"-style plays—those depicting "ghosts" or "emperors and princes, generals and ministers, gifted scholars and beauties"—were banned. Mao also proscribed Western music, both classical and contemporary. New works were written and old works rewritten to depict revolution in a way that Mao and Jiang Qing thought appropriate. For example, the opera *The White Haired Girl,* written shortly after the Communists came to power, was based on the true story of a young peasant woman kidnapped and raped by a landlord during the chaos of World War II. Her father then commits suicide. The landlord plans to murder the girl when she becomes pregnant. She flees and lives in a cave, stealing from a village temple where peasants leave offerings of food. She saves herself and her baby, but under such conditions, her hair turns white. Eventually, she is rescued by Communist soldiers who liberate the area from the Japanese and help her denounce the landlord. She returns to the boyfriend she had before her abduction and they live happily ever after.

Despite the fact that *The White Haired Girl* had been used to promote the positive qualities of the revolution since the Communists came to power, Jiang Qing criticized the drama because the peasants were depicted as too passive. In the version rewritten during the Cultural Revolution, the heroine is not raped and she successfully resists the landlord. She eventually flees from his oppression with the help of Communist soldiers. Her father does not commit suicide, but is killed by the Japanese. The goal of this revision was to portray peasants in greater control over their fate, however unrealistic that may seem.

There was criticism of such revisions, but Jiang Qing held tight control during the Cultural Revolution. As a result, many of China's best artists, writers, playwrights, and musicians were driven out of their professions, sent off to do other jobs in factories and on farms. The creativity and rich artistic tradition of the Chinese suffered greatly.

The Cultural Revolution also affected China's status internationally. With the exception of high-ranking Huang Hua in Cairo, every member of China's diplomatic corps was recalled. This was a direct consequence of a tirade against "traitors" carried on by the Red Guards. During the summer of 1967 Red Guards occupied the Foreign Ministry in Beijing, treating senior officers with contempt and rummaging through top secret files without consideration for security. Messages were transmitted to foreign missions without the consent of senior officials. The Red Guards condemned their compatriots living overseas for their "bourgeois" lifestyles and foreign connections. Diplomats, caught in a dilemma, had no way to determine whether orders coming from Beijing to vilify imperialism or to demonstrate for Mao were valid. Disobeying such orders could have been tantamount to treason. In one instance Red Guards were responsible for virtually inciting revolution in Cambodia. A cable from the Foreign Ministry to the Cambodian Association for Friendship with China ordered the group to overthrow reigning Prince Norodom Sihanouk. When Sihanouk threatened to cut off relations with China, Premier Zhou Enlai quickly apologized to avoid further complications.

In August, several incidents occurred involving representatives from countries with which relations were already strained. A Mongolian diplomat shopping in Beijing was attacked by groups of young Chinese. The Soviet Consulate was ransacked and a diplomatic automobile torched. Red Guards and their supporters pushed into the British colony of Hong Kong, demanding that the island and surrounding territories be returned to China. They provoked Hong Kong and other overseas Chinese into supporting cultural revolutions in their homelands throughout Asia. On August 22, following a series of anti-British demonstrations, the British mission in Beijing was attacked. A diplomat, Donald Hopson, was seized and publicly humiliated, and the legation was set on fire. Chinese employees of the various embassies were attacked and beaten. Witnesses later testified that PLA soldiers and local police tried to fight off the youths but were temporarily overwhelmed. By the time reinforcements arrived, the building had burned to the ground. Such actions were not approved by Mao and Zhou Enlai. Hong Kong remained a much-needed entrepôt for foreign exchange, and it did not want to strain relations with its neighbors at a time when China was relatively isolated from much of the world community. Although the Red Guards continued their disruptive activities for nearly a year, they were eventually evicted from the Foreign Ministry by Zhou.

The Cultural Revolution wreaked terrifying havoc on China, bringing wholesale destruction to lives and property. Throughout the late 1960s the foreign press published numerous accounts of mayhem perpetrated by Red Guard fanatics to an international audience. Testimony before a United States Senate committee by a Chinese musician and victim of the Cultural Revolution, Ma Sitson, who had managed to escape from China, helped reinforce the American opinion, especially among conservatives, that the PRC should not be recognized by the United States or allowed in the United Nations. One account was of Ma Sitson's encounter with Red Guards at a school in Beijing.

> . . . A platform was set up at one side of a large courtyard for the department head and his accusers. Many people came forward out of the crowd to level accusations. The rest of us were ordered to squat in the sun and watch. It was ugly. Red Guards dragged four or five men and women—friends and neighbors who had in the past defended the man—up to the platform and swore at them. Then a guard took a real whip and began beating them. The department head was beaten most savagely of all.
>
> Somebody screamed, "You see! Look what happens to those who oppose." The poor man lay there in the sun for at least an hour. I don't know how he got back to his cell. Later on during this same meeting the Red Guards were invited to beat us too, on the pretext that we were not bowing low enough. I was cut around the head with a metal buckle.
>
> This took place during the second or third week of August 1966, when the Red Guard frenzy was at its height in Peking [Beijing]. Physical violence slacked off after that. Elsewhere in the city there were many terrible

incidents during this period. Students at one high school actually beat to
death every one of their teachers. The woman who lived next door to us in
the west city was accused of having a radio transmitter and sending messages to Chain [*sic*] Kai-shek. Red Guards pulled her from her house into
the street and killed her. People spoke of heaps of unburied bodies rotting
in the mortuaries.

Fear of this same irrational violence caused my family to run away
from Peking.[17]

The violence of the Cultural Revolution was not confined solely to urban
areas. In Long Bow Village seven competing organizations that attacked a
variety of targets were formed in 1965. William Hinton explained,

The Cultural Revolution in Long Bow gradually polarized the population,
with everyone sooner or later lining up either as "rebels" . . . or as "loyalists"
behind the *Defend Mao Tse-tung [Mao Zedong] Thought Platoon* and its
allies in his defense. . . . No one should assume any important ideological
or political differences between the two groups. . . . It was a case of the
"outs" expressing dissatisfaction with the performance of the "ins," in part
because that performance was flawed, but mainly because this expression
gave the "outs" a chance to get in.[18]

The ultimate irony is that what was supposed to have been a cultural
revolution became instead a revolution against culture. For in the end the
Cultural Revolution destroyed culture, at least that part of the social matrix
that includes core values and beliefs. The wholesale assault on tradition, family, and personal relationships undermined any semblance of spiritual values,
honor, dignity, and social status. In short, the Cultural Revolution destroyed
everything that gives meaning to life.

The guilt felt by those who survived was pervasive and perverse. "None of
us are innocent, not even those who were victims," confessed Zhao Wenhao,
a Cultural Revolution survivor interviewed by the American historian Anne
Thurston. Why? Because all of us, said Zhao, had to speak things we did not
believe. And many innocent people were hurt by such lies. Even those who
had believed that Mao and the party were China's saviors ultimately saw the
errors of their thinking, and then felt guilt for having been so unthinking,
for having followed so blindly.[19] In Thurston's view, the Cultural Revolution represented not merely a "rupture in conscience" but also a failure in
morality. After Mao and his minions had destroyed all vestiges of traditional
culture, there were no absolute moral standards against which anything could
be measured. Of course the party was supposed to be the ultimate measure of

right and wrong, but the Cultural Revolution had questioned the integrity of that as well. The ethical bankruptcy of Communist China was captured by the writer Liang Heng, whose father, under the pressure of rectification, lost his moral compass. The only advice he could give his children was never to give their opinions on anything. It was too difficult to tell what is right or wrong: "Just believe Chairman Mao's words, they're the only thing that seems to be reliable anymore."[20]

The wide-scale violence and pandemic chaos of the Cultural Revolution raises a number of questions about its ultimate meaning and purpose. It is not entirely clear, for example, how Mao and a small number of loyal followers could have generated such highly motivated fury among millions of people. The emotional intensity and scale of popular anger that accompanied the Cultural Revolution may have some relationship with the administrative policies initiated by the party in the late 1950s and 1960s as it tried to achieve ambitious goals quickly but with scarce human and natural resources.

Immediately after liberation, the new regime was faced with a serious shortage of skilled personnel who were loyal to communism. Nor was the population as a whole sufficiently educated to serve the imperatives of modern economic development. The solution to these problems from the beginning was to mobilize the population through slogans, the employment of political labels, and violence calculated to frighten people into supporting the party's revolutionary social programs. In this context the "red versus expert" issue quickly became enmeshed in a "means-ends" problem. The mass campaigns were a short-term gain in that they cut the expense that a slow cultivation of mass compliance with revolutionary rule would have required. But they created serious problems for the long haul. The administrative resources generated by raising the hopes of career advancement through campaigns had a steep cost. When the state could not pay the bill, thereby satisfying the promises given to mass leadership groups, and moved on to other projects, the anger and popular energy that the party had roused could not be turned off easily. In this context Mao himself was simply one of several factors contributing to the maelstrom of discontent. By deciding to constrain the police apparatus against the Red Guards and their enemies, Mao became, in effect, the "spark" that ignited a conflagration of anarchistic violence. In the absence of a public security system, there was nothing to control the furies of frustrated individuals and status groups. In the words of Lynn White, Mao pulled "the pin on a grenade that he did not make alone, and whose effects no one could surely predict."[21]

The turmoil of the Cultural Revolution led many foreign observers to question the stability of the Chinese government and its leaders, particularly Mao Zedong. In the end, Mao regained authority at the expense of the lives of millions of Chinese. But the support Mao received from the military almost backfired on him with fatal results.

The Rise and Fall of Lin Biao

During the Cultural Revolution the army achieved a position within the government unprecedented in Chinese history. A characteristic of both traditional and post-1949 governments had been the dominance of the civilian sector over the military. In Confucian China the military was held in contempt. Although this changed somewhat in the modern period because of the need for a skilled army, civilian leadership always dominated the Chinese political scene. Moreover, in Leninist tradition the army was subservient to the Communist Party. These precedents were challenged during the Cultural Revolution by the accomplishments of Mao Zedong's chosen successor, Marshal Lin Biao.

In 1959 Mao and his supporters chose Lin to replace the purged Peng Dehuai as minister of defense. Lin was an ardent supporter of Mao and Mao's philosophy, and he used his considerable influence over his soldiers to ensure their political indoctrination. Like Mao, Lin Biao advocated the primacy of "correct" attitudes and political reliability. He was elevated to the position of a bona fide theorist and interpreter of Mao's philosophy with the publication in 1965 of a lengthy tract entitled "Long Live the Victory of People's War." Here he expounded on the validity of Maoist theory for the contemporary international scene. A major section of Lin's essay was a laudatory overview of Mao's military victories against the Japanese and the Nationalists. This was followed by an acerbic attack on the "Liuists," "Khrushchev revisionists" as Lin labeled them, who were deemed to be in league with imperialists like the United States in Vietnam because they peddled such "rubbish" as "peaceful co-existence, peaceful transition, and peaceful competition." Lin made an impassioned appeal to the masses, insisting that they could alter the world's injustices, just as Mao was urging them to rectify the problems at home with a Cultural Revolution.

To most observers, both in and outside of China, Lin Biao appeared to be one of Mao's closest comrade-in-arms, virtually his alter ego. It had been Lin who cleared the way for Mao's return to Beijing when the People's Liberation Army was ordered to the city at the outset of the Cultural Revolution. By 1966 Lin had become famous, if not notorious, for his unrelenting and consistent praise of Mao. But Mao was uneasy about this hagiologic barrage. In a letter to his wife, Jiang Qing, on July 18, 1966, Mao expressed doubts about Lin's trustworthiness. Lin had recently delivered a speech to the Politburo in which he cited many examples of bloody coups d'état in world history. This was followed by other similar speeches that caused both Mao and Jiang alarm. At this time Jiang had been working closely with Lin; indeed, Lin had been responsible for Jiang's appointment as cultural adviser to the army the previous February.

Lin's rise continued during the Cultural Revolution. As the Red Guards elevated Mao to a near deity, Lin assumed the role of court panegyric. Mao's *Little Red Book*, a collection of his quotations known as the Red Guard "Bible," was created and edited by Lin's staff. Lin's praise was endless and excessive. The flavor of such hyperbolics can be savored in a 1967 speech given in honor of Mao, later printed in the *Peking Review*:

> It is Comrade Mao Zedong, the great teacher of the world proletariat of our time, who in the new historical conditions, has systematically summed up the historical experience of the dictatorship of the proletariat in the world, scientifically analyzed the contradictions in the socialist society, profoundly shown the laws of class struggle in socialist society and put forward a whole set of theory, line, principles, methods and policies for the continuation of the revolution under the dictatorship of the proletariat. With supreme courage and wisdom, Chairman Mao had successfully led the great Proletarian Cultural Revolution in history. This is an extremely important landmark, demonstrating that Marxism-Leninism has developed to the state of Mao Zedong's thoughts.[22]

Meanwhile, Lin began to protect his exalted stature by surrounding himself with loyal followers and protégés. The march to Beijing and the subsequent arrest of Peng Zhen's supporters had allowed Lin to place loyal associates in strategic jobs, many of which were with the press. But this was merely the beginning. When the minister of culture and director of the Central Committee's Propaganda Department was purged in June 1966, Lin made sure that one of his protégés got the job. This gave him control of the media. Mao's decision in January 1967 to use the army to stop the Red Guards and quell the violence provided Lin with yet another opportunity to enhance his power. Now he had the opportunity to take over the leadership of the Red Guards, who had permeated virtually the entire country. Moreover, Lin had made certain that the PLA was well represented on the "revolutionary committees" that replaced CCP leadership in local, provincial, and national governing structures. As a result, much of the government, the media, industry, agriculture, and education came to be dominated by the military, and Lin managed to fill the vacuum created by the purged leadership several times during the Cultural Revolution. Now the military, under Lin's direction, found itself in the unprecedented position of being able to dominate the Chinese bureaucracy.

By mid-1967 it was clear to the Chinese public that Lin was Mao's devoted follower and obvious successor. Despite any misgivings Mao or Jiang may have had about Lin's true loyalties (and it remains uncertain whether Jiang's reminiscences recorded in 1981 after the failure of Lin's plot were distorted), his career continued to climb at a meteoric pace. At the Ninth Party Congress in April 1969, Lin was designated as Mao's successor. But Lin was at the top of a slippery slope, one that his mentor Mao was not inclined to make more secure. As early as the summer of 1966, Mao wrote to his wife about his concerns over the positions and responsibilities that both she and Lin had assumed during the Cultural Revolution. Prophetically he warned:

> Things always go toward the opposite side. The higher a thing is blown up, the more seriously it is hurt at the fall. . . . I suggest that you should also pay attention to this problem and should not become dizzy with success. You should remind yourself often of your weak points, shortcomings, and mistakes. On this I have talked with you numerous times. . . .[23]

In this correspondence Mao also revealed that he felt Lin Biao had inappropriately stirred up the Red Guards and others with his endless praise of Mao. By creating Mao, the deity, Lin was promoting his own career. Under Lin's guidance, Mao's thought, circulated widely in the *Little Red Book*, had become dogma. Mao commented on this unique phenomenon in Chinese history:

> I have never believed that a few small books of mine could have that kind of supernatural power, but under his [Lin's] sponsorship the whole country came to praise them. . . . I am forced to go along with him as it seems I have no choice but to agree. On questions of great importance, this is the first time that I agree with others against my own will.[24]

Anticipating a power struggle with Lin, Mao wrote:

> They [Lin Biao and the military] want to defeat our party and myself . . . but we cannot make this kind of talk public now, since the Leftists [supposedly Mao's supporters] are also speaking in the same manner. If we speak publicly, it will be like pouring cold water on them for the benefit of the Rightists [Liuists]. Our present task is to defeat the Rightists . . . , and then after seven or eight years we will start another campaign to sweep away the devils and demons. . . . [25]

Mao's prediction proved correct, but the showdown came sooner than expected. At the end of 1968 Mao made an appeal to the army asking its members to be responsible for rebuilding a new civilian party. This turned out to be a warning that the military's control over most of the institutions throughout the country would be temporary. Meanwhile, Mao joined with Zhou Enlai in revamping the CCP and restoring it as the primary political institution. Many former CCP leaders who had been mistreated during the Cultural Revolution returned to their former positions of power. Mao and Zhou drafted a new state constitution in which the party's power structure was revised, including the abolition of the office of president of the PRC, Liu Shaoqi's former position and a title that Lin Biao coveted. This office was important to Lin because, as heir-apparent to Mao's title of chairman of the party, he would eventually hold the two titles that Mao had held for many years. Lin then theoretically would become more powerful than Premier Zhou Enlai, who had maintained his stature and power by being consistent in his support of Mao throughout the Cultural Revolution. He voted for the dismissal of Liu Shaoqi and Deng Xiaoping, but he also squelched the Red Guards who took over the Foreign Ministry. Zhou survived these volatile years, although by the end of the Cultural Revolution he, too, had become a target of the Red Guards, a problem that apparently did not upset Lin Biao. Mao and Zhou presented the draft of the new constitution to the CCP in August 1970 at a conference in Lushan where, as a result, Mao and his supporters openly quarreled with Lin. Lin's group was charged, often by party stalwarts who had been victims of the Cultural Revolution, with promoting "revisionism," "splitism," and "conspiracy." Not to be outdone, Lin turned to his generals for support in an attempt to hold on to his position as Mao's successor by forcing CCP leaders to guarantee his succession. While Mao fought to deny these demands, Lin took action on his own. According to Zhou Enlai, Lin's group made an unsuccessful attempt to assassinate Mao at the conference.

Mao struck back. He began by attacking one of Lin's staunchest supporters, the former member of the Cultural Revolution Group Chen Boda. In this way, Mao temporarily could avoid directly confronting Lin, which would risk rebellion by the army. Lin, soon realizing that he himself would be the next target, organized several secret plans to do away with Mao and his supporters. Jiang Qing later recalled that Lin's men had drawn up maps of Mao's and others' residences with the intention of bombing them. She also claimed that he had intended to kidnap Mao's two daughters. Moreover, she alleged that Lin's men, for more than a year, had poisoned the food prepared for Mao and Jiang, making them both very ill. Jiang said her illness temporarily affected her brain and memory, and that it took her 2 years to recover completely.

During the spring of 1971 Lin took decisive action by planning a coup, the details of which still remain sketchy and secret. Lin's son, Lin Liguo, an air force general and deputy commander of the air operations command, allegedly drew up the plans. There was talk of using chemical or bacteriological weapons, bombs, an arranged car accident, assassination, kidnapping, or even urban guerrilla units. But the plans failed. It appears that Lin was counting on Moscow's support in the succession crisis, especially because he allegedly told the Soviets that he planned to thwart the upcoming Sino-American talks of 1971 and 1972. Soon after Lin and his supporters knew of Mao's impending challenge, they panicked. Lin ordered a plane to his summer residence; but his request was denied. When his son obtained a Trident Jet, Lin's family and six others took off for Mongolia on September 13, 1971. While landing to refuel in Mongolia, the wings struck the ground and the plane exploded. Lin's other supporters had left in a helicopter, but were forced down by the air force. According to the Chinese government, documents providing further evidence of the attempted coup were soon discovered.

Lin Biao's life and once brilliant career ended in disgrace. During the summer of 1972, Mao mounted the "Criticize Lin, Criticize Confucius" campaign to discredit Lin and his actions during the Cultural Revolution. Lin was blamed for many of the excesses of that tragic period and labeled a "closet Confucianist," "bourgeois careerist," conspirator, double-dealer, and ultimately an "ultra-rightist." These obviously contradictory criticisms were heaped on a man who had been a brilliant general and one of Mao's closest friends. Zhou Enlai's 1974 speech criticizing Lin virtually paraphrased Lin's 1969 denunciation of Liu Shaoqi. Lin Biao was blamed for nearly everything that went wrong in China during the late 1960s.

The Gang of Four

By the mid-1970s Mao Zedong's health was rapidly failing. He had begun to suffer from Parkinson's disease years before, and its debilitating effect on his coordination was exacerbated by a stroke that left him partially paralyzed. Premier Zhou Enlai, who headed the state apparatus, suffered from cancer. These circumstances allowed Jiang Qing to assume her most powerful role, carrying out Mao's as well as her own directives and making a bid to become Mao's successor. Her allies were three associates from Shanghai who had supported Mao during the Cultural Revolution: Wang Hongwen and Zhang Chunqiao, both members of the Cultural Revolution Group, and Yao Wenyuan, another group member who had helped Mao in the early stages of the Cultural Revolution by criticizing the play *Hai Rui Dismissed from Office*. Jiang Qing and these three men collectively became known as the "Gang of Four," a nickname coined by Mao himself.

The beginning of the succession crisis that pitted Jiang and her associates against the older and often more conservative CCP members came in January 1976 with the death of Premier Zhou Enlai. Zhou had enjoyed an impressive career in the CCP. Because of his birth into a gentry family, Zhou began his education in the best schools. He later studied in Japan and in 1920 traveled to France, where he was a student for 4 years. There he and his compatriot Deng Xiaoping joined the Chinese Communist Youth Corps, a group that organized Chinese laborers sent to France to aid in postwar reconstruction. An early CCP member, Zhou survived every power struggle and maintained a strong position among the upper echelons of the government and party leadership. Zhou also earned the respect of the international community. Many of his contemporaries considered him to be one of the world's most sophisticated and knowledgeable leaders.

In 1976, Zhou's awareness of his imminent death from cancer caused him to look for a successor. In 1973 he rehabilitated his old friend Deng Xiaoping, who had been purged during the Cultural Revolution. Mao agreed to the return of Deng, known to be a pragmatist who had never agreed with Mao on the need for permanent revolution, to restore order to the chaos resulting from the Cultural Revolution. Moreover, in 1973 the PLA had not yet relinquished its hold over government institutions. Deng's help was needed to counterbalance the power of the military. Once returned to a position of power, he immediately began a "reversal of verdicts" for victims of the Cultural Revolution like himself. This, of course, angered both the PLA and the Leftists led by Jiang Qing and her group. Deng nevertheless continued to be groomed for succession—a situation that caused serious problems for Jiang's plans to gain control of the CCP.

By the time of Zhou's death, Deng had already spent close to 3 years trying to solidify his former authority. But although he had replaced Zhou in carrying out many state functions and was thought by many of his followers in the CCP to be the obvious choice for the title of acting premier, Deng disappeared again only days after Zhou's death: Mao's illness had progressed to the point where Deng was unable to control the political maneuverings of Jiang Qing. Taking advantage of Mao's weakened state, Jiang and her associates published an article in the *People's Daily*, China's leading newspaper, attacking leaders such as Deng, who had taken the "capitalist road." Jiang pushed for the appointment of Zhang Chunqiao, a second vice-premier and member of the "Gang," to replace Deng. But she faced opposition from the entrenched CCP leadership and Mao, who, depleted in vigor and not prepared for yet another battle, arranged a compromise by designating Hua Guofeng as his successor. Hua, a Maoist, did not have a following among either the conservatives or Jiang's group. He was carefully groomed by Mao's supporters so that he would be perceived by the masses as Mao's chosen heir. Even his official portrait, including hairstyle and expression, were designed to show a physical resemblance to Mao.

Hua's term in office proved to be problematic. While Jiang continued to push her candidate, Zhang Chunqiao, for the position of premier, other forces surfaced reflecting widespread dissatisfaction with the Maoist leadership. The event that came to symbolize the conflict was the Tiananmen Incident on April 5, 1976. According to Chinese tradition, ancestral tombs are visited each spring, and in 1976 large numbers of people went to Beijing's Tiananmen Square to visit the Monument to the People's Heroes, which was widely known as Zhou Enlai's symbolic tomb. When police removed flowers placed at the tomb, protests began. On April 5, 100,000 demonstrators arrived at Tiananmen Square with placards praising Zhou and Deng Xiaoping and criticizing Mao and his followers. The crowd shouted, "The era of Qin Shihuang is gone," referring to the ancient first emperor of China with whom Mao had become identified. Soon becoming violent, the protesters battled fiercely with police and militia and attacked automobiles and military apparatus. Three days later, the CCP leadership lashed back at the "capitalist-roaders" like Deng, presumed responsible for the demonstration, with a staged counterdemonstration in support of Mao and Hua Guofeng. Meanwhile, the Gang of Four continued its intrigues against Hua.

On September 9, 1976, Mao Zedong died at age eighty-two after a long illness. His death was a shock to the Chinese people. No one could rival his prestige and power. Mao had become the symbol of Chinese communism. Moreover, a lack of standardized procedure through which high-level leadership could be transferred peacefully created a succession crisis that Jiang Qing was quick to manipulate. She used this opportunity to move against Hua, Mao's chosen successor.

Jiang and her associates held considerable power in 1976 as a result of their role in the Cultural Revolution and their connection with Mao. The Gang controlled much of the media and the schools, but this proved to be insufficient. Taking a page out of Mao's book on survival, Jiang hoped to use the military in her bid to depose Hua. Because the Gang's power base was in Shanghai, one of its first moves was to strengthen the one-million-strong Shanghai militia. Jiang also received the backing of Mao's nephew, Mao Yuanxin, who was the political commissar of the Shenyang Military Region in northeast China. He helped Jiang lay plans for a coup, which would involve a march south from Shenyang toward Beijing. But the ambitious Jiang overplayed her hand when she tried to enlist the support of other regional commanders. Not only did they spurn her offer but one even decided to inform Hua of the Gang's plans.

Hua's initial appointment had not been supported by either Jiang or the older CCP leaders, and now he found sufficient cause to move into the camp of Jiang's enemies, men in the Politburo who did not support her bid for power. Hua also joined forces with Deng Xiaoping, who had gone into hiding in Guangzhou (Canton) to escape Jiang's followers. Even though they held different political views, Hua and Deng were now drawn together by a common enemy. They proved to be a formidable force.

By September 1976 the swords were drawn. During a Politburo meeting Jiang openly attacked Hua Guofeng and other CCP leaders. She accused Hua of incompetence and demanded that she be appointed chairman of the Central Committee. Hua, in turn, warned that he had the power of several army generals behind him. After failing to make any headway in the Politburo, the Gang laid plans for a coup, which was to occur on October 6. Mao Yuanxin prepared to send reinforcements from Shenyang to Beijing, while Jiang's men planned to utilize one of the Beijing regiments to take over the government. But these plans were never carried out. On October 5 in a secret meeting Hua and the allies of Deng Xiaoping at PLA headquarters decided to arrest the Gang before they could strike. Hua invited Jiang and her three supporters to meet in emergency session at midnight on October 5. Two of the three men, Zhang Chunqiao and Yao Wenyuan, fell for the ruse and were promptly seized by the police. Wang Hongwen tried to resist and killed two guards before he himself was wounded. Jiang, who failed to show up for the meeting, was arrested at her home on the same night. They were then held in separate locations in Beijing. Mao Yuanxin and several others who allegedly cooperated with Jiang were also arrested.

Hua was now in what appeared to be a secure position, not only as premier but also as the newly appointed chairman of the CCP, the office previously coveted by Jiang. Three days after the arrests were made, the "smashing of the Gang of Four" was announced to the public at dozens of rallies throughout the country. On October 24 a celebration commemorating the Gang's fall and attended by more than one million people was held in Tiananmen Square. Jiang and her associates were publicly accused of a litany of crimes, including forcing the Chinese people to live in fear, attacking CCP members, attempting to destroy the economy, creating civil war, restricting foreign trade, ruining the education system, and adversely influencing Chinese cultural development. They were actually charged with four categories of crimes, which included persecuting CCP members and state leaders while plotting to overthrow the government; persecuting, killing, and torturing more than 34,000 people; plotting an armed uprising in Shanghai; and plotting to assassinate Mao Zedong.

Their trial was not held until November 1980. The Gang of Four, with six other co-defendants who had attempted to defect with Lin Biao, were tried together. Jiang was accused of being the mastermind behind the conspiracy. The proceedings were volatile. Jiang defiantly charged her accusers in the CCP with blaming her for supporting Mao's goals both during the Cultural

Revolution and after his death. After two months of testimony, the judges took three weeks to deliberate. The verdicts were handed down on January 25, 1981. Jiang Qing and Zhang Chunqiao received death sentences with 2-year suspended executions. Wang Hongwen was given life in prison. Yao Wenyuan received 20 years in jail, while the others were given sentences ranging from 16 to 20 years. Apparently, the Gang's association with Mao prevented the leadership from quickly executing all the defendants.

Conclusion

The era of the Cultural Revolution came to an end with the fall of the Gang of Four. Its sudden demise so soon after Mao's death demonstrated not only apprehension concerning Jiang's potential power but also the general dissatisfaction of the CCP leadership with Maoist policy. With the Gang out of power, many former leaders and intellectuals who had been purged during the Cultural Revolution were returned to their old positions, and gradually China's domestic and foreign policies began to change. The party leadership was faced with both a challenge and an opportunity to adapt Mao's thought to a "revolutionary modernization" for China. In 1976 Hua Guofeng stressed the need for "integrating theory with practice" in order to further economic development. The Gang, on the other hand, was criticized by one CCP leader for "completely ignoring the minimum common sense of Marxism."[26] It had promoted a program that so alienated the masses that it caused political chaos and a rapid deterioration of the socialist system; this brought home to the new administration the importance of being more sensitive to the needs and demands of the people.

The legacy of the Cultural Revolution haunted China for decades. Although the Chinese economy did not suffer the irreversible setbacks that many of Mao's detractors have claimed, long-term prospects for China's social well-being and economic growth were seriously compromised, as were the careers of many future leaders. The best and brightest among them were criticized and sent off to work in the countryside, at best postponing and at worst ending promising futures. Their revolutionary counterparts, supporters of the Maoist line, were often pushed through universities with a substandard education and by the 1980s constituted a "lost generation" of young to middle-aged men and women who were underqualified to hold the kinds of positions demanded by China's modernization program.

The experience also created a legacy of bitterness and a disillusionment with communism among the young who had been exploited for political purposes. Anger that was triggered by the consciousness-raising cultural upheavals would offer new possibilities for the future, none of which would bode well for hard-line party leaders. In the words of one former Red Guard who carefully surveyed the destruction of Mao's experiment:

> I began to ask questions about the fit between feudal Chinese culture and Mao's terrifying version of communism, about why there was a discrepancy between the beautiful words described in our books and the harsh reality around us. Many called us China's "lost generation," for we had awakened to the folly of our traditions, with their passion for hierarchy and obedience to authority.[27]

The impact of the Cultural Revolution on Chinese culture was not erased. The Marxist notion that the values and beliefs of the state reflect the interest of economically determined classes was the stimulus behind Mao's goal to produce a proletarian culture. Although the Maoists' plans were not completely successful, significant changes in the arts were made. The production of model plays, operas, dances, and musical compositions reflecting the plight of the masses or revolutionary themes continued. The post-Mao leadership did not completely erase this aspect of the Cultural Revolution, but brought back some of the old to accompany the new. For example, in 1976 the opera *The White Haired Girl* was restored to its original version based on the story of a rape of a peasant girl during World War II. This version was considered a more realistic portrayal of the brutal conditions in the countryside. Jiang's critics mocked her revision in which a young woman resisted the powerful landlord.

Another question that lingers from the era of the Cultural Revolution concerns the role Mao played in the crimes and abuses associated with the Gang of Four. Jiang brought up this issue at her trial. If they were merely carrying out his directives, then why was Mao not posthumously criticized for his conduct? The sensitivity of this issue for the CCP leadership was demonstrated by the fact that it took more than four years for the Gang's trial to take place. The new leadership was careful to assure that Mao remained the revered hero of the Chinese revolution throughout this period. Despite the fact that Deng Xiaoping wrote that the Cultural Revolution was a mistake for which Mao was responsible, Mao's thought still provides some of the theoretical underpinnings for China's present development. Just as Soviet leader Nikita Khrushchev criticized his predecessor Joseph Stalin's tactics while not undoing his accomplishments, China's post-Mao leadership kept many of the changes made during the Cultural Revolution as a way of building bridges to the future. The leaders then embarked on a revision of Mao's philosophy to launch a new modernization campaign now known as China's Second Revolution.

10

A Second Revolution

The Reforms of Deng Xiaoping

Deng Xiaoping (1904–1997)

After Mao's death in 1976, Deng Xiaoping came to the forefront among China's leaders and began a series of reforms that touched almost every segment of society. The changes in agriculture, industry, education, and even in party leadership had many China watchers writing about a "second revolution," one that would make China a serious competitor in the world economy and bring prosperity to greater numbers of Chinese than at any time since 1949. Moreover, Deng's policies opened China to Western culture. Deng's

"Four Modernizations"—in agriculture, industry, science and technology, and national defense—contrasted starkly with Mao's plans, and many of the changes were dramatic reversals of Mao's policies during the Cultural Revolution. Mao had stressed the need for ideological remolding, while Deng called for economic and technological change. Mao espoused class struggle, while Deng talked of unity among the classes. Mao demanded economic self-sufficiency, while Deng opened China to international trade, investment, and joint ventures—from capitalist and socialist nations alike. Mao taught that increased production, and therefore progress, could be achieved through ideological motivation. Deng used material incentives to get people to work harder. In 1978, the return to the "red" versus "expert" debate saw the experts at the helm once more. Even without his erstwhile colleague Liu Shaoqi, who died in prison in 1969, Deng's reforms during the 1980s went far beyond what Liu Shaoqi had envisioned 20 years earlier. Liu had endorsed a model for development more similar to that used in the Soviet Union, while Deng, with his support of private enterprise, created a new model for China.

Reforms in Agriculture

Of all the changes that comprise the "second revolution," agricultural reforms were clearly the most far-reaching and successful. China's farmers quickly became the most efficient in the world in terms of output per acre. They fed 22 percent of the world's population on 7 percent of the globe's arable land. In December 1978 the Third Plenary Session of the Eleventh Central Committee of the CCP heard that 150 million Chinese were starving. During the following decade, farm output grew by 4 percent per year for grain and 15 percent per year for cotton. China was transformed from a large grain importer to a net exporter. Visitors began to notice shops and open-air markets overflowing with fresh produce. Per-capita food consumption rose by almost 50 percent.

The party adopted a policy that called for "readjustment, restructuring, consolidation, and improvement" in the countryside. CCP economist Chen Yun, the architect of the 1957 rural revitalization program rejected by Mao, authored the plan. But the real force behind the changes was Deng Xiaoping, who finally implemented a proposal he had made to Mao back in the early 1960s and for which he was later purged: a program that championed the individual peasant household as the foundation of the Chinese economy. The program involved a series of changes in landownership, farm size, and price setting.

The 50,000 communes, which had been the chief economic unit since the Great Leap Forward, were eliminated by Deng's first major reform in the landownership system. From 1978 to 1984, village authorities were ordered to divide up communally held land into equal portions, based on size and quality. Each village household received one or more parcels, in many cases by drawing lots, so that every household controlled a farm. Farmers contracted with the government for long-term leases, perhaps fifteen to 20 years, and they could manage their land as they pleased, as long as they delivered a certain predetermined portion of their crops to the state for a prearranged price. Moreover, the leases could be passed on to their children.

Deng's experiment with "private" farming was a rapid and enormous success. Individual peasant households no longer saw their own hard work benefit their neighbors or the commune bureaucracy; they produced for themselves. Introducing a free market was the key to growth. Farmers sold their surplus at rural markets or transported produce to cities. They also were allowed to engage in sideline occupations. Entrepreneurial endeavors flourished, including privately run repair shops for televisions, radios, bicycles, and motorcycles; barbershops; shoe repair services; and various sorts of household service companies. One peasant from Hebei described his situation for the *China Daily*, an English-language newspaper.

> In 1982 I became prosperous on the sly. In 1983 I had to be brave to remain prosperous. In 1984 I can be prosperous without any worry.[1]

Creative peasants improved their lives; indeed, by Chinese standards they were becoming wealthy, giving credence to the popular slogan "To get rich is glorious." Some were able to buy televisions and refrigerators, out-of-reach luxuries just a few years earlier. Industrious peasants used a variety of innovations that helped create an economic miracle. Many peasants fused traditional methods with modern technology. While farming remained labor-intensive, backbreaking work done mostly by hand, peasants adopted some new technology, such as the application of transparent plastic sheeting, which protects crops and reduces the need for water in areas otherwise difficult to cultivate. In addition to the traditional animal and human wastes, chemical fertilizers are used as well. Veterinarians use acupuncture to treat animals, but instead of employing traditional needles, they work with laser beams.[2]

The ability of China's peasants to achieve enormous increases in productivity on their new small farms dazzled many foreign observers. China has only about 100 million arable acres of farmland. When the communes were divided, that translated into farms of about three-quarters of an acre for each peasant household. This, of course, drastically altered planting and harvesting methods. The small farms were intensively managed family gardens, replacing the 1,000-plus-acre tracts often farmed by more than 10,000 rural workers on communal land. The results of such changes were described by one anthropologist in 1984:

> When I first visited the Zengbu brigade there [in Guangdong], in 1979, there was virtually nothing in the market. When I went back in 1981, things had started to pick up. But when I returned in 1983 I couldn't believe what I saw. There were hundreds of people selling things. There were tanks of live fish, and piles of fruit and vegetables heaped up everywhere. Lots of pigs were being slaughtered for meat—something you rarely saw in the past. You could buy Coca-Cola, Budweiser beer, and foreign cigarettes at private shops. The prosperity was impressive.[3]

A combination of hard work and incentives led to profits for peasants during the first few years of Deng's program. However, the relatively small size of individual farms became a problem that threatened to undo the egalitarianism in the countryside. One of Deng's goals was to modernize farming techniques, employing chemical fertilizers, machinery, and large-scale irrigation projects, especially because the rapid increase in grain production leveled off by 1987. Efficient use of expensive technology requires vast acreage and less labor. This could lead to the necessity of recombining farms for the sake of greater efficiency, a process that began as a result of economic forces, not by CCP mandate.

Peasants who succeeded as a result of their family's hard work and/or good fortune can hire less successful farmers as wage laborers and rent their neighbors' land. The development of a new "class" of rich peasants has been an ironic result of Deng's reforms, and it has generated tension in the rural areas. Accusations against rich peasants have ranged from their unwillingness to cooperate with their neighbors in communal projects, such as irrigation canals and wells, to the exploitation of unsuccessful peasants as cheap labor. On the other hand, these efficient, hardworking peasants seem to be model farmers and are likely to be the beneficiaries in the future mechanization of the countryside. This process is reminiscent of the progress made by Russia's peasants during the 1920s under Lenin's New Economic Policy (NEP). But Lenin's successor, Stalin, had no tolerance for the "rich" Russian peasants, the kulaks, and in the 1930s they were destroyed as a class. So far, the CCP has been unwilling to reverse the development of "classes" in the Chinese countryside.

Price increases for farm products were another of Deng's significant reforms. From 1980 to 1985 the government raised the prices it paid for crops an average of 50 percent. Grain prices went up nearly 100 percent. This reform was long overdue, but even these apparently sizable increases did not bring prices up to what could be realized on the free market. As a result, farmers were forced to sell the amount contracted by the government at below market prices; refusal to do so would quite likely lead to government confiscation of their land. Although the government remains the largest purchaser of staples, such as grains, flourishing rural markets combined with the higher prices have been the source of increased peasant production and, therefore, incomes that have outstripped most predictions. The 1984 grain harvest, for example, overshot the target planned by the 1978 reform program for the year 2000.

After 1987 the rise in grain production leveled off. Several factors have been blamed for this. The efficiency of the small farms had been perfected after nearly a decade of "private" farming, so that the miraculous increases after the breakup of the communes came to an end. Price reforms also contributed to smaller grain harvests. The government kept contract prices low so that the 200 million urban workers on fixed wages did not have to cope with even more inflation than that caused by fluctuating free market prices. Despite this practice, Deng's government subsidized urban food prices in order to keep prices down. In 1984 alone, food subsidies cost about 17 billion *yuan*. (During the 1980s, one Chinese *yuan* was roughly equal in value to U.S. $0.50.) To avoid the less profitable government grain contracts, many farmers turned to raising vegetables or livestock, which brought higher prices. Moreover, livestock are often fed grains that could be used to feed the cities. After 1984, grain supplies declined by about 4 percent, and inflation caused food prices to increase consistently.

Intensive farming of relatively little land has resulted in other problems. Soil exhaustion threatens any gains made. The prevention of soil erosion has become a national concern, and it will take substantial investment to prevent future disaster.

Several additional destructive side effects of the agricultural reforms have had an impact on peasant life. Because an effectively managed farm can produce considerable wealth for rural families, the entire family's labor is exploited, often at the expense of the children's education. Many children are required by their families to work in the fields instead of attending school. Increased rural illiteracy, compared with the Maoist years, is an alarming trend that has accompanied Deng's reforms.

The one-child policy, pushed by the CCP since the late 1970s, is often ignored in the countryside because more children mean more farm labor and potentially more wealth. But a second or third child is heavily taxed under Chinese law, so some peasant families are not recording the births of their "extra" children. These unregistered children will eventually become adults who will not receive the benefits of an ordinary citizen, such as education, working papers, licenses, or health insurance. They constitute a fledgling "outlaw group" and could pose a serious threat to the stability of the countryside.

The one-child policy has also placed a premium on male children, which has led to the return of the age-old practice of female infanticide. Boys are not only considered better workers, but traditional marriage customs—the bride going to live with her husband's family, for example—are still practiced in many rural areas. A daughter is lost as a laborer to her husband's family once she marries, while a son brings an extra worker to the household. Moreover, the son has an obligation to care for his aging parents. A couple without a son has no security for their old age. In 1982 the *China Youth News* reported that in some parts of rural China, up to 80 percent of the surviving infants were male. In March 1983, the *People's Daily* wrote that a representative of the All-China Women's Federation claimed that:

> the drowning and killing of girl infants and the maltreatment of mothers of infant girls . . . have become a grave social problem. These phenomena are found not only in deserted mountain villages but also in cities; not only in the families of ordinary workers and peasants but also in the families of Party members and cadres.[4]

Reforms in Industry

The industrial sector was also a target of Deng's reform program, and the result was phenomenal growth in rural industry and some improvement in urban areas. China's centrally planned economy emphasized heavy industry and was tightly controlled by the CCP. Deng's plan, on the other hand, was characterized by a shift toward the production of consumer goods for sale both at home and abroad. In addition, Deng decentralized the economy. In the wake of these organizational changes, an unusual form of joint stock company emerged, in which shares are owned by various institutions controlled by the CCP. This new form of ownership resulted in a revitalization of stagnating industries, particularly in the countryside. The government also leased factories to workers and thus put responsibility for production in the hands of the producers. Worker-owned companies, for the most part, are smaller enterprises, many of which are found in suburbs or rural areas.

In 1987 approximately 4 million small companies produced about half of China's industrial output. They were largely responsible for the 266 percent increase in output from rural industry between 1982 and 1986. For example, the village of Yuwajai in Shaanxi Province produced only wheat before 1979. The peasants there earned a subsistence level of 130 *yuan* (approximately U.S. $65) per year and starved when the wheat crop failed. By 1987, 22 small factories, none of which existed before Deng's reforms, employed 1,100 out of 1,300 village workers, and income had risen to an average of 930 *yuan* per year.[5] Many factories were started with relatively little investment by peasants who had benefited from the reforms and answered demands for consumer goods and services. Other companies were subsidized by village, county, provincial, or army funds. Many companies expanded rapidly with reinvestment of profits.

Rural industry flourished, with 120 million peasants in 1987 employed in CCP-approved sideline jobs in small factories, repair shops, and cottage industries, but the heart of China's industry, the large state-owned factories, did not see much growth during the 1980s. Many remained inefficient, and some failed to make a profit. In 1986, for example, according to a CIA report, 20 percent of these factories recorded a loss. The problems of these failing industries were the legacy of the Maoist years. Nearly a decade later, in 1995, large state-owned industries were still responsible for approximately 60 percent of Chinese manufacturing.

One of the obstacles to change in the state-owned sector is the unique role Chinese factories played in the lives of their workers. The workplace, the unit, or *danwei*, was the source of a person's identity during the Maoist years. Until 1987, workers were assigned to a job for life with little chance of changing jobs or moving unless they somehow arranged for an exchange with another person working elsewhere. Most large factories continued to be responsible for employees' housing, recreational facilities, and various welfare benefits, including health care, unemployment insurance, and even birth control. The CCP used the workplace to control the urban working population. This means that in addition to a managerial bureaucracy every factory also paid the salaries and benefits for CCP cadres, who held significant power and determined factory policy. Party bureaucrats and the new factory managers often have conflicting goals. The bureaucrats frequently protect the workers' or CCP's interests, often at the expense of efficiency. Reforms in this area, therefore, threatened the entrenched power of the CCP. A member of the State Education Commission, Zhang Yingsi, commented in 1994 that it would not be practical to reform the state-owned enterprises because it would be impossible for the government to take over any time soon the broad range of school, hospital, and other social services that state enterprises provided their workers.

In 1988 a second phase of reform began that attempted to broaden reform to urban areas and support the establishment of large privately owned companies. Included in this phase were the special economic zones.

Special Economic Zones

By 1988, there were four special economic zones along the China coast where foreign firms set up industries or established joint enterprises with Chinese firms and could operate with a degree of economic freedom. The zones offer China foreign capital, technology, expertise, and ideas. They give foreigners tax incentives and plenty of cheap labor. While Deng Xiaoping is credited as being the mastermind behind the establishment of these zones, another CCP leader, Deng's protégé, Zhao Ziyang, is often credited with their success.

In 1987 Zhao was Deng's heir-apparent. He held both positions of premier and CCP general secretary. Like his mentor, Deng, Zhao Ziyang was mercilessly attacked during the Cultural Revolution. Deng rescued and then promoted Zhao after his own rehabilitation during his "reversal of verdicts" campaign in 1973. Zhao was considered a pragmatist who gave priority to economic development and international cooperation over orthodox ideology. In June 1984, while visiting Belgium, Zhao announced "China's door is open now, will be opened wider, and will never be closed again." At the October 1987 Party Congress, Zhao delivered a two-and-one-half-hour speech in which he outlined the Dengist vision for China's future. He said that the government would continue economic modernization and use techniques associated with capitalism so long as they promoted growth. Zhao stressed that China would continue to pursue economic reform and improve the climate for investors.

But foreign investment created problems that led to severe criticism of the reformers from CCP conservatives. The special economic zones reminded conservatives of the nineteenth-century treaty ports, where foreigners were not governed by Chinese laws. In those days, the foreigners exploited Chinese labor and natural resources and enjoyed privileged lives. Conditions in the new special zones, they noted, rapidly became remarkably similar. Chinese laws were routinely ignored by foreign business owners and their Chinese managers because the economic reformers promoting foreign investment supported business interests instead of Chinese labor unions. In May 1988 the Chinese press began reporting a series of horror stories involving underage workers, overcrowded working and living conditions, and twenty-four-hour-per-day shifts for teenage girls. Chinese law bans employment of youths under seventeen or making people work more than eight hours a day, six days per week. Officials found numerous violations of these regulations. For example, in July 1988, in the largest foreign economic zone, Shenzhen, inspectors found 40 out of 200 factories employing girls as young as 10 years old. Investigators dismissed nearly 500 underage workers from twenty-two Shenzhen factories. Young teenagers, 12 and 13 years old, were routinely recruited from poor villages by factory agents. Electronics, garment, and toy manufacturers were cited for providing poor living conditions; forcing teenagers to sleep in dormitories two or three to a bed; and forcing them to work fifteen hours a day, seven days per week.

Chinese authorities attempted to curtail the most flagrant abuses, but with difficulty. Foreign companies threatened to move elsewhere—to Thailand, for example—if conditions became too unfriendly. Moreover, the foreign companies, in theory, abided by Chinese rules, but violations of contracts and labor regulations remained difficult to police. The 1982 Chinese constitution bans strikes, but, by 1986, work stoppages began to plague the foreign economic zones. Complaints by unions fueled antiforeign, antireform sentiment within the CCP.

Deng answered his critics by promoting reform-minded younger CCP members such as Zhao Ziyang, and dismissing or retiring conservatives. In 1985 he persuaded ten of his older colleagues on the twenty-member Politburo and 340 Central Committee members to retire. During the following year, he replaced about half of the state and provincial party chiefs with younger leaders, answerable to him. Again in 1987, he attempted to provide for his reform programs, even after his retirement, by appointing additional young leaders loyal to his ideas. But even the accession to premier in 1987 of Deng's appointee, Zhao Ziyang, as well as the promotion of other reform-minded leaders, did not quell the controversy.

Deng and Zhao faced criticisms from their remaining Maoist colleagues, who blamed the reforms for a wide range of problems, such as increased urban crime, child labor, prostitution, and pornography, all of which they associated with capitalism. Conservatives also condemned the reformers for creating a generation of Chinese youth lacking in respect for communism. Most top CCP leaders, including Deng, demanded that China follow four basic principles: the leadership of the Communist Party; the adherence to socialism; the acceptance of Marxism, Leninism, and Mao Zedong Thought; and the dictatorship of the proletariat. The conservatives, in particular, despised Chinese intellectuals, who had been their most vociferous critics, for taking advantage of the increased freedom of expression allowed since Deng's return to power to demand even more freedoms, and they called for continued struggle against the "crime" of bourgeois liberalization. Deng and his reformist colleagues often were forced to bow to their pressure. An example of a compromise with this group was the dismissal of General Secretary Hu Yaobang, Zhao's predecessor and fellow reformer, in January 1987. CCP conservatives had pushed for Hu's ouster for his alleged failure to quash the 1986 prodemocracy movement.

Anti-Bourgeois Liberalism and the Prodemocracy Movement

Deng's reforms infused China with a wealth of new ideas. The closed society associated with the Cultural Revolution had dissipated by the late 1970s, when trade with the West and Japan began in earnest. The long process of reopening began in 1971 with U.S. Secretary of State Henry Kissinger's visit to China to begin negotiations for normalization of relations between the United States and China. President Richard M. Nixon traveled to China in 1972 and completed discussions leading to the "Shanghai Communiqué," in which the two governments "agreed to disagree" on certain issues, such as the future of Taiwan, and also formulated plans for American recognition of China. The process was not completed until 1979, when President Jimmy Carter extended diplomatic recognition to China, and commercial contact between the two nations was renewed after a nearly 30-year hiatus. Once Deng's reforms began, relations with capitalist nations grew far beyond mere trade. Foreign companies and their employees, teachers, students, and tourists flocked to China, while the Chinese sent thousands of students to Japan, Europe, and especially the United States. By 1989, Chinese intellectuals renewed their criticism of the CCP, demanding more freedoms and less control by the Communist Party. Their protests grew into an organized prodemocracy movement that proved to be an overwhelming stumbling-block for Deng's plans.

Disaffected intellectuals are not new to China. Confucius himself created his theory on meritocracy after being rebuffed in his quest for power in a society where influence was based on family connections instead of talent. Under CCP rule, intellectuals were given a brief chance to air their grievances with the CCP during the Hundred Flowers Movement in 1956. Their harsh criticisms were met with a harsher response—intellectuals were imprisoned or sent to the countryside to learn from peasants and workers. In the late 1960s and the 1970s, the Red Guards of the Cultural Revolution targeted "bourgeois rightist" intellectuals as enemies of the people. In the 1980s, however, Deng's reforms seemed to benefit and encourage intellectuals. China's desperate need for experts in all fields called for better educated citizens. Deng emphasized talent and hard work instead of proper ideology or class background. University admission was granted only to those who passed an extremely difficult entrance examination, and students no longer had to work on farms or in factories before going to college.

Protests by intellectuals began immediately with Deng's assumption of power. Intellectuals hoped that political change would accompany economic reform. In 1979, several Democracy Wall activists, so named for the posters and written statements they displayed next to public party bulletins and newspapers, were arrested and imprisoned. The most famous dissident of this group was Wei Jingsheng, who publicly suggested that Deng's Four Modernizations (agriculture, industry, science and technology, and national defense) should include a fifth: democracy. Charged as a "counterrevolutionary," Wei was sentenced to 15 years in prison. The government also imprisoned hundreds of other critics. Reports out of China alleged serious mistreatment of Wei and his fellow dissenters in prison.

Chinese intellectuals were assaulted in several ways. Demands for greater freedom of expression, more freedom of association, and more say in the government were condemned by the CCP leadership as "bourgeois liberalism." While the Chinese constitution allows for freedom of speech, publication, and democratic elections, the actual meaning of such terms has always been defined by the party. Critics of the government want the CCP to loosen its grip on politics and culture, while the party does not want to relinquish control.

Intellectuals also were dissatisfied with their obvious exclusion from the bounty of benefits that came with Deng's reforms. In 1978, state employees in knowledge-intensive occupations earned about 2 percent more than those performing primarily manual labor. By 1986, manual workers were earning about 10 percent more than their intellectual counterparts. A university professor's 1988 salary was lower than it had been during the 1950s, even if one does not consider inflation.[6] The 7 million Chinese who worked for state-controlled research institutes, schools, and universities were paid meager salaries. By 1988, an average illiterate laborer earned more than an average college graduate. Predictably, many graduate students working toward degrees in China dropped out of universities, while the best students went abroad to study and often did not return. After 1979, approximately 36,000 Chinese students traveled to the United States and fewer than 25 percent of them had returned home by 1988.

Student protests also focused on benefits enjoyed by foreigners in China. Foreign lifestyles contrasted sharply with those of the Chinese. The relatively few highly educated Chinese employed by foreign firms, about 10,000 in 1988, earned significantly higher salaries than their counterparts in Chinese companies, while most of the laborers employed by foreign companies were virtual slaves. This situation is reminiscent of the relationship between the despised nineteenth-century compradore class and Chinese laborers. Corruption appeared ubiquitous, and double-digit inflation undermined the buying power of the educated class, whose salaries are fixed by the government. The influx of foreign goods did not benefit those who could not afford them. In 1985, several thousand students held an anti-Japanese demonstration in Tiananmen Square. They talked of a "second" Japanese invasion—this time by Japanese products flooding Chinese markets. By 1984 Japan had become China's No. 1 trading partner, sending, for example, more than 400,000 color televisions a month to China. Although students shouted, "Down with Japanese militarism," they were really condemning Japanese consumer goods and the pervasive flashy billboards advertising the best of Japan's products.

By far the most troubling demonstrations for the CCP have been associated with the prodemocracy movement that had its roots in the earlier Democracy Wall protests of the late 1970s. The party's ban on the public display of posters and written statements shortly after Wei Jingsheng's arrest in 1979 did not end the protests for long. For Chinese intellectuals, the 1980s were characterized by both a new openness and leniency toward dissent and periodic crackdowns on particularly outspoken critics. This schizophrenic policy was a reflection of the struggle within the CCP between the reformers calling for tolerance and the conservatives stressing the need to maintain tight control. The Dengists, with their apparent acceptance of Western ideas, had instigated the protests by moving rapidly with economic reforms but too slowly for China's intellectuals in the direction of political change. The economic progress of the 1980s was not accompanied by a change in the political structure. The students' frustration was a reaction to the CCP's continued control over their lives, their deteriorating living conditions, and their sense of hopelessness about future progress. On the other hand, CCP conservatives viewed students as having been "spiritually polluted" by the introduction of capitalism and Western ideas into China. Demands by students and intellectuals for more say in the government's policies were a clear threat to the party's power.

In December 1986, tens of thousands of students in China's major cities took to the streets demanding democracy, freedom, and an end to corruption and party privilege. The Dengists were caught in the middle. The prodemocracy demonstrations came on the eve of Deng's planned implementation of more far-reaching economic reforms that would further limit state control over industry. Conservatives insisted that the protests showed that the reforms had already gone too far.

Official sources claimed that the first demonstration took place on December 5 in Hefei, the capital of Anhui, where students demanded a more open nominating process for local party congress candidates. The protests then spread to neighboring cities until, after several weeks, massive protests in Shanghai caught international attention.

By late December, the prodemocracy movement was responsible for the largest demonstration since the Cultural Revolution. The CCP leadership responded by threatening to arrest the demonstrators. A planned mass rally in Shanghai scheduled for December 22 fell far short of the students' expectations. Arrests of outspoken dissidents continued. By January, the protests had become smaller and fewer, and neither the conservatives nor the reformers seemed pleased by the outcome.

It appears that these potentially destabilizing outbursts of dissent were defused by party compromise. On the one hand, CCP leaders answered one of the students' demands by promising to allow more than one candidate, including those from non-Communist groups, to run for seats in local congresses. On the other hand, Beijing and Shanghai authorities tried to prevent future demonstrations by issuing regulations requiring groups to apply five days in advance for permission to assemble publicly. The state-controlled press also began to change its tone concerning the official attitude toward certain reforms, and a semiofficial campaign known as the "Criticism of the Tide of Thought of Bourgeois Liberalization" was soon inaugurated. In late December, for example, the *People's Daily* wrote of historian Zhou Gucheng's lectures to his students about the problems associated with "bourgeois democracy" and its inappropriateness for China. CCP general secretary Hu Yaobang chastised a group of intellectuals at a high-level party meeting for being "irresponsible" in their advocacy of total Westernization. He accused them of provoking the students into taking their divisive actions, although there had been no violence and few arrests. Many intellectuals were reassigned jobs with the goal of keeping them away from the political scene. Some were asked to relinquish their party membership. Hu's actions, however, did not go far enough for CCP conservatives. They demanded that reform-minded intellectuals be stripped of CCP membership. The conservatives got their way in January 1987 when numerous intellectuals were purged from the party and Hu Yaobang, Deng's heir-apparent, was dismissed from his position as CCP general secretary.

Hu had a long association of more than four decades with Deng Xiaoping. As a result, he had been attacked during the Cultural Revolution, was restored later to a position of power with Deng, and rose within party ranks after 1977. He demanded freedom of expression for Chinese intellectuals and wanted party control erased from the daily functions of the economic bureaucracy. In 1985 Hu created a major disturbance by asserting in a speech published in the *People's Daily* that "Marxism cannot solve any of our problems." Although an editor later "corrected" the statement to read, "Marxism cannot solve all of our problems," Hu had already provoked the wrath of the conservatives, who pushed for his expulsion. Hu's alleged leniency in dealing with the student protesters infuriated the conservatives, who then successfully pressured Deng into ousting Hu. This chapter of the prodemocracy movement was aptly summarized by reformist Politburo member Hu Qili when he gave CCP officials an ominous double warning in December: Do not purge intellectuals indiscriminately, and, on the other hand, do not allow protests to spread to the point where a crackdown is necessary.

The prodemocracy movement spread during the following two-and-a-half years. During this time, the demands for opening up the political system increasingly earned the respect of intellectuals, students, and workers, in other words, much of the urban population throughout the country, while it became a serious threat to CCP authority and prestige. Moreover, one of its best-known leaders, Fang Lizhi, captured world attention as a human rights advocate. Already recognized by the international academic community as one of China's most brilliant scientists, Fang in 1986 visited China's major universities, speaking out on the failure of socialism in China and the need to adopt democracy. By 1987, party conservatives had targeted Fang as an enemy. In the wake of the earlier prodemocracy crackdown, he had been stripped of his CCP membership. But CCP censure apparently strengthened Fang's resolve, and he continued his courageous and outspoken criticism of communism, thus becoming a hero for the prodemocracy movement.

Fang is unusual among China's intellectuals, not because of his uncompromising views, but because he dared to speak out openly, jeopardizing his career, if not his life. In the summer of 1988, Fang took his campaign abroad to Hong Kong and Australia where he stressed China's need for a two-party system, and he condemned the corruption rampant among CCP officials who abused the privileges associated with their rank. In response, the CCP, allegedly on orders from Deng Xiaoping himself, canceled Fang's exit visa to the United States, where he was scheduled to engage in scientific research and to lecture at several universities. On January 6, 1989, Fang commemorated the fortieth anniversary of the founding of the PRC and the seventieth anniversary of the May Fourth Movement with an open letter to Deng Xiaoping in which he suggested that a general amnesty for political prisoners be granted along with the release of Democracy Wall activist Wei Jingsheng and others. This was followed on February 16 by a letter addressed to the Standing Committee of the National People's Congress signed by thirty-three leading academics supporting Fang's request and stressing the need for the CCP to "conform to the universal trend toward human rights in the world today."[7] About a week later, another such letter of support was sponsored by forty-two prominent scientists. As the intellectuals began to speak out more openly, a conflagration of prodemocracy sentiment began to engulf the land.

An economic crisis that hit during the summer of 1988 provided a significant stimulus to the prodemocracy movement. This was a direct result of Deng's reforms and the rapid pace of economic growth during the previous decade. Although China's GNP continued to grow at an annual rate of between 7 and 9 percent, double-digit inflation had begun to cripple the urban economy. Monthly inflation averaged more than 10 percent during the summer, resulting in a 60 to 80 percent inflation rate for 1988. Consumers panicked and began hoarding essential goods; this predictably forced prices to spiral upward even further. As the CCP leadership convened to deal with the crisis, the division among the leadership became obvious. General Secretary Zhao Ziyang refused to slow the economy and instead accelerated an export drive, which further fueled inflation. By September Zhao had lost favor not only with the conservative leadership but also with Deng Xiaoping, and by the beginning of 1989 Zhao and his policies had been pushed aside. Conservative Prime Minister Li Peng enacted a series of regulations in a futile attempt to control inflation. In response, Zhao Ziyang tried to regain support from party liberals by calling for democratization to accompany economic reforms. While his outspokenness angered his conservative colleagues, it inspired disaffected urbanites throughout China. As it became clear that CCP unity had weakened, the prodemocracy movement was strengthened.

In late April 1989, immediately after the death of Hu Yaobang, prodemocracy demonstrations erupted on a scale that shocked China-watchers throughout the world. Hu's popularity among intellectuals, his outspoken criticism of party corruption, and his demands for greater intellectual freedom had made him popular as a victim of party oppression. Hu became a martyr for approximately 3,000 students who embarked on a hunger strike in Tiananmen Square, threatening to kill themselves rather than live without democracy. Marching through the streets and into the great square, the students chanted "Long live democracy! Long live freedom! Down with corruption."[8] Support for the students came from all classes in Beijing, and protests soon spread throughout the country. In fact, one party insider recently wrote that the Tiananmen affair ultimately culminated in what he called "the biggest, broadest, longest-lasting, and most influential prodemocracy demonstration anywhere in the world in the twentieth century."[9] In all, the demonstrations occurred in some 341 cities and brought out the participation of nearly a hundred million people in one form or another.[10] The demonstrators called for the resignation of Deng Xiaoping and his conservative premier, Li Peng. On May 18, Li Peng met with a contingent of student leaders of the hunger-strikers at the Great Hall of the People in Beijing, where he warned the students, "We cannot but defend the society, public property and personal safety." He added, "We have to defend socialism. I don't care if you like to listen to this or not."[11] On the following day, Zhao Ziyang visited Tiananmen Square just before dawn. Speaking through a bull horn in front of a Chinese television camera, he said, "I am too old, but you are still young. Live to see China's modernization."[12] He wanted the students to end the hunger strike. The CCP imposed martial law in Beijing. In his announcement on Chinese television, Li Peng declared: "I now call on the whole party, the whole army, and the whole nation to make concerted efforts and set immediately at all posts to stop the turmoil and stabilize the situation."[13] Convoys of troops rolled into Tiananmen Square to disperse the hunger-strikers and their millions of supporters. Initially, they failed. On May 29, a plaster-cast likeness of the Statue of Liberty, dubbed the "Goddess of Democracy," was paraded through the square and before television cameras from all over the world.

After seven weeks of peaceful protests, citizens kept troops temporarily at bay by imploring them not to attack the students. For several days in late May, convoys were halted, and some even turned back, by the millions of demonstrators. Meanwhile, Deng Xiaoping, who by this time was siding with the conservatives, was caught in a humiliating situation. He apparently had decided, by mid-May, to purge General Secretary Zhao Ziyang, his protégé, because of Zhao's "incorrect" approach to economic development and his conciliatory attitude toward the student protests. Deng and conservative Li Peng accused Zhao of counterrevolutionary policies. But Zhao refused to confess to any such crimes, and many of his CCP colleagues refused to vote for his ouster. The conservatives staged their own progovernment rallies, blaming student unrest on Chinese dissidents and foreign influence, particularly that of the United States, which they depicted as a villain dressed as Uncle Sam. But many party leaders were unimpressed, and a planned Central Committee meeting was postponed when Deng feared he would not have the backing to fire Zhao.

Moreover, the episode eclipsed what should have been one of the most historically significant meetings of two heads of state. On May 15, 1989, Deng Xiaoping hosted Soviet leader Mikhail Gorbachev, thus officially ending a 30-year feud between China and the Soviet Union. Ironically, it was Gorbachev's visit to China that provided the prodemocracy demonstrators their worldwide media coverage. As it turned out, the state visit became a source of great humiliation for Deng, especially when Gorbachev's itinerary had to be revised as a result of the occupation of Tiananmen Square by protesters.

Recently released documents (*The Tiananmen Papers*) reveal that the party was deeply divided over how to deal with what was clearly the most controversial event in Chinese Communist history. The ultimate decision to use force was made against the wishes of the Politburo Standing Committee, which urged continued dialogue with the students. The matter was settled by Deng and a group of semi-retired Communist "elders," who ordered martial law, fired Zhao Ziyang, and elevated to power in a constitutionally irregular procedure Jiang Zemin as successor to Zhao Ziyang.

The key player determining the course of events was Premier Li Peng, who manipulated information to lead Deng and the elders to see the demonstrations as a personal attack on them and as designed to overthrow Communist rule. In an emergency report to the Politburo on June 1, 1989 entitled "On the True Nature of the Turmoil," Li's group accused the students of perpetrating a "counterrevolutionary riot" in Tiananmen Square as a means of staging a final showdown with the party and government. Their aim, stated the report, was to provoke a crackdown so that "fresh blood will wake up the people and lead to a split and collapse of the government."[14] The report's usage of the word "turmoil" had serious consequences. Deng had been convinced to employ the label to describe the students' activities in an important editorial published in the April 26 edition of the *People's Daily*. In Chinese, "turmoil" (*dongluan*) has a particularly negative connotation because it was the term used to describe the upheavals associated with the Cultural Revolution between 1966 and 1969. Deng saw a clear correlation between the anarchy of the Cultural Revolution and the Tiananmen protests. If the instability in Beijing were not settled, claimed Deng, it would spread throughout "other provinces, regions, and cities." "Lying down on railroad tracks; beating, smashing, and robbing; if these aren't turmoil then what are they?" "If things continue like this, we could even end up under house arrest."[15] The students, for their part, were convinced that if they ended their demonstrations while the activity was officially classified as "turmoil," they would be subject to extremely harsh punishment. Only if their protests were termed "patriotic" or "democratic" could they withdraw safely from the square.[16] This, of course, did not happen. The emergency report to the Politburo of June 1, 1989, served to establish the legality and necessity of using military force to clear Tiananmen Square.

On June 3, two weeks after Gorbachev's departure, the crackdown began with a vehemence and brutality unpredicted by China experts. Troops in armored carriers and tanks crashed through barriers and attacked the demonstrators indiscriminately. Because much of the horror was witnessed by foreign correspondents and television cameras, the events shocked the world. Foreign analysts remain uncertain of the numbers of dead and wounded, but the casualties most likely totaled in the tens of thousands in Beijing and other cities throughout China. Soldiers attacked indiscriminately and, according to observers, their objective was to kill and cripple, not to disperse.[17] Chinese troops were ordered to burn bodies so that accurate figures of the death tolls would never be known.

On June 24 the Central Committee dismissed Zhao Ziyang from all of his posts. Outspoken dissident Fang Lizhi and his wife sought asylum in the U.S. embassy in Beijing, where they stayed until June 25, 1990, when the Chinese government allowed Fang and his family to leave for England.

Repression

Within a week of the Tiananmen Massacre, even as Chinese television portrayed PLA soldiers sweeping the streets and playing with children, a grim reign of terror settled over the land. Thousands of Chinese in Beijing and other cities were arrested. Official broadcasts preposterously claimed that the protesters were a mere "tiny handful" of looters and criminals who had been responsible for atrocities against the army. Chinese television repeatedly showed protesters attacking soldiers and vandalizing army vehicles. No one who witnessed these events on television would ever forget the brave young demonstrator who, single-handedly, tried to face down advancing tanks on their rampage through Tiananmen Square. Workers, as a group, were hardest hit in the early arrests and given harsh sentences. They could be found more easily than the thousands of students who fled the cities for their lives. But, more importantly, labor dissatisfaction and the establishment of autonomous workers' organizations during the preceding weeks terrified CCP conservatives, who could see the potential development of another Solidarity, the Polish labor union that toppled the Polish Communist government in September 1989. Hundreds of workers were tried by the courts and quickly found guilty of counterrevolutionary crimes. They were executed publicly. The public executions were used by the CCP to teach the nation a lesson.

A crackdown on intellectuals soon followed with the arrest, firing, and forced retirement of unknown numbers of students, teachers, journalists, writers, publishers, and artists. A list of the "Twenty-One Most Wanted," some of whom fled abroad, was broadcast over Chinese television. Under Chinese law, these people may be sent to labor camps without trial. Publications promoting "bourgeois liberalization" were banned. Sales of some foreign journals were halted and inventories confiscated. Hotels were ordered to disconnect satellite dish antennae to prevent access to foreign news broadcasts.

New requirements for college entrance and graduation were mandated. High school graduates had to work 1 or 2 years in factories, on farms, or enlist in the army before being admitted to universities. All entering university students were required to pass a course in "ideological remolding," with a reading list that included the most recent speeches of Deng Xiaoping. University graduates of the class of 1989 were obliged to pass a political ideology course and write politically appropriate essays describing their personal political views. In August, the government announced that those who graduated from college after 1985 would be enlisted in labor programs, mostly in the countryside, for 2 years before being allowed to continue their careers. Students who planned to enroll in three of China's major universities, Beijing University, Nanjing University, and Fudan University in Shanghai, had to first complete a year of military training or physical labor in the countryside. Only 10 percent of college graduates who came to major cities to study were allowed to remain there after graduation.

In September the CCP moved to inhibit further the spread of Western influence among students by restricting the number of graduate students it sent to the United States and other Western countries. Moreover, the number of graduate students allowed to study the social sciences was severely restricted. Vice Minister of Education He Dongchang explained that "a 'screen' must be placed over China's windows to the world to prevent 'flies and worms' from infesting the country."[18]

If the policies following the Tiananmen massacre sound familiar it is because they were the same hard-line tactics used against the "bourgeois rightists" during the Cultural Revolution. Ironically, back then Deng Xiaoping was a primary target instead of the attacker. As executions took place daily during the summer of 1989, Deng assured the Chinese people that yet another challenge to China's sovereignty had been rebuffed, just in time, by the Communist Party. In a speech on June 9 he commented, "In a word, this was a test, and we passed." He praised his octogenarian colleagues who, he said, "have experienced many storms and have a thorough understanding of things."[19] Presumably, what they understood was that they were in a struggle for survival, as they had been dozens of times since their own days of student activism.

In January 1990, martial law was lifted in Beijing, 575 dissenters were released from jail, and the troops moved out of the capital. But these actions were immediately followed by a crackdown on intellectuals and workers branded as activists. Months of imprisonment for many Chinese dissidents culminated in a series of trials and convictions in early 1991. Perhaps taking advantage of the world's preoccupation with war in the Persian Gulf, the Chinese government quickly gave prison sentences to participants in the Tiananmen movement for what the government referred to as inciting subversion, overthrowing the socialist system, interfering with martial law, and disturbing public order.

Despite continuous harassment and crackdowns by the government, Chinese dissidents remained committed to prodemocracy activity, leading one international human rights group to comment in 1995 that most dissidents who have tried to agitate for human rights since 1989 have been imprisoned. The fifth anniversary of the Tiananmen incident stimulated action by both dissident groups and the government. Activists arrested in 1994 were often given "appallingly severe" prison sentences, according to Human Rights Watch–Asia.

In the spring of 1995 an intensification of prodemocracy activity coincided with the UN's fiftieth anniversary of its founding. The "Year of Tolerance," as 1995 was dubbed by the United Nations, was marked in China by the boldest antigovernment move since 1989—a demand for tolerance by some of China's most prominent intellectual leaders. Forty-five protesters, including Wang Ruoshui, a former editor of *People's Daily*; Wang Gancheng, a designer of China's first atomic bomb; and other former members of the Chinese Academy of Sciences and the Communist Party petitioned President Jiang Zemin and chairman of the national legislature Qiao Shi to "release all those who have been imprisoned because of their thoughts, religious beliefs, or acts of speech." The letter asserted that China, as one of the UN's founders and a permanent member of the Security Council, should "consistently implement this resolution so that this spirit of tolerance, a spirit with which our country is relatively unfamiliar, may take root and flourish in areas such as politics, thought, religion, culture, and education."

While this petition was signed by the largest number of dissidents to protest publicly since the Tiananmen incident, it was only one of at least a dozen released by prodemocracy activists and families of political prisoners during early 1995. All urged the government to stop labeling the unarmed Tiananmen protest as an antigovernment riot and to release political prisoners.

The government reacted by stepping up surveillance and harassment of activists. Several drafters of the letter to Jiang were immediately arrested and detained. Others, who had been involved in the 1989 protests but who had not participated in more recent activities, were brought in for questioning by local police. Representatives from Human Rights Watch–Asia criticized the Chinese government for its determination to stamp out dissent.

11

The Era of Jiang Zemin

Jiang Zemin (b. 1926)

The prodemocracy activity of the 1990s appeared to be less of a threat to the stability of the Chinese government than the economic strain caused by the continuation of Deng Xiaoping's reforms. Following the Tiananmen incident, Deng announced that he would press for economic growth at an even faster pace. The Central Committee's election of economic reformer Jiang Zemin as the party's general secretary in June 1989 assured that Deng's open door policy and free market experiment would continue. Jiang Zemin was chosen president in March 1993.

In order for Deng Xiaoping to assure political stability and economic growth for China, it was necessary to engineer a smooth transition of leadership to the next generation. This was an especially crucial issue because Deng's previously appointed successors, Hu Yaobang and Zhao Ziyang, had fallen from grace because of their destabilizing liberal policies. Conservatives within the party resented Zhao's progressive ideas on political and economic reform, which they saw to have opened up avenues of change that threatened social anarchy as well as the continued existence of the party itself. Deng had sided with the hardliners when the Tiananmen protesters had crossed the line, but the crackdown weakened his own prestige and called into question the wisdom of the free market reforms that he had encouraged. Deng realized that such progressive economic policies had to be continued if the party were to survive and China find her rightful place as a world power.

Conservatives were convinced that the steep trajectory of Deng's reforms had created conditions that led to the Tiananmen troubles and that the party needed to reverse direction. They hoped that one of their own, perhaps Premier Li Peng or economic planner Yao Yilin, would replace the discredited Zhao Ziyang as general secretary and pursue a more orthodox Marxist domestic agenda and a harder line toward the United States. Deng thought otherwise, and he began to build his case against the conservatives by making reference to what he called "the core" of the party. This notion had its roots in Mao's struggles to establish a special Chinese "path to revolution" and referred to the leader as being at the center of a web of personal relationships that shaped essential policy decisions. A "core leader" was one who commanded the formal and informal authority to be the ultimate arbiter on party matters. As the Chinese put it, he possessed the capacity to "strike the table" and end debate.[1] Mao's designated successor, the more obscure Hua Guofeng, who was not a veteran of the Long March, had lacked such pedigree and thus lost out to Deng. Deng was able to push Hua aside because he could claim to represent the legitimate "core" of the "second generation" of CCP leadership.

As the party struggled to find its way after the disruptions of 1989, Deng used his status as "core leader" to promote the continuity of reformist economic development and designate a successor. After consulting with some of the "party elders" (a coterie of power brokers and former Politburo Standing Committee members with whom he had a close working relationship), Deng announced that the party boss of Shanghai, Jiang Zemin, would become the "core" of the "third generation" of CCP leaders and thus claim the rank of general secretary.

Jiang Zemin was not well known outside party circles, but he satisfied

Deng's criteria for the next generation of leadership. China's new leader, unlike Hu Yaobang and Zhao Ziyang, would have to be a political authoritarian yet fight tenaciously for liberal economic reform. This disqualified Li Peng and company because their immediate involvement in the Tiananmen crackdown and conservative economic thinking would complicate China's relations with Western governments and investors as well as exacerbate social and political unrest at home. The new leadership, said Deng, "should represent an entirely new look so that people will feel there is a promising new lineup that will carry out reforms. . . . If the people feel that the leadership is hidebound, conserva- tive or mediocre . . . there will be many more disturbances and never peace."[2] The times called for a fresh face, someone who could reconcile contending political factions and reassure the nation and the international community that China was prepared to move forward as a major player in world affairs.

A Rising Star of the Third Generation

Much like Deng, Jiang Zemin was no Marxist ideologue limited by the tunnel vision of the dialectic. Like Deng, he read more widely in the broader corpus of Chinese and Western history than in Marxist theory. Jiang was essentially a patriotic pragmatist, deeply committed to advancing the development of the Chinese nation. He also was someone who could work effectively with a myriad of personality types and had a natural instinct for siding with political winners. His career owed much to the economic reforms of Deng. Jiang's first job after working as a machine engineer, for example, was with a government commission charged with plans for the creation of special economic zones (SEZs) in Guangdong and Fujian provinces. After several trips abroad to study industrial and trade development, Jiang became a convert to opening China to foreign investment. His group submitted a report to the Politburo recommending far-reaching reforms designed to encourage joint Chinese– foreign industrial and financial ventures. Their proposal was bitterly opposed by party conservatives who feared that the zones would undermine domestic pay scales and state-owned industry. Jiang made a special appearance before the National People's Congress to defend the report, which ultimately played a key role in winning its approval. His inspired promotion of the SEZs brought exposure to senior party officials and marked him as an effective advocate of Deng's economic plans.

Jiang was trained as an engineer and was soon promoted to a leading position in the newly created Ministry of Electronics, yet another outgrowth of China's expanding interest in global trade. Success as vice-minister of electronics soon led to important party promotions, eventually giving Jiang a seat on the Central Committee. By 1982 it was clear that Jiang had been selected as one of the rising stars in the "third generation" of leaders who would follow in the footsteps of Deng Xiaoping.

In 1984 Jiang was selected by Premier Zhao Ziyang to draw up plans for a new economic development program for Shanghai. After roughly six months on the job studying the political and economic dynamics of the city, leaving ministerial duties to subordinates while he roamed the markets disguised in a leather jacket and baseball cap, Jiang was appointed mayor of Shanghai in July 1985. As mayor and later municipal party boss, Jiang promoted foreign investment, worked to establish Shanghai as a center for international banking, and encouraged experiments in free market economics. When Shanghai university students protested about inflation and the rising costs of living, Jiang, following the directives of Zhao Ziyang, went to the city's campuses and explained the rationale for economic reform policies. He had notable success in quelling disturbances. On the other hand, student demands for more democracy were forcibly resisted by Jiang, as he drew an indelible line between political and economic reform.

As Jiang detected the tide turning against the liberal policies of party chief Hu Yaobang because of a failure to mitigate countrywide student unrest that broke out in the winter of 1986, he began to see the efficacy of taking a stronger stand against what the conservatives called the insidious influx of "bourgeois liberalization." Jiang, it seems, had a gift for knowing which way the political winds were blowing and adjusted his positions accordingly—a talent possessed by all successful Chinese leaders in the unpredictable atmospherics of Beijing politics. This is what earned him the nickname "Weathercock." Now Jiang claimed that leaning too far in the direction of capitalism was a dangerous thing. The party must instead, remarked Jiang on Shanghai Radio in March 1987, "march forward unswervingly along the road to Chinese-style socialism."[3] As part of his campaign against political liberalization, Jiang moved quickly to assert party control over Shanghai's media organizations, going so far as closing down the prestigious *World Economic Herald* when it praised the discredited liberal Hu Yaobang. This won accolades from the party hardliners in Beijing, who by this juncture were growing apprehensive over the popular demands for more democracy.

When the country was fixated on the student demonstrations in Tiananmen Square in May 1989, the good soldier Jiang followed Zhao Ziyang's instructions to pursue a policy of conciliation through dialogue. Jiang by this point had been promoted to the Politburo and made Shanghai CCP secretary. The economic reformer Zhu Rongji had been given the position of mayor. Although they allowed the deputy party secretaries to meet with the students, neither Jiang nor Zhu attended the sessions, possibly expecting a policy change in Beijing. Whatever the reason, the decision proved fortuitous because the hardliners led by Li Peng convinced Deng to dump Zhao and impose martial law in Beijing. As the army marched into Tiananmen Square, Jiang, Zhu Rongji, and other top leaders in Shanghai went to their students and pleaded for restraint, promising to work toward reform and economic development. This show of moderation and understanding, along with promises not to punish protesters, served at least temporarily to mollify the Shanghai students.

Although Jiang was one of the first local leaders to endorse Li Peng's crackdown, he made his own subordinates employ persuasion instead of coercion to deal with Shanghai protesters. Official notices went out that the party would continue to have dialogue with students "so as to improve CCP work." Instead of making threats, Jiang's officials appealed to decency and common sense. Thus, throughout the turbulence of the Tiananmen protestations Jiang showed his ability to navigate skillfully between the conservatives in Beijing and the reformist demonstrators in Shanghai. For purposes of addressing the concerns of those who feared the political anarchy threatened by the Tiananmen disturbances, Jiang was quoted in the front page of the *People's Daily* a few weeks after the crackdown: "Toward these cruel enemies there must not be even one percent of forgiveness. If we go easy on them, we shall commit an error of historic proportions."[4] In short, Jiang could threaten the iron fist when it came to holding the line on political reform, yet from the beginning he had also committed himself to advancing Deng's economic agenda. Jiang quickly got behind Deng's seminal 1992 southern tour to promote economic liberalization and convinced the leader that he could be trusted to promote progressive industrial and market reforms. Yet, at the same time, he showed himself to be firm enough to resist the kinds of dangerous liberal political flirtations that proved fatal to Deng's previously anointed successors.

Economic Reforms Continue

Ever since the Tiananmen incident Deng had been under pressure from the so-called CCP "left," conservatives who cleaved to a more orthodox Marxist-Leninism. They contended that reformist policies were largely responsible for the student unrest and if continued could lead to the downfall of the party itself. In order to defuse his critics, Deng asserted that planned and market systems were simply "methods" employed pragmatically by both socialist and capitalist nations to stimulate economic growth. Market mechanisms were sometimes required in both to unleash the requisite "productive forces." What distinguished the two systems, Deng claimed, was the principle of ownership (private versus public). The distinctive features of the socialist system, which Deng assured the conservatives he supported, were its capacities to liberate maximum social productivity, increase the collective strengths of the nation, and raise society's standard of living. These were the criteria by which any economic system had to be measured. Deng went so far as to claim that the achievements of reform and the opening up of economic relationships with the outside world had actually saved the party from falling victim to the Tiananmen disturbances. As he told local officials:

> and if we had failed to pass the test, there would have been a chaotic situation that might have led to civil war, as was the case during the Cultural Revolution. The reason our country remained stable after the June 4 incident was that reform and opening up had already promoted economic development and improved people's livelihood. Therefore both the army and the state government must continue to safeguard the line, this system, and these policies.[5]

After chastising the leftists for their overwrought concerns about creeping capitalism, Deng went on the offensive. Drawing on one of Mao's famous metaphors, he accused the leftists of acting like "women with bound feet," their timidity holding back the productive forces that needed to be unleashed if China were to advance. In a sharp reversal of the criticism of bourgeois liberalization that had dominated official party propaganda since 1989, Deng declared that both the "right" and "left" could bury socialism, but the main threat, he warned, now came from conservatives who resisted imperative economic changes. This was a remarkable proclamation, for Deng was essentially declaring that Maoist "leftism" was more dangerous than capitalist "rightism." Those who oppose reforms should resign their posts. Whoever challenges the reformist line, declared Deng, "will be stopped by the common people and will be struck down."[6]

In the early morning of January 17, 1992, Deng left Beijing in an unmarked train heading south to Guangzhou. The journey was kept secret. Deng had not made a public appearance in more than a year, and given the temper and tone of the Beijing government and party media it seemed at this juncture that the leftists were on the ascendancy. Now at the age of 88 years, Deng knew that his time was limited. This was his last opportunity to make a mark on history; all stops had to be pulled out in the battle to reform China's economy. Thus he embarked on what has been called the *nanxun,* or "southern sojourn," a visit to the economically dynamic SEZ of Shenzhen. The purpose of the journey was to send a bold new signal to the country that Deng was supporting a further push to marketize China's economy. To the hardliners it was meant as a sign that Deng would not give way to their caution on economic reform, although he would remain with them in wielding dictatorship over the party's political foes. The boomtowns of the south coast were now to serve as models for a high-octane, foreign investment–driven industrialization.

Deng and his group crisscrossed Guangdong province for several days promoting new economic growth, praising the idea of stock markets, and urging the SEZs to join the ranks of the "Asian Tigers" (Singapore, South Korea, Hong Kong, and Taiwan), Deng's economic models for China. The "southern sojourn" bolstered the position of Jiang Zemin because he had sided with Deng in the 1991 economic debates and was an early booster of the SEZ concept. There is evidence to suggest that Jiang was informed about Deng's trip in advance. A few days before Deng's train departed for the south, Jiang notified his colleagues in Shanghai to make more vigorous public moves for deeper reforms. Jiang was in constant contact with Deng's entourage as they moved through the south, and he continued to prod the cadres to cut back on their bureaucratic functions and concentrate on economic matters. Jiang even made his own self-criticism, admitting that he had moved too cautiously on reforms and underestimated the dangers of "leftism." By May he was urging party officials to build "a brand-new social system" by "making use of all productive forces and superior cultural fruits created by capitalist societies."[7] Jiang was well protected from criticism concerning the other abiding concern of Deng's, namely to uphold party control over the political process. Jiang had already earned his credentials as a firm believer in political authoritarianism.

Deng had worked behind the scenes with party elders to secure Jiang Zemin's appointment as general secretary. The hardliners (namely Li Peng and Yao Yilin) were told not to take advantage of Jiang's relative lack of experience at the center of party politics. It should be pointed out, however, that Jiang was the third leader of the Chinese Communist Party to have come to power through a coup (after the purge of Zhao Ziyang).[8] Other than Deng's fuzzy references to "the core," there were as of yet no formal procedures for leadership transition. Jiang's claim to power would ultimately depend on his ability to satisfy the expectations of Deng, who at least for a time would wait behind the proverbial bamboo screen to offer a helping hand when needed.

Jiang Gains Control Over the Military

In order for Jiang to secure his leadership it would be imperative to have the full support of the military. Jiang had never served in the army and therefore it was difficult for Deng the kingmaker to have him assume the chairmanship of the Central Military Commission (CMC), an office that provided Deng with a powerful weapon over factions within the party and ultimately allowed him to carry the day on policy matters. It was assumed that the general to whom

Deng had turned to put down the Tiananmen disturbances, Yang Shangkun, would succeed him as the next head of the military. On the other hand, Deng seems to have had reservations about the loyalty of the army to the party if Yang and his associates were given such power. Soon after Jiang Zemin's elevation to general secretary, Deng began to make the argument that because Jiang was qualified to be head of the party he was equally qualified to be in charge of the military, thus making explicit the long-held Marxist-Leninist principle that the party commands the gun. Throughout the autumn of 1989 Deng lobbied for the retirement of General Yang Shangkun and the elevation of Jiang as head of the Central Military Commission. The thrust of his argument was that the nation needed younger, more flexible leadership. In short, it was time to make way for the third generation, even in military matters. Although Yang objected to a civilian politician who had never fired a gun being placed in charge of the army, he was partially mollified by being allowed to remain at his post as vice-chairman of the CMC, while his half-brother, Yang Baibing, was given charge of running the military on a day-by-day basis.

Jiang candidly admitted his lack of experience in military affairs but expressed a willingness to learn from the veterans. For the next 2 years he immersed himself in study, touring the country with senior military officers. He visited more than one hundred army units and mingled with the troops, assuring them that the party would address their most mundane needs while fully supporting the drive to strengthen and modernize every branch of the military. Jiang allowed the Yang brothers to lead the reform efforts, while he worked to increase the defense budget. Jiang's persistent message to the troops was that the party needed army support to resist attempts to overthrow socialism at home and to defend the nation from enemies abroad.

Despite Deng's ability to have Jiang appointed chairman of the Central Military Commission, it was soon apparent that the new general secretary's supreme authority was being compromised by the activities of Yang Baibing, the half-brother of General Yang Shangkun, who was using his position as secretary general of the CMC to build up an empire within the army by appointing cronies to fill influential posts in the PLA headquarters and in China's seven military regions. This politicization of the promotion process flew in the face of Deng's efforts to professionalize the military after the disasters of the Cultural Revolution and the policies of Lin Biao. In order for the Chinese military to modernize (it was still an essentially 1940s-style fighting machine), officers would have to be promoted on the basis of merit. Besides challenging Jiang's power, Yang Baibing's empire building threatened the meritocratic imperatives of modernization, while his accompanying cronyism alienated young officers who were imbued with the values of professionalism. Jiang himself, being a technocrat and especially appreciative of modernizing the

Chinese military after witnessing the success of the U.S. 1991 invasion of Iraq, was fully committed to reforming the military.

Jiang and the Yang brothers maneuvered behind the scenes to win over various elements within the military to their respective sides, but when Yang Baibing gave evidence of his political agenda by making promotions without consulting Jiang, the threat to the paramount position of party rule was clear. Jiang then succeeded in winning over the support of high-ranking Politburo members, veterans of the New Fourth Army, and Deng himself in order to have Yang removed from power. Yang Baibing was dismissed from his military positions in October 1992. Yang Shangkun was also removed from his military post, and thus ended what some have called the "Yang family army." After this purge several hundred senior and regional commanders were retired or reassigned.

Closely associated with the problems presented by the Yang brothers, and an additional cause of the military's deterioration in discipline and morale in the lower ranks, was the People's Liberation Army's involvement in a myriad of business transactions. As a means of compensating for a decline in the military budget, the PLA since 1985 had invested in a diverse array of entrepreneurial ventures, ranging from telecommunications to health and real estate businesses. The profits from such investments had supplemented the official defense budget by as much as a third.[9] The management of these business ventures took the military far from the tasks of soldiering. Corruption and crime spread, while the army's revenue bases allowed it to become more autonomous of party control. There were also complaints from the private sector of unfair competition. Jiang launched a "rectification" campaign in early 1994 to restructure the PLA business empire. The goal was to tighten up control over the many powerful junior commanders who served as business executives. The campaign targeted "money worship, pleasure-seeking, and extreme individualism" and shut down some 5,000 firms. The PLA continued its business activities but now the party increased its control over such enterprises.

The "Yang wars" represented Jiang's first forceful move to assert his leadership. In all probability, losing control of the army would have started a chain reaction down the leadership line, and Jiang may well have lost authority within the party itself. His success in defeating the Yang brothers and increasing discipline over the PLA's business activities undoubtedly bolstered Jiang's self-confidence and signaled that he would be more than simply a transitional figure to get the party through the challenge of Tiananmen. Yet the outcome of the battle still depended on the intervention of Deng Xiaoping. Jiang had passed his initial test, but he still was not his own man.

As a follow-up to his victory over the Yang brothers, Jiang at the 1992

Party Congress took control over several key policy-making bodies and appointed a number of younger, technologically trained, college-educated men to various ministries and the Politburo. Most significantly, he managed to get his old colleague Zhu Rongji, mayor of Shanghai, appointed to the Politburo Standing Committee (PBSC). Jiang could rely on the managerial skills and economic acuity of Zhu to implement his desired reforms. Another important addition to the power line at this time was Tibet party secretary Hu Jintao, a rising star of the younger generation who as a trusted associate would work closely with Jiang for the next few years. These younger men, all highly educated technocrats, replaced several members of the old guard and served to further check the power of the most significant conservative threat to Jiang's policies, Premier Li Peng. Finally, culminating his climb to the top, Jiang was elected president by the delegates of the National People's Congress in March 1993. Although this was largely a ceremonial title, it did mean that Jiang now had the top posts in state government, the CCP, and the military.

Jiang Zemin as President

The most pressing challenge for Jiang as the new boss was to heal the wounds of the Tiananmen Massacre, and this, as Deng Xiaoping had repeatedly emphasized, depended directly on continued economic growth. There were two serious obstacles to achieving such objectives: resistance from the party's leftists and the corrosive effects of corruption. Much as Deng had to refrain from destroying the legacy of Mao for purposes of transition and legitimacy (thus we see the "good" early Mao and the later "bad" Mao who made "mistakes" in his dotage), Jiang could not place all the blame on Zhao Ziyang for the Tiananmen uprising. Both Deng and he needed to protect the economic legacy of Zhao's programs. Consequently, party leaders placed part of the blame on "party failures," the rectification of which mandated a "cleansing" of the ranks. The media also had to be brought into line so as to complement and support party policy. And of course it would be necessary to mend fences with the international community, especially the United States.

The single most important way of winning back respect for the party was to root out corruption, a poison that was quickly killing public support for Deng's economic reforms. Indeed, frustration with corruption had been the fuel that fed the fires of the Tiananmen protests in the first place. In the summer of 1993 Jiang unleashed a major anticorruption campaign that resulted in substantial arrests and convictions. The so-called "red princes," children of high-ranking cadres whose business operations profited from family connections, were a major target of Jiang's crusade. Even Deng Xiaoping's son, Deng Pufang, was exposed for profiteering. The anticorruption campaign was not simply a matter of swatting "flies"; no "tigers" (party big shots) would be allowed to roam free under the new regime either. Jiang for his part strictly forbade his own two sons from involvement in either politics or business, thus largely avoiding the prospect of his immediate family being tarred with the brush of corruption. By the winter of 1994–95, Jiang's anticorruption crusade would move virtually into the tiger's den.

Ever since the Communists came to power, Beijing had been under the iron hand of a single party official who ran the municipality as his own fiefdom. Mao himself had described the capital as "an independent kingdom, impenetrable and watertight."[10] One of Beijing's more powerful bosses was Peng Zhen, whom Mao had struggled to dislodge during the Cultural Revolution. Only by removing Peng was Mao able to gain complete control of the city. After the demise of Mao, Beijing in the early 1980s became the satrapy of mayor and party secretary Chen Xitong. The operation of the city's business and financial infrastructures was greased by a labyrinthine scheme of bribes and kickbacks known as the "Chen system" that provided its participants with harems of mistresses, fleets of luxury automobiles, and fancy villas. The Chen operation functioned as a well-oiled machine, its finely meshed gears of cronyism creating a barrier that not a single investigation of corruption could penetrate.

The situation in Beijing was a double threat to Jiang Zemin. Chen Xitong had openly questioned his legitimacy as Deng's heir apparent, and the elaborate scheme of municipal spoils made a mockery of Jiang's anticorruption campaign. The Chen system was itself a glaring example of the central government's incapacity to lead, a tenacious holdover of the kind of regionalism that had proved lethal to previous Chinese dynasties. What ultimately led to the unraveling of Chen's power was an investigation in 1992 of an illegal fund-raising scheme in southern Jiangsu province. Once police broke up the scam in mid-1994 they found an official who, after promises of leniency, provided inside information on a trail of bribes and kickbacks that led directly to the highest levels of Beijing's leadership. Chen's officials at the time were trying to illegally revoke a lease of the Beijing McDonald's franchise, the largest hamburger outlet in the world and a symbol of the post-Tiananmen foreign investor confidence. This was to make way for a huge Hong Kong–financed real estate deal that Chen and his cronies had much to gain from because of bribes they coerced from the project's investors. Although this was what initially attracted public attention, it was only the first of a plethora of disclosures involving the diversion of huge amounts of city money to friends and relatives for the acquisition of villas, fast women, and jewelry. Once the noose tightened, Beijing's vice-mayor committed suicide, and with his disgrace the Chen system came crashing to the ground. Chen Xitong was charged with corruption and in September 1995 became the first Politburo member in the history of Communist China to be dismissed for corruption. After a 2-year period of exile in Inner Mongolia, Chen was expelled from the party and prosecuted for embezzlement and dereliction of duty (the highest official to stand trial since the Gang of Four in 1980). Chen received a 16-year jail sentence (he was later released for medical reasons), and his playboy son was given a 12-year sentence for bribery and misuse of public funds. Scores of others received a variety of penalties ranging from life-term imprisonments to execution.

The purge of Chen Xitong gave a significant boost to Jiang Zemin's anointment as Deng's successor. The successful attack on corruption into the highest levels of the party greatly improved Jiang's public image as a force for justice, and the party's insistence on playing by the rules pushed China further toward implementing the rule of law. The fundamental principle upon which the prosecution made its case was that everyone should be held to the highest standards of discipline and that party members who violated rules would be punished severely. Finally, besides showcasing the general secretary's political skills, the dismantling of the house of Chen showed that Jiang as party boss was now able for the first time to make a seismic political move without having to depend on the support of Deng.

As a reformer, Jiang Zemin departed from Deng's single-minded economic thinking by pioneering what he called a "third way," meaning he was prepared to draw on Deng's liberal economic vision but reject the Westernized proto-democratic political trajectory of Zhao Ziyang. His objective was to carve out a middle course that could be defended against critics from both the left and right. Jiang's "neoauthoritarian" political tendencies became more hardened in the wake of the collapse of Communist regimes in Eastern Europe and the Soviet Union. The passing of those regimes was blamed on permissive bourgeois political ideas. There would be no loosening of party political controls under Jiang's watch.

A major series of economic initiatives was launched in 1994 under the banner of the "Year of Reforms." The goal was to bring fundamental changes in tax laws, banking, pricing, and state industry so that markets, instead of bureaucratic planners, could drive China's economy. By the mid-1990s the state had largely relinquished price controls and some two-thirds of the economy was guided by market principles. However, this was not to be confused with capitalism, the Jiangists asserted, because in line with Deng's definition of socialism, "public ownership" would remain the economic core.

Considerable infusions of foreign capital, the formation of joint stock companies, and spectacular increases in real estate investments produced unprecedented economic gains following Jiang Zemin's reform drive. But they also generated serious regional disparities. In fact, much of the capital for funding real estate development on the coast was diverted from local banks and the budgets of officials that were supposed to service the purchase of agricultural products from the inner provinces. This had the effect of exacerbating regional economic discrepancies and increasing hostility between the highly developed coastal areas and the agrarian hinterland. The "Year of Reforms" prepared the ground for waves of rural protests and riots; within a mere two months (May and June 1997), for example, half a million farmers and workers were involved in such actions.[11] One critic referred to the real estate boom that accompanied Jiang's reforms as "China's enclosures movement" (a reference to the wholesale displacement of common people in seventeenth-century England) because rising prices made the purchase of land and affordable housing beyond the reach of ordinary citizens.[12] Much of this economic disparity was a direct consequence of the growth of China's private economy. For example, between 1991 and 1993, after Deng's heralded trip to the south, the government reported that the number of private enterprises more than doubled and the amount of registered private capital increased fivefold. Most Chinese scholars believe these official figures vastly understated the increases because there were thousands of "hidden" private enterprises in 1994. They said that by the end of the century there might well have been more than 2 million such enterprises that employed 17 million people.[13]

The economic success of the private sector, especially the joint Chinese-foreign ventures, stood in stark contrast to the increasing unprofitability of the state-owned enterprises (SOEs) and the huge amounts of government funds required to keep them in operation, an expense that became a serious drain on the state budget. In 1996, for example, government subsidies to the SOEs exceeded their total profits. There were also considerable disparities in income between those who worked for private enterprises and laborers in the state sector, and this created resentment (what the Chinese call "red eye disease") and anger. The party feared that closing down the unprofitable SOEs would produce massive unemployment and social unrest.

The economic reforms also brought about unprecedented social changes, most notably the emergence of a nascent bourgeoisie and another class of immensely wealthy entrepreneurs. Many of the latter had important political connections, making possible sweetheart business deals and opportunities for fraud. In many respects the massive increase in corruption targeted by Jiang was a by-product of his own liberal economic reforms.

These profound social and economic changes raised the ire of a cross-section of China's population. The increasing commercialization of society encouraged by the influx of Western values led leftists to criticize Jiang for deviating from Marx and spawning capitalism. In early 1995 there appeared the first of what were called the "10,000-character manifestos" (so called because of their length and subject matter). The first document asserted that the growth of private companies at the expense of state enterprises had contributed to the creation of a "new bourgeoisie" as a class unto itself. The authors complained of technocrats taking over leadership positions in the party and warned that China's sovereignty was being undermined by economic dependence on the West. A second 10,000-character manifesto circulated in the autumn of 1995 coinciding with growing tensions over Taiwan. The thrust of its criticism was directed at the party's failure to appreciate the danger of Western imperialism. Economic liberalism had compromised China's social stability and threatened national security. China's reliance on the international economy, it argued, had weakened the domestic industries and thereby made the nation more vulnerable to Western demands. A continuation of such policies might well lead to the emergence of a "Chinese Gorbachev" and the end of the CCP.

A major source of firepower behind the manifestos was a group of intellectuals distinct from the more conservative ideologues who cleaved to an orthodox version of Marxism. Known as the "new left," they, ironically, had been influenced by Western critics of capitalism and imperialism who argued that Westernization itself is a force inimical to democracy. Capitalism, these neo-Marxist and postmodernist critics assert, is essentially a tool for exploiting nations on the periphery of the global market. The Chinese new left critiques globalization from a nationalist perspective, believing international markets will undermine Chinese sovereignty.[14] The leftist tracts have been severely repudiated by the "rightists," that is Chinese liberals, who assert that their arguments stir up ideological confusion and represent a hopeless call for another cultural revolution. The leftist proposals, they warn, would set China back into the 1950s.

Although both the new and old left were probably a minority, the latter included more of the older, non–college-educated cadres. These nationalistic and conservative elements were an important force to be dealt with because they had played a pioneering role in the establishment of the party and were the standard bearers of Marxism, which the party needed for purposes of legitimation. Also, both the new and old leftists could claim to speak for a broad public constituency, namely China's masses, who have not benefited from liberal economic reforms.

Jiang Zemin tried to steer a middle path between his critics on the left and those on the right who were pushing for more political and economic reform than he thought prudent. In order to legitimate his "third way" (i.e., authoritarian politics/liberal economics), Jiang and his intellectual advisers purposively grounded their program on patriotic values, asserting that a continuing economic relationship with the international community and the harnessing of market forces would bolster the strength of the Chinese nation. In the long run, China's economy would expand, benefiting all social groups. Yet, Jiang insisted, growth could not be at the expense of "spiritual civilization." Cadres must be aware of the social effects of their work. All this would be secured by strengthening party control of opinion so as to firm up the public's will to preserve "Marxism, Leninism, and Mao Zedong Thought."

A significant dimension of Jiang's campaign for spiritual rejuvenation was a call for cadres to "pay attention to politics." By this Jiang meant a concerted effort to make the party work more effectively by combating corruption, laziness, and internal bickering, and promoting higher ideological standards. The party now became more selective about promoting cadres. It was determined that a large number of those promoted through the ranks in the 1990s were woefully deficient in ideology and work style, which meant that they could command little support and respect from the masses over whom they were to rule.

Opposition to Jiang

The Jiangists' concern with spiritual values was a reflection of what seemed to be a widespread sense of moral confusion that beset the nation in the mid-1990s. The manifestations of cultural crisis ranged from a growing nostalgia for Mao (in Shaoshan, his birthplace, there is a lavish and highly esteemed display of Mao's underwear) to religious revivalism, the most difficult to contain being that associated with Falun Gong, which according to official estimates has attracted possibly as many as 80 million adherents. The deification of Mao appears to have been a direct consequence of the disruptions brought about by Jiang's economic reforms. In the popular mind, Mao stood for egalitarianism and moral rectitude, whereas the current elite seemed corrupt, greedy, and disdainful of the masses.[15]

The Chinese government was particularly worried about Falun Gong's capacity to mobilize supporters for collective action. For example, between April and July 1999 alone it mounted 307 protest demonstrations. One such gathering involved some 10,000 practitioners from several provinces in front of Zhongnanhai, a strategic compound near Beijing's Forbidden City that serves as party and government headquarters. The protestors demanded official recognition as a religious group, a policy the government refused to consider. The official media deemed this demonstration to be the most serious threat to public order since the Tiananmen incident of 1989.[16] After that event, as many as 10,000 Falun Gong leaders were arrested and sent to brutal labor camps. Another dramatic incident occurred in late January 2000 when several members of the banned organization set themselves on fire in Tiananmen Square. The success of Falun Gong in gaining adherents as well as the recent increase in conversions to Christianity throughout China point to the poverty of party ideology, communism itself having been largely discredited in the public eye since the disasters of the Cultural Revolution and the Tiananmen Massacre.

Falun Gong emphasizes the use of ancient breathing and related exercises known as *qigong* that are supposed to promote spiritual sensitivity as well as physical and mental healing. Its leader is a charismatic, mystical figure named Li Hongzhi who currently resides in New York City. Li is considered a grand master of *qigong* techniques, claiming to have perfected these powers to the point of experiencing free flight. The CCP asserted that Falun Gong was a formal, highly disciplined organization aiming to create public disorder and regime change. Consequently, the government classified the movement as an illegal organization, essentially seeing Falun Gong as a powerful secret society, a traditional harbinger of dynastic collapse.

What made Falun Gong especially dangerous in party opinion was its organizational and communication capacities (it has more than eighty Web sites), giving leaders the ability to call out millions of practitioners at short notice virtually anywhere in China. The CCP has had few effective remedies to the challenges of such cults or the riots of farmers and workers protesting factory closures and poor wages, other than falling back on the old bromides of redoubling the study of Marxist dogma and giving battle to "classism" and foreign imperialists. Such measures did relatively little to reinforce the party's legitimacy, which rests on its claims to represent the will of the nation. Those who protested its policies, from frustrated peasants to unemployed workers, religious cultists, and intellectuals, were calling into question the party's mandate to rule. These voices of dissonance rested their case on a higher morality (much as did the "early" Mao), an alternative dogma that directly threatened the legitimacy of Communist Party rule.

Jiang Zemin tried to lay out a vision for the future that would help deal with the challenges of dissident groups, meet the "complaints" of his predecessor's policies, and capture the imagination of the nation in an effort to remake China as a major power for the next century. In order to counter "spiritual pollution," the party encouraged the revival of Confucian teachings and what it calls "traditional Chinese values" (thrift, honesty, and even filial piety, among other such virtues) in order to strengthen the nation's moral fabric. Jiang also called on the party to filter out the negative attributes of Western culture ("when the windows are opened, flies can come in") through tighter control of the media and popular culture. There was even an attack on Mickey Mouse, a cartoon character as popular with Chinese adults as with children because it was deemed an example of decadent "cultural colonialism."

Despite limited success on the cultural front, Jiang's efforts at consolidating his own style of leadership and thought were sufficient to assure a continuity in power when his patron Deng Xiaoping suffered a stroke and died on February 19, 1997. At the Fifteenth Party Congress the following September, plans were put in motion to have Jiang's old ally Zhu Rongji replace the conservative and unpopular hardliner Li Peng as premier, a reward for having spearheaded China's economic modernization efforts. Zhu's replacement of Li Peng also made it easier for Jiang to initiate a more progressive foreign policy, especially with regard to improving relations with the United States. Engaging Washington on a more positive footing would facilitate liberal domestic economic reforms and raise Jiang's international stature. Another promotion was that of Hu Jintao, who was made vice-president. Hu was an avid supporter of Jiang's efforts at improving the work style of cadres through ideological indoctrination and discipline. Yet another significant move was the appointment of Wen Jiabao to the position of vice-premier. All those who received promotions shared Jiang's views concerning political authoritarianism and liberal economic reforms. As a means of opening up elite leadership positions, it was decided in the summer of 1997 that those aged 70 and older by the end of June should retire (Jiang excluded). The ruling was a convenient means of moving the more conservative old guard into the background.

The Fifteenth Party Congress was a watershed in the history of the CCP in that it marked the first peaceful transition of power from those who made the revolution to a postrevolutionary generation. The smooth way in which this took place owed much to the leadership style of Jiang Zemin. Unlike Mao, Jiang operated by consensus, not confrontation. He realized that the party could no longer afford the political instability that came with purges. Jiang was more interested in building institutions and establishing rules for party business and economic and political reforms.

Once Jiang's new team was in place, the issues of economic and government reconstruction once again took center stage. On the economic front, China had to decide to what extent it wished to become linked to the global economy. A fuller integration with international markets called attention to the fate of SOEs, the inefficiencies of which were impeding economic growth. Reforming the SOEs was a highly sensitive issue. Closing down unprofitable state companies would lead to a massive loss of jobs and call into question a core principle of socialism itself, namely the viability of planned economies.

The decision to lift restrictions on foreign ownership in the mid-1990s resulted in substantial increases in investment, but it also stimulated economic nationalism. Many Chinese-owned enterprises had difficulty competing with the more efficient foreign firms. Such concerns added fuel to the debate about whether China should join the World Trade Organization (WTO). The leftists feared that more engagement with the international economy would lead China into a capitalist snare and increase its vulnerability to American global hegemony.

Under Zhu Rongji's bureaucratic reform plans many ministries were downsized or eliminated as the state prepared to retreat from managing the economy so private industries would have a chance to grow. The government hoped that the rapidly expanding private sector would absorb workers who lost employment because of cutbacks in the SOEs. Jiang's team wanted to integrate the Chinese economy more closely with international markets and therefore pushed for China's entrance into the WTO. Although Zhu Rongji was out front pushing for WTO membership, he had considerable opposition from Li Peng and the leftists who feared "bourgeois liberalization." Meanwhile, relations between the United States and China went sour, owing to highly credible allegations of China's nuclear espionage, accusations that China had tried to influence American politics by making illegal contributions to the Democratic Party, and American displeasure over renewed political crackdowns. China, for its part, was apprehensive about what it regarded as Washington's interventionist policies regarding Serbian president Slobodan Milosevic. When his government refused to accept an agreement to end ethnic conflict in Kosovo province, in March 1999 the United States led a NATO-sponsored bombing campaign in Serbia.

The United States initially refused to support WTO membership for China unless Beijing made several broad concessions concerning international trading norms. After Zhu Rongji failed to win support from President Clinton during a special visit to Washington in April 1999 despite what Beijing believed were generous concessions on its part (regarding telecommunications and computer technology), all hell broke loose on the Chinese domestic front. Adding to the nationalist fury was the unfortunate American bombing of China's Belgrade embassy, clearly a planning error in the campaign against the Milosevic government, but not believed so by an already agitated Chinese public. Jiang and Zhu now came under severe criticism from Chinese nationalists and the followers of Li Peng. Zhu's compromises with President Clinton were equated with Yuan Shikai's concessions to the 1915 "Twenty-one Demands," which had aimed to reduce China to a colony of Japan. The WTO issue, along with the American bombing, triggered an unprecedented outpouring of popular patriotic emotion. In some ways, Jiang had been hoist by his own petard: now he had to ride the tiger his previous appeals to nationalism had aroused. Those on the left who spoke out against the WTO warned that it and the World Bank, the International Monetary Fund (IMF), NATO, and even the United Nations were part of a web of institutions designed to promote American corporate interests and other capitalist multinational enterprises.

Although there was serious opposition to joining the WTO within the ruling elites and among the general public, Zhu Rongji realized that China's economic future depended on membership. Moreover, there were several immediate problems that could be remedied by joining that international body. The Asian financial crisis (1997–98) had undercut demand for Chinese exports and foreign investment was beginning to slacken. Entry into the WTO and American granting of Permanent Normal Trade Relations (PNTR) would reassure investors and help revive China's export markets. Zhu hoped that the increased global market competition that came from WTO membership would pressure reluctant bureaucrats to carry out the necessary restructuring of the dysfunctional SOEs. All this would buttress Zhu's plans to weed out the more inefficient industries. Finally, without a reasonably good relationship with the United States, which WTO membership would facilitate, additional resources would be required for building up the military, thereby diverting much-needed revenues for modernizing the economy.

After long and arduous negotiations between the Clinton administration and Jiang Zemin's government, agreement on the WTO was finally reached in November 1999; within the month the Politburo Standing Committee voted to accept conditions for membership (Li Peng was the lone voice of dissent). China's accession to the international trade body owed much to the skillful hand of Jiang in quelling the squabbles unleashed by the leftists and the voices of popular nationalism.

For the rest of his tenure as president and general secretary, Jiang Zemin had additional problems with corruption, the social and economic fallout of the SOEs, a volatile popular nationalism fanned by the left, and intellectual dissidents who chaffed under authoritarian political restrictions. As a means of meeting these challenges and struggling to show himself to be a leader with vision, Jiang in a speech in late February 2000 introduced a new thesis to guide the party, a formulation summed up as the "Three Represents." Jiang asserted that the party had always represented "the most advanced productive forces, the most advanced culture, and the fundamental interests of the broad masses of the Chinese people."[17] The task now, he claimed, was to absorb the achievements of foreign countries and meld them with the finest cultural traditions of China. This would permit China as a member of the WTO to adjust to the demands of a global economy and rapid developments in science and technology, yet be guided in the world of "broad and profound changes" by fundamental Chinese values. The most important and new theoretical dimension to Jiang's ideology was the insistence that the party must represent the interests of all Chinese people, a modification of the older formulation that the CCP represents the vanguard of the working class. An "all people's party" not only lacks precedence in Chinese Communist history but it also runs contrary to orthodox Marxist ideology. This definition of the party's mission leaves room for potential political reform, if such is defined as promoting the broad interests of the Chinese citizenry.

The leftists failed to come up with a comparable political vision or viable economic plan of their own, and therefore Jiang and his supporters were able to accelerate the pace of economic reform as China struggled to adjust to the norms of a global market and position herself for international leadership in the twenty-first century.

12

China in the World

Shenzhen, across the river from the Hong Kong Special Administrative Region, was the first special economic zone designated in 1980 and became one of the fastest growing cities in the world.

Many of China's international objectives today are continuous with those of previous Communist, and even pre-Communist, periods. Although the reforms of Deng Xiaoping opened China to the world economically, and thus were a radical departure from policies associated with the Mao years, the values that shape China's foreign policies have deep roots. A study published by the Council on Foreign Relations more than a decade ago identified five major objectives (listed below in italics) that underlie China's international behavior.[1]

1. *Protecting China's sovereignty*. This "sacred principle" has determined Beijing's attitude toward the return of jurisdiction over Hong Kong, its relations with Taiwan and Tibet, and the quest for sovereignty over various offshore islands. Its defense of territorial integrity and national independence has strengthened the Communist Party's commitment to determine its own views on human rights, protection of the environment, and the utility of foreign values for the Chinese people.

2. *Maintaining national security*. For the Beijing government the development of global interdependence is secondary to protecting and enhancing national interests. As a result, China often does not openly endorse cooperative security arrangements and has demonstrated an aversion to joining international or regional security efforts. One example is seen in China's role in the 1991 Gulf War when Iraq invaded Kuwait: As a permanent member of the Security Council, China did not join the United Nations coalition forces, yet did not act as obstructionist. The goal of maintaining national security has also caused Beijing to ignore international pressure to limit its advancing military capabilities.

3. *Eroding Taiwan's international status*. Chinese Communist leaders, like their predecessors, hold fast the principle that Taiwan is part of China. Taiwan's status remains problematic as its political, economic, and cultural separateness from the mainland appears to widen. The 2000 election of Chen Shui-bian, the island's first non-Guomindang (GMD) president, brought Taiwan closer to achieving democracy. As a result, prodemocracy supporters worldwide became willing critics of Beijing's attempts to reunify with Taiwan. Taiwan's status remains a contentious issue for the Communist government in dealing within the international arena.

4. *Cultivating a favorable image*. Although China is among the nations that most often oppose the positions of the United States and its allies in the United Nations, for the most part it has not sought to undermine Western positions within the international organization. Beijing is reluctant to use its veto power to dispute an international consensus because it seeks the advantages of being perceived as cooperative and responsible within the international community.

5. *Promoting economic interests*. Deng's successors are committed to China's full participation in the international economy and a continuation of reforms to enhance China's market-based system. Beijing's admission to the World Trade Organization (WTO) in 2002 was a huge step in that direction and its developing ties with Taiwan and South Korea are part of the plan.

Hong Kong: Special Administrative Region of the People's Republic of China

The return to China of territories lost to imperialism was one of Deng Xiao-ping's top priorities. In January 1980, in one of his major policy announcements to high-level Communist Party leaders, Deng emphasized the importance of China's reunification with Hong Kong, Macao, Taiwan, and several offshore islands to accompany his broader goals of economic modernization. The recovery of Hong Kong would be tackled first, and subsequently the process would serve as a model for future negotiations concerning other territories.

In 1982, talks between Beijing and London began, with the goal of renego-tiating the 99-year lease on the New Territories of Hong Kong, due to expire on July 1, 1997. Within 2 years, a Joint Declaration on the Question of Hong Kong was reached, announcing that the entire Hong Kong territory (includ-ing Hong Kong Island, Kowloon Peninsula, and the New Territories) would be ceded to China in 1997. Hong Kong would then be designated a special administrative region of China, allowed to maintain its capitalist economic system for 50 years, while the local government would be autonomous, as long as Hong Kong laws did not conflict with China's laws. This agreement served as the basis for Jiang Zemin's "one country, two systems" principle later applied to Taiwan.

A Joint Sino-British Liaison Group was established in May 1985 to ensure a smooth transition for the transfer of power to China, but the group ran into difficulty when relations quickly deteriorated after the Tiananmen Massacre in 1989. The massive prodemocracy demonstrations that erupted in Hong Kong were accompanied by a sharp increase in applications for emigration out of the colony. Hong Kong governor Chris Patten increased tensions by is-suing several actions considered controversial by Beijing, the most significant of which was the establishment of an elected Legislative Council in 1995. This would have been the first time in the colony's history that Hong Kong's leaders were elected and not appointed. The infuriated Beijing government countered by announcing that the elected council would be dismantled and replaced by a Beijing-appointed provisional government upon the transfer of Hong Kong to Chinese rule, but Beijing and Hong Kong authorities worked out a compromise. On April 4, 1990, the Basic Law, whereby Hong Kong enjoys some degree of autonomy except in defense and foreign policy, was adopted by Beijing's Seventh National People's Congress. The law provides that Hong Kong will be ruled by a chief executive who "shall be selected by election or through consultation held locally and be appointed by the Beijing government." It went into effect on July 1, 1997.

President Jiang Zemin considered the return of Hong Kong to be of the utmost significance, especially because he made little headway in negotiations concerning reunification with Taiwan during the 1990s. In 1996, Jiang commented, "A successful resolution of the Hong Kong issue will surely have a splendid impact on prospects for national reunification."[2] The July 1, 1997, transfer of power went smoothly. An estimated 2 billion people around the world watched the televised ceremony, and in attendance were CCP and British dignitaries, including Jiang, British Prime Minister Tony Blair, and Prince Charles. According to one observer:

> Both sides had scripted everything, right down to when the reverberations of the cymbals from the British ceremonial band would die out as the British flag was lowered at midnight. "The eyes of the world are on us at this moment," Jiang said with both literal and figurative accuracy shortly after the Chinese flag was raised in the convention center hall and began to flutter in air piped through the base of the flagpole. "This is both a great event for the Chinese nation as well as a victory for the universal cause of peace and justice."[3]

On the following day, Jiang hosted a "spectacular extravaganza" in Beijing's Workers' Stadium, celebrating Hong Kong's return. A cast of tens of thousands performed a series of historical skits depicting China's development from a weak nation victimized by imperialism starting with the Opium Wars to a strong power under the leadership of the Communist Party. Jiang's opening speech traced how the Chinese people had "tragically but heroically traversed a long and rugged road, a road full of humiliation and hardship. . . ." The occupation of Hong Kong was, he said, "the epitome of the humiliation China suffered in modern history."[4] The success of Hong Kong's reunification would bolster Chinese patriotism while achieving a significant first step toward regaining all territories still claimed by Beijing.

Although the ceremony commemorating the transfer went smoothly, the transition that followed did not. Despite Jiang's attempts to assure the people of Hong Kong and the rest of the world that the 4,000 PLA troops and 21 armored antiriot tanks that entered the territory on July 2, 1997, were no threat, many were unnerved by their presence. Beijing's critics have complained that the freedom enjoyed by Hong Kong residents has been fading. The United States government weighed in with its support for Hong Kong's autonomous status. During the Clinton administration, Congress passed the U.S.–Hong Kong Policy Act (1992), which asserts that "The human rights of the people of Hong Kong are of great importance to the United States and are directly relevant to U.S. interests in Hong Kong."[5] Although the United States has not threatened to impose the sanctions provided for in the act, it has served notice that the new Chinese administration in Hong Kong would be closely monitored.

The fifth anniversary of Hong Kong's handover was marked by anti-Beijing, prodemocracy protests. Demonstrators campaigned for improved human rights for China and an end to the one-party state. Their slogan was "Down with Jiang Zemin."[6] The Beijing government downplayed the complaints; it highlighted the development of closer economic ties instead. On the following year's anniversary, July 1, 2003, the government of Hu Jintao was shocked by a 500,000-strong prodemocracy march. The protest came as a response to a proposed internal security bill pending before Hong Kong's Legislative Council and supported by Beijing-backed Chief Executive Tung Chee-hwa. Nearly one-tenth of the city's population rallied for the march, asserting that the security laws symbolized the "true transition to Chinese rule," a more direct takeover, occurring 6 years after the initial reunification. Although the vote on the bill was postponed indefinitely in September 2003, representatives of Hong Kong's Civil Human Rights Front, a coalition of prodemocracy organizations, expressed pessimism about the future.[7] Protesters again voiced their concerns by organizing another prodemocracy march on New Year's Day, 2004. The events served as a setback to Jiang and Hu's "one country, two systems" model, not only for Hong Kong, but for Taiwan as well.

"One Country, Two Systems": The Issue of Taiwan

Jiang Zemin openly promoted negotiations on the reunification of China and Taiwan in his report to the Fourteenth National Congress of the Communist Party in October 1992 where he proclaimed, "On the premise that there is only one China, we are prepared to talk with the Taiwan authorities about any matter, including the form official negotiations should take, a form that would be acceptable to both sides."[8] Therefore, it is no coincidence that Jiang's ascension to the presidency in March 1993 was soon followed by an historic and controversial move: the April 1993 meeting between representatives from China and Taiwan in Singapore, the first official dialogue between the two enemies since 1949. The "Taiwan-China Talks" were organized by two semiofficial organizations, Taiwan's Straits Exchange Foundation (SEF) and China's Association for Relations Across the Taiwan Straits (ARATS). It was not until July 2000 that both the Beijing and Taibei governments admitted to holding a series of secret talks leading up to the 1993 meeting. From 1988 to1992 representatives from both sides met a total of nine times, working out details for a conference. Apparently, Beijing made the first move, initiating the highly secret meetings in January 1988 when Jia Yibin, a member of the Chinese People's Political Consultative Conference, contacted Nan Huai-chin, a mainland-born historian and philosopher from Taiwan, telling Nan that Beijing leaders wanted to consult with Taiwan's new president, Lee Teng-hui. Lee had replaced Chiang Ching-kuo, Chiang Kai-shek's son, in January 1988 following Chiang Ching-kuo's death. Despite apparent high-level support from both sides, the talks failed to produce any significant political agreements. A document calling for "peaceful coexistence and reunification through negotiations"[9] drafted by Nan Huai-chin has not yet been signed.

On January 30, 1995, in a celebratory New Year's address entitled "Continue to Promote the Reunification of the Motherland," President Jiang acknowledged the ongoing attempts at cross-Straits negotiations. The speech continues to serve as China's official policy toward Taiwan, promoting "one country, two systems" and outlines an eight-point proposal describing the Communist Party's intentions to pursue peaceful reunification while acknowledging Taiwan's continuing right to develop "non-governmental economic and cultural ties" with other countries. The Communist Party shows no signs of abandoning the goal of reunification. Jiang emphasized, "It remains the sacred mission and lofty goal of the entire Chinese people to achieve the reunification of the motherland and promote the all-round revitalization of the Chinese nation. . . . [T]here is only one China, and Taiwan is part of China. We will never allow there to be 'two Chinas,' or 'one China, one Taiwan.'"[10]

Talks between representatives of China and Taiwan stalled in May 1995 when the United States granted a visa to Taiwan's president Lee Teng-hui to attend his college reunion. The visa was granted after intense pressure on the administration by the Republican-dominated Congress. Beijing reacted by recalling the Chinese ambassador to the United States and stepping up pressure on Taiwan by holding military exercises near the island. Two American officials were arrested and expelled from China for allegedly spying on Chinese military installations. In the midst of controversy, President Clinton renewed China's most-favored-nation trading status. In June 1995, Harry Wu, an American citizen and human rights advocate, was arrested in China while investigating the labor-camp system. He was charged with espionage and sentenced to 15 years in prison. Wu was an outspoken critic of the Chinese government, having spent 19 years in prison before immigrating to the United States. He claimed to have proof of China's flagrant human rights abuses, including the sale of executed prisoners' organs and the use of slave labor to produce exports. On the day following his sentencing, Wu was expelled from China and flown home to California. At the time, the Clinton administration considered this action a gesture of Beijing's willingness to smooth relations with the United States. But problems soon reemerged when China held intensive military exercises during the spring of 1996, just prior to Taiwan's national presidential elections. China's show of force this time was answered by the Clinton administration when a portion of the U.S. Seventh Fleet was deployed off Taiwan's coast. Harsh mutual condemnation by China and the United States coincided with the show of military force, but after Taiwan's elections were over and President Lee was reelected, the hostilities ceased, in part because Lee used his inaugural speech on May 20, 1996, as an olive branch to Beijing. He claimed that Taiwan's independence was both impossible and unnecessary, and he offered to journey to Beijing to discuss peace.

In July 1999, tensions were renewed when President Lee began to waiver in time for the March 2000 elections and spoke of a "two-state" approach to negotiation, but Lee's heir apparent, the GMD candidate Lien Chan, was defeated, and the election of Chen Shui-bian, Taiwan's first non-GMD president, only exacerbated the conflict. Chen's party, the Democratic Progressive Party (DPP), supports the independence of Taiwan. The DPP's platform "Let Taiwan decide its own future" and Chen's campaign speeches promising the people of Taiwan that they will determine their own destiny brought threats from Beijing. But Chen soon faced the realities of Taiwan's internal politics: the DPP won the election with only 39 percent of the popular vote. GMD candidate Lien received 23 percent, and a second GMD associate, James Soong, won 36.8 percent. Thus Chen ruled with no popular mandate and no majority in Parliament. By the time of his inaugural address, Chen had acquiesced to the GMD's position on Taiwan's future: There will be no declaration of independence, and negotiations will continue. In April 2001, new talks were announced based on Jiang's "one country, two systems" policy, even though Chen and the DPP claimed the policy is unacceptable.

The DPP's provocative platform that angered Beijing and worried the United States was rejected by voters in a landslide victory for GMD presidential candidate Ma Ying-jeou in March 2008. The Harvard-educated Ma supports expanding economic ties with China and avoiding political confrontation with Beijing. His campaign platform focused on improving Taiwan's faltering economy through cultivating closer ties to China.

"Get Mad and Then Get Over It": The Relationship between Washington and Beijing

Diplomatic relations between China and the United States have been characterized as troubling. On the one hand, strong economic ties helped forge closer business relationships between Americans and Chinese; on the other hand, political and military confrontations occurred with alarming frequency as China made headway in challenging American hegemony in East Asia. On July 28, 2001, a Chinese journalist asked Secretary of State Colin L. Powell, in Beijing preparing for a visit by President George W. Bush, about one of

"Powell's Rules" cited in his autobiography. The journalist commented that it seems Rule No. 2, "Get mad and then get over it," best describes bilateral relations between China and the United States. Powell agreed.[11] At the heart of the conflict is Washington and Beijing's shared objective to be the dominant power in East Asia. The continued presence of strong U.S. military forces throughout the Pacific has served as an obstacle to some of Beijing's ambitions. For example, since 1950 the U.S. Navy has prevented the Communists from using force to retake Taiwan. The deployment of the U.S. Seventh Fleet by President Clinton, during the March 1996 Taiwan Straits Crisis, affirms Beijing's concerns. Nationalistic Chinese, from leaders to ordinary citizens, increasingly identify the United States as the "global hegemonist."[12] Jiang's Foreign Minister Qian Qichen explained that for the foreseeable future the United States "will create much trouble. . . . The major obstacle to our foreign relations will come from the United States."[13]

One of the turning points in U.S.-China relations was caused by American reactions to the Tiananmen Massacre because of continuing tensions between those who support human rights and democracy for China and adherents of closer trade ties. Human rights activists, including some members of Congress, demanded that the U.S. government impose economic sanctions against the Chinese government following the massacre in 1989. But just days later, it was business as usual in the cities adjoining the coastal special economic zones. President George H.W. Bush did not want China's domestic conflicts to have an impact on trade agreements with U.S. companies. He dispatched two top aides, Lawrence Eagleburger and Brent Scowcroft, to meet secretly with CCP leaders to assure continuation of friendly relations. Within weeks of the massacre, the Bush administration renewed China's most-favored-nation trading status, which allows for relatively unrestricted trade between the two nations. In June 1989, the president of the U.S. China Business Council, Roger W. Sullivan, commented that "[American] companies are loath to abandon the joint ventures that are already in effect. They spent a lot to get them in place. These joint ventures are, by and large, directed at selling into the Chinese market. So they want to keep it alive."[14] But trade relationships grew tense during the first Bush administration when the U.S. government blamed its accelerating trade deficit in part on the Chinese refusal to open its markets to American products. Sanctions on nearly $4 billion in Chinese goods were threatened but never took effect because the Chinese agreed to a series of market-opening procedures.

Trade conflicts continued to plague U.S.-China relations to the point where journalists were writing of a "trade war" by 1995. President Bill Clinton, like his predecessor, faced a growing trade deficit with China—$30 billion in 1994, second only to the U.S. trade deficit with Japan. Although some areas of China's market remained closed to American goods, the more problematic issues involved accusations of intellectual property theft and other violations of copyright laws by Chinese manufacturers. The American Recording Industry Association claimed that in 1994 twenty-six Chinese factories were capable of producing 70 million pirated compact disks to be sold to foreign markets. American computer software manufacturers and film producers made similar claims. These practices potentially cost American manufacturers more than $1 billion in losses annually. Human rights advocates also pressured the U.S. government to stop buying Chinese products allegedly made by prison labor. In response, Clinton's trade representative, Mickey Kantor, proposed sanctions on some of China's more popular exports. The Chinese government retaliated by threatening to impose a 100 percent tariff on U.S. consumer products exported to China, but after months of negotiations, both sides backed down. Sanctions were dropped while the Chinese government assured the United States that it would crack down on copyright violations. But these actions proved ineffective: One week before the U.S. computer giant Microsoft Corporation released its new software, Windows 95, in mid-1995, vast quantities of bootlegged versions were produced in China.

Yet another controversy for the Clinton administration involved Chinese sales of advanced military equipment to countries banned from such sales by international agreements. When U.S. intelligence agencies found evidence that China had shipped missile components to Pakistan in 1993, the Clinton administration blocked sales of satellite systems to China. These limited sanctions had no effect on China's sales practices, but American manufacturers complained bitterly of losing out to foreign competitors. Ironically, the CCP's most effective lobbyists have been American corporate heads who do not want to be excluded from the Chinese market by their own government. One example of this can be seen in Jiang Zemin's appeal to the American business community made in 1993 at the Seattle Asia-Pacific Economic Cooperation forum, where he promoted the benefits of China trade for American job security. Jiang's claim that China trade supported 250,000 American jobs, effectively resonated with Clinton's concerns for the U.S. economy. The following year, Clinton announced that the United States would no longer link trade with China's progress on human rights. U.S.-China trade grew at an average rate of about 25 percent annually, the U.S. deficit reached $256 billion in 2007, and political disputes between the two nations continued.

Among the more serious disputes between the United States and China have been potential military conflicts whose underlying cause involves Beijing's increasing sensitivity over the presence of the U.S. military in East Asia. In 1994, the Chinese Air Force confronted American planes sent from the U.S.

aircraft carrier, *Kitty Hawk*, as they were tracking a Chinese submarine allegedly located in China's territorial waters. The Beijing government warned the U.S. government that violations of Chinese air space will result in American planes being shot down.[15] In 2001, another such incident occurred, resulting in the holding of 24 American military personnel on Hainan Island for 11 days, after a mid-air collision left a Chinese pilot dead and the American EP-3 aircraft crash-landed on the island. The U.S. aircraft was allegedly on a routine surveillance flight over international waters when the Chinese Air Force challenged its position, claiming the air space as Chinese. The standoff was eventually resolved, and the 24-member crew was released after the Bush administration apologized for the Chinese pilot's death.[16] American military presence continues to be an irritant for Beijing.

The Bush administration made little progress on resolving political or economic conflicts with the Chinese, but an outwardly amicable relationship was forged after numerous state visits for presidents Bush and Hu Jintao. In 2006, in preparation for one of Hu's U.S. tours, one senior Foreign Ministry official commented, "We believe the China-U.S. relationship is one of the most important bilateral relationships in the world."[17]

Balancing Contradictions: China and Japan

Stability in East Asia depends on good relations between China and Japan, two nations sure to remain economic and military powers for the foreseeable future. Yet, "contradictions" in Sino-Japanese relations are part of the continuing development of political and economic ties. On the one hand, China and Japan share a centuries-old cultural heritage, adopted by Japan from China; on the other, Japanese aggression and cruelty in China from 1894 through World War II leave a bitter historical legacy. As Deng Xiaoping's program began to open China to the world in 1972, the Communist Party found itself uncomfortably dependent on Japanese technology, investment, and loans. This reality remains a source of frustration for nationalistic Chinese.[18] As the relationship continues to grow, the main goals of Beijing's policies toward Japan include (1) preventing a remilitarized Japan from having the ability to threaten, challenge, or coerce China by military means again; (2) keeping Tokyo from acquiring the role of regional leader in East Asia, a role that should be Beijing's; (3) acquiring as much investment, economic assistance, and advanced technology from Japan for as long as possible; and (4) minimizing Japanese relations with Taiwan. Consequently, Chinese relations with Japan reflect the dilemma of dependency coupled with fear of Japan's regional political and military clout, especially because the United States has pushed Japan into playing a greater regional role.[19]

China and Japan also dispute the ownership of the Diaoyudao Islands, located about 100 miles northeast of Taiwan. (Taiwan also claims ownership.) The islands are rich in resources, including substantial offshore oil and natural gas deposits. For nationalistic Chinese, recovery of the islands is an important goal, not only for economic reasons, but also for the historical legacy the islands represent. The Diaoyudao (Fishing Islands) were named by Chinese officials during the fifteenth century. The Japanese later claimed that they were part of their Ryukyu island chain, although the feudal-era Ryukyu kingdom recognized the Diaoyudao as Chinese. The Japanese formally took the islands, along with Taiwan and other concessions, in the 1895 treaty marking the defeat of China in the Sino-Japanese War (1894–1895). In 1900 they were named the Senkaku Islands by Japan. Today, Japan controls the islands because they were grouped with the Ryukyus by the U.S. occupation administration after World War II.

There have been numerous incidents during the past 50 years in which Chinese from both China and Taiwan have staged protests, raised Chinese flags, and confronted Japanese authorities on the islands. In 1996, for example, when a group of Japanese erected a lighthouse adorned with Japanese flags on one of the islands, protestors from Hong Kong and Taiwan sailed to the islands, only to be rebuffed by the Japanese coast guard. The governments of Beijing, Tokyo, and Taibei have downplayed the significance of such incidents, not wanting to jeopardize their lucrative economic ties, but Beijing continues to claim that China's sovereignty over the Diaoyudao is indisputable.[20]

Another recent area of contention between China and Japan resulted from a renewal of intense nationalism based on their shared histories. The Chinese harbor resentment of Japanese conduct in China before and during World War II. More than 60 years since the end of the war, popular media in both countries still flame suspicions and prejudices. The publication of Iris Chang's *The Rape of Nanking: The Forgotten Holocaust of World War II* in 1997 on the occasion of the 60th anniversary of the Nanjing Massacre reignited old animosities. Chang documented the horror experienced by Chinese in 1937 and 1938 in what historians have called "the rape of Nanjing." The bestseller was vilified by Japanese, but its story was hailed by Chinese all over the world. Other sources of antagonism included Tokyo's approval of Japanese history public school textbooks that, according to the Chinese, gloss over wartime atrocities by the Japanese in China. In addition, the annual visits to Japan's war memorial and symbol of its militaristic past, the Yasukuni shrine, by former Prime Minister Junichiro Koizumi sparked widespread anti-Japanese demonstrations in China. Such expressions of often violent public outrage, the Japanese sarcastically observed, have been the few that authoritarian CCP leaders permit. One indication of how serious the Chinese and Japanese consider interpretations of history can be seen in the creation of a special academic commission whose goal is to resolve historical arguments, including those surrounding World War II. In 2007 both governments appointed ten academic specialists assigned the daunting task of reconciling the different points of view. The commission may take years to complete its findings.

Seeking Stability: China and the Two Koreas

The Chinese government did not establish diplomatic relations with the Republic of Korea (South Korea) until 1992, but ties between the two former enemies have continued to expand since then. Bilateral trade flourished, growing at a rate of about 20 percent annually, reaching the point where China became South Korea's number one trading partner, surpassing the United States by mid-2002. China has become a target for investment by South Korean businesses, especially small and mid-sized companies that have been bankrolling the automobile, textile, technology, and chemical sectors of the Chinese economy.[21]

The developing relationship between China and South Korea has obvious implications for the Democratic People's Republic of Korea (North Korea), whose government protested China's rapprochement with the South in 1992. Until the 1990s, China and North Korea were close allies, sharing a legacy of Communist leadership and partnership in the Korean War. But the personal ties between Chinese and North Korean leaders of the past are gone, now that both Deng Xiaoping and Kim Il-sung are dead. Hu Jintao's "Fourth Generation" and Kim Jong-il appear to have little in common. Beijing's response to the sensitive situation was to employ an "equidistance policy" and attempt to "balance political interactions between Seoul and Pyongyang. Both North and South Korea were treated in equivalent fashion on issues of politics and public symbolism, including overt use of the Chinese media to reinforce the political message of equidistance by providing equal space to events related to North and South Korea."[22]

The balancing act proved difficult for Beijing, especially because China has begun to take more of a leading role in regional security and Beijing's relations with South Korea moved beyond bilateral trade. By the mid-1990s, the Chinese began to stray from the "equidistance" policy in order to focus on "stability" for the Korean peninsula, attempting to preserve the status quo. Several issues forced the transition. A famine in North Korea threatened to destabilize the peninsula by severely weakening North Korea's economy. Moreover, refugees streamed into northeast China, taxing the local economies. Beijing responded with humanitarian contributions of food and aid through both private and public sources reported to have amounted to one quarter to one third of China's total foreign aid budget. Analysts conclude that the Chinese aid program may have delayed a possible North Korean collapse.[23]

Another conflict involves North Korea's nuclear weapons program, perceived as threatening and destabilizing by all of Korea's neighbors as well as the United States. In August 1998, Pyongyang successfully tested a ballistic missile with a range of 3,000 miles, capable of hitting Beijing, Seoul, Taibei, and Alaska. Western intelligence analysts agree that North Korea is capable of arming its vast arsenal of ballistic missiles with nuclear warheads. A crisis over North Korea's military capabilities came to the forefront following a speech made by President George W. Bush, in which he referred to North Korea as part of an "Axis of Evil." North Korea's Foreign Ministry Deputy Director, Ri Pyong-gap, responded with the warning that North Korea would be willing and capable of launching preemptive strikes. Following the threat, Pyongyang began full-scale operations at the Yongbyon nuclear plant, the suspected site of weapons-grade plutonium production, kicked out international inspectors, and withdrew from a global treaty to stop the spread of nuclear weapons. In response, the Chinese government called for a conference, held in Beijing in August 2003, to discuss the North Korean nuclear weapons program. Representatives from North Korea, the United States, Russia, and South Korea joined the Chinese. A series of talks resulted in a multinational agreement in which Pyongyang consented to provide an accounting of its nuclear programs and eventually disable its nuclear reactors. By the end of 2007 the Yongbyon plant was shut down. In return, North Koreans received oil and other aid.

In the long term, China's quest for stability and peace in East Asia to promote economic growth may push the Communist Party into supporting a reunified Korea. As Beijing forges closer ties with Seoul it remains to be seen whether the PRC will continue to prop up North Korea. Meanwhile, Beijing has served as a leader in attempting to avoid potential disaster by remaining one of the few governments that can effectively influence North Korean leaders.

No Longer a Threat: Russian Relations with China

For China, Russia has been a rival, ally, and enemy. China's relations with Russia during the leadership of Jiang Zemin were a reflection of economic and political conditions in Russia: With its armed forces in disarray and its economy in transition, Russia did not pose a challenge to China. Yan Xuetong of the China Committee of the Council of Security Cooperation represented the opinion of many Chinese analysts when he commented in 1995, "Russia is in need of a long period of time to stabilize its domestic political order and to extricate itself from its present economic crisis, and so has neither the will nor the strength to exercise military expansion in East Asia."[24] Yan also predicted that two other factors contribute to Russian interest in actively improving relations with China. The enlargement of NATO, a phenomenon Moscow has been reluctant to support, and the conflict in Chechnya should encourage the Russian government to seek a strategic cooperative partnership with China.[25]

In November 1997, Russian President Boris Yeltsin met with President Jiang Zemin at a summit to discuss the two nations' futures. Negotiators from both sides quickly rejected any revival of the formal alliance from the 1950s while they worked out closer political and economic ties. President Jiang described the new relationship: "I think the bilateral relationship is a strategic partnership of equality and mutual respect. We will not form an alliance, and this kind of long-term relationship is not directed against another country."[26] In July 2001, a Treaty of Friendship reflecting Jiang's perspective was signed in Moscow.

Among the most difficult issues for the two governments to resolve has been the continuous dispute over the borders between Russia and China. Eight years had passed since Soviet leader Mikhail Gorbachev visited Beijing in 1989 to renew relations between the two nations and negotiate a peaceful end to the decades-old border war. In 1997, 6 years of talks finally concluded an agreement that delineates the 2,670-mile-long eastern frontier from Mongolia to the Tumen River near the Sea of Japan. But a shorter 31-mile western border between Kazakhstan and the western tip of Mongolia is still in dispute. In January 2003, Russian President Vladimir Putin expressed confidence that the problem would soon be solved through compromise: "There are reasons to believe that in the near future the issue will finally be settled."[27] At the heart of the issue is territory ruled by Russia but claimed by China. Meanwhile, Moscow wants to maintain, if not strengthen, investment in the area.

China's trade with Russia has also grown, but not to the extent that it has with the United States or East Asian nations. At a 1996 summit held in Beijing, Presidents Jiang Zemin and Boris Yeltsin optimistically projected that by 2000, bilateral trade should exceed $20 billion per year.[28] In 2002, bilateral trade had increased to only $12 billion annually, an increase of more than $2 billion from 2001.[29] One of the main components has been Beijing's importation of Russian military hardware, especially because Moscow placed fewer restrictions on arms sales to China than its Western trading partners. Beijing and Moscow also planned a $12 billion, 30-year-long project to build a pipeline connecting natural gas sources in Siberia to China's Pacific coast. The fuel will be sold throughout China, South Korea, and Japan.

Under the leadership of Russian president Vladimir Putin, relations with

China became somewhat warmer. In 2005 Beijing and Moscow announced new bilateral agreements that called for "pragmatic cooperation in trade" and "significant coordination" in international affairs. Putin and Hu Jintao approved initiatives aimed at deepening bilateral ties, enhancing mutual understanding, and expanding trade called "The Year of Russia in China," 2006, followed by "The Year of China in Russia," 2007. The election of Putin's former deputy prime minister Dmitry Medvedev to the presidency in 2008 should signal the continuation of Putin's cooperative policies.

A Pragmatic Relationship: China and the European Union

During the presidency of Jiang Zemin, China's relationship with several European nations underwent a period of recovery after bilateral trade plummeted in the wake of the Tiananmen Massacre in 1989. Relations with France were severely strained when the French government granted political asylum to numerous Chinese dissidents involved in the prodemocracy movement. The British reaction to Tiananmen affected ongoing negotiations with Beijing over the planned return of Hong Kong to Chinese sovereignty in 1997. In December 1989, after months of debate in Parliament, the British government passed a law granting British passports to 50,000 heads of Hong Kong households and their family members. The Chinese government unsuccessfully opposed this move. Despite the acrimony, by the summer of 1990, most of the year-old sanctions imposed by Western European nations on trade with China were lifted, and bilateral trade with European nations recovered steadily. China's recent ties with Europe can be described as a "businesslike and pragmatic pursuit of bilateral interests." The relationship is less "emotionally charged"[30] than that with the United States, primarily because Chinese leaders do not perceive the European Union (EU), unlike the United States, as a threat to Beijing's ambitions in East Asia.

The absence of serious conflict between China and the EU during the 1990s, however, does not mean that the relationship was free from controversy. In 1996, China's Prime Minister Li Peng visited France with the goal of convincing European governments to halt criticism of China's human rights policies. Li Peng's overture was reinforced by Chinese promises of lucrative trade deals for EU states made at an EU-Asia summit held in Bangkok in March 1996. Subsequently, the EU adopted a more conciliatory approach, resulting in Chinese exports expanding to the point where several EU import quotas were consistently saturated by Chinese products. By 2002, the EU's Trade Commissioner, Pascal Lamy, was forced to negotiate market-opening measures with Beijing. Each side accused the other of imposing discriminatory trade barriers. After several months of talks, the two sides reached mutually satisfactory trade arrangements, including the promise that the EU would vote in favor of China's entrance into the WTO.

From Beijing's perspective, EU leadership also has taken a meddlesome stand toward the status of Tibet. In March 2002, the EU's External Affairs Commissioner, former Hong Kong governor Chris Patten, visited Shanghai to urge Chinese leaders to begin a dialogue with the exiled leader of Tibet, the Dalai Lama. According to Patten, " . . . [T]here was no argument in Europe that Tibet was a Chinese province, there were concerns about whether Tibetan linguistic and cultural traditions were being preserved."[31] On the other hand, EU leadership adheres to the one-China principle, and encourages a reunification of China with Taiwan based on the principles associated with President Jiang Zemin's "one country, two systems" policy. At the Fifth EU-China Summit, held in Copenhagen in September 2002, representatives from both sides welcomed continued expansion of EU-China trade and foreign investment in both directions. The conference reiterated a commitment "to promote the development of a comprehensive partnership" based on equality and mutual benefit between the EU and China.[32]

Tibet

The Chinese Communist Party has come under fire for its policies toward Tibet. The status of Tibet remains problematic as long as the international community continues to pressure the Beijing government to support Tibetan freedom, culture, and language. The western province, comprising approximately 13 percent of the PRC's total territory, is organized into the Tibet Autonomous Region, but for the past two decades Tibetan autonomy has gradually eroded. Perhaps the most significant threat to the claim for Tibetan independence is that by the mid-1990s, Han Chinese outnumbered Tibetans in their home province by more than a million. The demographic change came as a result of Beijing's resettlement program, which provided lucrative financial incentives to Han Chinese to emigrate to Tibet.[33]

Tibet is strategically significant for China's security because it borders on India and Russia, providing a buffer in case of attack. Moreover, the Beijing government has legitimate concerns that an independent Tibet may provide military access or even bases for foreign powers. During the 1960s, the CIA trained Tibetan exiles in guerrilla war at a base in Colorado.[34] More recently, the "Tibetan government-in-exile," representing the exiled head of Tibet's religious autocracy, the fourteenth Dalai Lama, Tenzin Gyatso, maintains close ties to Western powers. In July 2000, the European Parliament called on the governments of EU member states to consider recognizing the government-in-exile as the legitimate representative of the Tibetan people.[35] Also significant is the fact that Tibet is rich in natural resources, many of which have supported China's continuing economic development.

The Tibetan claim for independence is based on Beijing's record of human rights violations and the failure of the Communist Party to allow Tibet's traditional theocracy under the Dalai Lama to rule. While the claim is supported by three resolutions adopted by the United Nations General Assembly in 1959, 1961, and 1965, it should be noted that Beijing was not represented in the UN at the time. Tibet was ruled by the Qing dynasty from the early eighteenth century, but gained independence in 1913 during the period when China's central government faced disintegration under warlord rule. When the Republic of China was established in 1927, the GMD government reclaimed Tibet and other lost Chinese territories, but did not restore effective control. Shortly after the Communist victory in 1949, the People's Liberation Army reestablished authority over Tibet, "liberating" the Tibetans from feudal theocratic rule. The Dalai Lama traveled to Beijing in 1954, meeting with Mao Zedong and Zhou Enlai to negotiate a peaceful settlement to the dispute, but all efforts failed. Beijing's takeover of eastern Tibet ignited a popular resistance movement that spread throughout the province. After a 1959 proindependence demonstration in Lhasa was brutally crushed by the People's Liberation Army, the Dalai Lama fled, leaving those who remained in his government to negotiate with the Communists. The two sides reached a compromise resulting in Tibet's military and foreign affairs coming under Beijing's control, while Tibetans were to be allowed a high degree of autonomy and cultural freedom.

Relations between the Chinese and Tibetan opposition groups have never been smooth. When Tibetan guerrilla fighters attacked Chinese troops, the Chinese retaliated, burning villages and temples, and abducting Tibetans for forced labor and "reeducation." The Cultural Revolution brought new intensity to Tibetan persecution by Red Guards focused on destroying the symbols of Tibetan Buddhism. Tibetan opposition groups have charged the Chinese with abuse of human rights and attempted cultural genocide.[36]

Under the leadership of Deng Xiaoping, the Chinese government declared a willingness to discuss any issue with the exiled Dalai Lama, except independence for Tibet. But the thaw was short-lived because Beijing declared martial law in Tibet shortly before the Tiananmen Massacre. Tibetan dissidents were imprisoned in large numbers. Later in 1989, the Dalai Lama won the Nobel Peace Prize, helping to generate widespread support and publicity for the Tibetans' cause. In the months leading up to Beijing's Olympic Games in the summer of 2008, Tibet came to the forefront of international controversy yet again after Chinese troops cracked down on Tibetan protesters, attempting to silence the most widespread anti-Chinese activities seen for several years.

The Chinese government has reopened talks with the Dalai Lama's representatives from time to time, but the issue of independence remains closed. China's leaders have made it clear that no serious dialogue will take place unless the Dalai Lama and his followers acknowledge that Tibet is an inalienable part of China.

The Beijing Olympics

Of the five objectives driving China's international behavior that were listed at the beginning of this chapter, the last two were most evident in Beijing's hosting of the 2008 summer Olympic games, but all of them were in play. With some 80 heads of state and government in attendance, and tens of thousands of international journalists reporting and broadcasting events, China presented itself to the world as a global power capable of great feats of organization and spectacle as well as athletic prowess. Although when bidding to host the games, Chinese authorities had assured the International Olympic Committee that human rights would be respected if Beijing were chosen as the 2008 site, when the time came those promises were subject to interpretation. Maintaining tight security and a façade of domestic harmony meant that the suppression of protests or even potential demonstrations of dissent was intensified in connection with the games, while the world press got to experience firsthand the Chinese state's ability to block all access to electronic media and web sites considered subversive. Overall, however, China's successful hosting of the games represented a proud triumph over a century and a half of national humiliation.

13

The Fourth Generation

Hu Jintao (b. 1942)

In mid-November 2002, after a formal election of the Central Committee following the Sixteenth Party Congress, the CCP announced the coming to power of a new group of leaders. They were given membership on the Politburo Standing Committee (PBSC) and would succeed Jiang Zemin and his associates. Known as the fourth generation—Mao's was the first, Deng Xiaoping's the second, and Jiang's the third—these men constituted the "core leaders" chosen to navigate China's journey into the new century.

As a group, the fourth generation is composed of dedicated economic modernizers, committed to moving China into the global market and maintaining good relations with the United States. The new leaders are all experienced, pragmatic managers with technological backgrounds. Another distinguishing feature of this generation is that they came of age during the Cultural Revolution. They are accustomed to hardship, politically so-phisticated, and deeply suspicious of ideology.[1] The mental and physical traumas they experienced have given this generation a sense of identity and group consciousness that is perhaps as strong as that which shaped the mind-sets of those who made the revolution. They have personally felt the pains of ideologically driven economic experiments. Yin Hongbiao, a former Red Guard and current professor of international politics at Beijing University, has argued that the lessons of the Cultural Revolution trans-formed his associates from "the generation of sloganeers" to the "genera-tion of down-to-earth practitioners."[2] Mao's disastrous utopianism made the Cultural Revolution generation politically and intellectually mature; they have largely abandoned Marxist idealism for pragmatism. Because many current political leaders were "sent down" to the countryside, they have a deeper appreciation of rural conditions and peasant needs than their predecessors. This "grass-roots consciousness" suggests that they will be more accessible and practical-minded than previous leaders. Finally, the chaos brought by the Cultural Revolution makes this generation especially sensitive about social and political stability. Although aware of the need for change, the fourth generation is fearful of mass movements and will insist on close oversight of any moves toward political reform. Like their predecessors, the new leaders are political authoritarians, wedded to the death penalty as a tool for fighting crime, and prepared to use brute force to quell ethnic disturbances in Tibet and Xinjiang. Although supportive of certain free market economic ideas, they are harsh critics of what they see to be the permissive moral values of the West and are determined to preserve the political power of the Communist Party. China, they insist, must draw on its communal and paternalistic traditions to withstand the shock waves of modernization. In fact, some of the new generation of leaders have even called for a reincorporation of Confucianism into Chinese nationalism as a means of strengthening the nation's cultural unity.

Much of what we currently know about the new leaders and the process by which they were selected comes from internal reports prepared by the CCP's Organization Department. Such information has generally been kept secret, but in late 2001 portions of the dossiers on each candidate for membership on the Politburo Standing Committee were given to a Chinese writer living outside China, apparently with some official approval, for a book that would better acquaint Western audiences with the fourth generation. Two Ameri-cans, Andrew J. Nathan and Bruce Gilley, collaborated with this author and published the information in English.[3]

What is remarkable about the emergence to power of the fourth generation is that it transpired in a relatively smooth and orderly fashion, absent the usual purges associated with previous transitions. Much of this, it seems, was due to the managerial skills of Jiang Zemin, who assured that factional struggles would be restrained and muted by consensus.[4] Since Jiang lacked the power of his predecessors (Mao and Deng), he was not able to simply designate a successor but instead was obliged to promote new leaders through coalition building and compromise in order to create consensus. However, there is some evidence that Jiang was able to wield a considerable amount of clout in promoting his own favorites.

The Influence of Jiang Zemin

In 2002 Jiang was seventy-six years of age and had served two-and-a-half terms as general secretary. As of 1997 it had become party policy that central leaders should step down after reaching the age of seventy. Although Jiang had been made an exception to the rule (he was seventy-one at the time), the general consensus of the party was that he should not stand for another term as leader. The only unresolved question was whether he would give up his position as chairman of the Central Military Commission, a post that has no rule for succession. Deng Xiaoping kept the position for himself some two years after retirement so as to assure the smooth transition of leadership to Jiang Zemin.

The fourth generation leaders are the product of a meritocratic process of selection started by Deng Xiaoping in 1980. According to what was known as Deng's "Four Transformations" program, the party was to put in place procedures to discover future leaders who were "more revolutionary, younger, more knowledgeable, and more specialized" so as to "transform" China into a world power. Jiang Zemin continued Deng's program and ordered senior officials across the country to search for young party activists with the above four qualities of leadership. Instead of relying on the customary seniority system, which had produced considerable mediocrity and sycophancy, officials now promoted young cadres with good educations, talent, and administrative know-how.

Among several who benefited from this accelerated system of advancement in the 1980s were Hu Jintao (b. 1942), Li Ruihuan (b. 1934), and Wen Jiabao (b. 1942). Jiang's heir apparent was Hu Jintao. Hu was educated as an engineer at Qinghua University, one of China's most prestigious institutions of higher learning. Over the years Hu showed himself to be a consummate networker. He cultivated a diverse group of senior backers ranging from conservatives to liberal reformers. Despite his association with some influential conservatives, Hu became a favorite of the progressive General Secretary Hu Yaobang, with whom he had a close personal relationship. After the fall of Hu Yaobang, Hu Jintao's loyalty to the party was such that he won over Deng Xiaoping, who became his third major patron. Hu gained administrative experience by serving as party secretary in two of China's poorest and most troubled provinces, Guizhou and Tibet. He gained the attention of the powerbrokers on the Politburo when in March 1989 he instituted martial law to manage disturbances in Tibet, which became a paradigm for dealing with the later Tiananmen protesters. In 1992, as part of his plan to develop a younger core of leaders to assure China's long-term stability, Deng Xiaoping appointed Hu Jintao to the Politburo Standing Committee. At the age of forty-nine, Hu was the youngest person in party history to have been promoted to such a position. Finally, Hu began to cultivate an enduring relationship with Jiang Zemin while serving as president of the Central Party School. There he actively promoted Jiang's "three represents" program and assisted the party propaganda chief in the compilation of *The Selected Works of Jiang Zemin*, a document intended to establish Jiang's legacy as a worthy successor of Mao and Deng Xiaoping. Hu Jintao later played an important role in Jiang's anticorruption drive against Chen Xitong, party boss of Beijing. It was this episode that ultimately solidified Hu's relationship with Jiang Zemin. Hu's reward for loyalty and good service came in March 1998 at the Ninth National People's Congress when at the age of fifty-six he was made vice-president, once again the youngest in party history. In that capacity Hu showed his reformist administrative skills by successfully closing down several of the army's business enterprises, many of which were pools of corruption, and transferring the assets to local authorities. Within a year Jiang finally succeeded in having Hu appointed vice-chairman of the Central Military Commission. Besides Jiang himself, Hu was only the second civilian to be given such power over China's military.[5]

Outgoing premier Zhu Rongji made way for Wen Jiabao. Wen was a protégé of Zhu's and had been burdened with some of the most demanding responsibilities. These included, among a myriad of other assignments, the management of rural affairs, poverty relief, flood control, and the administration of financial affairs. As premier, Wen is responsible for China's economic development. Wen indicated that he wants to give more encouragement to China's domestic market and put less emphasis on the export sector. He also has expressed a desire to offer more aid to the struggling rural areas and to give special attention to China's severe environmental problems.

A similar fast track was provided Li Ruihuan, who was advanced from a mid-level job in Beijing to the post of vice-mayor of Tianjin, one of the largest industrial port cities in China. The same speed-up selection was given Wen Jiabao and other younger men of quality promoted to the Politburo. In addition to competence, talent, party loyalty, and a strong work ethic, the leaders of the fourth generation, as exemplified in the career of Hu Jintao, constantly required the support of influential sponsors along the way.

Another among the top potential leaders was Li Ruihuan who, at just under seventy years old, was one of the oldest of this group. Li was scheduled to take over the chairmanship of the National People's Congress and was a proponent of opening up the political system through semi-competitive elections for government positions at the provincial level. As opposed to Jiang Zemin, whom he frequently had criticized for lack of imagination and inherent political conservatism, Li also wanted to give greater freedom to the Chinese media. However, on November 15, 2002, the plenary session of the Sixteenth Central Committee completed its one-day session and Li was unexpectedly dropped from the Standing Committee of the Politburo. This suggests that Jiang was able to use his power to thwart the advancement of one of his more prominent critics. In fact, Jiang was very successful in getting the men of his choice appointed to the Politburo Standing Committee. One of the most significant promotions was that of one of Jiang's favorites, Zeng Qinghong, son of the former interior minister, who was expected to play a prominent role in the years ahead running the party secretariat.

The new leadership was not expected to diverge substantially from the policies of either Deng Xiaoping or Jiang Zemin. All are committed to maintaining the party's monopoly of political power. Their chosen model for emulation is the politically authoritarian but open market system of Lee Kuan Yew's Singapore, until recently also operative in Taiwan and South Korea. However, some modification is expected concerning policies for economic development. Wen Jiabao, for instance, is concerned about raising domestic demand and improving living standards in rural China. The new leaders are convinced that such reforms will increase the popularity of the party, improve the environment for both foreign and domestic investment, and diminish China's dependency on exports. There will also be ongoing efforts to phase out the unprofitable state-owned enterprises (SOEs). Unlike former premier Zhu Rongji, Wen Jiabao is prepared to be more hard-nosed about cutting back on state support for the larger state enterprises, and he is willing to sell them as long as they are not strategically important. One of Hu Jintao's major concerns is the party's failure to keep a sufficiently close relationship with China's masses. The CCP is in the process of losing the support of its traditional base. The source of this problem, in Hu's view, has been corruption and abuse of power by party officials. Although there is common agreement about the seriousness of such issues, there does not appear to be a consensus about how to address them. Hu Jintao and Wen Jiabao favor reforms in party recruitment and promotion. Others advocated external public supervision, including limited elections and giving more freedom to newspapers, radio, and television.

Will the new leaders enact the kinds of far-reaching political reforms necessary to move the country in the direction of democracy? Although they are united in recognizing the wisdom of continuing the ban on political opposition, fearing that a premature opening up of the political system will destabilize a country as poor and diverse as China, there is agreement that some political reforms are necessary. Jiang Zemin emphasized that he rejected "copying the model of the Western political system wholesale," but he called for a number of limited political reforms. He has spoken of the need to guarantee "human rights" and of opening up the political process at the village level. The fourth generation recognizes the interrelatedness of institutions in a modern society and that a change in any one sector (economics, society, or politics) will have a deep impact on all aspects of culture. The myriad problems confronting the nation are well known by the public and widely discussed in the domestic media. The open debates generated by such problems are in themselves a catalyst for opening the political system to broader participation. Another encouraging factor that offers some potential for thinking beyond the conventional Marxist-Leninist lock box is that the new elites for the most part have not been the recipients of the rigid Soviet-style educations that in many ways stultified the thinking of their elders. They have had considerable exposure to Western culture, some having studied in the United States and Europe. Although they may have serious reservations about Western cultural values, many of the new generation appreciate Western social and economic dynamism and are better prepared to communicate with Westerners than were their predecessors. But it is unlikely that the new elites will advocate changes that disperse power, authority, and control at their own expense.

On the other hand, the prerequisites for a civil society, without which democracy cannot exist (there must be independent institutional bodies to check governmental power), are gradually emerging in China.[6] Throughout the 1990s, for example, China made substantial progress toward the creation of a legal system, issuing more laws and regulations during that time frame than any other country. In order to satisfy its obligations for membership into the World Trade Organization (WTO), China was obliged to establish legal procedures for creating stronger economic and civil rights. Chinese citizens now have a better platform from which to broadcast their rights and grievances. And there is presently a sizable coterie of legal professionals to help them: the number of lawyers increased from 3,000 in the early 1980s to 150,000 in 2001.[7]

Chinese society itself has also become more pluralistic, as can be seen in the new regard and respect for professionalism in a variety of fields (the social sciences, medicine, science and technology, law). The growth of such professions has contributed to the emergence of a distinct Chinese bourgeoisie, a sector of society that over the course of centuries was the seminal force for the development of democracy in the West. Even the CCP has come to grips with such professionalism, having recently permitted businessmen—"private entrepreneurs"—to join the party. In fact, Jiang Zemin has gone on record as favoring the creation of a middle-class society. Finally, the fourth generation understands the importance of improving China's international image. Progressive political reform would be an important way of meeting that objective, but the emphasis continues to be placed on China's economic development, not its political development.

China's Economy in the Twenty-first Century

In 2007 the World Bank estimated China's trade surplus at more than $250 billion. The United States' 2006 trade deficit with China was approximately $232.5 billion and is projected to continue to grow annually. The New York investment bank Goldman, Sachs and Co. predicted that China would have the world's largest economy by 2027. The policies of China's fourth generation leadership have made such remarkable achievements possible. President Hu Jintao remains committed to the goals of his predecessors Deng Xiaoping and Jiang Zemin to grow China's economy while also having it serve as a model for other developing nations. But China's recipe for success may be difficult to emulate.

James McGregor in *One Billion Customers* (2005) described China's recent rapid growth:

> If you think about the last decade of China's economic and social development in terms of comparable changes in the history of the United States, you can feel the wind on your face. China is undergoing the raw capitalism of the Robber Baron era of the late 1800s; the speculative financial mania of the 1920s; the rural-to-urban migration of the 1930s; the emergence of the first-car, first-home, first-fashionable clothes, first-college education, first-family vacation, middle-class consumer of the 1950s, and even aspects of social upheaval similar to the 1960s.[8]

How has this happened? We have already examined the initial successes of Deng Xiaoping's special economic zones (SEZs) and Jiang Zemin's reform drive of the 1990s, which led to an infusion of foreign capital and formation of joint ventures, but the Chinese economy continues to surge under Hu Jintao's leadership because of the impact of membership in the WTO and the corresponding adjustments in China's economy. China's success can, in part, be attributed to vast amounts of foreign direct investment (FDI), more than US$ 60 billion from 2001 to 2005. The main targets for foreign money and venture capital have been economic and technological development zones (ETDZs), initially created in the mid-1980s as smaller, more specialized counterparts to SEZs. Located along China's coast or in cities already open for international trade, they are areas where government policies specifically encourage high-tech industries over more traditional manufacturing firms through tax incentives and other benefits. By 2000 there were fifty-four national government-sponsored ETDZs and hundreds more supported by provincial and municipal authorities throughout China. They received 15 percent of China's total FDI for 2006 when more than 200 multinational high-tech companies sponsored 400 industrial projects. China's relative advantage in procuring foreign investment continues to be based on the promise of low wages; low taxes; rapid licensing; a large domestic market; and fewer regulations concerning working conditions, and health and accident insurance. The expanding ETDZs are the focal point for China's continued growth.

Under Hu Jintao's leadership, the Chinese also have demonstrated considerable creativity in accessing much-in-demand resources overseas. Under the guise of foreign aid and development, China has made inroads into capturing both markets and raw materials from many Third World nations often ignored by Western powers. The 2006 Forum on China and Africa Cooperation was one example of China's new international role. Delegates from forty-eight African nations endorsed Beijing's "Action Plan" to facilitate strategic and economic partnerships. In 2006 Hu Jintao promised to double China's annual aid packages to African nations while also committing hundreds of millions of dollars to other developing nations, particularly those in Southeast Asia. As a result, the Chinese have become major competitors for the world's resources. A few examples include Chinese sponsorship of Zambia's copper industry; oil and gas exploration in Ethiopia, Nigeria, and Sudan; railways in the Philippines; and roads and infrastructure development in Brazil and Cambodia.

The 11th Five-Year Plan (2005) and Future Development

While China's expanding middle class purchases vast quantities of the world's resources, and its entrepreneurs inevitably benefit as consumers seek the trappings of wealth and modernization, there are also many who have been left behind. Hu Jintao's government has addressed the divisive issues that could undermine China's future prosperity and threaten CCP power. In October 2005, the CCP's Central Committee approved its 11th Five-Year Plan for Economic Development in which the Beijing government outlined its goals into the second decade of the twenty-first century. According to political scientist Barry Naughton, the plan is remarkable because, unlike previous plans, it omits production targets. Instead it focuses on a program that promotes sustainable growth driven by market forces whose benefits allegedly will be more equitably shared by the Chinese people. Its specific targets include a doubling of China's gross domestic product (GDP) per capita from 2000 to 2010 while also calling for "putting people first," especially those who have not benefited from the prosperity associated with the rapid urbanization of the past decades—China's rural population. Hu's policies call for investing in rural infrastructure and technology, reducing taxes, making nine years of school compulsory, and supporting a revitalized health care system. The CCP also claims to be committed to protecting farmers' land rights. China's farmers were granted thirty-year, inheritable leases under Deng Xiaoping's original reforms in 1978 and prospered for nearly a decade. More recently, however, farmers' rights have been violated by local party officials and entrepreneurs who have expropriated or underpaid for land that they in turn have developed for profit. One of Hu Jintao's goals is to allow farmers increased freedom in selling or leasing their land, a policy the CCP has referred to as "building a new socialist countryside." But his proposals did not garner the support of high-level officials within the CCP.

In 2007 the National People's Congress again addressed the issue of property rights. Since the 2005 Third Session of the Tenth People's Congress, leftists had successfully blocked the passage of laws that would grant legal protection for private property, despite the embarrassing reality that nearly two-thirds of China's GDP was produced by privately owned enterprises. In a victory for Hu Jintao's views, the National People's Congress approved a property law granting individuals the same legal protections as enjoyed by the state. Like many Communist Party edicts, its efficacy is limited. Critics have commented that the law will be difficult to enforce. The primary beneficiaries of the new law are urban homeowners, who can more freely buy/sell property and pass it on to their children. Farmers whose land is being stolen or exploited by developers, both foreign and domestic, are not necessarily protected. The social costs of the deepening class divisions exacerbated by Hu Jintao's economic policies as China's economy continues to grow in the twentieth-first century are yet to be measured.

Social Costs

Some of the most serious challenges for China's leadership are the deep social divisions created by rapid increases in wealth. In some respects, China is taking on the appearance of what Benjamin Disraeli observed of England in the Industrial Age: the country, said he, was becoming "two nations between whom there is no intercourse and no sympathy."[9]

We find in Guangdong, for example, the spectacular Mission Hills

Golf Club built at the cost of $250 million during the mid-1990s and host to the World Cup of golf in 2007. It is one of more than seventy resorts near Shenzhen where dozens of factories belch smoke into the air as they create products that fuel China's export boom. While about 60 percent of the club's members, who must pay $315,000 to join, are from Hong Kong, the balance is increasingly shifting to mainland Chinese who have become rich as a result of the free market reforms.

More than one thousand miles to the north in Hebei Province, not simply in another part of China but almost literally in another world, are the remnants of the site of Baoding No. 1 Paper Mill. A model of Chinese socialism for more than thirty years, the factory was closed under Zhu Rongji's reforms, leaving its workers without jobs. Like millions of middle-aged and older workers whose state-owned factories cannot compete in China's part-socialist, part-capitalist economy, pensions and access to medical care disappeared with their jobs. "I never imagined it would get this hard," a seventy-two-year-old woman told a Western reporter. In 2000, she had to live on a pension of US$6.00 per month; in 2001 even that was not paid.[10] Many of Baoding's industries became targets for foreign investment. As a result, the once-state-owned enterprises are in the hands of private owners, both foreign and Chinese. Ironically, one of Baoding's thriving commercial centers is at No. 1 Paper Mill Road.

Older workers from defunct factories are not alone in their insecurity. In the countryside, the end of the collective farm system has displaced many young people, especially those without educations. According to *People's Daily*, in 2003 more than 140 million migrant laborers wandered between villages and cities looking for work, double the number from 1993. Often referred to as China's "floating population," they account for 30 percent of the rural labor force. With 80 percent falling between the ages of fifteen and thirty-five, these unfortunate workers survive on part-time low-paying jobs. Their employers call them "one-day mules." Companies that employ such laborers often ignore laws that limit work hours and set minimum wages. Beginning in 2005, the government-sponsored All-China Federation of Trade Unions began recruiting migrant workers, especially for construction jobs. According to Chinese government sources, approximately 35 percent of construction workers have joined, thus helping to give a small part of the "floating population" a modicum of security. In China, however, there are no independent trade unions. Despite having signed international agreements calling for free labor unions, the CCP does not allow workers to organize themselves. Past attempts by workers to set up their own independent trade unions have been crushed, the organizers sent to prison or labor camps. Western companies, subject to pressure at home, have sometimes improved working conditions in their Chinese factories; this is not the case in factories owned by companies based in Hong Kong, Taiwan, or China.

Industries in China continue to offer workers some of the lowest wages in the world. The apparently endless supply of "one-day mules" has meant that companies get away with paying workers about 50 cents an hour, or one-twentieth of the average American manufacturing wage.

There also has been little effort made to satisfy even minimal safety standards in privately owned companies and state-sponsored projects. The irony for a nation whose leaders still claim adherence to the principles of Marxism-Leninism is that working conditions are among the worst in the world, in many instances comparable to those that raised the moral condemnation of Marx at the dawn of the industrial age. This has resulted in endemic workplace casualties. According to the State Administration of Work Safety, nationally some 140,000 people died in work-related accidents in 2002, up from about 109,000 in 2000. In 2003 the CCP enacted the Safety Production Law in an attempt to address the issue, but the CCP's efforts have been feeble, amounting to little more than occasional propaganda campaigns, isolated crackdowns on more egregious bosses, and attempts to pay off families of those who died. For example, in early 2008, the CCP's Deputy Minister of Supervision, Wang Wei, announced disciplinary actions taken against 183 managers allegedly responsible for workplace injuries. The managers were charged with dereliction of duty, abuse of power, and bribery. Most were fined. Relatively little has been done to solve such fundamental problems in China's emerging capitalist culture because high rates of injury and death are considered part of the cost of doing business and maximizing profits. In 2007, Li Yizhong, head of the State Administration of Work Safety, claimed that workplace deaths have decreased annually since 2005, but he also acknowledged that the approximately 100,000 deaths each year is a number that must be reduced.[11]

Nor are China's citizens safe in their own homes, at least not if they reside in a thriving city like Shanghai, where unrestrained capitalism has changed the urban landscape. In the summer of 2001, a fifty-five-year-old factory worker named Song Houfu spoke to a Western reporter in his tiny one-room apartment in a half-demolished apartment building near the center of Shanghai. The man had already lost his job to economic change. "I'm a true Communist," he said, but that allegiance to China's ruling party was not helping him. The CCP was doing nothing to save the home he shared with his wife and daughter. Thousands of neighbors shared the man's problems. All of them lived in a working-class residential neighborhood that was leveled to make way for corporate offices and luxury homes that will cost millions of dollars each.[12] Since Shanghai won the bid for the 2010 World Expo, even more extensive urban renewal projects are on the drawing board. The city government called for large-scale clearance of slum housing and obsolete industrial buildings. Additionally, Shanghai's land use will continue to be transformed from residential and industrial to commercial, high-end residential, and office space.[13] Only one old structure was saved from the wrecking ball: the gray brick building where thirteen men, among them Mao Zedong, founded the Chinese Communist Party in 1921. The First Congress Meeting Hall, surrounded by an upscale entertainment area, was renovated in 1999 and soon reopened as a tourist attraction complete with life-size wax figures of the CCP founders.

Injustices and rampant commercialism have not always met with the stoicism shown by Mr. Song. By 2001, in addition to the disruptive activities of the Falun Gong, the government could not hide the fact that other social protests involving as many as 10,000 people have been common. Farmers, workers, business people, and even officials and former soldiers have been among the protesters. These demonstrations frequently have been militant and even violent, with protesters blocking roads and bridges, storming party or government offices, and destroying property. The state-controlled media have done their best to keep such disturbances from dominating the news, often contradicting visual evidence circulated on the World Wide Web.

Crime and Punishment

In addition to producing glaring discrepancies in income and lifestyles, the opening of China's economy produced waves of crime that the government has been unable to control. Rising inequality and the growing crime rate have the same underlying cause. From the 1950s through about 1980, most of China's people were closely supervised and unable to move around freely. In the countryside, they were bound to communes, whose officials regulated most aspects of their lives. In the cities, factories and other places of work did much the same thing. For example, factories provided their workers with living quarters, medical care, vacations, and almost every other basic need. A system of residence permits kept people rooted in one place. These and other levers of totalitarian control virtually stamped out activities like drug use and prostitution, as well as many other criminal activities. Deng's economic reforms allowed people to move around, and by removing the social safety net provided by the state-controlled communes and factories, forced them to strike out on their own. The old system of supervision was fatally compromised, and with so many people suddenly having to rely on their wits to survive, crime almost immediately became, and has remained, a national problem. The government's main strategy for controlling crime has been a series of "strike hard" sweeps to round up tens of thousands of suspects, rush the suspects through perfunctory and meaningless trials, and execute tens of thousands of them, unconcerned that many might in fact be innocent. The first strike hard campaign from 1983 to 1986 claimed an estimated 30,000 lives; the regime refuses to reveal the actual toll. Torture was commonly used to extract confessions. Other campaigns followed, including a "fourth" beginning in 2001 and lasting for two years, allegedly focused on drug dealers and prostitutes. Since the September 11, 2001, terrorist attacks, China's "strike hard" campaigns have fanned out to include suspected "terrorists" and others who challenge social order. In 2005, for example, the CCP announced a "strike hard" campaign against dissidents in the largely Muslim province of Xinjiang. During "strike hard" campaigns, China's criminal procedure law is all but ignored by police and court officials eager to meet punishment quotas. According to the human rights organization Amnesty International, the Chinese government continues to execute more people than all the other countries of the world combined.

Huge public rallies attended by as many as one million people witnessed public trials and executions. The police meanwhile were enthusiastic about what they were doing: "There's a strong sense of pride between provinces, and we compare ourselves to each other," one of them told a Western journalist. The public, apparently more worried about criminals than the prospect of innocent people being executed, seemed to support the "strike hard" campaigns. As one college student remarked, "They [criminals] are the termites of society. They deserve the death penalty."[14]

Health Scandals

Beijing's lurid practices regarding corporal punishment and the widespread use of the death penalty have hurt China's international image. One response to world opinion came at the end of 2001 when China's Supreme Court urged officials in the country's largest cities and provincial capitals to begin using lethal injections to carry out executions by the end of the year. Meanwhile, the execution of thousands of prisoners per year, often young and healthy people, unwittingly gave birth to a new "business" that reaches from China's execution fields to doctors' offices in the United States and other countries. In 1998 a Chinese official was arrested in New York, accused of trying to sell organs from executed Chinese prisoners for transplant operations. In fact, since the mid-1980s, government policy allows organs—including kidneys, livers, lungs, and corneas—to be extracted from executed prisoners for transplant operations. While many who receive these organs are wealthy Chinese, foreigners also have benefited. The thousands of dollars foreign patients pay for their operations—often much more than local patients can afford—have earned Chinese hospitals, especially military hospitals with close ties to government prosecutors, tens of millions of dollars per year. Many new transplant centers have opened, sometimes with special wards for foreign patients who pay top dollar for treatment.

In 2006 officials from China's Foreign Ministry admitted that organs are taken from prisoners, but only from those who have volunteered to donate them after their deaths. But there is convincing eyewitness testimony to the contrary. Even worse, there has been eyewitness evidence that organs have been removed from prisoners who were still breathing after being shot. Such practices have in turn created ethical dilemmas for American doctors whose patients received organ transplants in China and who need follow-up care. Should they treat patients who have received organs under circumstances that violate American medical standards, legal norms, and fundamental assumptions about human rights? As of 2002, more than 78,000 Americans were awaiting organ transplants, and that number was growing rapidly. American doctors, and the United States itself, now face a moral question without an easy answer that will have to be confronted with increasing frequency. Organ transplants remains big business in China, especially in coastal cities with large numbers of tourists. According to a BBC report, in 2006 a liver could be purchased for just under US$100,000, and the wait was less than three weeks at a Tianjin hospital.

Yet another source of embarrassment for the Chinese government has been the spread of HIV/AIDS. As in many countries in Asia, Africa, and the former USSR, HIV/AIDS in China has been spreading at an epidemic rate. Many factors worked to make the situation far grimmer than it needed to be. Beginning in the late 1980s, tens of millions of people were on the move in search of work, and they were shockingly ignorant about how the disease is contracted. As intravenous drug use and prostitution spiraled out of control, HIV/AIDS also spread. Greed on the part of unscrupulous people, as well as poverty, compounded the problem.

One notorious example of this deadly coupling was a scandal that took place in Henan. During the 1990s, several state-sponsored companies used unsterile collection methods to gather blood plasma from donors, mainly poor farmers trying to make a little extra money (the average Henan farmer survived on 78 cents per day). Villagers were paid roughly US$6.00 for an 800 cc blood donation, enough to feed a family for a week. Realizing that it was more profitable to sell blood than tend fields, Henan farmers lined up by the hundreds to cash in on the bonus. By the mid-1990s the province had become China's plasma farm for hospitals throughout China. One poor peasant from Xiongqiao Village, ground zero of what is one of the world's worst HIV/AIDS epidemics, claimed to have given four donations in a single day. Multiple donations were possible because the donors' red blood cells were replaced after the plasma was removed to avoid anemia, but the mixing of tainted blood, the overuse of unsanitary equipment, and the fact that few could afford the price of a condom (equivalent to half a day's wages) produced a lethal scourge in which virtually everyone in the village contracted HIV/AIDS. "It is our custom for strong male adults to carry the coffin, but so many people are sick or dead that there aren't enough of us left," bemoaned a thirty-five-year-old farmer. "So now it is the old people who are doing the burying."[15] In 2006, the Henan government announced that the province had more than 35,000 HIV/AIDS cases as a result of the illegal blood trade of the 1990s.

HIV/AIDS spread as peasants from the poor countryside flocked to China's major cities in search of work; countless numbers of them were not even aware that they carried the deadly virus. Dr. Gao Yaojie, an eminent retired gynecologist in Henan Province who has won numerous international awards for her efforts to expose the Henan crisis, feared that it was already too late to stop the spread of the disease. The Chinese government used tactics of intimidation and harassment, bugged her telephone, and placed her under house arrest to keep her from publicizing the government's failures to deal with what rural Chinese called the "nameless fever." It was not until 2007 that the Beijing government gave in to pressure to allow Dr. Gao to travel to the United States to receive the coveted "Vital Voices-Global Leadership" award at Washington DC's Kennedy Center.

Others who tried to expose the crisis in Henan have experienced similar treatment. One journalist who spoke on condition of anonymity to the British newspaper *The Guardian* claimed that he had been fired by three different newspapers in Henan for trying to get the story of Xiongqiao Village published. A Henan official who was questioned about the government responded, "Who will invest in our province if they believe we have a huge number of HIV cases?"[16]

Nobody knows how many people in China are infected with HIV/AIDS. The case studies of Henan are just the tip of the iceberg. In fact, the province with the largest percentage of HIV/AIDS cases in 2006 was Yunnan, located at the heart of international drug trafficking routes. In 2006, China's Ministry of Health claimed 650,000 HIV/AIDS cases, but World Health Organization (WHO) scientists argued that the figure is closer to 1.5 million. Beijing denied the seriousness of the AIDS epidemic until 1998 when, after extraordinary international pressure, including a prediction by UNAIDS (United Nations Joint Programme on HIV/AIDS) scientists that China could have between 20 and 30 million HIV/AIDS cases within a decade, government leaders admitted that China had a problem. The CCP's State Council enacted a long-term plan to 2010 focused on preventative action, drug use, and prostitution. By 2004 provincial governments were required to enact AIDS awareness educational programs and provide medication and facilities for HIV/AIDS patients. In 2007 an international team of AIDS researchers praised the administration of Hu Jintao for responding "in a big way" to the HIV/AIDS challenge after China's early policies not only failed to stop, but most likely hastened the spread of the disease. Since 2006, the Chinese government has offered a variety of free programs nationwide, including testing, medication for the uninsured, education for AIDS orphans, and awareness programs with internationally famous spokespersons such as the NBA star Yao Ming.[17]

Whether the Chinese government learned anything from the AIDS scandal in Henan Province is another question. An example of another failure to react in a timely way was the 2002–3 Severe Acute Respiratory Syndrome (SARS) epidemic that infected approximately 8,000 people and killed 900. Fear of punishment was one of the reasons that compelled officials with the Henan Health Bureau to cover up for several years the province's AIDS outbreak, directly contributing to the infections of thousands of unsuspecting new victims. The government's tight control of the media further stymied reports about the lethal epidemic. Given the nature of China's authoritarian political system, decisive action of any kind can only be taken when intervention comes from the very top of the leadership pyramid. This procedure is justified on the grounds of assuring stability and popular confidence. Yet this very process was directly responsible for the dilatory and disastrous Chinese response to the outbreak of SARS.

SARS first appeared in Foshan, in Guangdong Province's Pearl River delta, in November 2002, when one man developed what seemed to be an extreme case of pneumonia. He recovered, but health workers assisting him fell ill, and soon many throughout Guangdong Province died from what was described as "a disease with no cure, which kills in a day."[18] People panicked, and there was a stampede to buy vinegar, a popular disinfectant, and other medications to hold back the sickness. The outbreak coincided with the start of the Chinese New Year. Millions were on the move, but authorities failed to take public action. Even after word of the lethal affliction had spread to the provincial capital, Guangzhou, and then to Hong Kong, no official warnings were issued. The Guangzhou *Southern Capital* newspaper received 2,700 phone calls within a few days from worried readers and intended to publish its own investigation. Official pressure blocked its publication. The stonewalling continued, as the CCP prohibited disturbing news in the media to avoid disrupting the National People's Congress that was preparing to meet in March 2003. Meanwhile, the virus spread to Hong Kong and then to Canada, Vietnam, Singapore, and Taiwan. This prompted WHO to demand to know what was happening in China.

Chinese health authorities initially tried to deflate WHO concerns by stating that the virus was under control and that it probably had not originated in China in the first place. Officials blamed it on the pangolin, a scaly anteater, which had the advantage of being an inhabitant of Indochina, not native to

China proper. The charade did not work, and it became clear that for six months Chinese authorities had sat on crucial information and failed to take preventative measures to check the epidemic, thereby allowing it to spread around the world. It was only WHO and international pressure that forced the leaders at the top to intervene, allowing an outside investigation of the problem and the disclosure of medical records. Beijing then reluctantly revised upward the number of deaths, admitting that the situation in China was nearly ten times worse than reported. It also ordered the cancellation of the week-long May Day holiday in an effort to stop the spread of the disease. At the urging of President Hu Jintao, the ruling Central Committee sacked the health minister, Zhang Wenkang, and the mayor of Beijing, Meng Xuenong, and expelled them from the party as well.

There were apparently important domestic economic reasons for the regime to take forceful action to address the SARS epidemic. Beijing's commitment to opening the economy had resulted in a serious deterioration of China's social infrastructure to the point where health services could not cope with the SARS outbreak. Local people took matters into their own hands and set up roadblocks to prevent outsiders from entering their communities. There were riots opposing the establishment of quarantine centers. Finally, a highly critical editorial in the most popular newspaper in Guangdong, the *Southern Metropolitan Daily*, called on government to be more open and forthcoming with the people: "This crisis illustrates the need for timely and clear reporting of the truth to the people. . . and the clear communication of what the government is doing to deal with the crisis and the problems it might face."[19]

President Hu Jintao's limited toleration of media criticism and the unprecedented access given WHO inspectors to Chinese health records suggest that Hu may have been using the crisis to promote his own agenda for more transparency and also to weaken the power of some of the more conservative holdovers from the Jiang Zemin regime. The Chinese government continued to work with WHO scientists on SARS prevention. In 2004 WHO designated China as the first nation in which human trials of a SARS vaccine could be tested.

Environmental Challenges

Initiated three decades ago, Deng Xiaoping's economic reforms have produced stunning industrial and urban growth. In the process, hundreds of millions of Chinese have been lifted from poverty, and the country today is the world's leading producer of consumer goods. In 2006 China replaced Japan as the world's second largest manufacturer of trucks and cars after the United States. China's tremendous economic growth has not only been confined to industry.

According to the U.S. Energy Information Administration over the past several years China has built each year some 7.5 billion square feet of commercial and residential space. This is more than the combined floor space of all the malls in America. Yet all this economic expansion is seriously compromised by dramatic environmental degradation, one of the most serious challenges yet to the political control of the ruling Communist Party. The leadership depends on continuing economic expansion to legitimize its rule, but sustaining such growth does significant damage to China's air quality, water supply, and limited energy resources. This has resulted in serious health problems and even social unrest.

Pollution from coal-fueled power plants and factories along with automobile exhaust means that China's cities are continually engulfed in haze, enveloping their occupants in a noxious envelope of fumes that in some cases permanently blocks out the sun. Sixteen of the world's twenty most polluted cities are in China. Approximately 14,000 new automobiles arrive on China's overcrowded roads each day.

A major culprit of poor air quality is China's reliance on coal. Although a relatively abundant and cheap fuel resource, coal has the distinction of being one of the dirtiest sources of energy. China relies on coal for about two-thirds of its energy needs and burns more than the United States, Europe, and Japan combined. The Chinese are building new power plants at a staggering pace, but for economic reasons continue to rely on obsolete coal-fired technology. According to economist Paul Roberts, many operating plants lack emissions-control technology altogether and waste most of the energy they generate.[20] The World Bank reports that China's steel manufacturers on average use one-fifth more energy per ton than the international average. Cement production requires 45 percent more power, and ethylene producers utilize 70 percent more than producers elsewhere. In general, China's industries are seven times more inefficient than those in the United States.

Compounding China's nonrenewable energy inefficiencies is the deleterious impact manufacturing has had on the nation's water supply. China has only one-fifth as much water per capita as the United States. The necessity of water for industrial production and coal mining has seriously depleted the country's supplies of ground water. Farmers in the north once used shovels to dig wells. Today many aquifers in Beijing and Hebei Province have been so depleted that wells must be dug more than one-half mile deep.[21] In fact, the water table has dropped so significantly that many coal-producing and coastal area cities are actually sinking. In the past fifteen years, for instance, Shanghai has sunk six feet, and the city's skyscrapers are beginning to tilt. Cracks have appeared in the foundations of several factory buildings as they sink into the earth. The overuse of water and the cutting down of forests (China has lost twice as much forested land over the centuries as it now possesses) have rapidly increased desertification. Currently, more than one-fourth of China is desert. These sands have encroached so rapidly that today the desert has expanded to within seventy-five miles of Beijing. Some villages have become so devastated by desertification that their entrepreneurial citizens have turned them into sand-based theme parks.

Beijing's efforts to address many of these problems have not been successful. The Xinhua News Agency reported in the autumn of 2007 that China's showcase engineering project, the Three Gorges Dam, the world's largest hydroelectric plant designed to both limit the country's dependence on coal power and improve flood control, has created enormous environmental problems. Upstream water quality has deteriorated because of decreasing water flows, leading to outbreaks of algae, and rising levels of water in the dam's reservoir have eroded the banks of the Yangzi, causing landslides. Such environmental degradation already has rendered 30 percent of the water from the Yellow and Yangzi rivers, along with three of China's largest lakes—the Tai, Chao, and Dianchi—unfit for even industrial or agricultural use. Tap water is simply not potable anywhere in China (600 million people drink contaminated water daily). And little is being done to rectify the problem, as many factories and farms dump waste into rivers and lakes without compunction and with virtually no penalties. Indeed, two-thirds of the household waste dumped into China's rivers goes without treatment.[22] The impact of pollution has taken a heavy toll on the nation's health. The disease level is so high from imbibing impure water that many settlements along China's rivers are called "cancer villages." Air and water pollution are major causes of China's soaring cancer rate. The government is sensitive about publishing data on the problem for fear of inciting social unrest. But independent studies by Chinese non-governmental organizations (NGOs) indicate that there has been a 19 percent increase in urban cancer rates and 23 percent increase in rural rates since 2005. A 2007 World Bank study calculated that 750,000 people die annually directly from air pollution alone. Another study reported that only one percent of the country's 560 million city dwellers breathe air considered safe by the European Union. In an interview with *China Daily*, cancer researcher with the Chinese Academy of Medical Sciences, Chen Zhizhou, commented in 2007, "The main reason behind the rising number of cancer cases is that pollution of the environment, water, and air is getting worse day by day."[23]

The environmental and health situation may only get worse because up to the year 2000 China relied mostly on light industry and small-scale enterprises for economic growth. In the current cycle of development, the government is dedicated to quadrupling the size of the economy, and for this it has decided to rely mainly on energy-intensive heavy industry. This will place even greater stress on the country's tattered environmental infrastructure.

A major political problem for CCP leaders is that the citizenry have begun to fight back. In 2007 Beijing witnessed an increase in riots, violent protests, and petitions across the country (a 30 percent increase over the previous year) as the people protested in anger over health issues caused by pollution. Both President Hu Jintao and Premier Wen Jiabao have officially declared the government's commitment to cleaning up the environment. The head of China's environmental agency, Zhou Shengxian, has called for a "struggle" against polluters and admitted that the public has refused to accept increasing degradation of the environment.[24] Yet at this point the government has not matched rhetoric with action. It appears that environmental officials like Zhou have little influence in the government's bureaucracy. His agency has only about 200 full-time employees, compared with 18,000 in the U.S. Environmental Protection Agency. China's central planning agency, the Energy Bureau of the National Development and Reform Commission, has only 100 full-time staff. The Energy Department in Washington has 110,000 full-time staff members.

Although the current CCP leadership claims it is committed to curbing environmental degradation (Prime Minister Wen Jiabao made forty-eight references to the environment in his 2007 state of the nation address), its hold on power has been assured by rapid economic growth. Prosperity satisfies the public's material expectations, provides economic windfalls for well-connected officials, and forestalls demands for political change. What is required is a balance between growth and environmental protection, but this is seriously compromised by Beijing's failure to control officials and industrialists at the local level. In fact, the central government, concerned about the poor air quality for the 2008 Olympic Games in Beijing, ordered local factories to close during the games and heavy-polluting vehicle traffic was restricted. The problem of weak environmental protections is partly structural. The economic initiatives of the 1980s were designed to weaken socialist policy by giving lower-level officials more freedom to stimulate economic growth. Local leaders gained broad powers over lending, taxes, and land regulation. Many of these officials since then have made sizable investments in industrial enterprises, whose continued growth, despite environmental degradation, provides them with great wealth and power. Factory owners who violate environmental laws are frequently protected by local officials, and in many cases regulations are flaunted completely. In fact, the head of Beijing's environmental protection agency has claimed that several plants have installed secret pipes to discharge polluting chemicals. Even when enforcement does take place it is frequently tainted by corruption. In the spring of 2007, for example, officials in Yunnan

Province addressed the mandated reconstruction of Laoshou Mountain, which was used as a quarry, by spraying green paint over acres of rock.

Although CCP leaders appear unable to meet environmental challenges, there is a growing green movement among China's citizenry that intends to hold the country's industrialists accountable for their errant ways. In 2002 China had fewer than fifty registered green NGOs. In 2007 that number had grown to almost 3,000. One such group, the Institute of Public Environmental Affairs, which is dedicated to cleaning up the nation's air and water, has published an online water pollution map identifying and shaming the worst offenders. In order to have their names removed from the list, polluting companies must accept third-party audits and address identified problems. Many companies have responded, and a few have even agreed to audits. Some other such greens have been able to shut down development projects altogether, but there is still the ever-present threat of arrest by both local and national government officials. Some activists have been incarcerated in secret, but as environmental issues have increasingly become the focus of public attention, officials have been forced to move more cautiously.

The Problem of Corruption

Another critical issue confronting China today, in some respects even more volatile than environmental degradation, affecting everything from the distribution of economic resources and wealth to the legitimacy of the Communist Party leadership, is endemic corruption. This was a scourge that led to the demise of past dynasties and fatally crippled the regime of Chiang Kai-shek. One of Mao Zedong's first priorities in taking power in 1949 was to extirpate corruption. The notorious Green Gang, for example, was put out of business, and the CCP proudly proclaimed that the brothels and gambling dens of Shanghai were shut down for good. All this was part of the Communist Party's promoting "New Democracy" and putting in place the infrastructure for a socialist economy. However, since the acceleration of Deng Xiaoping's economic reforms, necessary both to overcome the economic setbacks of the Great Leap Forward and the Cultural Revolution and to legitimize CCP leadership after the disaster of the Tiananmen Massacre, corruption once again has become an entrenched feature of China's economic and political landscape.

China's modern criminal activity has taken on particular patterns. The Chinese economist He Qinglian has observed that corruption during the 1980s and 1990s was chiefly characterized by individuals on the take. An example of this was the general manager of Guizhou International Trust and Investment who embezzled billions of dollars and was later executed. By the mid-1990s, corruption evolved from individual criminality to a more organized form. Communist Party officials in government agencies and in state-owned companies took the lead. Their method of operation was to use state resources to bribe high-level officials for either financial support or special-interest projects. He Qinglian cites the actions of the People's Liberation Army as the best example of what she calls "organized corruption." Several generals set up a smuggling ring. The party responded by executing one of the top generals after a quick trial. Since 1998, however, corruption in China has morphed into a more systematic form, ultimately infesting every sector of the political, industrial, educational, and financial systems.

Rarely do China's leaders wash their dirty linen in public, but data recently released by the Supreme People's Procuratorate (SPP) reveal the extent to which corruption is threatening political and economic stability. From 2002 to 2005, more than 42,000 government officials on average were investigated for corruption every year. More than 30,000 per year faced criminal charges. These figures do not include crimes in the private economic sector. According to the director-general of the SPP, "almost every type of financial institution has seen the emergence of criminal cases involving the solicitation of bribes in return for loans."[25]

In the autumn of 2006 the official Xinhua News Agency reported that an "anti-graft storm" had washed over China. In August 2006 the Central Committee issued new regulations forbidding senior party cadres, government officials, and members of the judiciary from working in their native counties and prefectures, a policy strikingly reminiscent of the Qing dynasty's "law of avoidance." The new regulations also banned the employment of spouses, children, and relatives in any unit supervised by a state official. In the spring of 2007 Shanghai First Party Secretary Chen Liangyu, a member of the Politburo, was arrested for illegally lending US$475 million worth of municipal social security funds to local real estate developers. In December, Beijing's Vice Mayor Liu Zhuhua was expelled from the Communist Party for accepting US$10 million from contractors working on the 2008 Olympics project and maintaining a "pleasure palace" of concubines. During the fall and winter of 2007 the retired director of the State Food and Drug Administration was accused of accepting bribes, and senior officials in three provinces were detained on corruption charges.

Meanwhile, private sources indicate that the level of corruption reported is far greater than has been admitted by the government. A French journalist, for instance, reported in December 2007 that citizens in Gaoyang and other small towns in the Chongqing region watched helplessly as their homes were bulldozed by government officials to make way for the huge Three Gorges Reservoir. Despite promises of government-funded relocation, thousands have remained homeless as officials embezzled or misused funds set aside for town reconstruction. One Gaoyang resident complained that "money goes down through seven different government levels, with everyone taking a cut, so by the time it gets to us there is nothing left." This man was given a harsh prison sentence for speaking out about the problem.[26]

The husband-and-wife team of Chen Guidi and Wu Chuntao in their book *Will the Boat Sink the Water?* focused primarily on Anhui Province and detailed how a legion of local Communist Party officials leveled illegal and unfair taxes on peasants, rigged audits of local accounts, and unleashed hooligans to terrorize those who had the temerity to complain. Although the government has reported large-scale arrests of those accused of such crimes, Chen and Wu asserted that 80 percent of corrupt officials have been given suspended sentences and were exempted from criminal penalties. They also alleged that local Communist Party officials were "ring-fenced"; that is, protected from charges of criminality by superiors. Their book quickly sold 250,000 copies before it was banned by the government, but it went on to sell almost 10 million copies in a pirated edition sold underground throughout China.

The leaders who followed Deng Xiaoping have frequently fulminated against corruption. In 2002, for example, Jiang Zemin in his political report to the National Party's Congress declared that if his colleagues failed to crack down on corruption, "the flesh-and-blood ties between the party and the people will suffer a lot and the party will be in danger of losing its ruling position, or possibly leading to self-destruction."[27] President Hu Jintao has been even more vocal in his determination to stanch this scourge, recognizing that public anger over corruption could lead to mass protests and destabilize the country. The problem has become especially worrisome because party officials have increasingly sided with the privileged, further exacerbating the yawning gap between rich and poor. In fact, in 2007 several large-scale peasant riots broke out after it was revealed that local officials stole public money meant to compensate impoverished farmers for land taken for development projects. Because those who are victimized have no recourse to legal means, they have often resorted to extra-legal measures such as strikes, demonstrations, and sit-ins to attract media attention. In 1993 the Ministry of Public Security reported 8,700 of these disturbances. By 2005 such action increased ten-fold to 87,000.

In the autumn of 2007, as a response to such matters the government after four years of bureaucratic dithering, finally launched a National Bureau of Corruption Prevention (NBCP) under the control of Premier Wen Jiabao's cabinet. The organization is headed by a new Minister of Supervision charged with the task of ending graft and enhancing international cooperation against corruption, as stipulated in the United Nations Convention against Corruption. The plan is to use public campaigns and training programs to better prepare

China's citizens to battle malfeasance. As part of its public relations campaign as state crime buster, the NBCP thought it would be a good idea to open up a Web site for citizens to denounce crooked officials. Indeed, the idea was so good that the site was quickly deluged by angry Chinese, and the system overloaded and crashed after merely two days of operation. This outpouring of popular rage was a clear signal of how deeply corruption has infected the Communist Party in the three decades of liberal economic policies.

Yet the party continues to highlight its crime-fighting commitments. In the weeks leading up to the 2007 National People's Congress the government stepped up its anti-corruption campaign and publicized reports of numerous arrests of crooked party cadres and officials at banks and other state-owned enterprises. The government announced that it had disciplined more than 150,000 corrupt party members over the year and uncovered more that US$300 million in misused public funds.

The much publicized arrest and conviction in 2007 of Shanghai party boss Chen Liangyu in a social security fund scandal is an example of what the government says is part of its new campaign against "tigers," corrupt high-ranking officials (as opposed to what the people used to call "flies," lower-ranking corrupt officials). Wang Yukai, a scholar with China's National School of Administration, which trains mid-level and senior civil servants, boasted that since the beginning of 2007 "we have seen a lot of tiger-beating in the country, instead of merely fly swatting."[28]

According to independent reporters and non-party-affiliated scholars both in China and the West the much-vaunted "tiger" campaigns have more to do with public relations than hunting expeditions. A few high officials have been arrested and given severe penalties (resulting in executions in some cases), but they function chiefly as showcases to convince the public that the CCP is serious about stanching the corruption problem. In many respects this seems to be a revisiting of Mao's policy of selectively punishing the miscreant official or "class enemy" to send a message to the people, what he called "killing the chicken to teach the monkey."

Some analysts have claimed that the Communist Party has purposely tolerated a certain level of corruption in combination with selective anti-criminal enforcement as tools for inducing local officials to promote economic reform. China's traditional reliance on *guanxi* (connections), the customary way of using personal connections to get things done by "going through the back door," serves as a lubricant for economic enterprises. This is especially effective in China's two-tracked economy, which combines private and state-owned businesses. Traditionally, *guanxi* required firm managers to maintain good relations with government officials to assure resource provisions, guarantee timely deliveries of necessary raw materials, and satisfy their intermediate production goals. Because the incomes of local Communist Party officials are nominally fixed and government servants are forbidden to moonlight as employees of either private or state-owned firms, their only means of compensation for services rendered are bribes, kickbacks, or nepotistic favors. The party's tolerance of such forms of corruption not only serves to fuel economic growth but also enhances control over local officials by creating a situation in which the leaders hold the threat of punishment over everyone. One astute observer has noted: "Because an individual knows that higher-ups could charge him with corruption at any time, lack of exposure is in effect special treatment for which the official gratefully exchanges his political support."[29]

This mechanism of compensation has the benefit of strengthening the Communist Party's political power. In this respect, corruption in China today appears to serve the same function as the customary forms of "squeeze" in imperial China, in which the official scholar-gentry's modest and inadequate salaries were supplemented by various forms of bribes and economic kickbacks. Both Communist Party propaganda and Confucian ideology present their respective officials as "selfless servants of the people." The persistent threat to traditional dynastic legitimacy was "excessive squeeze," which went well beyond acceptable boundaries and thereby led to peasant insurrections. The same dilemma now confronts the Communist Party leadership. As Simon Cartledge, owner of a Hong Kong-based research and publishing firm has observed, the challenge facing the Chinese party-state is not to eliminate corruption but to manage it:

> Corruption helps regulate the relationship between political and economic actors, and its continued existence—within limits—enables the state to: increase the resources at its disposal through economic growth without sacrificing political power to business interests; enhance central government authority by selective crackdowns on local governments; and bolster the party's legitimacy by giving it sole right to define the moral dimensions of and solutions to the corruption problem.[30]

The primary task for the CCP is to attempt to balance the threat of punishment with selective enforcement. This means employing sufficient sanctions to deter local officials from excessive corruption and a willingness to punish corrupt officials who either cross the permissible threshold or whose political allegiance has fallen under suspicion. Here is where the arrest of Shanghai party boss Chen Liangyu fits into the political calculus.

Despite President Hu Jintao's stepped-up campaign against corruption, evidence suggests that the CCP is rapidly losing control of the situation. A report delivered in the autumn of 2007 by Minxin Pei, director of the China

Program at the Carnegie Endowment for International Peace, examined the root causes of China's chronic corruption. Pei concluded that corruption had surpassed the party's ability to contain it and is one of the most serious threats to China's future economic and political stability. Corruption, he argued, not only fuels social unrest and economic inequality but also undercuts the government's environmental reforms and "has spillover effects beyond its borders." It threatens the security of foreign investment and thereby the stability of the global economy. Although the Chinese government has more than 1,200 laws and regulations against corruption, enforcement is lax and ineffective. There is less than a 3 percent chance of a corrupt official going to jail, rendering such behavior a profitable and low-risk activity. The Carnegie report's findings include the following: corruption is concentrated in economic sectors with extensive state involvement (real estate, infrastructure projects, government-procurement, and financial services), and the absence of political pluralism and a free press render these areas particularly susceptible to all types of fraudulent activity; the direct costs of endemic corruption could be as high as US$86 billion annually; indirect costs to the environment, public health, education, and other areas of public life are incalculable. The system of institutional corruption not only raises the cost of doing business in China for foreign firms but illicit behavior by local officials opens up these companies to environmental, human rights, and financial liabilities.[31]

Minxin Pei and George Zhibin Gu, an influential investment banker educated at Nanjing University with a Ph.D. from the University of Michigan, both concluded that corruption could well destroy China's economy. The astute financier Warren Buffet commented that outsiders should be wary of investing in China.

Public statements by President Hu Jintao and Prime Minister Wen Jiabao indicate that they are well aware of the problem, but despite the tough rhetoric they have been unable or unwilling to curb it. If President Hu comes down too hard on corruption he risks losing the support of high-ranking members of the party congress who have elected him to office. The vast majority of these delegates are drawn from party officials at the local and provincial levels.

Thus far, China's crime-busting reforms have focused on internal adjustment and control within the system. However, evidence suggests that the only realistic way to resolve the endemic corruption is to separate completely the private and state economic sectors and to employ external forces of control. This means taking enforcement out of the hands of government bureaucracies. Rather than an anti-corruption agency controlled by the CCP, there needs to be an independent organization to police all forms of economic behavior. A likely model for this would be the Independent Commission Against Corruption that exists in Hong Kong, which has had notable success in monitoring and curbing financial malfeasance.

In sum, the only way to eliminate the potentially destabilizing consequences of corruption is through fundamental structural change. This requires the separation of business from party and government jurisdiction, fundamental political reform, and the abandonment of the one party-state. Zheng Yongnian, head of research at the China Policy Institute, University of Nottingham, insists that fighting corruption must arise from a change in China's political structures: "Only if there is political reform can people's participation be guaranteed. Effectively fighting corruption depends on establishing a new and democratic relationship between state and society, between the government and the people."[32] Yet there seems little likelihood that such reforms are in the future. As Minxin Pei has noted, the ability of Communist regimes to use the power of patronage and coercion to keep power provides insufficient incentive to give up such capacity by introducing gradual democratic change from above.[33]

Future Prospects

China at the beginning of the twenty-first century remains a land where contradictions, improvements, and setbacks go hand in hand. Despite remarkable economic progress since 1980, it still has a fragmented economy. The areas that are modernizing at a rapid pace are becoming increasingly integrated with the rest of the world and will continue to benefit from international trade and WTO membership. According to China's National Bureau of Statistics, in 2007 well over half of China's industrial output came from the private sector as opposed to less than a quarter in 1998.[34] On the other hand, government programs that have been phasing out state-owned industries since 2002 have contributed to a rising unemployment rate unheard of before 1980. Furthermore, the agricultural sector remains primitive and subject to the exploitation of unscrupulous developers. The Chinese government, despite its economic reform efforts, has not come close to meeting the needs of its people, especially in rural areas where unemployment and underemployment are substantial. The Chinese Communist Party appears well aware of the problems and contradictions it faces and has attempted to address many potentially destabilizing problems. For example, Premier Wen Jiabao announced in early 2007 that the Beijing government plans to set up a comprehensive medical insurance program over the next three years that will cover all urban citizens, including children and the unemployed. Such a program would expand the government's 2003 rural health care program and, in theory, provide coverage for those Chinese not employed by the private sector.

Despite significant and ongoing modifications to China's economic structure, its political system remains largely unaffected. Although the CCP's leadership no longer aspires to totalitarianism, striving to control all aspects of human behavior as under Mao, the party operates as an authoritarian dictatorship that claims to look back to the legacy of Marxism/Leninism for inspiration. This presents yet another contradiction. On October 21, 2007, the 17th National Congress of the CCP amended and adopted a new constitution for the first decade of the twenty-first century. In it is enshrined the fourth generation's new mantra, the "Scientific Outlook on Development," associated with Hu Jintao's economic development policies. The Fourth Generation's economic principles became the latest official stage in its long-range program. The Constitution also references the principles that serve China's development process: "The Communist Party of China takes Marxism-Leninism, Mao Zedong Thought, Deng Xiaoping Theory, and the important thought of the Three Represents [of Jiang Zemin] as its guide to action." The CCP continues to adhere to the view that China remains "in the primary stage of socialism and will remain so for a long time to come," despite evidence to the contrary, as seen in the daily lives of capitalist Chinese. The Constitution outlines the party's current economic goal to "realize modernization . . . by the time of the centenary of the People's Republic of China." In a revision of goals announced in 2002 that called for the quadrupling of economic output from 2000 to 2020, the CCP proposes the more ambitious target to bring the per capita GDP up "to the level of moderately developed countries." The subtle change in focus from the economy as a whole to per capita goals is an acknowledgment of the growing trend toward individualism and economic independence in China today, characteristics that are not associated with Marxism/Leninism.

In his opening address to more than 2000 National Party Congress representatives in 2007, President Hu Jintao also credited the CCP's past accomplishments as he outlined the party's future aims:

> The theme of the congress is to hold high the great banner of socialism with Chinese characteristics, . . . thoroughly apply the Scientific Outlook on Development, continue to emancipate the mind, persist in reform and opening up, pursue development in a scientific way, promote social harmony and strive for new victories in building a moderately prosperous society in all respects.

While Hu spoke of the CCP's achievements, he also warned of future problems whose solutions may be hindered by the CCP's inability to meet new challenges. "Some primary party organizations," Hu explained, "are weak and lax." Corruption, dishonesty, waste, and "other undesirable behaviors" obstruct progress. Yet, nowhere in Hu's two-and-a-half hour speech were suggestions for substantive political reform. Instead Hu advocated endeavors to strengthen the CCP through education, training, and combating corruption. The CCP will keep its monopoly on power under the new Constitution. The Chinese government continues not to recognize human rights as understood in the West. While the press has more latitude than in the past, all newspapers remain under party control. Journalists who stray too far from the accepted party views risk their careers. Academics and others who have delved too deeply into issues that the CCP leadership finds threatening do so at the risk of their freedom.

President Hu also addressed other issues of concern to the international community, such as pollution, competition for energy resources, and the potential for the spread of disease, promising the party's commitment to cooperate with international agencies. In addition, Hu examined his government's support for an "independent foreign policy of peace." He specifically included the CCP's continued efforts to meet challenges posed by outstanding territorial issues with Hong Kong, Macao, and Taiwan. But the promise of talks and cultural and economic exchanges was tempered by his reference to upholding the Anti-secession Law directed at Taiwan enacted by the PRC in 2005. Issues that the CCP leadership views as threats to China's sovereignty will continue to be a source of conflict. The CCP has the support of much of the Chinese population, including China's youth, who have developed a sense of nationalism, in part due to the success of China's economic reforms.

China's younger generations, especially its current university students, present another contradiction. To outside observers they seem Westernized. They behave in many ways like Western youth; they frequent the discos that have become extremely popular, not only in major cities like Beijing (which claims to have the largest disco in the world), Shanghai, and Guangzhou, but even in much smaller cities and towns throughout the country. They flock to Internet chat rooms, wear the latest European/Japanese fashions and American footwear, and avidly watch American and European sports teams. Yet their attitude toward the West, and especially the United States, is fundamentally different from the outlook of the generation that bravely demonstrated for democracy in Tiananmen Square in 1989. The government crackdown since then and Beijing's tireless trumpeting of Chinese nationalism and anti-American propaganda, as evidenced by the spontaneous explosion of anger against the United States after the errant bombing of China's Belgrade embassy in 1999, have crippled the prodemocracy movement. The propaganda begins in primary school, continues through college, and is reinforced by the media. China's university students in their early twenties have little knowledge of the Great Leap Forward and the Cultural Revolution. What happened in Tiananmen Square is also a topic for history, one that is largely ignored in the public schools. Current university students appear to agree with the government claim that it is protecting the social order when it curbs freedom of expression and represses dissenters. Many Chinese students are interested in the United States, and often want to study or visit there, but they also view the American government as a bully trying to push China around. Even those young Chinese who have become socially alienated do not show an interest in politics. Many of China's young people today are part of what is known as a "gray culture," zones of alternative thought and lifestyle bleached of Communist "redness" and beyond party control; they celebrate money-making, material goods, foreign music, and generally anything that does not touch on the established political structures.

The Communist Party still rules with an iron hand. But a quarter of a century after Mao Zedong's death, the ideals that constituted the core of Communist promises to the Chinese people are as cold and dead as that waxed cadaver of the Great Helmsman presently residing in his glass sarcophagus in Tiananmen Square. Aside from the CCP dictatorship itself, nationalism is what holds the country together. Nationalism draws strength from resentment the Chinese still feel from more than 150 years of foreign mistreatment. It is rooted in a regal history 4,000 years old and it is a strong glue. The ultimate question touches on the title of this very book: Can the Communist Party's revolutionary imperatives satisfy the demands of modernization? Can communism wedded to nationalism, the latter a universal progeny of modernization itself, prevent the rifts caused by deep social, economic, and political problems from deepening to the point where they threaten the country's stability and usher in yet another swing of the dynastic cycle?

Notes

Preface

1. Anne Thurston, *Enemies of the People: The Ordeal of the Intellectuals in China's Great Cultural Revolution* (Cambridge, MA, 1988), xx.

2. "First-comers" and "latecomers" are terms used by the scholars working with the Center of International Studies, Princeton University. For a further discussion and analysis of social change outside the West, see the extended essays in Cyril E. Black, Marius B. Jansen, et al., eds., *The Modernization of Japan and Russia* (New York, 1975) and Gilbert Rozman, ed., *The Modernization of China* (New York, 1981).

3. Paul A. Cohen, *Discovering History in China: American Historical Writing on the Recent Past* (New York, 1984), ix.

Chapter 2

1. Raymond Dawson, *The Chinese Experience* (New York, 1978), 35.

2. Kang Chao, *Man and Land in China: An Economic Analysis* (Stanford, CA, 1986), 5–6, 29–32, 222–27.

3. Mark Elvin, *The Pattern of the Chinese Past* (Stanford, CA, 1973), 301–2.

Chapter 3

1. Hsin-pao Chang, *Commissioner Lin and the Opium War* (Cambridge, MA, 1964), 96.

2. Jack Beeching, *The Chinese Opium Wars* (New York, 1975), 35.

3. Ibid., 330.

4. See John King Fairbank, *Trade and Diplomacy on the Chinese Coast: The Opening of the Treaty Ports, 1842–1854* (Stanford, CA, 1969).

5. For an elaboration on this issue, see Owen Lattimore, *Inner Asian Frontiers of China* (New York, 1951).

6. Franz Michael, *The Taiping Rebellion: History and Documents* (Seattle, 1966), 3.

7. Frederic Wakeman, Jr., *Strangers at the Gate: Social Disorder in South China, 1839–1861* (Berkeley, CA, 1966), 3.

8. Stanley Spector, *Li Hung-chang and the Huai Army: A Study in Nineteenth-Century Chinese Regionalism* (Seattle, 1964), 15.

9. Ting-yee Kuo and Kwang-ching Liu, "Self-Strengthening: The Pursuit of Western Technology," in Denis Twitchett and John King Fairbank, eds., *The Cambridge History of China,* vol. 10 (Cambridge, UK, 1978), 495.

10. Mary Clabaugh Wright, *The Last Stand of Chinese Conservatism: The T'ung Chih Restoration, 1862–1874* (Stanford, CA, 1957), 154.

11. Quoted in J. Martin Miller, *China: Ancient and Modern* (Chicago, 1900), 321.

12. Abraham Yarmolinsky, trans. and ed., *The Memoirs of Count Witte* (New York, 1921), 103.

13. Hu Shih, *The Chinese Renaissance* (Chicago, 1934), 9.

14. As quoted in Franz Schurmann and Orville Schell, *Imperial China* (New York, 1967), 30–31, from Evariste Regis Huc, *The Chinese Empire* (London, 1855).

Chapter 4

1. Sun Yat-sen, "The Three People's Principles," in William Theodore De Bary, Wing-tsit Chan, and Chester Tan, eds., *Sources of Chinese Tradition,* vol. 2 (New York, 1960), 113.

2. Sun Yat-sen, *Memoirs of a Chinese Revolutionary* (London, 1918, reprinted Taipei, 1953), iv.

3. Quoted in James Sheridan, *China in Disintegration* (New York, 1977), 91–92.

4. Lee N. Feigon, *Chen Duxiu: Founder of the Chinese Communist Party* (Princeton, NJ, 1983), 32.

5. Chen Duxiu, "The Way of Confucius and Modern Life," in De Bary, Chan, and Tan, eds., *Sources of Chinese Tradition,* 153.

6. Chow Tse-tsung, *The May Fourth Movement* (Cambridge, MA, 1960), 276.

7. Ibid., 277.

Chapter 5

1. Quoted in Lloyd Eastman, *The Abortive Revolution: China under Nationalist Rule, 1927–1937* (Cambridge, MA, 1974), 1.

2. Quoted in Lloyd Eastman, "Nationalist China during the Nanking Decade," in John King Fairbank and Albert Feuerwerker, eds., *The Cambridge History of China,* vol. 13 (Cambridge, UK, 1986), 145–46.

3. Lucien Bianco, *Origins of the Chinese Revolution, 1915–1949,* trans. Muriel Bell (Stanford, CA, 1971), 128.

4. John King Fairbank, *The United States and China,* 4th ed. (Cambridge, MA, 1979), 253.

5. Mao Tse-tung, "Report on an Investigation of the Peasant Movement in Hunan," in Franz Schurman and Orville Schell, eds. *Republican China: Nationalism, War, and the Rise of Communism 1911–1949* (New York, 1967), 125–26.

6. Edgar Snow, *Red Star over China* (New York, 1938), 157–58.

7. Mao Tse-tung, *Selected Works,* vol. 1, 1926–1936 (New York, 1954), 27.

8. Quoted in Jean Chesneaux et al., *China: From the 1911 Revolution to Liberation* (New York, 1977), 227.

Chapter 6

1. Theodore White and Annalee Jacoby, *Thunder Out of China* (New York, 1946), 174–75.

2. Maria Hsia Chang, *Return of the Dragon: China's Wounded Nationalism* (Boulder, CO, 2001), 82.

3. Lucien Bianco, *Origins of the Chinese Revolution* (Stanford, CA, 1971), 159.

4. Quoted in Lyman Van Slyke, "The Chinese Communist Movement during the Sino-Japanese War, 1937–1945," in John King Fairbank and Albert Feuerwerker, eds., *The Cambridge History of China,* vol. 13 (Cambridge, UK, 1986), 689.

5. See Dai Qing, *Wang Shiwei and "Wild Lilies": Rectification and Purges in the Chinese Communist Party, 1942–1944* (Armonk, NY, 1994).

6. Suzanne Pepper, *Civil War in China: The Political Struggle 1945–1949* (Berkeley, CA, 1978), 26.

7. Jonathan D. Spence, *The Gate of Heavenly Peace: The Chinese and Their Revolution, 1895–1980* (New York, 1981), 315.

8. U.S. Department of State, *United States Relations with China* (Washington, DC, 1949), 845–46.

9. See Douglas J. Macdonald, "Communist Bloc Expansion in the Early Cold War," *International Security* 20.3 (winter 1995/96), 152–88; Sergei N. Goncharov, John W. Lewis, and Xue Litai, *Uncertain Partners: Stalin, Mao, and the Korean War* (Stanford, CA, 1993); Odd Arne Westad, *Cold War and Revolution: Soviet-American Rivalry and the Origins of the Chinese Civil War* (New York, 1993).

Chapter 7

1. Mao Tse-tung, *Selected Works,* vol. 4 (Peking, 1969), 374.

2. Dennis Bloodworth, *The Messiah and the Mandarins: Mao Tse-tung and the Ironies of Power* (New York, 1982), 71.

3. Dick Wilson, *The People's Emperor* (New York, 1980), 292.

4. Ibid., 294.

5. Mao Tse-tung, *Selected Works,* vol. 1 (Peking, 1969), 147–50.

6. Bloodworth, 106.

7. See Jacques Guillermaz, *La chine populaire* (Paris, 1964), 47.

8. Jacques Guillermaz, *The Chinese Communist Party in Power: 1949–1976* (Boulder, CO, 1976), 72.

9. Bloodworth, 111.

10. Craig Dietrich, *People's China: A Brief History* (New York, 1986), 88.

11. See Bloodworth, 113.

12. Quoted in Merle Goldman, "The Party and the Intellectuals," in Roderick MacFarquhar and John King Fairbank, eds., *The Cambridge History of China,* vol. 14 (New York, 1987), 241.

13. Mao, *Propaganda Conference Speech,* 14, cited in Roderick MacFarquhar, *The Origins of the Cultural Revolution. 1: Contradictions among the People 1956–1957* (New York, 1974), 187.

14. Quoted in a joint article in the *People's Daily, Red Flag,* and *Liberation Army News,* September 1, 2, and 3, 1968. As cited in MacFarquhar, 194.

15. Jonathan D. Spence, *The Search for Modern China* (New York, 1990), 569.

16. See Liao Kai-lung, "Historical Experiences," *Issues & Studies* (October 1981), 80–81.

17. See Lynn T. White III, *Policies of Chaos: The Organizational Causes of Violence in China's Cultural Revolution* (Princeton, NJ, 1989), 6–9.

18. Liang Heng and Judith Shapiro, *Son of the Revolution* (New York, 1983), 178.

19. Wilson, 347.

20. This was the reverse in the Soviet Union, in which 70 percent of the party membership came from urban areas.

21. MacFarquhar, 311.

22. This was what researchers discovered from interviews with Chinese citizens. See Kenneth Lieberthal, *Governing China: From Revolution through Reform* (New York, 1995), 68.

Chapter 8

1. Stuart R. Schram, *The Political Thought of Mao Tse-tung* (New York, 1963), 253.

2. Stuart R. Schram, ed., *Chairman Mao Talks to the People; Talks and Letters: 1956–1971* (New York, 1974), 92.

3. Quoted in Edward Rice, *Mao's Way* (Berkeley, 1972), 164.

4. Mark Selden, *The People's Republic of China: A Documentary History of Revolutionary Change* (New York, 1978), 413.

5. Schram, *Chairman Mao Talks to the People,* 119–20.

6. Dennis Bloodworth, *The Messiah and the Mandarins: Mao Tse-tung and the Ironies of Power* (New York, 1982), 130.

7. Richard C. Thornton, *China: A Political History, 1917–1980* (Boulder, CO, 1982), 254.

8. Schram, *Chairman Mao Talks to the People,* 145–46.

9. Quoted in Maurice Meisner, *Mao's China: A History of the People's Republic* (New York, 1977), 245.

10. Quoted in Roderick MacFarquhar, *The Origins of the Cultural Revolution,* vol. 2 (New York, 1983), 10.

Chapter 9

1. Quoted in Jack Gray and Patrick Cavendish, *Chinese Communism in Crisis* (London, 1968), 124–25.

2. Quoted in Bob Avakian, *Mao Tse-tung's Immortal Contribution* (Chicago, 1979), 232.

3. Roxane Witke, *Comrade Chiang Ching* (Boston, 1972), 362.

4. Dick Wilson, *Zhou Enlai* (New York, 1984), 239.

5. "Long Live the Revolutionary Rebel Spirit of the Proletariat," *Peking Review* (September 9, 1966), 20–21.

6. Stuart R. Schram, ed., *Chairman Mao Talks to the People* (New York, 1974), 258.

7. Quoted in Witke, 325.

8. *Mao Zedong sixiang wan sui!* (Long Live Mao Zedong Thought!) (no city of publication or publisher provided, 1969), 195, quoted in Kenneth Lieberthal, *Governing China: From Revolution through Reform* (New York, 1995), 71.

9. Neale Hunter, *Shanghai Journal* (Boston, 1971), 88.

10. William Hinton, *Shenfan* (New York, 1983), 542.

11. Hunter, 165.

12. Immanuel C.Y. Hsu, *The Rise of Modern China* (New York, 1975), 851.

13. Anne F. Thurston, *Enemies of the People: The Ordeal of the Intellectuals in China's Great Cultural Revolution* (Cambridge, MA, 1988), 124.

14. See Andrew J. Nathan, *Chinese Democracy* (New York, 1985), 5.

15. Nien Cheng, *Life and Death in Shanghai* (New York, 1986), 76.

16. Witke, 310.

17. Richard L. Walker, "The Human Cost of Communism in China," in U.S. Senate, Subcommittee to Investigate the Administration of the Internal Security Act and Other Internal Security Laws of the Committee on the Judiciary (Washington, DC, 1971), 23.

18. Hinton, 521.

19. Thurston, 246–47.

20. Liang Heng and Judith Shapiro, *Son of the Revolution* (New York, 1983), 76.

21. Lynn T. White III, *Policies of Chaos: The Organizational Causes of Violence in China's Cultural Revolution* (Princeton, NJ, 1989), 310.

22. Lin Piao, "Long Live the Victory of People's War," *Peking Review*, no. 32 (August 4, 1967): 13.

23. Quoted in Witke, 358.

24. Quoted in Hsu, 862.

25. Ibid.

26. CCP member Xiang Jun said this in a 1977 speech.

27. Liang Heng and Judith Shapiro, *After the Nightmare* (New York, 1986), 5–6.

Chapter 10

1. Quoted in Orville Schell, *To Get Rich Is Glorious,* 2nd ed. (New York, 1986), 16.

2. See Sylvan Wittner, Sun Han, Yu Youtai, and Wang Lianzheng, *Feeding a Billion* (East Lansing, MI, 1987).

3. Quoted in Schell, 54.

4. Ibid., 96.

5. *The Economist* (August 1, 1987), 10.

6. Ibid., November 26, 1988, 36.

7. Orville Schell, "An Act of Defiance," *New York Times Magazine,* April 16, 1989, 30.

8. Immanuel C.Y. Hsu, *The Rise of Modern China,* 6th ed. (New York, 2000), 928.

9. This is the view of Zhang Liang, a pseudonym used by a Chinese official who smuggled out of the PRC a trove of secret documents on the party deliberations leading up to the decision to crush the student-led Tiananmen protestors in the spring of 1989. The documents were translated into English by two American China scholars, Andrew J. Nathan of Columbia University and Perry Link of Princeton University. For Zhang Liang's assessment see Andrew J. Nathan and Perry Link, eds., *The Tiananmen Papers* (New York, 2001), xi.

10. Andrew J. Nathan, *"The Tiananmen Papers:* An Editor's Reflections," *The China Quarterly,* 167 (September 2001), 724. This number is not given in the book, but was later calculated by Zhang Liang from data in the secret documents.

11. Donald Morrison, *Massacre in Beijing* (New York, 1989), 152.

12. Ibid., 153.

13. Ibid.

14. Nathan and Link, 330–31.

15. Ibid., 189.

16. Ibid., xxxvi.

17. Recent documents indicate that the army was given clear orders to minimize bloodshed, but inadequately trained troops lost control of the situation. See Nathan and Link, 354–62; 420–25; 436–37.

18. David E. Sanger, *New York Times,* September 3, 1989, 1.

19. *Beijing Review* (July 10–16, 1989), 19.

Chapter 11

1. Joseph Fewsmith, *China Since Tiananmen: The Politics of Transition* (Armonk, NY, 2001), 63.

2. Bruce Gilley, *Tiger on the Brink: Jiang Zemin and China's New Elite* (Berkeley, CA, 1998), 131.

3. Ibid., 94.

4. Orville Schell, *Mandate of Heaven: The Legacy of Tiananmen Square and the Next Generation of China's Leaders* (New York, 1994), 173.

5. Ibid., 344.

6. Fewsmith, 56.

7. Schell, 360.

8. Mao had to overcome the Twenty-eight Bolsheviks, Li Lisan, and the Comintern, while Deng ousted Hua Guofeng.

9. Gilley, 226.

10. Ibid., 241.

11. Cited in Thomas P. Bernstein and Xiaobo Lü, "Taxation without Representation: Peasants, the Central and the Local States in Reform China," *The China Quarterly,* 163 (September 2000), 753.

12. Fewsmith, 171.

13. Ibid., 173.

14. For a fuller treatment of the Chinese new left, see Fewsmith.

15. See Ian Buruma, "Cult of the Chairman," *The Guardian Weekly,* March 15–21, 2001.

16. For more, see James Tong, "An Organizational Analysis of the Falun Gong: Structure, Communications, Financing," *The China Quarterly,* 171 (September 2002), 636–60.

17. For a fuller treatment of this, see Joseph Fewsmith, *China since Tiananmen,* 229–31.

Chapter 12

1. The "five objectives" are adapted from a study conducted by the Council on Foreign Relations in 1999. Michel Oksenberg and Elizabeth Economy, "Introduction: China Joins the World," in Oksenberg and Economy, eds., *China Joins the World* (New York, 1999), 20–21.

2. Quoted in Bruce Gilley, *Tiger on the Brink: Jiang Zemin and China's New Elite* (Berkeley, CA, 1998), 299.

3. Ibid., 302.

4. Jasper Becker, "Beijing Extravaganza Charts China's Historic Path to Glory," *South China Morning Post,* July 2, 1997.

5. Denny Roy, *China's Foreign Relations* (Lanham, MD, 1998), 223.

6. "Protests Surround Hong Kong Handover Anniversary," *The Guardian,* July 1, 2002.

7. Keith Bradsher, "Hong Kong Delays Security Bill after Cabinet Member Resigns," *New York Times,* July 7, 2003.

8. Jiang Zemin, "Continue to Promote the Reunification of the Motherland," January 30, 1995, http://www.chinaembassy.dk/links/taiwan-jiang8.htm.

9. Agence France-Presse. "Historic 1993 China, Taiwan Talks Took Five Years of Groundwork," July 19, 2000, Taiwan Research Institute, http://taiwansecurity/.org/AFP/AFP-071900.htm.

10. Jiang Zemin, January 30, 1995.

11. United States Department of State International Information Programs, "Transcript: Powell Stresses U.S. Wants Friendly Ties with China." Interview on CCTV-China's State Television, July 30, 2001, http://usinfo,state,gov/regional/ea/uschina/pulectv.htm.

12. Richard Bernstein and Ross H. Munro, *The Coming Conflict with China* (New York, 1997), 20.

13. Qian Qichen (1994). Quoted in Roy, 135.

14. Quoted in the *New York Times,* June 18, 1989.

15. Roy, 140.

16. Linda D. Kozaryn, "U.S. Air Crew Detained in China Head Home," U.S. Department of Defense, April 2001, http://www.dod.mil/news/Apr2001/n04122001–20010421.html.

17. Edward Cody, "Chinese Leader Coming to U.S. Well Prepared," *Washington Post Foreign Service*, April 18, 2006, A14.

18. Allen S. Whiting, "China and Japan: Politics versus Economics," in *The Annals of the American Academy of Political and Social Science*, ed. Richard D. Lambert, 519 (January 1992), 40.

19. Roy, 159; 163.

20. Ibid., 169.

21. Scott Snyder, "Sino-Korean Relations and the Future of the U.S.-ROK Alliance," *National Bureau of Asian Research*, 14.1 (June 2003), 54.

22. Ibid., 59.

23. Ibid., 60.

24. Yan Xuetong (1995). Quoted in Roy, 129.

25. Yan Xuetong, "Security Will Top World Agenda," *China Facts and Figures 2002*, http://www.china.org.

26. Rebecca MacKinnon, "China and Russia: Mutual Trust, But No Alliance," November 10, 1997, CNN Interactive, http://www.cnn.cn/WORLD/0711/10/russia.china/.

27. "Vladimir Putin: Border Demarcation Between Russia and China to Be Settled Soon," *Pravda,* January 22, 2003, http://english.pravda.ru/politics/2003/01.

28. Ibid.

29. "China-Russia Trade to Get Stronger," *Pravda,* October 7, 2002, http://english.pravda.ru.economic/2002/10/07/37823.html.

30. David Shambaugh, "China and Europe," in *The Annals of the American Acad-*

emy of Political and Social Science, ed. Richard D. Lambert, 519 (January 1992), 110–11.

31. Canada Tibet Committee, World Tibet News, "European Union Urges China to Begin Dialogue with the Dalai Lama," March 29, 2002, http://www.tibet.co/wtarchive/2002/3/30–4.html.

32. Europaische Union-China, Press Release, "The Fifth EU-China Summit Took Place in Copenhagen on 24 September 2002," September 24, 2002, http://www.europa-web.de/europe/03euinf/05CHINA/euchisum.htm.

33. Roy, 49.

34. Ibid., 50.

35. "Europe Waits for Progress—July 2003," *Tibetan News,* http://www.sakya-centre.org/sakya_news.tibetan.chinese.discussion.May.2003htm.

36. Roy, 47–48.

Chapter 13

1. For an analysis of the nature, character, and expectations of the Cultural Revolution generation, see Cheng Li, *China's Leaders: The New Generation* (London, 2001).

2. Ibid., 183.

3. Some of what follows draws from Nathan and Gilley's two articles in the *New York Review of Books* (September 26 and October 10, 2002) and their subsequently published *China's New Rulers: The Secret Files* (New York, 2002).

4. This is the picture that emerges from Nathan and Gilley's analysis. For a different view, see Joseph Fewsmith, "The Sixteenth National Party Congress: The Succession That Didn't Happen," *The China Quarterly,* 173 (March 2003), 1–16. Fewsmith asserts that Jiang was a more prominent force than Nathan and Gilley suggest, and that he got his way after a good deal of arm-twisting and backroom dealing. Others, and especially the Central Committee, Fewsmith argues, had little substantive influence on the promotions of the new leaders.

5. For an outline and discussion of Hu Jintao's career, see Richard Daniel Ewing, "Hu Jintao: The Making of a Chinese General Secretary," *The China Quarterly,* 173 (March 2003), 17–34.

6. An excellent contemporary explication of the importance of a civil society for the creation of liberal democracy can be found in Fareed Zakaria's *The Future of Freedom: Illiberal Democracy at Home and Abroad* (New York, 2003).

7. Li, 238.

8. James McGregor. *One Billion Customers: Lessons from the Front Lines of Doing Business in China* (New York, 2005), 3.

9. Quoted in Asa Briggs, *The Making of Modern England 1783–1867: The Age of Improvement* (New York, 1959), 294.

10. *New York Times,* December 8, 2001.

11. "China Reports Major Decline in Accidents," Associated Press, November 5, 2007.

12. *New York Times,* July 16, 2001.

13. Salvatore Diglio, "Urban Development and Historic Heritage Preservation in Shanghai," University of Naples "L'Orientale" 2005, http://www.webjournal.unior.it.

14. *New York Times,* December 26, 2001.

15. Jonathan Watts, *The Guardian Weekly,* October 30–November 5, 2003.

16. Ibid.

17. "China Praised for Its AIDS Efforts." *China Daily,* February 23, 2007.

18. John Gittings, "Inside Asia," *The Guardian Weekly,* April 17–23, 2003.

19. Jonathan Watts, *The Guardian Weekly,* June 26–July 2, 2003.

20. Paul Roberts, *The End of Oil: On the Edge of a Perilous New World* (New York, 2004).

21. Joseph Kahn and Jim Yardley, "As China Booms, Pollution Reaches Deadly Extremes," *New York Times,* August 26, 2007.

22. Much of these data come from Elizabeth Economy, "The Environmental Challenge of China," a lecture delivered at the Chautauqua Institute, June 11, 2007, and her book *The River Runs Black: The Environmental Challenge to China's Future* (Ithaca, NY, 2004).

23. *China Daily,* May 21, 2007, 1, http://www.chinadaily.com.cn.

24. Jonathan Watts and David Adam, *The Guardian Weekly,* July 13, 2007, 3.

25. Friedrich Wu, "China's Losing Battle Against Corruption," *Institute of Defense and Strategic Studies* (October 17, 2006), 6.

26. Dan Martin, "China's Three Gorges Migrants Decry Corruption, Abuse," Agence France-Press, December 9, 2007.

27. Quoted by Will Hutton, "Power, Corruption and Lies," *The Guardian,* January 8, 2007.

28. "Anti-corruption Storm Rages Through China," http://www.nyconsulate. prchina.org/eng/xw/t274156.htm.

29. Quoted in Chengze Simon Fan and Herschel I. Grossman, "Entrepreneurial Graft in China," *The Providence Journal,* May 3, 2001.

30. Rowan Callick, "China Needs to Tackle Corruption," *The Australian,* December 17, 2007.

31. Minxin Pei, "Corruption Threatens China's Future," Carnegie Endowment, Policy Brief No. 55, October 2007. It should be noted that Pei's think tank in Washington, DC is affiliated with a number of Chinese universities in Beijing. The report's findings are based on official audits, press reports, government anti-corruption enforcement data, and estimates based on international norms.

32. Zheng Yongnian, *Lianhe zaobao,* September 4, 2007, Translated by Michael Rank, http://www.zaobao.com/special/forum/pages5/forum zp 070904a.html. Willy Wo-Lap Lam makes the same assessment regarding the necessity of fundamental political reform as the only means of extirpating China's systematic corruption. See his *Chinese Politics in the Hu Jintao Era: New Leaders, New Challenges* (Armonk, NY, 2006), 107.

33. Minxin Pei, *China's Trapped Transition* (Cambridge, MA, 2006), 18.

34. Sean Dougherty, Richard Herd, and Ping He, "Has a Private Sector Emerged in China's Industry? Evidence from a Quarter of a Million Chinese Firms," *China Economic Review* 18.3 (2007), 309–34.

Suggested Readings

The Middle Kingdom and Patterns of Chinese Life

Buchanan, Keith, Charles P. Fitzgerald, and Colin A. Ronan. *China: The Land and People*. New York, 1980.

Buck, Pearl S. *The Good Earth*. New York, 1972.

Cotterell, Arthur. *China: A Cultural History*. New York, 1988.

Dawson, Raymond. *The Chinese Experience*. New York, 1978.

————, ed. *The Legacy of China*. Oxford, UK, 1964.

Ebrey, Patricia Buckley, ed. *Chinese Civilization and Society: A Sourcebook*. New York, 1981.

Elliot, Mark C. *The Manchu Way: The 8 Banners and Ethnic Identity in Late Imperial China*. Stanford, CA, 2001.

Elman, Benjamin A. *On Their Own Terms: Science in China, 1550–1900*. Cambridge, MA, 2005.

Elvin, Mark. *The Pattern of the Chinese Past*. Stanford, CA, 1973.

Gentzler, L. Mason. *An Introduction to Chinese Civilization*. Lexington, MA, 1973.

Gernet, Jacques. *A History of Chinese Civilization*. Cambridge, UK, 1982.

Hucker, Charles O. *China's Imperial Past: An Introduction to Chinese History and Culture*. Stanford, CA, 1975.

Kang, Chao. *Man and Land in China: An Economic Analysis*. Stanford, CA, 1986.

Shaughnessy, Edward, general editor. *China: Empire and Civilization*. New York, 2000.

Sickman, Laurence C.S., and Alexander Soper. *The Art and Architecture of China*. Harmondsworth, UK, 1971.

Spence, Jonathan. *The Death of Woman Wang*. New York, 1978.

Imperial Breakdown and Western Invasion

Chan, Wellington K.K. *Merchants, Mandarins, and Modern Enterprise in Late Ch'ing China*. Cambridge, UK, 1977.

Chang, Hsin-pao. *Commissioner Lin and the Opium War*. Cambridge, MA, 1964.

Davis, Fei-ling. *Primitive Revolutionaries of China: A Study of Secret Societies in the Late Nineteenth Century*. Honolulu, 1977.

Esherick, Joseph. *The Origins of the Boxer Uprising*. Berkeley, CA, 1987.

Fairbank, John K. *Trade and Diplomacy on the China Coast: The Opening of the Treaty Ports, 1842–1854*. Cambridge, MA, 1953.

Fay, Peter Ward. *The Opium War, 1840–1842*. London, 1975.

Feuerweker, Albert. *China's Early Industrialization: Sheng Hsuan-huai and Mandarin Enterprise*. Cambridge, MA, 1958.

Hao, Yen-p'ing. *The Commercial Revolution in Nineteenth-Century China: The Rise of Sino-Western Mercantile Capitalism*. Berkeley, CA, 1986.

Kwong, Luke. *A Mosaic of the Hundred Days: Personalities, Politics and Ideas of 1898*. Cambridge, MA, 1984.

Purcell, Victor. *The Boxer Uprising: A Background Study*. London, 1963.

Rawski, Evelyn. *The Last Emperors: A Social History of Qing Imperial Institutions*. Berkeley, CA, 1998

Shih, Vincent. *The Taiping Ideology: Its Sources, Interpretations, and Influences*. Seattle, 1967.

Wagner, Rudolf. *Reenacting the Heavenly Vision: The Role of Religion in the Taiping Rebellion*. Berkeley, CA, 1982.

Wakeman, Frederic, Jr. *Strangers at the Gate: Social Disorder in South China, 1839–1861*. Berkeley, CA, 1966.

Wehrle, Edmund S. *Britain, China, and the Antimissionary Riots, 1891–1900*. Minneapolis, 1966.

The New Chinese Republic

Bergère, Marie-Claire. *Sun Yat-sen*. Stanford, CA, 1998.

Chow, Tse-tsung. *The May Fourth Movement: Intellectual Revolution in Modern China*. Cambridge, MA, 1960.

Dirlik, Arif. *The Origins of Chinese Communism*. New York, 1989.

Eastman, Lloyd E. *The Abortive Revolution: China under Nationalist Rule, 1927–1937*. Cambridge, MA, 1974.

Fung, Edmund. *The Military Dimension of the Chinese Revolution*. Vancouver, Canada, 1980.

Gasster, Michael. *Chinese Intellectuals and the Revolution of 1911*. Seattle, 1969.

Grieder, Jerome. *Hu Shih and the Chinese Renaissance: Liberalism in the Chinese Revolution, 1917–1937*. Cambridge, MA, 1970.

Lary, Diana. *Warlord Soldiers: Chinese Common Soldiers, 1911–1937*. New York, 1985.

Price, Don. *Russia and the Roots of the Chinese Revolution, 1896–1911*. Cambridge, MA, 1974.

Rankin, Mary. *Elite Activism and Political Transformation in China*. Stanford, CA, 1986.

Schiffrin, Harold. *Sun Yat-sen and the Origins of the Chinese Revolution*. Berkeley, CA, 1970.

Schoppa, R. Keith. *Chinese Elites and Political Change*. Cambridge, MA, 1982.

Schwarcz, Vera. *The Chinese Enlightenment: Intellectuals and the Legacy of the May Fourth Movement of 1919*. Berkeley, CA, 1986.

Sheridan, James. *Chinese Warlord: The Career of Feng Yu-hsiang*. Stanford, CA, 1966.

Wilbur, C. Martin. *Sun Yat-sen: Frustrated Patriot*. New York, 1976.

Nationalists and Communists

Bianco, Lucien. *The Origins of the Chinese Revolution, 1915–1949*. Stanford, CA, 1971.

Eastman, Lloyd E. *The Abortive Revolution: China under Nationalist Rule, 1922–1937.* Cambridge, MA, 1971.

Harrison, James. *The Long March to Power.* New York, 1973.

Isaacs, Harold. *The Tragedy of the Chinese Revolution.* Palo Alto, CA, 1951.

Israel, John. *Student Nationalism in China, 1922–1937.* Palo Alto, CA, 1966.

Kim, Ilpyong. *The Politics of Chinese Communism: Kiangsi under the Soviets.* Berkeley, CA, 1973.

Schwartz, Benjamin I. *Chinese Communism and the Rise of Mao.* Cambridge, MA, 1951.

Sheridan, James. *China in Disintegration.* New York, 1975.

Snow, Edgar. *Red Star over China.* Revised and enlarged ed. New York, 1968.

Tien, Hung-Mao. *Government and Politics in Kuomintang China, 1927–1937.* Palo Alto, CA, 1972.

Wilbur, C. Martin. *The Nationalist Revolution in China, 1923–1938.* Cambridge, UK, 1983.

Wilson, Dick. *The Long March of 1935: The Epic of Chinese Communism's Survival.* New York, 1982.

China at War

Barnett, A. Doak. *China on the Eve of the Communist Takeover.* New York, 1963.

Chassin, Lionel M. *The Communist Conquest of China: A History of the Civil War, 1945–1949.* Cambridge, MA, 1965.

Eastman, Lloyd. *Seeds of Destruction: Nationalist China in War and Revolution: 1937–1949.* Palo Alto, CA, 1984.

Hinton, William. *Fanshen: A Documentary of Revolution in a Chinese Village.* New York, 1966.

Johnson, Chalmers A. *Peasant Nationalism and Communist Power: The Emergence of Revolutionary China, 1937–1945.* Palo Alto, CA, 1962.

Levine, Steven. *Anvil of Victory: The Communist Revolution in Manchuria, 1945–1948.* New York, 1987.

Pepper, Suzanne. *Civil War in China: The Political Struggle, 1945–1949.* Berkeley, CA, 1978.

Selden, Mark. *The Yenan Way in Revolutionary China.* Cambridge, MA, 1971.

Shaller, Michael. *The U.S. Crusade in China.* New York, 1979.

Sih, Paul, ed. *Nationalist China during the Sino-Japanese War, 1937–1945.* New York, 1977.

Tuchman, Barbara. *Stilwell and the American Experience in China, 1911–1945.* New York, 1971.

White, Theodore, and Annalee Jacoby. *Thunder Out of China.* New York, 1946.

Creating the New Order, 1949–1957

Barnett, A. Doak. *Communist China: The Early Years, 1949–1955.* New York, 1955.

Chang, Jung, and Jon Halliday. *Mao: The Unknown Story.* New York, 2005

Chang, Maria Hsia. *Return of the Dragon: China's Wounded Nationalism.* Boulder, CO, 2001.

Ch'en, Jerome. *Mao and the Chinese Revolution.* New York, 1965.

Kao, Michael Y.M., comp. *The People's Liberation Army and China's Nation-Building.* White Plains, NY, 1973.

Li, Zhisui. *The Private Life of Chairman Mao.* New York, 1994.

Lieberthal, Kenneth. *Revolution and Tradition in Tientsin, 1949–1968.* Stanford, CA, 1980.

———. *Governing China: From Revolution through Reform.* New York, 1995.

Lifton, Robert. *Thought Reform and the Psychology of Totalism: A Study of "Brainwashing" in China.* New York, 1961.

MacDonald, Callum. *Korea: The War before Vietnam.* Basingstoke, UK, 1986.

Meisner, Maurice. *Mao's China and After: A History of the People's Republic.* New York, 1986.

Rawski, Thomas. *China's Transition to Industrialism.* Ann Arbor, MI, 1980.

Shapiro, Judith. *Mao's War against Nature: Politics and the Environment in Revolutionary China.* Cambridge and New York, 2002.

Short, Philip. *Mao: A Life.* New York, 1999.

Solomon, Richard. *Mao's Revolution and the Chinese Political Culture.* Berkeley, CA, 1971.

Vogel, Ezra. *Canton under Communism: Programs and Politics in a Provincial Capital, 1949–1968.* Cambridge, MA, 1969.

The Great Leap and the Bad Fall

Chan, Alfred L. *Mao's Crusade: Politics and Policy Implementation in China's Great Leap Forward.* Oxford, UK, 2001.

Goldman, Merle. *Literary Dissent in Communist China.* Cambridge, MA, 1967.

———. *China's Intellectuals: Advise and Dissent.* Cambridge, MA, 1981.

Li, Zhisui. *The Private Life of Chairman Mao.* New York, 1994.

MacFarquhar, Roderick. *The Origins of the Cultural Revolution.* Vol. 2: *The Great Leap Forward, 1958–1960.* New York, 1983.

Schurmann, Franz. *Ideology and Organization in Communist China.* Berkeley, CA, 1966.

Thaxton, Jr., Ralph A. *Catastrophe and Contentions in Rural China.* Cambridge, UK, 2008.

Wilson, Dick. *The People's Emperor, Mao: A Biography of Mao Tse-tung.* New York, 1980.

The Cultural Revolution

An, Tai-sung. *Mao Tse-tung's Cultural Revolution.* Indianapolis, IN, 1972.

Butterfield, Fox. *China: Alive in the Bitter Sea.* New York, 1982.

Chang, Jung. *Wild Swans: Three Daughters of China.* New York, 1991.

Chen, Jack. *A History of the Chinese Cultural Revolution.* New York, 1974.

Cheng, Nien. *Life and Death in Shanghai.* New York, 1987.

Daubier, Jean. *A History of the Chinese Cultural Revolution.* Trans. Richard Seaver. New York, 1974.

Gray, Jack. *Chinese Communism in Crisis: Maoism and the Cultural Revolution.* New York, 1968.

Hunter, Neale. *Shanghai Journal: An Eyewitness Account of the Cultural Revolution.* New York, 1969.

Jiang, Yarong, and David Ashley. *Mao's Children in the New China: Voices from the Red Guard Generation.* London, 2000.

Luo, Ziping. *A Generation Lost: China under the Cultural Revolution.* New York, 1990.

MacFarquhar, Roderick, and Michael Schoenhals. *Mao's Last Revolution.* Cambridge, MA, 2008.

Min, Anchee. *Red Azalea.* New York, 1994.

Niu, Niu. *No Tears for Mao: Growing Up in the Cultural Revolution.* Trans. Enne and Peter Amman. Chicago, IL, 1995.

Thurston, Anne F. *Enemies of the People.* New York, 1987.

Wen, Chihua. *The Red Mirror: Children of China's Cultural Revolution.* Boulder, CO, 1995.

Wheelwright, E.L. *The Chinese Road to Socialism: Economics of the Cultural Revolution.* New York, 1970.

A Second Revolution

Cheng, Chu-yuan. *Behind the Tiananmen Massacre: Social, Political, and Economic Ferment in China.* Boulder, CO, 1990.

Ding, Yijiang. *Chinese Democracy after Tiananmen.* Vancouver, Canada, 2001.

Evans, Richard. *Deng Xiaoping and the Making of Modern China.* New York, 1994.

Fewsmith, Joseph, *China since Tiananmen.* Cambridge, UK, 2001.

Friedman, Edward. *National Identity and Democratic Prospects in Socialist China.* Armonk, NY, 1995.

Gilley, Bruce, *Tiger on the Brink: Jiang Zemin and China's New Elite.* New York, 1994.

Harding, Harry. *China's Second Revolution: Reform after Mao.* Washington, DC, 1987.

Lam, Willy Wo-Lap. *The Era of Jiang Zemin.* New York, 1999.

Li, Cheng, *China's New Leaders.* London, 2001.

Ma, Jun. *The Chinese Economy in the 1990s.* London, 2000.

Marti, Michael E. *China and the Legacy of Deng Xiaoping: From Communist Revolution to Capitalist Evolution.* Washington, DC, 2002.

Nathan, Andrew. *Chinese Democracy.* New York, 1985.

Oksenberg, Michel, Lawrence R. Sullivan, and Marc Lambert, eds. *Beijing Spring, 1989: Confrontation and Conflict: The Basic Documents.* Armonk, NY and London, 1990.

Oksenberg, Michel, and Elizabeth Economy, eds. *China Joins the World.* New York, 1999.

Overholt, William H. *The Rise of China: How Economic Reform Is Creating a New Superpower.* New York, 1993.

Roy, Denny. *China's Foreign Relations.* Lanham, MD, 1998.

Salisbury, Harrison E. *Tiananmen Diary: Thirteen Days in June.* Boston, MA, 1989.

Schell, Orville, *Mandate of Heaven: The Legacy of Tiananmen Square and the Next Generation of Chinese Leaders.* New York, 1994.

Shanor, Donald R. *China Today: How Reform Is Changing the Way Chinese Live and Work.* New York, 1995.

Spence, Jonathan D. *The Search for Modern China.* New York, 1990.

Unger, Jonathan, ed. *The Nature of Chinese Politics from Mao to Jiang.* Armonk, NY, 2002.

Zhang, Liang, compiler. *The Tiananmen Papers.* Ed. Andrew J. Nathan and Perry Link. New York, 2001.

Foreign Policy Issues for the Twenty-First Century

Bush, Richard C. *Untying the Knot: Making Peace in the Taiwan Strait.* Washington, DC, 2005.

Chang, Maria Hsia. *Return of the Dragon: China's Wounded Nationalism.* Boulder, CO, 2001.

Goldstein, Avery. *Rising to the Challenge: China's Grand Strategy and International Security.* Palo Alto, CA, 2005.

Gries, Peter Hays. *China's New Nationalism: Pride, Politics, and Diplomacy.* Berkeley, CA, 2004.

Keller, William W., and Thomas G. Rawski, eds., *China's Rise and the Balance of Influence in Asia.* Pittsburgh, PA, 2007.

Shambaugh, David. *Modernizing China's Military: Progress, Problems, and Prospects.* Berkeley, CA, 2002.

Shirk, Susan L. *China: Fragile Superpower.* New York, 2007.

Tsang, Steve. *A Modern History of Hong Kong.* London, 2007.

Zheng Yongnian. *Discovering Chinese Nationalism in China: Modernization, Identity, and International Relations.* Cambridge, UK, 1999.

The Fourth Generation

Cai Yongshun. *State and Laid-Off Workers in Reform China: The Silence and Collective Action of the Retrenched.* New York, 2006.

Economy, Elizabeth C. *The River Runs Black: The Environmental Challenge to China's Future.* New York, 2004.

Finkelstein, David, and Maryanne Kivlehan, eds. *Chinese Leadership in the 21st Century.* Armonk, NY, 2003.

Lam, Willy Wo-Lap. *Chinese Politics in the Hu Jintao Era: New Leaders, New Challenges.* Armonk, NY, 2006.

Naughton, Barry. *The Chinese Economy: Transitions and Growth.* Cambridge, MA, 2007.

Pei, Minxin. *China's Trapped Transition.* Cambridge, MA, 2006.

Qiu Ping. *Fifth-Generation Leaders of the Chinese Communist Party.* Hong Kong, 2005.

Sang Ye. *China Candid: The People on the People's Republic.* Berkeley, CA, 2006.

Suettinger, Robert L. *Beyond Tiananmen: The Politics of U.S.-China Relations, 1989–2000.* Washington, DC, 2003.

Zong Hairen, *China's New Leaders: The Fourth Generation.* New York, 2002.

Index

Africa, 284
Agrarian Reform Law, 137
Agricultural Producers' Cooperatives (APCs), 146–149
Agriculture
  breadbasket in Yangzi valley, 20–21
  collectivization of, 145–150, 158, 160, 169–171
  communes and, 170–171
  First Five-Year Plan and, 144
  grain production declines and, 223
  Great Leap Forward and, 170–171, 175
  under Guomindang government, 96
  in Imperial China, 4
  Liu Shaoqi's policies on, 179
  in Moscow's modernization drive, 158
  peasants and, 11
  reforms, 127, 137–141, 145, 158–161, 219–224, 285
  Second Five-Year Plan and, 158–160
  technological innovations in, 4, 16, 21
  water and, 12, 170
  Yan'an Way and, 119
AIDS epidemic, 290–292
All-China Federation of Trade Unions, 286
Alliance Society (Tongmenghui), 67, 69–70
Anticorruption campaigns, 248–250, 297–299, 300, 302
Antirightist campaigns, 155–157, 160, 180, 202
Antis-Movement, 141–142
Arts and culture, 4, 21, 184, 202, 204–205, 207, 218
Asian financial crisis (1997–98), 257
Astronomical achievements, 5
Autumn Harvest uprising, 102
"Axis of evil," 271

Banking system, 96
Baoding No. 1 Paper Mill, 286
Basic Law, 261
Beijing, 40–41, 50, 57–59, 87, 128–129, 154, 195, 199, 243, 249, 276, 296
Beijing University, 194
Bianco, Lucien, 94, 115
Blair, Tony, 262

Blue Shirts, 93–94
Bogue Treaty, 37
Bolshevik Revolution, 77, 82
Bolshevik Right Opposition, 159
Borodin, Mikhail, 82, 84–85, 87
Bourgeois, 132–133, 152, 190, 205, 227, 229–231, 236–237, 242, 256
Boxer Protocol, 58
Boxers and Boxer Rebellion, 56–59
Braun, Otto, 109
Brezhnev, Leonid, 184
Britain. *See* Great Britain
British East India Company, 27–28
Buddhism, 17–18, 20, 183
Bukharin, Nikolai, 159
Bureaucracy, 13–15, 21–25, 55, 59, 66, 186, 256
Bush, George H.W., 266
Bush, George W., 265–266, 268, 271

Cambodia, 136
Capitalism, 30, 60–61, 77, 182, 185–187, 202, 252
Carter, Jimmy, 228
Cartledge, Simon, 301
Censorate, 22–24
Central Military Commission (CMC), 245–246, 279
Chang, Iris, 269
Charles, Prince, 262
Chen Boda, 184, 193, 198, 212
Chen Duxiu, 77–81, 85–87
Chen Guidi, 299
Chen Liangyu, 298, 300–301
Chen Shui-bian, 260, 265
Chen system, 249–250
Chen Xitong, 249–250
Chen Yun, 159–160, 177, 187, 220
Chiang Ching-kuo, 264
Chiang Kai-shek
  China's Destiny and, 95
  civil war and, 124, 127–129
  Communists and, attacks on, 87, 97–98, 109–110

Chiang Kai-shek *(continued)*
  exile of, 129
  Guomindang and, 83–87
  Guomindang government and, 89–94
  Japan's invasion of China and, 113, 123, 127
  Manchuria issue and, 124
  Mao Zedong meeting and, 123–124
  modernization and, 93–94
  New Life Movement and, 94–95
  Northern Expedition and, 85–87, 89
  political background of, 83–84
  retreat of, 128
  revolution and, 83
  turning point for, 86
  United States and, 115
  warlords and their allies and, 85, 90
  Whampoa Military Academy and, 83, 85
  White Terror and, 87, 98, 102, 104
  World War II and, 112
China Democratic League, 126
China's Destiny (Chiang Kai-shek), 95
Chinese Communist Party (CCP). *See also*
      Cultural Revolution; Great Leap Forward
  agrarian reforms of, 145, 158–160, 219–224
  Agricultural Producers' Cooperatives and,
      146–149
  antirightist campaign of, 155–157, 160, 180,
      202
  cadre's role in, 135
  challenges facing, 98–100
  Chiang Kai-shek's attacks on Communists
      and, 87, 97–98, 109–110
  civil war and, 123–129
  Comintern and, 81–84, 99
  Common Program and, 133
  corruption and, rooting out, 248–250, 301
  counterrevolutionary campaigns of, 139,
      151–152
  current power of, 306
  development of, 81–85
  disputes within, 107–109, 175–176, 178,
      191–193
  Eighth Party Congress of, 150, 158, 163–164
  Eleventh Five-Year Plan of, 284–285
  expelling of Communists from Guomindang
      and, 87
  Fifteenth Party Congress of, 255
  First Five-Year Plan of, 142–144, 158, 165
  First National Party Congress of, 82
  First United Front and, 87
  founding of, 80–81, 288
  four-class alliance and, 133, 141–142
  Fourth Five-Year Plan and, 284–285
  Guomindang and, 82
  Hu Jintao and, 281, 304–305
  Intellectuals' criticism of, 151–152, 228
  Japan's invasion of China and, 111–115

Chinese Communist Party (CCP) *(continued)*
  Korean War and, 138, 140
  land reform and, 127, 139–140
  leaders of, early, 99–100
  Mao Zedong and, 121–122, 186–187, 212,
      288
  Marxism and, 99
  May Thirtieth Incident and, 84
  "May Zedong Thought" and, 122
  Mutual Aid Teams and, 146
  nationalizing private sector and, 142, 145,
      225, 251, 256, 281
  Ninth Party Congress of, 211, 280
  Northern Expedition and, 85–87
  prodemocracy movement and, 229–235
  professionals and, 282–283
  revival of Confucianism and, 254
  Russian Communists and, 131–132, 136
  Second Five-Year Plan of, 158–160
  Seventh Party Congress of, 122
  Sixteenth Party Congress of, 277
  Sixth Congress of, 108
  socialist transformation and, 144–150,
      160–162
  strengthening of, 119–122
  Taiwan and, 264, 305
  Third Congress of, 82
  three-thirds system of government in, 116
  "to the villages" policy and, 120
  traditional base of, loss of, 281
  Twenty-second Congress of, 183
  union organization and, 86
  victory of, over Guomindang government,
      128–129
  World War II and, 116–119
  xiafang program and, 157
  Yan'an Way and, 119–122, 134
  Zhou Enlai and, 86, 212
Chinese Eastern Railway, 53
Chinese League for the Protection of Civil
      Rights, 93
Chinese republic. *See* Chinese Soviet Republic;
      New Chinese Republic; People's
      Republic of China (PRC)
Chinese Soviet Republic, 107–110
Christianity, 43–45, 57
Civil war in China, 123–129, 143
Cixi, Empress Dowager, 52, 55–56, 66, 71
Class. *See* Social class and structure
Clinton, Bill, 256, 264, 266–267
Cohen, Paul, ix
Cohong, 27
Cold War, 143, 181
Collectivization of agriculture, 145–150, 158,
      160, 169–171
Comintern (Communist International), 81–84,
      99

Common Program, 133
Communes, 167–172, 220
Communist Manifesto, 105
Compradores, 41, 59, 138
Confucianism
  Chen Duxiu and, 78
  emperors and, 24
  flexibility of, 19–20
  government and, 18–19
  Han Chinese and, 20
  in Imperial China, 4, 18–20
  li concept in, 18–19, 34
  New Life Movement and, 94–95
  opium use and, 34
  rivals of, 17–18
  scientific achievements and, 29
  social class and structure and, 18–19
  Taiping Rebellion and, 44–47
  three bonds and, 19
  trade and, 15, 63
  views of, 15, 18–20
  women and, 18
Confucius, 17–19, 228
Copyright violations, 267
Corruption, 92, 96, 248–250, 297–303
Counterrevolutionary campaigns, 139, 151–152
Crime and punishment, 23, 288–289
Cuban Missile Crisis, 183
Cultural Revolution
  culture and, 202, 204–205, 207, 218
  Deng Xiaoping and, 195–198, 200–201, 218
  economy and, 217
  education and, 203–204
  end of, 217
  foreign policy and, 205–206
  Fourth Generation and, 277–278
  Gang of Four and, 213–217
  groundwork for, 156
  impact of, 202–209
  Jiang Qing and, 198, 205
  legacy of, 217–218
  Lin Biao and, 194–195, 209–213
  Liu Shaoqi and, 122, 195–201
  Mao Zedong and
    cultural impact of, 204–205
    reasons for, 190–191
    regaining of power and, 191–202,
      208–209
    role in violence of, 218
  morality and, failure of, 207–208
  period immediately after, 208
  reasons for, 189–191
  Red Guards and, 196–200
  Sixteen-Point Directive and, 195–196
  Tibet and, 275
  turning point of, 195
  universities and, 191

Cultural Revolution *(continued)*
  violence of, 197–202, 206–208
  wall poster campaigns and, 194
  Zhou Enlai and, 193–194
Cultural Revolution Group, 188, 193, 198–199

Dalai Lama, 274–276
Daoism, 17–19
Democracy Wall activists, 228
Deng Pufang, 248–249
Deng Xiaoping. *See also* Reforms
  antirightist campaign and, 155
  Central Military Commission and, 245–246,
    279
  Communist errors and, admission of, 153
  Cultural Revolution and, 195–198, 200–201,
    218
  Dali Lama and, 275
  death of, 255, 270
  education and, 236
  foreign investment in China and, 227
  Four Transformations program and, 279
  Fourth Generation and, influence on, 279
  Gorbachev and, 234–235
  hiding of, 215–216
  Hu Jintao and, 280
  Hua Guofeng and, 215
  intellectuals and, crackdown on, 236
  Jiang Qing and, 214
  Jiang Zemin and, 234, 239–241
  Liu Shaoqi's leadership and policies and,
    177, 179–180
  Long March and, 110
  Mao Zedong and, 187, 220
  nanxun (southern sojourn) of, 244–245
  purge of, 201
  repression under, 235–238
  rise of, 219–220
  as successor to Zhou Enlai, 214
  successors to, 240–241, 245
  Tiananmen Square protests and massacre
    and, 234–235
  transition of leadership and, 240–241
Diaoyudao Islands, 269
Disraeli, Benjamin, 285
Dixie Mission, 122
"Double Ten," 69, 89
Duan Qirui, 72–75, 78
Dutch in China, 27
Dynastic cycle, 15–18
Dynasties. *See* Imperial China; *specific name*

Eagleburger, Lawrence, 266
Economic and technological development
    zones (ETDZs), 283–284
Economy
  Asian financial crisis (1997–98), 257

Economy *(continued)*
    crisis of 1988 and, 232–233
    Cultural Revolution and, 217
    foreign ownership and, 255–256
    Fourth Generation and, 283–284
    future prospects, 304
    of Great Britain, 31
    under Guomindang government, 95–96
    of Imperial China, 29–30, 51
    nationalizing private sector and, 142,
        145
    reforms and, 224–227, 239–240, 243–245,
        250–251, 283, 288, 293
    special economic zones and, 225–227, 241,
        244, 283–284
    Tongzhi Restoration and, 51
    in twenty-first century, 283–284
Education
    Cultural Revolution and, 203–204
    Deng Xiaoping and, 236
    eight-legged essay and, 25, 52, 55, 118
    literacy campaigns and, 119
    Mao Zedong on, 167
    modernization in, 66
    pro-democracy movement and, 228–230
    Red Guards and, 197
    scholar-gentry and, 13–15
    service examination system and, 13–15, 22,
        55, 58, 66
    Yan'an Way and, 119
Eight-legged essay, 25, 52, 55, 118
Elgin, Lord, 39
Elites, 24, 59, 63–64, 133, 190
Elliot, Charles, 36
Emperors of China, 3–4, 24, 39
Energy inefficiencies and resources, 294–295,
    305
Engineering achievements, 5, 21, 169, 295
Entrepreneurship, 221
Environmental issues, 293–297
Ethnic groups, 6–8. *See also specific name*
European Union, 273–274
Explorations by Chinese, 25
Extraterritoriality, 37–38

Fairbank, John K., 94–95
Falun Gong, 253–254, 288
Family, 12–13, 63–64, 136, 223–224
Famines, 33, 47, 149, 175, 270
Fang Lizhi, 231–232, 235
Fascism, 94
First Five-Year Plan, 142–144, 158, 165
First opium war, 35–39
First United Front, 82–87
Five Antis-Movement, 141
Floods, 7, 33, 69
Footbinding, 13

Foreign investment in China, 60–61, 71,
    226–227, 283–284
Foreign policy
    Cultural Revolution and, 205–206
    European Union, 273–274
    Hong Kong, 37, 206, 261–263
    international incidents and, 205–206
    Japan, 268–270
    Korean Peninsula, 270–271
    objectives, 259–260
    Russia, 271–273
    Taiwan, 260, 263–265
    Tibet, 183–184, 274–276
    United States, 265–268
    Zhou Enlai and, 201
Forum on China and Africa Cooperation,
    284
Four-class alliance, 133, 141–142
Four Modernizations, 220, 228
Four orders, 11–15
Four Transformations program, 279
Fourteen Points of Wilson, 76, 81
Fourth Generation
    composition of, 277–278
    corruption and, 297–303
    crime and, 288–289
    Cultural Revolution and, 277–278
    Deng Xiaoping's influence on, 279
    economy and, 283–284
    Eleventh Five-Year Plan and, 284–285
    emergence of, 278–279
    environmental issues and, 293–297
    future development of China and, 284–285
    future prospects and, 303–306
    health scandals and, 289–293
    Hu Jintao and, 270, 280
    Jiang Zemin and, 279–283
    social class and structure and, 285–288
France, 39, 41, 53, 74–76, 273

Gang of Four, 213–217
Gao Gang, 148
Gao Yaojie, 291
Genghis Khan, 8, 25
Gentry, 13–15, 23, 47, 59, 66, 137, 140
Geography of China, 6–8, 10–11
Germany, 53, 53–54, 74, 94
Gilley, Bruce, 278
Gold Coin rebels, 47
Gong, Prince, 49, 51
Goodnow, Frank J., 72
Gorbachev, Mikhail, 234–235, 272
Government, 5, 18–19, 21–24, 33, 46, 147.
    See also Chinese Communist Party
    (CPP); Guomindang (GMD) government;
    specific dynasty
Grand Canal, 21

Great Britain
arrival in China, 27–28
economy of, 31
Hong Kong and, 37, 206, 261–262, 273
investment in China, 60–61
Kowloon Peninsula and, 41, 53
trade with China and, 27–28, 34–35
Versailles Treaty and, 76
warlords and, 75
Weihaiwei and, 53
World War I and, 74–75
Great Depression, 100
Great Leap Forward
agriculture and, 170–171, 175
announcement of, 163–164
anti-intellectualism of, 166–167
aura surrounding, 165
backyard steel furnaces and, 166, 168–169
communes and, 167–172, 220
crisis of, 172–175
failure of, 173–174, 176
ideal of, 167
ideology, 164, 169–170
industry and, 171, 175
Liu Shaoqi and, 172, 177–181
Mao Zedong and, 187
national euphoria and, 168–169
objectives of, 164–165
premise of, 164
renewed, 175
reversal of, 172
Great Proletarian Cultural Revolution. *See*
Cultural Revolution
Great Wall, 5, 8
Greece, 17
Green Gang, 87, 92, 141, 297
Gros, Baron, 39
Gu, George Zhibin, 302
Guangxu, Emperor, 54, 56
Guangzhou, 27, 35–36, 47, 75
Guangzhou System, 27
Guanxi (connections), 300–301
Gulf War (1991), 260
Guomindang (GMD) government
agriculture under, 96
Blue Shirts of, 93–94
capital of, 89
Chiang Kai-shek and, 89–94
civil war and, 123–129
Communists and, attacks on, 87, 97–98, 109–110
conservatism of, 91, 96
corruption in, 92
economy under, 95–96
fall of, 128–129
Japan's invasion of China and, 112–115
New Life Movement and, 94–95

Guomindang (GMD) government *(continued)*
peasants and, 114–115
reforms of, 95–96
regime of, 89–94
repression under, 93–94, 126
World War II and, 112–115
Guomindang (Nationalist Party), 70, 82–87, 102

Hai Rui Dismissed from Office (Wu Han), 180–181, 188, 191–193
Hakkas, 43–44
Han Chinese, 6, 8, 13, 20, 43, 65–66, 274
Han dynasty, 20–21
He Dongchang, 236
He Qinglian, 297–298
Health scandals, 289–293
Henan HIV/AIDS crisis, 290–291
Hinton, William, 198, 207
Hitler, Adolf, 93–94
HIV epidemic, 290–292
Hong Kong, 37, 206, 261–263, 273
Hong Xiuquan, 43–46
Hopson, Donald, 206
Hu Feng, 151–152, 154
Hu Jintao
Africa and, 284
agrarian reform and, 285
anti-corruption campaign of, 299, 302
biographical information about, 279
Chinese Communist Party and, 281, 304–305
Deng Xiaoping and, 280
economic reform and, 283
environmental issues and, 296
Fourth Generation and, 270, 280
Jiang Zemin and, 280
political background of, 279–280
Putin and, 273
rise of, 255
SARS epidemic and, 293
Hu Qili, 231
Hu Shi, 77, 79
Hu Yaobang, 202, 231, 233, 240–242, 279
Hua Guofeng, 214–217, 240
Huc, Abbé, 62
Human rights, 238, 264, 267, 289
Human will, 106–107
Hunan Army, 48, 50
Hundred Days Reform, 54–56, 71
Hundred Flowers Movement, 152–155, 157, 161, 228
Hundred Regiments campaign, 118
Hungarian Uprising against Soviet Union, 149–150, 153, 183

Imperial China. *See also specific dynasty*
agriculture in, 4

Imperial China *(continued)*
  Boxer Rebellion and, 56–59
  bureaucracy in, 21–24
  centralized states in, 17
  civilization of, 4–6, 11, 17, 21
  Confucianism in, 4, 18–20
  decline of, 28–34
    analysis of, 59–64
  dynastic cycle in, 15–18
  economy of, 29–30, 51
  elites in, 24, 59, 63–64
  emperors in, 3–4, 24, 39
  ethnic groups in, 6–8
  explorations of, 25
  family in, 12–13, 63–64
  famines in, 33, 47
  foreign investment in, 60–61
  four orders and, 11–15
  gentry in, 13–15, 23, 47
  government in, 5, 21–24
  highpoint of, 26
  Hundred Days Reform and, 54–56, 71
  intellectuals in, 17
  last dynasties of, 24–26
  legal system, 23
  merchants in, 15
  military in, 25
  modernization in, failure of, 59–60, 63–64
  nomadic invasions of, 8, 16, 25–26
  opium trade and, 28, 34–35
  opium wars in, 35–41
  peasants in, 11–12, 33
  population in, 5–6, 30, 32–33, 62
  poverty in, 62
  rise of, 20–21
  Sino-Japanese War and, 52–54
  social class in, 4
  Taiping rebellion and, 42–48
  technological innovations in, 4–5, 16–17, 21, 25
  tributary system in, 26–31
  unequal treaties and, 37–39, 41–42, 60
  unity in, 10–11, 24
  value system of, 12
  Westerners and, 8–9, 48–52
  women in, 13
Imperialism, 60–61, 67, 75, 80–81
Imperialism, the Highest Stage of Capitalism (Lenin), 60, 80–81
India, 183–184
Individualism, 12, 179
Industrial Revolution, 29
Industrialization, 161
Industry
  entrepreneurship and, 221
  environmental issues and, 293–297
  First Five-Year Plan and, 144

Industry *(continued)*
  foreign investment in China and, 226–227
  future prospects and, 303
  Great Leap Forward and, 171, 175
  Liu Shaoqi's policies on, 180
  problems, 286–287
  productivity and, 180
  reforms of Deng Xiaoping and, 224–225
  safety standards, 287
Infanticide, female, 223–224
Intellectual property theft, 267
Intellectuals
  criticism of Chinese Communist Party by, 151–152, 228
  Deng Xiaoping's crackdown on, 236
  Great Leap Forward attacks on, 167–168
  in Imperial China, 17
  Liu Shaoqi's policies and, 180–181
  May Fourth Movement and, 76
  new left and, 252
  in People's Republic of China, 151–152
  prodemocracy movement and, 228–229, 236
Italy, 53–54, 94

Japan
  atomic bombing of, 122
  China invasion by, 111–115
  Chinese students in, 66–67
  Diaoyudao Islands and, 269
  Duan Qirui and, 75
  foreign policy of China and, 268–270
  Korean Peninsula and, 52–53
  Manchuria invasion by, 90–91
  rape of Nanjing and, 113
  recognition of People's Republic of China and, 227
  Russia and, 53, 66
  Shandong Peninsula and, 72
  Sino-Japanese War and, 52–54, 269
  Tokugawa Shogunate in, 63
  Triple Intervention and, 53
  Twenty-one Demands of, 72, 256
  warlords and, Chinese, 75
  World War I and, 75–76
  World War II and, 115
  Yasukuni shrine and, 269
Jia Yibin, 263–264
Jiang Qing
  arrest of, 216
  charges against, 216
  Cultural Revolution and, 198, 205
  in Cultural Revolution Group, 192–193
  culture and, 184, 204–205
  death sentence of, 217
  Deng Xiaoping and, 214
  in Gang of Four, 213–217
  Hua Guofeng and, 216

Jiang Qing *(continued)*
  Lin Biao and, 209–212
  Mao Zedong and, 184, 192
  power of, 213, 215, 217
  trial of, 216–218
Jiang Zemin
  anticorruption campaign of, 248–250, 299
  biographical information about, 241–242
  challenges facing, 257
  criticisms of, 251–253, 256
  Deng Xiaoping and, 234, 239–241
  dissidents of prodemocracy movement and,
    237
  Falun Gong and, 253–254
  Fourth Generation and, 279–283
  Hong Kong and, 261–263
  Hu Jintao and, 280
  ideology of, 257–258
  leadership style of, 255
  Li Ruihuan and, 281
  as mayor of Shanghai, 242
  middle-class society and, 283
  military and, 245–248
  National People's Congress and, 248
  opposition to, 253–258
  as president of China, 248–253
  purge of Chen Xitong and, 250
  real estate boom under, 251
  reforms of, 243–245, 250–251, 282
  rise of, 241–243, 245, 250
  Selected Works of Jiang Zemin, The, 280
  spiritual rejuvenation and, 253
  student protests and, 242–243
  as successor to Deng Xiaoping, 240–241, 245
  Taiwan and, 263–264
  third way of, 250
  Three Represents thesis and, 257
  Tiananmen Square protests and massacre
    and, 242–243, 248
  trade with United States and, 267
  Westerners and, 273
  Yang brothers and, 246–247
  Yeltsin meeting and, 272
Joffe, Adolf, 82
Joint Sino-British Group, 261

Kang Sheng, 184–185
Kang Youwei, 54–56, 66–67
Kantor, Mickey, 267
Khitans, 8
Khrushchev, Nikita, 149–151, 153, 159,
    173–174, 182–183, 218
Kiakhta Treaty, 28
Kim Il-sung, 138, 270
Kissinger, Henry, 227–228
Koizumi, Junichiro, 269
Korean Peninsula, 52–53, 270–271

Korean War, 138–141
Kowloon Peninsula, 41, 53
Kublai Khan, 25

Labor. *See* Workers
Lamy, Pascal, 273
Land reform
  Chinese Communist Party and, 127, 139–140
  consequences of, political and social, 140
  of Deng Xiaoping, 221
  modernization and, 96
  1911 Revolution and, 67
  in People's Republic of China, 139–140
  Tongmenghui and, 67
Land Reform Law, 144–145
"Land System of the Heavenly Kingdom, The,"
    44
Landlords, 16, 127
Law of avoidance, 23, 298
Lee Kuan Yew, 281
Lee Teng-hui, 264–265
Legal system in Imperial China, 23
Legalism, 17–18, 20
Lenin, V.I., 60, 77, 80–82, 99, 120, 132, 134, 222
Leninism, 80–81
Li concept, 18–19, 34
Li Dazhao, 77, 80–82, 87, 101, 103, 107, 118
Li Hongzhang, 48–53, 58, 62, 73
Li Hongzhi, 254
Li Lisan, 99–100, 103, 107–108
Li Peng, 232–234, 240, 243, 245, 248, 255,
    257, 273
Li Ruihuan, 279–281
Li Yizhong, 287
Li Zongren, 128
Liang Heng, 208
Liang Qichao, 54, 56, 66–67
Liaodong Peninsula, 53
Liberalism, anti-bourgeois, 227–235
Lien Chan, 265
Lijin (levy), 48, 95
Lin Biao
  Beijing and, march on, 195
  civil war in China and, 128
  coup planned by, 212–213
  Cultural Revolution and, 194–195, 209–213
  fall of, 212–213
  Jiang Qing and, 209–212
  Long March and, 110
  Mao Zedong and, 106, 174, 176, 185, 188,
    195, 209–211
  Nie Yuanzi and, 194
  political background of, 185
  purge of, 213
  Red Guards and, 210–211
  rise of, 195, 209–212
  as successor to Mao Zedong, 211

Lin Zexiu, 35–36
Literature, 4, 12, 25, 79–80
"Little Red Book," 188, 210–211
Liu Shaoqi
  collectivization of agriculture and, 148
  Communist errors and, admission of,
      153–155
  Cultural Revolution and, 122, 195–201
  death of, 220
  Great Leap Forward and, 172, 177–181
  "How to Be a Good Communist," 187
  Long March and, 110
  Mao Zedong and, 122, 172, 186–187, 189
  policies of, 177–181, 183
  purge of, 200–201
  Soviet Union and, 183
  Zhou Enlai and, 177, 200
Liu Zhuhua, 298
Long March, 97, 109–110
Lu Dingyi, 154
Lu Ping, 194
Lu Xun, 151
Lushan Conference, 174–176

Ma Sitson, 206
Ma Ying-jeou, 265
MacArthur, Douglas, 138, 140
MacFarquhar, Roderick, 161
Manchukuo, 90–91, 97
Manchuria, 8
Manchus, 25–26, 29, 33–34, 39, 42, 65. *See
    also* Qing (Manchu) dynasty
Mandarin, 22–23
Mandarinate, 22–24, 45
Mandate of Heaven, 16, 24
Mao Yuanxin, 215–216
Mao Zedong. *See also* Chinese Communist
    Party (CPP); Cultural Revolution
  Autumn Harvest uprising and, 102
  Beijing of, return to, 129
  biographical information about, 101
  birth of, 82, 101
  bureacracy and, 186
  Changsha and, attack on, 108
  Chiang Kai-shek meeting and, 123–124
  Chinese Soviet Republic and, 108–110
  collectivization of agriculture and, 148–149,
      160
  Communist errors and, admission of,
      153–155
  constitution and, opposition to, 147
  corruption and, eradicating, 297
  Cultural Revolution group and, 188
  Dali Lama and, 275
  death of, 215
  Deng Xiaoping and, 187, 220
  on education, 167

Mao Zedong *(continued)*
  emergence of, 100–107
  Great Leap Forward and, 187
  Guomindang and, 83, 102
  health of, deteriorating, 213
  human will and, 106–107
  Hundred Flowers Movement and, 152–155,
      157, 161
  Jiang Qing and, 184, 192
  Khrushchev and, 150, 159, 173, 182
  Korean War and, 138, 140
  Li Dazhao and, 80, 101, 103, 107
  Lin Biao and, 106, 174, 176, 185, 188, 195,
      209–211
  Liu Shaoqi and, 122, 172, 186–187, 189
  Long March, 109–110
  Marxism and, 102–103, 133–134
  mass campaigns and, 135, 161–162
  mass line ideology and, 119–120, 135
  May Fourth Movement and, 101
  military and, 104–106, 109
  nationalism and, 117
  "On New Democracy," 116
  "On the People's Democratic Dictatorship,"
      132
  party-building and, 116–117
  Peasant Movement Training Institute and,
      82–83, 103
  peasants and, 102–104, 109, 133–134
  Peng Dehuai and, 106, 173–174
  Peng Zhen and, 192–195
  People's Liberation Army and, 173, 188
  political background of, 101–107
  principles of, 102–107
  purges by
      Deng Xiaoping, 201
      Lin Biao, 213
      Liu Shaoqi, 200–201
      Peng Dehuai, 174–175, 209
      Peng Zhen, 193–194, 210
  quotations by, book of, 188, 210–211
  Red Guards and, 196–197
  regrouping of, 184–188
  "Report on an Investigation of the Peasant
      Movement in Hunan" and, 103–104
  revolution and, 119–120, 131
  Selected Works, 134
  semi-retirement of, 173, 185
  Sinification of Marxism and, 118
  Socialist Education Movement and, 187–188
  socialist transformation and, 160–162
  Soviet Union and, 140–141, 159
  Stalin and, 143, 181–182
  state-owned enterprises and, 142
  successors of, 211
  thought reform campaigns and, 133,
      135–136, 152–157

Mao Zedong *(continued)*
  three magic weapons of, 116–117
  United States and, 143, 182
  "use value" and, 134
  violence and, 105–106
  World War II and, 116–119
  Wu Han's play and, 191–193
  Yan'an Way and, 119–122, 134
  Zhou Enlai and, 109–110, 143, 212
  Zhu De and, 102
Maritime Customs Service, 38, 41
Marriage Law, 136
Marshall, George C., 123, 126–127
Marx, Karl, 134
Marxism
  Chinese Communist Party and, 99
  Communist Manifesto and, 105
  concrete, 118
  elites and, 190
  Hu Yaobang and, 231
  imperialism and, 60
  Lenin's modifications of, 99
  Li Dazhao and, 80–81
  Mao Zedong and, 102–103, 133–134
  peasants and, 99
  revolution and, 99, 102
  Sinification of, 118
  socialism and, 106–107
Mass campaigns, 135–136, 142, 147, 161–162, 208
Mass line ideology, 119–120, 135
Mathematical achievements, 5
May Fourth Movement, 75–81, 101, 232
May Thirtieth Incident, 84
McGregor, James, 283
Medical achievements, 5
Medvedev, Dmitry, 273
Mencius, 17
Meng Xuenong, 293
Merchants, 15
Michael, Franz, 43
Middle Kingdom, 3–9. *See also* Imperial China
Mif, Pavel, 108
Military
  in Imperial China, 25
  Jiang Zemin and, 245–248
  Mao Zedong and, 104–106, 109
  navy, 53
  of Qing (Manchu) dynasty, 33, 36
  of Taiping commonwealth, 45
  U.S.-China conflicts involving, 267–268
  warfare innovations and, 21
  warlords and, 73
  Zeng Guofan's army, 48, 50
Miners' rebellion, 47
Ming dynasty, 25–26, 45
Ming Tombs Reservoir, 169

Minxin Pei, 301–303
Missionaries, 39, 41, 57
Modernization
  challenges to, vii–viii
  changes wrought by, viii
  Chiang Kai-shek and, 93–94
  compradores and, 41
  Constitution's outline of, 304
  current history and, ix
  defined, viii
  in education, 66
  Four Modernizations, 220, 228
  in Imperial China, failure of, 59–60, 63–64
  imperialism and, 61
  land reform and, 96
  onset of, viii
  revolution and, viii
  Second Revolution and, 218, 220
  by Soviet Union, 144
  Tongzhi Restoration and, 50–52
  westernization versus, viii–ix
Mongolia, 7–8
Mongols, 8, 25
Most-favored-nation trading status, 37, 266
"Mourning" rule, 23
Mukden (Shenyang) Incident, 97
Mussolini, Benito, 93, 94
Mutual Aid Teams, 146
Myrdal, Gunnar, 60

Nan Huai-chin, 263–264
Nanjing, 86, 89, 97, 113, 269
Nanjing Assembly, 70–71
Nanjing Treaty, 37
Nathan, Andrew J., 278
National Bureau of Corruption Prevention (NBCP), 299
National People's Congress, 248, 281, 285, 300
National security issues, 260, 274
Nationalism, 67, 117, 132, 269, 306
Nationalist Party (Guomindang), 70, 82–87, 102
Nationalizing private sector, 142, 145, 225, 251, 256, 281
Naughton, Barry, 284–285
Nerchinsk Treaty, 28
New Chinese Republic
  founding of, 69
  limitations of, 69–70
  May Fourth Movement and, 75–81
  New Culture and, 79
  1911 Revolution and, 68–71
  Qing (Manchu) dynasty and, end of, 69
  Sun Yatsen as provisional president of, 70
  Twenty-one Demands and, 72
  vernacular literature campaign and, 79–80
  warlords and, 73–74

New Chinese Republic *(continued)*
　World War I and, 74–77
　Yuan Shikai as president of, 70–73
New Culture, 79
"New Democracy," 132–136, 297
New Economic Policy (NEP) of Lenin, 222
New left, 252
New Life Movement, 94–95
New Youth, 78–80
Nian horsemen, 47
Nie Yuanzi, 194
1911 Revolution, 65, 68–71, 78
Ningbo, 36–37, 47
Nixon, Richard M., 228
North China, 6–8
North Korea, 270–271
Northern Expedition, 85–87, 89
Northern Song dynasty, 13, 21–22
Nuclear research and tests, 184, 203, 271

Olympic Games (2008), 276, 296
"On New Democracy" (Mao Zedong), 116
"On the New Life" (pamphlet), 94
"On the People's Democratic Dictatorship"
　(Mao Zedong), 132
One-child policy, 223–224
Opium trade, 28, 34–35
Opium wars, 35–41
Organ transplant scandal, 289–290
Orwell, George, 176

Pakistan, 267
Palmerston, Lord, 36
Panthay Muslims, 47
Party-building, 116–117
Patten, Chris, 261, 274
Peasant Movement Training Institute, 82–83,
　103
Peasants
　agrarian reform and, 221–222
　agriculture and, 11
　in communes, 169–171
　in four orders, 11
　in Guomindang army, 114–115
　Guomindang government and, 114–115
　in Imperial China, 11–12, 33
　Mao Zedong and, 102–104, 109, 133–134
　Marxism and, 99
　mass campaigns and, 135
　mass line ideology and, 119–120
　one-child policy and, 223
　Peasant Movement Training Institute and,
　　82–83, 103
　in People's Republic of China, 137–138,
　　140, 157
　poverty of, 62, 157
　productivity of, improved, 221–222

Peasants *(continued)*
　Red Army and, 104–105
　taxes on, 33, 96, 299
Peng Dehuai, 102, 106, 140, 173–176, 187,
　191–192, 209
Peng Pai, 83, 103
Peng Zhen, 153–155, 188, 192–195, 197, 210,
　249
People's Liberation Army (PLA) [formerly Red
　Army]
　business transactions and, involvement in,
　　247
　civil war and, 128
　cultural pride and, 161
　Korean War and, 138
　Mao Zedong's plans for, 173, 188
　Quotations from Chairman Mao and, 188
　Soviet aid and, 173
　Tibet and, 275
People's Livelihood concept and program, 68,
　91
People's Republic of China (PRC). *See also*
　Chinese Communist Party (CCP);
　Cultural Revolution; Foreign policy;
　Great Leap Forward
　Africa and, 284
　challenges facing, in early years, 138
　Diaoyudao Islands and, 269
　family in, 136
　founding of, 129
　gentry in, 137
　history and, vii
　human rights and, 238, 264, 267, 289
　industrialization and, 161
　intellectuals and, 151–152
　Japan's recognition of, 227
　Khruschchev and, 149–151
　military conflicts with United States and,
　　267–268
　modernization and current history of, ix
　most-favored-nation trading status with
　　United States and, 266
　national security issues, 260, 274
　"New Democracy" and, 132–136
　peasants in, 137–138, 140, 157
　piracy of copyrighted material in, 267
　population in, 132
　questions surrounding, 9, 306
　repression in, 155–157
　sovereignty of, protecting, 260
　Soviet Union and, 143–144, 181–184
　urban renewal projects in, 287–288
　violence in, 139
　women in, 136
Permanent Normal Trade Relations (PNTR),
　257
Piracy of copyrighted material, 267

Pol Pot, 136
Pollution, air and water, 294–295, 305
Population, 5–6, 30, 32–33, 62, 132
Portuguese in China, 25, 27
Poverty, 62, 157
Powell, Colin L., 265–266
Prodemocracy movement
  Chinese Communist Party and, 229–235
  dissidents in, 228, 237
  economic crisis of 1988 and, 232–233
  education and, 228–230
  intellectuals and, 228–229, 236
  intensification of, 237–238
  protest demonstrations and, 228–231
  reforms of Deng Xiaoping and, 227–235
  threat of, versus economic strain, 239
  Tiananmen Square protests and massacre
    and, 229, 233–235
Property rights, 13, 136. *See also* Land reform
Putin, Vladimir, 272–273
Puyi, Emperor, 90–91
Pye, Lucian, 70

Qian Qichen, 266
Qiao Shi, 237
Qigong, 254
Qin dynasty, 20–21
Qin Shihuangdi, 20
Qing (Manchu) dynasty
  Boxer Rebellion and, 57–59
  challenges of, in nineteenth and twentieth
    centuries, 62–63
  checks and balances in, 23, 33, 46
  decline of, 28–29, 31–34
    analysis of, 59–64
  end of, 65, 69, 89, 91
  Hundred Days Reform and, 54–56
  Manchus as rulers of, 8, 25
  military of, 33, 36
  reforms of, 68–69
  Sino-Japanese War and, 53
  Taiping Rebellion and, 42–48
  Tibet and, 275
  Tongzhi Restoration and, 50–52
  unequal treaties and, 37–39, 41–42, 60
  warlords and, 73
  Westerners and, 32–34, 50
  White Lotus Rebellion and, 33
Qu Qiubai, 99–100
Quotations from Chairman Mao, 188, 210–211

Railroads, 53, 69
Railway Protection League, 69
Rape of Nanjing, 113, 269
Re-education, 121–122, 133, 135–136,
  152–157
Real estate boom, 251

Rectification (*Zhengfeng*), 121–122, 133,
  135–136, 152–157
Red Army, 104–106, 109–110, 116. *See also*
  People's Liberation Army (PLA)
Red Guards, 196–200, 202, 205–207, 210–211,
  228
"Red princes," 248
Red Turbans, 47
"Red Versus Expert" issue, 178, 208
Reforms
  agrarian, 127, 137–141, 145, 160–161,
    219–224, 285
  bureaucratic, 256
  of Deng Xiaoping
    agriculture, 219–224, 285
    economic, 224–227, 239–240, 243–245,
      288, 293
    impact of, 239–240, 259, 268
    industry, 224–225
    land, 221
    new ideas and influence of, 227–228
    prodemocracy movement, 227–235
    special economic zones, 225–227
  economic, 224–227, 239–240, 243–245,
    250–251, 283, 288, 293
  First Five-Year Plan and, 145
  of Guomindang government, 95–96
  of Jiang Zemin, 243–245, 250–251, 282
  political, 282
  Qing (Manchu) dynasty efforts, 68–69
Religion, 17, 20, 41, 43–46, 57
"Report on an Investigation of the Peasant
  Movement in Hunan" (Mao Zedong
  report), 103–104
Repression, 93, 126, 155–157, 235–238
Revive China Society (Xing Zhonghui), 67
Revolution. *See also* Cultural Revolution
  Bolshevik, 77, 82
  Chiang Kai-shek and, 83
  elites and, 59
  groundwork for, 66–68
  Mao Zedong and, 119–120, 131
  Marxism and, 99, 102
  modernization and, viii
  1911, 65, 68–71, 78
  Peasant Movement Training Institute and,
    82–83
  proletarian, 81
  Qing (Manchu) dynasty and, end of, 65
  reform efforts and, 66–68
  in Russia, 77, 82, 131
  Second, 71, 218, 220
  Sun Yatsen and, 66–68, 70
  violence and, 105
Ri Pyong-gap, 271
Righteous and Harmonious Fists, 57
Rites of Zhou, The, 45

Roberts, Paul, 294
Roman Empire, 5–6, 21
Roosevelt, Franklin D., 115
Roy, M.N., 87
Rural revitalization program, 220–224
Russia. *See also* Soviet Union
  Amur region of China and, 41
  Bolshevik Revolution in, 77
  foreign policy of China and, 271–273
  Japan and, 53, 66
  Mao Zedong and, 140–141
  Mongols in, 25
  revolution in, 77, 82, 131
  second opium war and, 41
  trade with China and, 28
  warlords and, 75
  World War I and, 75

Safety issues, 287
SARS epidemic, 292–293
Scholar-gentry, 13–15, 24, 56
Science and scientific achievements, 5, 29,
    202–203
Scientific socialism, 106
Scowcroft, Brent, 266
Second Five-Year Plan, 158–160
Second opium war, 39–41
Second Revolution, 71, 218, 220. *See also*
    Reforms, of Deng Xiaoping
Second United Front, 98, 118
Selected Works (Mao Zedong), 134
Self-strengthening program, 49–50, 52, 55
Service examination system, 13–15, 22, 55,
    59, 66
Shandong Peninsula, 53, 72, 75
Shang dynasty, 4, 16
Shanghai, 47, 81, 84, 86, 112, 141, 154, 242,
    287–288
Shanghai Commune, 199
Shanghai Communiqué, 228
Shimonoseki Treaty, 54
Sichuan Province, 6–7, 69
Silk trade, 4
Sinification of Marxism, 118
Sino-Japanese War, 52–54, 269
Sixteen-Point Directive, 195–196
Social class and structure. *See also* Bourgeois;
    Peasants
  Confucianism and, 18–19
  elites, 24, 59, 63–64, 133, 190
  family and, 12, 63–64
  Fourth Generation and, 285–288
  gentry, 13–15, 23, 47, 59, 66, 137, 140
  in Guangdong, 285–286
  in Imperial China, 4, 11–15
  legal system in Imperial China and, 23
  merchants, 15

Social class and structure *(continued)*
  middle class, 283
  Orwell's dictum on, 176
  scholar-gentry, 13–15, 24, 56
  women, 13, 18, 136
Socialism, 106–107, 140, 144–150, 160–162,
    177–178, 232, 286
Socialist Education Movement, 187–188
Society of God Worshipers, 44
Song Houfu, 287–288
Song Jiaoren, 70–71
Soong, James, 265
Soong, Meiling, 96
Soong Qingling, 87
Soong, T.V., 96, 124
South China, 7
South Korea, 270
Southern Song dynasty, 24–25
Soviet Union. *See also* Russia
  capitalism, slide into, 185–186
  Cold War and, 143
  de-Stalinization campaign in, 149–150, 153,
    183
  First Five-Year Plan of, 143–144
  Hungarian Uprising against, 149–150, 153,
    183
  Liu Shaoqi and, 183
  Mao Zedong and, 140–141, 159
  modernization by, 144
  People's Liberation Army aid and, 173
  People's Republic of China and, 143–144,
    181–184
  United States and, thaw of relations, 182–184
Special economic zones (SEZs), 225–227, 241,
    244, 283–284
Stalin, Joseph, 87, 99, 123, 128, 136, 141, 143,
    149, 181–182, 218, 222
State Administration of Work Safety, 287
State-owned enterprises (SOEs), 142, 145, 225,
    251, 256, 281
Status groups, 156
Steel furnaces, backyard, 166, 168–169
Stilwell, Joseph, 115
Stock market crash (1929), 100
Strike Hard campaigns, 288–289
Study societies, 56
Sui dynasty, 21
Sullivan, Roger W., 266
Summer Place, looting of, 40–41
Sun Yatsen, 66–70, 75, 82, 83–84, 91, 95, 112
Supreme People's Procuratorate (SPP), 298
Supreme State Conference, 149

Taipings and Taiping Rebellion, 44–48
Taiwan, 53, 260, 263–265, 269
Taiwan-China Talks, 263
Taiwan Straits Crisis, 266

Tang dynasty, 21–22
Taxes, 33, 48, 95–96, 299
Technological innovations
    agricultural, 4, 16, 21
    in Imperial China, 4–5, 16–17, 21, 25
    warfare, 21
    of Westerners, 25, 29, 31
10,000–character manifesto, 252
Tenzin Gyatso, 274
Terrorist attacks (September 11, 2001), 289
Thought reform campaigns, 121–122, 133,
        135–136, 152–157
Three Antis-Movement, 141
Three bonds, 19
Three Gorges Dam, 295, 298–299
Three Principles of the People, 67, 70
Three rules and eight points, 104–105
Thurston, Anne, 200, 207
Tiananmen Incident (1976), 215
Tiananmen Square protests and massacre (1985
        and 1989), 229, 233–236, 242, 248, 266
Tianjin Treaties, 39, 50
Tibet (Xizang), 7–8, 183–184, 274–276
"Tiger hunt," 142
"To the villages" policy, 120
Tokugawa Shogunate, 63
Tongmenghui (Alliance Society), 67, 69–70
Tongzhi Restoration, 50–52
Trade
    cohong and, 27
    Confucianism's view of, 15, 63
    early, 4, 27–28, 34–35
    with Great Britain, 27–28, 34–35
    most-favored-nation trading status, 37, 266
    opium, 28, 34–35
    with Russia, 28, 272–273
    silk, 4
    tea, 27–28
    Tongzhi Restoration and, 51
    unequal treaties and, 37–39, 41–42, 60
    with United States, 257, 266–267
    with Westerners, early, 27–28
Treaty of Friendship, Alliance, and Mutual
        Assistance, 143, 272
Tributary system, 26–31
Triple Intervention, 53
Trotsky, Leon, 99
Truman, Harry, 123, 126–127
Tung Chee-hwa, 263
Tungus people, 8
Twenty-eight Bolsheviks, 99–100, 107, 109,
        121
Twenty-one Demands, 72, 256
Twenty-One Most Wanted list, 236

Unequal treaties, 37–39, 41–42, 60
United Front, 82–87, 98, 116–118

United Nations, 206, 237, 260, 275, 291
United States
    atomic bombing of Japan by, 122
    Chiang Kai-shek and, 115
    civil war in China and, 123, 126–127, 143
    Cold War and, 143
    Dixie Mission of, 122
    foreign policy of China and, 265–268
    Fourteen Points of Wilson and, 76, 81
    Great Depression in, 100
    Hong Kong and, 262–263
    Korean War and, 138–141
    Mao Zedong and, 143, 182
    military conflicts with China and, 267–268
    normalizing relations with China and,
        227–228
    North Korea and, 271
    Permanent Normal Trade Relations with
        China and, 257
    Soviet Union and, thaw of relations, 182–184
    stock market crash (1929) in, 100
    Taiwan and, 264–265
    trade with China, 257, 266–267
    in Vietnam, 201
    violence of Cultural Revolution and, impact
        on, 206
    warlords and, 75
    World War I and, 74–75
    World War II and, 115
    younger generations in China and, 306
Universities, 191, 194, 197, 203–204, 236. See
        also Education
U.S.-Hong Kong Policy Act, 262
"Use value," 134

Value system of Imperial China, 12
Vernacular literature campaign, 79–80
Versailles Treaty, 75–76, 80–81
Vietnam, 201
Voitinsky, Gregory, 81

Wakeman, Frederic, Jr., 47
Wall poster campaigns, 194
Wang Gancheng, 237
Wang Guangmei, 199–201
Wang Hongwen, 213, 216
Wang Jingwei, 84–87
Wang Ming, 121–122
Wang Ruoshui, 237
Wang Shiwei, 121
Wang Wei, 287
Wang Yukai, 300
Warlords and their allies, 73–75, 85, 90, 92
Weber, Max, ix
Wedemeyer, Albert, 115
Wei Jingsheng, 228, 230
Weihaiwei, 53

Wen Jiabao, 279–281, 296, 299, 302–303
Westerners. *See also specific country*
    arrival in China, 25, 27
    Boxer Rebellion and, 58–59
    extraterritoriality and, 37–38
    Guangzhou System and, 27
    Hundred Days Reform and, 54–56
    Imperial China and, 8–9, 48–52
    Jiang Zemin and, 273
    opium trade and, 34–35
    opium wars and, 35–41
    Qing (Manchu) dynasty and, 32–34, 50
    Sino-Japanese War and, 52–54
    Taiping Rebellion and, 42–43
    technological innovations of, 25, 29, 31
    trade with China, early, 27–28
    unequal treaties and, 41–42
    younger generations in China and, 305–306
Westernization, viii–ix
Whampoa Military Academy, 83, 85
White-Haired Girl, The (opera), 204, 218
White Lotus Rebellion, 33
White-Lotus secret society, 33
White, Lynn T., 156, 208
White Terror, 87, 98, 102, 104
Wilson, Woodrow, 76, 81
Witke, Roxane, 193
Women, 13, 18, 136
Woodblock printing, 21
Workers. *See also* Peasants
    displacement of, 286
    jobless, 286
    labor unions, 286–287
    migrant, 286
    pay of, versus professors, 229
    strikes by, 84, 100
World Health Organization (WHO), 292–293
World Trade Organization (WTO), 255–257,
    260, 283
World War I, 72, 74–77
World War II, 112–119, 122
Writing system, 4
Wu Chuntao, 299
Wu Han, 180–181, 188, 191–193
Wu, Harry, 264

Xia dynasty, 4
Xiafang (down to the countryside) program,
    157, 180, 202
Xiamen, 47
Xian Incident, 98
Xing Zhonghui (Revive China Society), 67
Xinjiang, 7–8
Xizang (Tibet), 7–8, 183–184, 274–276

Yan Xuetong, 271–272
Yan'an Way, 119–122, 134
Yang Baibing, 246–247
Yang Shangkun, 246–247
Yang wars, 247
Yangzi River and Valley, 5–7, 20–21, 46, 69
Yao Wenyuan, 191–193, 199, 213, 216–217
Yao Yilin, 240, 245
Yasukuni shrine, 269
Yellow River, 6–7, 10, 20, 33
Yeltsin, Boris, 272
Yin Hongbjao, 278
Yuan dynasty, 8, 25
Yuan Shikai, 70–73, 78, 90, 256
Yunnan, 47

Zeng Guofan, 47–48, 50, 73
Zeng Qinghong, 281
Zhang Chunqiao, 193, 199, 213–217
Zhang Wenkang, 293
Zhang Yingsi, 225
Zhao Wenhao, 207
Zhao Ziyang, 226–227, 232–235, 240–242,
    248, 250
Zheng He, 25
Zheng Yongnian, 303
Zhengfeng (rectification), 121–122, 133,
    135–136, 152–157
Zhou dynasty, 16
Zhou Enlai
    antirightist campaign and, 156
    biographical information about, 214
    Chinese Communist Party and, 86, 212
    Communist errors and, admission of, 153,
        156
    Cultural Revolution and, 193–194
    Dali Lama and, 275
    death of, 213–214
    foreign policy and, 201
    health of, deteriorating, 213
    Liu Shaoqi and, 177, 200
    Mao Zedong and, 109–110, 143, 212
    Red Guards and, 202, 206
    sciences and, 202–203
    successor to, 214
Zhou Gucheng, 231
Zhou Shengxian, 296
Zhu De, 102, 108
Zhu Rongji, 242–243, 248, 255–257, 280,
    286
Zongli Yamen, 50
Zoroaster, 17
Zunyi Conference, 110

About the Authors

June Grasso is associate professor of social science at Boston University's College of General Studies. She is the author of Truman's Two-China Policy (1987). She holds a Ph.D. in modern Chinese history from Tufts University.

Jay P. Corrin is professor and chairman, division of social science at Boston University's College of General Studies. He is author of G.K. Chesterton and Hillaire Belloc: The Battle against Modernity (1981), and Catholic Intellectuals and the Challenge of Democracy (2002) and conducts research and writes on Catholic social and political ideas in Great Britain and the United States.

Michael Kort is professor of social science at Boston University's College of General Studies. He is author of The Soviet Colossus: History and Aftermath (6th ed., 2006), The Columbia Guide to the Cold War (1998), The Columbia Guide to Hiroshima and the Bomb (2007), A Brief History of Russia (2008), and many books for high school students.